P9-DUN-297

The Multilateral Investment System and Multinational Enterprises

The Multilateral Investment System and Multinational Enterprises

Thomas L. Brewer and Stephen Young

OXFORD UNIVERSITY PRESS

1998

Mumbai Nairobi Paris São Paolo Singapore
Taipei Tokyo Toronto Warsaw

and associated companies in
Berlin Ibadan

Oxford is a trade mark of Oxford University Press

Published in the United States
by Oxford University Press Inc., New York

British Library Cataloguing in Publication Data
Data available

Library of Congress Cataloging in Publication Data
Brewer, Thomas L., 1941–
Multilateral investment system and multinational enterprises /
Thomas L. Brewer and Stephen Young.
p. cm.
Includes bibliographical references and index.
1. Investments, Foreign. 2. International business enterprises
—Finance. I. Young, Stephen, 1944– . II. Title.
HG4538.B674 1998 658.15'54—dc21 97–46978
ISBN 0–19–829315–1

1 3 5 7 9 10 8 6 4 2

Typeset by Hope Services (Abingdon) Ltd.
Printed in Great Britain
on acid-free paper by
Bookcraft (Bath) Ltd,
Midsomer Norton, Somerset

To our parents, with thanks

Acknowledgements

We gratefully acknowledge the generous assistance we have received in the preparation of this book. We note in the introduction the formal and informal discussions we have held with investment-related organizations, companies, and colleagues. Our thanks, however, extend to the wide range of organizations with which we have worked as consultants over the years, ranging from the World Bank to Scottish Enterprise, and the accumulated knowledge we have gained from these studies; and both to the reviewers of our previous articles and to the Oxford University Press reviewers of this volume.

We would also like to acknowledge the contribution of our institutions—Georgetown University and the University of Strathclyde—to our research work. This goes well beyond the normal facilities for research, to include funding for transatlantic travel and for research visits to Continental Europe and the USA.

Finally, we would like to recognize the special contribution of a number of individuals: first, Alan Rugman, whose suggestion led to the conception of this volume; second Neil Hood, to whom Stephen Young, in particular, owes a considerable debt over many years; and to Monty Graham and Steve Guisinger, who have enriched our understanding of many issues. Finally, our sincere thanks go to Dorothy Sykes in the Georgetown University School of Business Faculty Services staff for word processing services; and especially to Betty McFarlane in the Department of Marketing at Strathclyde University who bore the brunt of the typing of this work in its numerous drafts, and coped with our idiosyncrasies and the frustrations of the electronic age with good humour.

Our work together has been 'quite good' or 'fantastic' depending on which side of the Atlantic one lives. It has enabled Tom Brewer to discover the delights of the Scottish Highlands and Steve Young to rediscover blueberry muffins for breakfast. Long may this continue.

T.B.
S.Y.

Acknowledgements

Contents

Part II Evolution of the System

Part III Policy Problems

List of Figures

List of Tables

List of Boxes

List of Appendices

Abbreviations

APEC	Asia Pacific Economic Cooperation [forum]
ASEAN	Association of South East Asian Nations
BIT	bilateral investment treaty
BOP	balance of payments
DSU	Dispute Settlement Understanding
EC	European Community
EU	European Union
FCN	friendship, cooperation, and navigation [treaty]
FDI	foreign direct investment
FIRA	Foreign Investment Review Agency [of Canada]
GATS	General Agreement on Trade in Services
GATT	General Agreement on Tariffs and Trade
IBRD	International Bank for Reconstruction and Development
ICSID	International Centre for the Settlement of Investment Disputes
IFC	International Finance Corporation
ILO	International Labour Organization
IMF	International Monetary Fund
IPR	intellectual property rights
ITA	Information Technology Agreement
ITO	International Trade Organization
MAI	Multilateral Agreement on Investment
MFN	most favoured nation
MIGA	Multilateral Investment Guarantee Agency
MNC	multinational corporation
MNE	multinational enterprise
NAFTA	North American Free Trade Agreement
NIEO	New International Economic Order
NTB	non-tariff barrier
OECD	Organization for Economic Cooperation and Development
RBP	restrictive business practice
RIA	regional integration agreement
SCM	Subsidies and Countervailing Measures
TNC	transnational corporation
TPRM	Trade Policy Review Mechanism
TRIMs	Trade Related Investment Measures
TRIPs	Trade Related Intellectual Property Rights
UNCTAD	United Nations Conference on Trade and Development
WTO	World Trade Organization

Introduction

The multinational enterprise (MNE) has been one of the foremost economic, political, and social influences in the world economy for many decades. As a response to its expansion, there have been historically important developments in the evolution of the international regime for investment, especially foreign direct investment (FDI); they include, for instance, the creation of the World Trade Organization (WTO) and the subsequent negotiations of additional agreements with provisions concerning FDI. These and other developments have worldwide implications for governments and firms, as well as workers, consumers, and the non-governmental organizations that represent their interests. Investment issues have thus emerged as key items on the agenda of international economic policy-making and international business–government relations, and those issues will become increasingly important well into the twenty-first century.

Public awareness of the emergence of investment issues has been heightened at the regional level through the creation of the North American Free Trade Area (NAFTA), the integration process in the European Union (EU), and in other developments. Further, many of the substantive issues have been evident periodically in countries' bilateral relations and in the work of international organizations for half a century. At the multilateral level, in particular, however, the issues have not received sustained attention—except among a small number of policy-makers, industry representatives, and academic specialists concerned with investment issues in the Organization for Economic Cooperation and Development (OECD), United Nations, and recently in the WTO.

This research-based volume aims to provide a comprehensive assessment of international investment policies since the 1940s, to analyse current policy problems, and to identify major policy dilemmas for the future. It is based on several years of research undertaken individually and jointly by the present authors; this has included formal and informal discussions with a wide range of officials in organizations such as the WTO, UNCTAD, OECD, and EU, as well as with multinational companies and colleagues in the international business community. The analyses, derived both from economics and from politics, concern developments at bilateral, regional, and multilateral levels. Aside from investment issues, moreover, this volume reflects the ubiquitous nature of the MNE by analysing questions of trade and technology, competition, and economic development. Trade policy is especially important, since international agreements on investment can often only be understood in relationship to international agreements on trade—and in fact because investment and trade are often inextricably mixed together in single agreements. *However, whereas books on international trade policy typically treat investment issues only quite marginally if at all, those issues are the central concern of the present volume.*

Investment is still often considered one of the 'new' issues on the international economic agenda and is thus frequently regarded as one among many ancillary questions in the context of an increasingly wide-ranging 'trade' agenda. For instance, investment is regarded as one of several types of 'trade' relationships in the General Agreement on Trade in Services (GATS), which is in fact an agreement on international investment as well as trade. Similarly the North American Free Trade Agreement and other regional economic agreements, by their names, obscure the important fact that they are also investment agreements. Yet these and other international agreements include important provisions about governments' investment policies and thus about governments' treatment of multinational enterprises.

In their totality, recent changes in the international regime for investment will have significant tangible consequences for international trade and technology transfer, as well as for international investment flows. Patterns and trends in production, employment, and prices will be affected at all levels of economic activity—within national economies as well as among them. The structure of entire industries will change at the global level, and the competitive positions of individual firms within those industries will also change as a result of these agreements. Individual consumers and individual workers, then, have much at stake as existing agreements are implemented and as new agreements are reached in the future. Though many of the agreements are phased in over long periods (more than ten years in some instances), and though the applicability of the agreements to particular circumstances may be uncertain, they often require significant changes in governments' policies. All of the agreements, it should be noted, affect firms' practices, either directly or indirectly.

The effects of the agreements are thus real and tangible, but they are often misunderstood or not even recognized at all. The following examples are intended not only to illustrate the nature and scope of some of the agreements but also to demonstrate that they do in fact have tangible impacts at many different levels:

- The telecommunications industries of more than a hundred countries are being opened to significant degrees of foreign ownership, and in many instances even control by a few large foreign corporations—as a result of investment provisions in the General Agreement on Trade in Services (GATS).
- Individual FDI manufacturing facilities of MNEs in the motor vehicle industry will be able to source their parts by importing without having to meet domestic content requirements of countries—as a consequence of the agreement on Trade Related Investment Measures (TRIMs).
- Many countries that host investment projects are required to develop entirely new national intellectual property rights regimes that will, among other things, protect the patents, copyrights, and other types of intellectual property rights of foreign parent corporations and their local affiliates—because of the agreement on Trade Related Intellectual Property Rights (TRIPs).

- Individual employees of MNEs in most service industries will have a right to enter countries for temporary stays to work for their MNE employers despite immigration policies that would otherwise impose highly restrictive visa requirements on them—also a result of the GATS.
- Conflicts about governments' policies concerning firms' and individuals' foreign direct investments can be addressed through dispute settlement procedures within the auspices of numerous organizations. Depending on whether the dispute is between governments or between investors and governments, these procedures can include, for instance, the WTO, the International Centre for the Settlement of Investment Disputes (ICSID) at the World Bank, or NAFTA.

Despite many delays and uncertainties in their implementation and regardless of the particular industries, government policies, or firm practices to which a given agreement applies, the agreements tend to be grounded on basic principles such as national treatment and most favoured nation treatment. These principles have been expressed in numerous international legal instruments over the years. Many of the principles, concepts, and even specific investment topics have, therefore, actually been on the multilateral agenda of economic negotiations for more than half a century. Yet the issues are still often considered to be among the 'new issues' of international economic relations, and they are relatively unfamiliar to many specialists in the traditional issues of international *trade*. The book is thus intended *inter alia* for international economists, lawyers, business executives, and government officials who must become conversant with the multilateral efforts to develop a new institutional framework for investment, even though they may have detailed familiarity with many traditional trade issues.

Questions

Diverse types of questions are addressed in the book. Many of them concern the *contents of agreements*: what are the particular manifestations of principles such as national treatment, and how are they limited by the agreements? What variations are there across industries and sectors in the applicability of a particular agreement? How has the balance of liberalization of government policies and regulation of firms' practices changed over time? What are the relationships among agreements affecting trade and technology transfer policies? What is typically included in bilateral investment treaties (BITs)? Do regional agreements, such as the EU and NAFTA, facilitate or retard progress in the development of a multilateral regime?

In addition, a variety of questions are addressed concerning the *economic and political context* of the agreements: what were the circumstances in which policy-makers developed the ambitious plan to create an International Trade Organization (ITO) that would have had authority to deal with investment and competition policy issues as well as trade issues in the 1940s? Why was the ITO defeated by the US Congress, and what were the consequences for the evolution of the international investment regime? Why have both the WTO and the OECD put investment issues on their agendas in the 1990s, and what are the similarities and differences in their activities on investment issues?

Further, questions about *economic efficiency as well as the equity and effectiveness* of the agreements are considered: what are the economic and political rationales for the creation of a multilateral regime for investment? What are the weaknesses of the Uruguay Round agreements, such as the Anti-dumping agreement and the Subsidies and Countervailing Measures agreement, from the viewpoint of their effects on investment-related issues? Why are the investment provisions of NAFTA often considered to be state-of-the art? What are the consequences for developing and developed countries of unrestrained competitive bidding for FDI projects in the absence of an effective international agreement that would impose limits on such government policies?

Structure

The analysis in Chapter 1 begins with a discussion of the nature of multinational enterprises and international investment policy; the economic theory of MNEs and international production, and the implications for international investment agreements, are also discussed in that chapter. In Chapter 2, long-term patterns and trends in FDI flows are traced, together with changes in public policies and landmark events that have affected investment policy from the mid-1940s to the late 1990s. In the chapters of Part II, the history of investment issues on the agendas of numerous fora during more than half a century is discussed and evaluated. The historical review covers the efforts to create the International Trade Organization plus the early history of the GATT, the IMF, the World Bank, and the OECD (Chapter 3), the numerous activities of various UN agencies, including UNCTAD and the ILO (Chapter 4), the creation of NAFTA and of the WTO (Chapter 5), and developments in these and other international fora during the late 1990s (Chapter 6). The policy balance in terms of liberalization/regulation, level (national to multilateral), and issues is also analysed in these chapters. Part III focuses upon selected key issues that are especially important and problematic at the present time and that promise to remain so for several years into the future. These include, in particular, interactions among multilateral and regional agreements (Chapter 7), policy linkages among trade, technology transfer, and investment (Chapter 8), linkages between competition (i.e. anti-trust) policy and investment policy (Chapter 9), and issues associated with investment in developing countries (Chapter 10). In Part IV, the concluding chapter presents an overview, highlights key policy problems needing priority attention and provides a politically focused interpretation of the past and the future.

Terminology

The term 'multilateral' refers to organizations and agreements that include most countries in the world, or are even nearly universal in the scope of their memberships in some cases. The WTO is a multilateral organization in that sense, as are the UN, the IMF and the World Bank. Although the OECD is not technically a multilateral organization because of its limited membership, it is commonly referred to as one, and we have followed that usage here. As the size and geographic diversity of its membership have increased, it has become more nearly like other multilateral organizations, and in any case, it has had negotiations in progress on a 'Multilateral Agreement on Investment' in the 1990s. The term 'plurilateral' refers to agreements such as those on civil aircraft and government procurement that include only a subset of the WTO's membership; the term is also used to refer to a US government approach to international economic policy-making that encourages sector-specific agreements and agreements at all levels, i.e. bilateral and regional as well as multilateral. The term 'international' is generic and includes any agreement or organization involving two or more countries.

We have used the term 'multinational enterprise' (MNE) in the title and throughout the book rather than 'global corporation' for reasons that are discussed in Chapter 1. Similarly, the conceptual and semantic distinctions associated with the term 'transnational corporation' (TNC) are discussed in Chapter 4.

Clarification is also required concerning the terms 'international investment' and 'foreign direct investment' (FDI). The former encompasses the latter, and in that sense is generic. The terms are used in this volume in their conventional international business sense without exact definition. However, as will become evident in the discussion of the nature of various agreements, the precise, legal definition of these terms and thus the scope of coverage of the agreements are themselves substantive issues. For what is at stake in the definitions is the types of international business transactions and relationships that are included in or excluded from the agreements. Furthermore, there remain differences in official national governmental practices, despite much analytical work by international agencies to establish uniformity in the definition and information collection procedures associated with investment in general and FDI in particular.

A theme which dominates the book concerns the changing balance, as between 'liberalization' and 'regulation' policies, through time and at different levels, and clarification of the usage of the terms is essential. Market efficiency requires policy liberalization to create internationally open economies that facilitate MNEs' activities, together with international rules (described as 'governance policies') to encourage competition and discourage restrictive business practices, to remedy market failure in other areas such as environmental protection, and to prevent wasteful competitive bidding as in the case of investment incentives. These conditions for maximizing world welfare are described throughout the book as 'liberalization conditions', but it should be noted that very little progress has been made to date at an international level, for example, in curbing monopolies and restrictive business practices or in controlling incentives. MNEs are unlikely to be neutral in terms of their impacts on income distribution between and within countries. On grounds of equity, therefore, there may be attempts to regulate and control multinationals, mainly at national but conceivably also at multilateral levels. These 'regulatory conditions' can be harmful to market efficiency and world welfare. Nevertheless the sovereignty of national governments needs to be recognized in respect of interventions to remedy stabilization problems and market imperfections and to redistribute income. And it is desirable that these rights of countries be taken into account in international investment policies, in terms of behavioural obligations or guidelines for MNEs.

Target audiences

This volume has been written primarily for scholars and specialists in the public and private sectors—including those with interests and responsibilities concerning international trade, technology transfer, and finance issues that are related to investment. It will be of value to officials in governmental and non-governmental organizations at national, regional, and international levels who are concerned with policy formulation and implementation. For example, at national level the attraction of foreign direct investment has become a major and highly competitive activity; and in many countries MNEs play a major role in economic development strategies. In addition, it is highly relevant to executives in multinational companies who have to come to terms with the realities of implementing investment rules and thus understand their context as well as their details.

The volume will also be useful for graduate students in a variety of courses, including international business, international economics, international politics, and international law. The topic of international investment policy is most likely to be taught as a module within more widely based courses. However, there are a growing number of courses, focusing upon, for instance, public policy in international business, in various subject departments, where this volume should be of core relevance. Hopefully it will stimulate research interest at doctoral level.

Additional reading

Although there is now a very extensive literature on MNEs and foreign direct investment, there are far fewer studies on investment policy issues than, for example, on trade policy. In order to keep abreast of latest developments, therefore, regular reading of newspapers and magazines (especially the *Financial Times* and *The Economist*) is essential. *Inside US Trade* is a valuable weekly newsletter with a supplementary electronic service, dealing with all international economic policy issues with a US focus.

The annual studies from UNCTAD, *World Investment Report* (*WIR*), Geneva, contain a wealth of data and analysis concerning FDI and MNEs with a policy and developing country focus. Regular statistical series on inward and outward FDI stocks and flows by country are included, together with sectoral and company information, etc. Individual reports are devoted to in-depth analysis of particular topics: *WIR* 1996 analysed the multilateral investment regime at the mid-1990s. In addition, reports by other international organizations (WTO, OECD, and World Bank) as well as the texts of investment agreements themselves are important. Recent relevant OECD publications include: OECD (1996), *Market Access after the Uruguay Round*, Paris.

With the growing interest in investment policy issues, there is an increasing number of relevant articles in journals such as *Transnational Corporations*, *Journal of World Trade*, *World Economy*, and *International Trade Journal*. The *Journal of International Business Studies* is the leading academic journal in the area of international business and multinational enterprises; see especially the symposium on 'Multinational Enterprise and Economic Analysis' in the March 1998 issue (Vol. 29, No. 1).

Significant books:
Caves, R. E. (1996), *Multinational Enterprise and Economic Analysis*, 2nd edn. (Cambridge: Cambridge University Press).
Dunning, J. H. (1993), *Multinational Enterprises and the Global Economy* (Wokingham: Addison-Wesley).
Graham, E. M., and Krugman, P. (1995), *Foreign Direct Investment in the United States*, 3rd edn. (Washington: Institute for International Economics).

The first two of these books contain a wealth of information on the economics of multinational enterprises. Graham and Krugman is the classic work on FDI in the United States.

Graham, E. M. (1996), *Global Corporations and National Governments* (Washington: Institute for International Economics) provides an insightful, brief analysis of the case for and constituents of multilateral investment rules.

Hoekman, B., and Kostecki, M. (1995), *The Political Economy of the World Trading System* (Oxford: Oxford University Press). This provides a historical review and analysis of the world trading system, including the establishment of the WTO. It facilitates comparison between the issues and challenges for the multilateral system when viewed from a trade as opposed to investment perspective.

Sauvé, P., and Schwanen, D. (eds.) (1996), *Investment Rules for the Global Economy* (Toronto: C. D. Howe Institute) contains a series of writings on current and new issues in international investment rule-making.

There are a number of books which deal with regional or national dimensions of FDI rules, e.g. C. J. Green and T. L. Brewer (eds.) (1995), *Investment Issues in Asia and the Pacific Rim* (New York: Oceana); A. M. Rugman (ed.) (1994), *Foreign Investment and NAFTA* (Columbia: University of South Carolina Press); and A. E. Safarian (1993), *Multinational Enterprises and Public Policy: A Study of the Industrial Countries* (Basingstoke: Edward Elgar).

More detailed reading is contained in the extensive citations within individual chapters of this volume and the full References.

Part I

Context

1

Multinational Enterprises and Foreign Direct Investment Policy

Theory and Issues

Chapter 1 in this introductory section provides an overview of explanations for the growth of the multinational enterprise (MNE) and foreign direct investment (FDI). Based on the implications of theory for economic impact, the chapter presents the basic arguments for an international framework of rules for FDI. The basic policy instruments applied at national, bilateral, regional and multilateral levels are reviewed, illustrating the problems associated with the complexity and patchwork of rules existing at present.

1.1 The Nature of the Multinational Enterprise

Definitions

The *multinational enterprise* may be defined as an enterprise which owns (in whole or in part), controls, and manages value-adding activities in more than one country. In so doing it engages in production and/or service activities across national boundaries, financed by *foreign direct investment* (Hood and Young, 1979; Dunning, 1993). The essential elements of multinational operations are, first, direct, as opposed to portfolio investment abroad, giving the power of control over decision-making in the foreign enterprise. From a managerial perspective, the degree of equity ownership required to ensure control will vary. Similarly, there are variations in country definitions of direct investment (in terms of minimum percentage of equity ownership) as opposed to portfolio investment, for inclusion in their international payments statistics. A second key element is the collective transfer of a package of resources, involving factor inputs such as capital, technology, entrepreneurial and managerial skills, and access to markets for trade and foreign production. A third element of the definition is that the value-adding activities of the enterprise are located in at least two countries.

In the present-day world, the ownership issue is less significant in that the MNE is likely to be involved in a variety of cross-border non-equity ventures, such as licensing agreements, non-equity joint ventures, and strategic alliances. Dunning (1991: 6) has thus portrayed the multinational as 'an orchestrator of a set of geographically dispersed but interdependent assets'. While such relationships and networking activities more generally are important features of MNE strategies at the dawn of the third millennium, it is still true that ownership of undertakings which possess core competencies is vital. Nevertheless, there is an enormous range and diversity of multinational firms, from those which have operations in only one country outside their home nation to those operating on a world scale. But the broad definition presented above is simpler to implement than others which employ a structural criterion (the number of countries in which a firm operates); a performance criterion (e.g. the share of assets, employees, or sales outside the home country); or a behavioural criterion (the top management 'thinks internationally'). In the context of devising multilateral investment agreements, a precise, legal definition is necessary to encapsulate the relevant areas of international investment.

Orthodox explanations for the emergence of the multinational enterprise link the theory of the firm and location theory (Caves, 1996). Thus the enterprise, possessing certain firm-specific assets, finds some cost advantages in internalizing the use of these assets within the organization on a cross-border basis. Knowledge is one such key asset where the internal market is commonly preferable to the external market and arm's length transactions, because of the problems of pricing technology and the risks of opportunistic behaviour. The locational incentive to establish operations abroad may derive from tariff or non-tariff barriers which act as deterrents to trade, lower unit labour costs, or host government policies (such as offers of investment incentives or nationalistic procurement policies which favour enterprises located within the market).

The evolution of the MNE

In high-technology sectors especially, some companies may be multinational almost from day one of their existence. In other industries there are examples of enterprises establishing production or services operations abroad as their first overseas ventures, and hence becoming multinational as soon as they engage in international business. For smaller and medium-sized enterprises in particular, however, an evolutionary internationalization process could be involved (Johanson and Vahlne, 1977), with exporting through agents or distributors, the establishment of sales subsidiaries, licensing, and manufacturing. According to this model, companies would focus first upon foreign markets where 'psychic distance' (on the basis of cultural, business, and geographic factors) was low. Empirical studies have shown that the linear internationalization sequence has frequently been replaced by leap-frogging of stages (especially for small, high-tech companies), while other firms may remain as exporters throughout their existence; in general, choice of modes of entry is sector-specific and often very limited (e.g. for non-tradable services); the outward internationalization stage is often preceded by inward internationalization as companies import goods and services, buy or license in technology, etc.; and choice of markets is influenced as much by 'customer pull' as by 'psychic distance' (Bell and Young, 1998).

For the large international enterprise, the choices are different ones. Experience in managing multi-plant firms domestically may be transferred internationally. Initially plants were established in major markets abroad to replicate operations at home (albeit with a more truncated product line), with exports continuing from the parent company to fill out the product range (horizontal integration) (see Vernon's (1966) product life cycle—PLC—model of international trade and investment). Signs of integration on a multi-plant and multi-country basis were evidenced in the EC after the accession of the UK in 1973 (vertical integration with specialization by product or process). Enhanced regional integration was stimulated by the EU's Single Market programme from the early 1990s. By this time, however, there were also nascent signs of global integration by some companies in some sectors. What is important to stress is the reduced significance of some established models and concepts to explain the modern MNE. These include Porter's 'diamond of competitive advantage' (Porter, 1990) which is predicated on the basis of the generation of competitive advantages in the company's home base. Rather the global MNE may generate competitive advantage anywhere in its constellation (Rugman and Verbeke, 1997). The product cycle model (Vernon, 1966) also assumes a one-way flow of innovation from parent to subsidiary, home to host nation; whereas MNE-owned R & D centres in specialist agglomerations around the world may be important sources of product or process innovations. For MNEs which are pioneering new structures and strategies, 'hierarchy' may be replaced by 'heterarchy', and 'country-centred' or 'multi-domestic' strategies by 'global' strategies.

The multinational enterprise and international investment agreements

For the debate on international investment agreements, there are a variety of highly significant implications of the above. First, the MNE has a major involvement in international trade as an exporter (and importer) of final goods and services from its home base and its subsidiary companies. Integrated companies also organize and coordinate the flows of intermediate products and services across national boundaries. Given its multinational status, the enterprise internalizes these cross-border markets, with internal transfer pricing mechanisms replacing arm's length trade. Trade and foreign direct investment are as complementary as they are competitive. There are obvious difficulties, therefore, in trying to separate out international trade and international investment agreements.

Second, the multinational enterprise is a principal source of innovation in the world economy. The desire to appropriate fully the returns from its R & D investment in proprietary assets is a major reason for the internalization of know-how within the enterprise and hence for the very *raison d'être* of the multinational corporation. MNEs will patent some know-how (other types of intellectual property will be retained as trade secrets) and in certain cases formally license this within the firm, as well as externally (for mature technologies usually). Therefore, the company has an overwhelming interest in rules for the protection of intellectual property rights (IPR). As will be discussed, this issue was included within international agreements for the first time in the Uruguay Round negotiations. It continues to be a major source of contention between developed and developing nations, essentially over the public goods nature of technology. As a public good, the conditions for optimality would require know-how to be openly available without charge, apart perhaps from a price to cover the costs of circulating it (as developing countries would like). But to do this would discourage new investment in information creation. This is why home countries support their MNEs in demands for a strengthened international legal system. The latter would permit firms to appropriate the returns from their R & D investments through the temporary monopoly offered by patents.

A third issue (and one linked to the second point above) concerns the multinational enterprise and technology transfer. Later sections of this chapter discuss this topic in more detail but the point is worth making here that there is again a conflict between the goals of host nations (mainly but not solely developing countries) which emphasize the technology transfer potential of MNEs, and those of the firm which stress internalization as the route to profitability. The tradition of joint ventures in developing countries from the 1960s and 1970s has its roots in the attempt to capture some of the potential technology transfer benefits of MNEs. Translated into an issue for multilateral investment agreements, it draws attention to the debate over the relative rights and obligations of enterprises and nation-states in such agreements.

Fourth, and more conventionally, the MNE has a major role in global financial flows through its initial and sequential investments, through remittances of profits, dividends, royalties, management fees, etc., and through its foreign exchange exposure management measures. From an international policy perspective, there are important issues concerning capital controls and foreign exchange controls which historically have been maintained by national governments for balance of payments, exchange rate, and national security reasons but which may severely hamper market access through FDI.

Fifth, many MNEs are large firms operating in imperfectly competitive markets. Important issues arise for international competition policy, which ultimately must represent a constituent of a comprehensive trade and investment agreement. But they are highly problematic in an era of strategic alliances, networking, and other forms of what has been referred to as quasi-internalization (Dunning, 1993). Related problems arise in respect of defining the country of origin of enterprises. While the nationality of most MNEs can be readily identified, complexities emerge as the shares of the major MNEs are quoted in the principal stock exchanges across the world, board membership is multinational and an increasing proportion of value-added activity is undertaken outside the MNEs' home countries.

Sixth, the growth of tertiary activities means that, even within manufacturing MNEs, the service element in companies' intermediate and final activities is expanding rapidly. For example, it has been estimated that 80 per cent of investment in the information technology (IT) industries is in services and software rather than hardware (Peters, 1995). This is quite separate from the expansion of services MNEs themselves, but means that market access issues (as in telecoms, financial services, etc.) are critically important to the growth of multinational service operations. The slow pace of the growth of multinationality in services historically has been linked to government regulation and state ownership: hence deregulation and privatization questions are rolled into multilateral investment agreements.

1.2 The Economics of Multinational Firms and Foreign Direct Investment

The theory of international production and the multinational enterprise

In the main, writers seeking explanations for the existence and growth of MNEs have focused upon the level of the firm rather than the macroeconomic perspective (but see, for example, Kojima, 1978, 1990) as in the case of trade theory. A full explanation for MNE activity has, nevertheless, to take account both of locational dimensions (the domain of classical and neo-classical trade theory) and of ownership and organizational factors.

Despite the rapid growth of foreign direct investment in the early post-war years, prior to the 1960s there was no established theory of international production or of the MNE. From the work of Hymer in 1960 (eventually published in 1976), however, a continuing thrust in the international business literature has related to explanations for the emergence and growth of the multinational enterprise. The principal question being asked was 'what are the factors explaining multinationality and for choosing international production as opposed to exporting?' Hood and Young (1979; see also Dunning, 1993) traced a variety of themes in the early literature, most of which had their roots in market imperfections and the sources of ownership advantages which MNEs acquired within this imperfectly competitive environment. The work of Hymer (1976), Kindleberger (1969), and Caves (1971) initiated explanations for the MNE in the industrial organization tradition, revolving around a structure–conduct–performance paradigm (following Bain, 1956). Others focused more specifically on technological advantage and technological accumulation, a theme pursued most recently within a competitive international industry context by Cantwell (1989). And there were a number of contributions by financial economists, most notably Aliber (1970).

In the mid-1970s, efforts were directed at more holistic explanations of the activities of MNEs. Based on Coase's (1937) work, Buckley and Casson (1976) presented an internalization theory to explain why cross-border transactions were organized by hierarchies rather than by the market. Essentially firms would undertake foreign direct investment when the transaction costs of an administered exchange were lower than those of a market exchange. The authors' major contribution included the identification of situations in which the markets for intermediate products were likely to be internalized, including government intervention, inequalities between buyers and sellers with respect to knowledge, the inability of the market to ensure sufficient control over the quality of the final products, etc. Much of the subsequent orthodox economics literature on explanations for international production has followed this internalization/transaction cost tradition, including the work of Williamson (1985), Teece (1986), and others.

Dunning's eclectic (or OLI) paradigm (1988) took a somewhat different path but has probably had more influence even though there are question marks over whether the variables in the model are independent of each other. Dunning included ownership-specific advantages (e.g. technology, marketing, and finance know-how; advantages of common governance), internalization incentive advantages (e.g. avoidance of search and negotiation costs, buyer uncertainty, quality protection), and location-specific variables (e.g. input prices, quality and productivity, transport and communication costs, tariff and non-tariff barriers) as the constituents of his framework. The level and form of FDI will depend upon the possession of ownership-specific advantages, the advantages gained from internalizing these, and the extent to which the global interests of the MNE are served by creating or utilizing its ownership advantages in a foreign location (Dunning, 1993).

Much of the above work has focused upon the discrete investment decisions of multinational enterprises, within a rationalist, profit-maximizing framework. Challenges for theory concern the need to provide explanations for joint ventures, strategic alliances, and other kinds of cross-border relationships between and within firms, and for the choice between greenfield ventures and acquisitions. An even greater challenge is to incorporate globalization and systems of transactions as opposed to individual transactions within the analysis, where strategic variables have a major influence. Whether a uniquely economics-based approach is up to these challenges is doubtful; although Dunning (1995) has attempted to incorporate 'alliance capitalism' within the eclectic paradigm. In response to the criticism that the theoretical approaches reviewed above are static in nature, Gray (1996) has presented some ideas on a dynamic analysis. There is in addition increasing interest in uncertainty and evolutionary decision-making on FDI issues (e.g. Rivoli and Salorio, 1998).

The introduction to this section explained the important role of Stephen Hymer (1976) in the early efforts to develop a theory of international production. Hymer's particular perspective focused upon internationalization as a mechanism by which producers increased their market power. MNE activity is, therefore, not so much an independent response to competition as a means of further extending collusive networks, raising barriers to entry, and increasing the efficiency of foreign plants (Cantwell, 1991). This tradition, which is linked to a variety of dependency and Marxist models, has been pursued by authors such as Newfarmer (1985), Cowling and Sugden (1987), and Pitelis and Sugden (1991). To such writers multinational enterprise activity is a means not only of raising the market power of firms but also of raising the share of profits. This is achieved through the greater bargaining power of the MNE over wages and working conditions derived from its ability to switch production. In addition, organized trade union activity in large plants is weakened by outsourcing to local and international networks of subcontractors. A combination of an increasing share of profits and greater market power leads to slower demand growth and stagnation domestically and ultimately internationally (along the lines of the monopoly capitalism arguments of Baran and Sweezy, 1966).

While the above perspectives on industrial organization stress the negative dimensions of oligopolistic behaviour, Cantwell (1991) identifies another 'conventional' stream of thought in this tradition. Beginning with Kindleberger (1969), writers again highlighted oligopolistic market structure and behaviour, emphasizing the advantages associated with economies of scale and scope. Size was also seen as an important attribute both for successful innovation and for defending intellectual property rights. In his interpretation of multinational oligopoly behaviour, Graham (1978) focused upon 'exchange of threats' in transatlantic cross-FDI as a mechanism for preserving stable competition. Cross-investments by MNEs in the same sector were also believed to accelerate new product development and launch.

Such notions have been taken further by Cantwell (1989) in his model of technological accumulation: here innovation and the growth of international production are regarded as mutually supportive; but the actual technological path of each firm is to some degree unique and differentiated, in part reflecting the locational spread of the multinational enterprise. Cantwell's (1989) model has also been applied in a national economic development context, with MNE technological activity being strengthened by but also strengthening local technological capabilities and facilitating economies of agglomeration. Within this framework, however, it is recognized that MNE technological activities may in some circumstances have anti-competitive effects in host country industries. Where indigenous firms were internationally competitive, the entry of MNEs in the same sector could provide a competitive stimulus which encouraged an increase in local research-related activity. Conversely, where indigenous firms were weak, MNEs might displace domestic enterprises and replace them with assembly-only foreign affiliates: in the process, the research capability of the country's industry would be downgraded. In this formulation, the orthodox and 'radical' industrial organization approaches provide some similar conclusions.

The economic impacts of multinational enterprises

The growth of the MNE has been shown to be a consequence of imperfections in both goods and factor markets internationally, but particularly in the market for knowledge. By overcoming such imperfections, MNEs operate, albeit unconsciously, to improve worldwide economic efficiency and world welfare. Graham and Krugman (1995) distinguish two categories of potential gains from FDI. The first group represent the benefits from increased integration and may be analysed in the same way as the gains from international trade. The sources for these gains are comparative advantage, with trade enabling countries to specialize in their different attributes; increasing returns to scale, where trade permits states to produce a narrower range of products or services and in this way generate a larger and more efficient scale of production; and greater competition through trade, thereby reducing the oligopoly power of large enterprises. Trade in relation to FDI is regarded as including trade in goods, services, and knowledge, the latter being most interesting given the problems of appropriating the benefits from investment in R & D. It is argued that by producing the particular goods itself, this will permit *de facto* trade in the results of R & D and, therefore, improve the returns from research and development work. Overall, the MNE will expand the gains from trade to the extent that FDI encourages trade in goods, services, and knowledge. An equivalent situation is one where tariff and non-tariff barriers restrict trade by preventing a company from exporting from its home country. By establishing a production operation inside the host nation, the enterprise is able to avoid these government-induced barriers (imperfections). It is true, nevertheless, that the import substitution operations are second best, since the manufacturing costs of the import substitutes will be higher than those of the imports themselves.

Alongside these direct benefits from integration are a second group of indirect (external) benefits (and costs) associated with FDI. These take the form of spillovers to the domestic economy in the form of technology of various types, through backward, forward, and horizontal linkages; the upgrading of workforce skills, which may then transfer elsewhere, and perhaps some encouragement to entrepreneurship.

The general conclusion is that, as with trade, increased international flows of FDI should be encouraged since they generate both global and national benefits. Growth would be stimulated through more efficient production and prices lowered through stronger competition.

Nevertheless, the theoretical discussion above (and not simply that derived from 'radical' models) highlights instances where MNEs could have adverse effects upon the welfare of home or host countries. Host multinational activity until recently was characterized by large enterprises operating in oligopolistic industries. Their behaviour could, therefore, result in sub-optimal efficiency with excessive discretionary spending, wasteful advertising, and the like; and predatory tactics could stifle domestic competition. In a similar vein, Cantwell (1989) showed how MNEs in host countries might contribute to a vicious cycle of technological decline rather than a virtuous cycle of technological rejuvenation and development. And, in respect of regional free trade groupings, Dunning and Robson (1988) have argued that MNE internalization, which might be optimal from the perspective of the global corporation, might not necessarily be so from the standpoint of the individual affiliate, host country, or regional group.

1.3 Public Policy and the Multinational Enterprise: Rationales for International Agreements

There are several implications for public policy that emerge from the economic analysis of MNEs and foreign direct investment. All suggest the need for a multilateral regime for investment issues.

There are two complementary liberalization conditions for market efficiency. The first emphasizes the volume and diversity of the international economic transactions of MNEs and their ability to operate complex internationalized production systems relatively efficiently. Foreign direct investment is an important vehicle for obtaining technology, management skills, and capital; for improving the international competitiveness of firms and the economic performance of countries; and ultimately for improving world welfare. The latter is a presumption because of the second-best nature of the situation. In a situation where restrictions on trade and factor movements exist, not every move to overcome such restrictions will result in an improvement in real output and incomes. The general assumption is, however, that MNE operations are hampered by a variety of government-created obstacles, which inhibit the firms' actual contributions to economic welfare compared with what they could be in the absence of the government-created obstacles. The implication for public policy, therefore, is that *government policies should be liberalized*; if firms were liberated from the constraints imposed on their operations by governments, they could be even more efficient.

The second and complementary line of analysis emphasizes oligopolistic industry structure and firms' anti-competitive behaviour and their rent-seeking tendencies based on the internalization of transactions. The implication for public policy is that *government policies should be devised to encourage competition and discourage restrictive business practices*. Policies to remedy market failure in areas such as environmental protection and to prevent wasteful competitive bidding as in the case of investment incentives are also necessary. In regard to MNE behaviour which is not oligopolistic but, say, part of a strategy of exploiting the international division of labour, the optimal solution at host government level is not restrictionist policies. Rather the solution lies in the removal of distortions, and the provision of infrastructural conditions by which both indigenous and multinational firms can upgrade the competitiveness of domestic resources and aid long-term dynamic comparative advantage.

Consideration also needs to be given, however, to policy interaction and conflicts. Julius (1990) has shown that the gains from multilateral policy could best be achieved in a policy environment of neutrality or non-discrimination. For public policy, this means, therefore, *national (equal) treatment of foreign and indigenous firms in the domestic market; and non-discrimination between trade and investment as market servicing methods*. An interesting illustration which links trade and investment policy concerns is the instance where anti-dumping and countervailing duty measures are introduced following pressure from domestic firms seeking to erect entry barriers against foreign rivals (see Rugman and Verbeke, 1990 on what they term the 'theory of shelter'). These measures have led on occasion to a switch by foreign firms from the exporting to FDI mode. But in the process some of their firm-specific advantages may be dissipated by, for example, the need to use local suppliers. There is, therefore, an overall reduction in economic efficiency. The solution here lies in tightening anti-dumping rules and, more importantly, internationalizing competition policy.

The application of unilateral national policies to facilitate the objectives identified above may reduce world welfare, and hence provides the basic argument for an international investment regime. Despite the degree of policy convergence and of policy liberalization which has occurred in the recent past, considerable differences still exist in national policy regimes, reflecting the diversity of country objectives and priorities. National governments cannot effectively regulate MNEs through unilateral policies because the effectiveness of their policies is generally limited to their own territory in a political system of legally sovereign nation-states. They therefore lack the political and administrative ability to solve MNE-related problems unilaterally. (This important issue of national government policies towards MNEs is discussed more fully later in the chapter.) International cooperation is thus necessary, and the solution is an international regulatory regime.

While the case for international investment rules has always existed (and was recognized half a century ago in the plans of the Havana Charter for an International Trade

Organization), a number of features of the present-day world economy greatly strengthen the case for multilateral rules.

Globalization

There is considerable debate about the exact meaning of terms such as 'globalization', 'global business', 'global strategy', and 'global economy'. To many commentators a 'global firm' is simply post-1985 terminology for what would have been previously described as a 'multinational firm'; to others, such as Ohmae (1990), the global corporation is one that has shed its national identity and has 'made traditional national borders almost disappear, and pushed bureaucrats, politicians, and the military toward the status of declining industries' (Ohmae, 1990: p. xi). The latter view is much exaggerated, the former inaccurate. The modern multinational enterprise has been around since the nineteenth century. The number, size, nationality, and geographical spread of MNEs has increased enormously since that time; however, the 39,000 parent multinationals (with 270,000 foreign affiliates) (UNCTAD, 1996*a*) mostly still have a clear geographic centre or home country and top management in these enterprises is largely national.

Yet the process of globalization is an emerging reality, involving a widening of the extent and form of cross-border transactions, and a deepening of the economic interdependence of enterprises, other private and public institutions, and governments located in different countries (Dunning, 1993). Key features of globalization at the enterprise level include (UNCTAD, 1994):

- Global manufacturing or service activities, global sourcing, and global customers.
- The emergence of integrated international production systems. Geographically dispersed affiliates and fragmented production systems are being replaced initially by regionally and then by globally integrated production and distribution networks.
- New forms of corporate governance. More complex integration has been associated with a breakdown of the value chain into discrete functions; and the establishment of assembly, procurement, R & D functions, etc. in optimal locations around the world. In such systems, decision-making units may be widely spread geographically with integrated flows of technology, skills, and finance as well as goods and services. Hierarchical relationships between headquarters and subsidiaries may be partially replaced by heterarchical and network relations.
- Networks are not self-contained but are connected to other business and corporate networks through a variety of forms of cooperation and alliances.

The extent of these developments is uncertain, but there appear to be integrated global companies in industries such as microelectronics and consumer electronics, office machinery, household appliances, instruments, pharmaceuticals, and financial services. And in other sectors, some elements of globalization, such as global sourcing, are in place.

The major drivers of globalization are well known, including technoglobalism (the requirement for a global market to spread research and development costs and assist commercialization); major innovations in information and communications technologies, and increasing specialization and differentiation of products, especially in service sectors which represent the largest component of foreign direct investment flows; government policies of deregulation and privatization; and liberalization of trade and investment regimes at both unilateral and multilateral levels. And the most visible signs of globalization at the enterprise level appear in global manufacturing or service activities, global sourcing, and global customers.

Globalization seems likely to accentuate further many of the economic impact issues discussed in previous paragraphs. On the one hand, the potential for greater worldwide economic efficiency is increased as MNEs exploit a global division of labour. On the other, both stronger positive and negative contributions are possible at country level, depending upon the integration of the nation within MNE global production systems, and on the ability to anchor FDI projects within local clusters of technological advantage. As a consequence, the efficiency versus equity debate seems bound to be higher up the policy agenda.

Moreover, as UNCTAD (1994: 156) note, 'the challenges to international governance posed by an integrated international production system are even greater than those already experienced with the formation of an international trading and monetary framework'. The issues are much wider, including labour and environmental standards, investment and technology policies, and social provisions, and they are more difficult to resolve.

Strategic alliances and networks

Although essentially part of the globalization process, it is worth commenting separately on international strategic alliances. This is not only because they bring together large and commonly competitive firms for specific purposes, but also because in the process alliances potentially complicate relationships and negotiations between Triad countries on FDI matters. Alliances are particularly common in new, high-technology industries such as information technology, biotechnology, autos, and new materials. Their objectives include the achievement of economies of scale; technology development and specialization; risk reduction, through sharing resources and reducing the costs of R & D; providing access to global markets and distribution systems, and circumventing trade restrictions; and the shaping of competition by influencing participating firms' cost structures, technology, and market competitiveness. Thus companies share complementary assets to gain particular advantages, but without the commitment and risk involved in FDI since strategic alliances do not necessarily imply equity involvement.

Strategic alliances are, arguably, part of a wider process of increased networking within and among enterprises. Within the company, networks involve changes in reporting arrangements, flows of information, and incentives linked to a departure from hierarchical organization structures. Bartlett and Ghoshal (1997), indeed, rejecting conventional organization structures, have suggested a new management approach in terms of three core processes—entrepreneurial, integration, and renewal processes—which mean very different roles for front-line, middle, and top-level managers. The required mind-set changes and implementation problems may prove an insuperable barrier to the adoption of such an approach in many companies. In truth, the fashion for lesser, flatter structures is already causing significant problems because of the loss of management capacities.

Networking does not only involve intra-firm relationships or alliance relationships but also links with customers, competitors, suppliers, and the non-business infrastructure (universities, research institutions, governments, etc.) (D'Cruz and Rugman, 1993). Particularly significant has been the trend from vertically integrated mass production to lean production and vertical disintegration, which became widely adopted in response to the environmental conditions facing companies in the 1970s and 1980s. The evolution of this process into the 1990s may see the outsourcing of not only peripheral but possibly core functions, leaving the company to concentrate on its true core competencies (*Financial Times*, 1996*a*).

If international corporate networks and alliances are to function efficiently, a liberal and stable environmental framework is critical; an important component of the latter is obviously an international investment regime.

Alliance capitalism

Dunning (1994*a*) identified three eras in the development of capitalist economies, namely entrepreneurial capitalism (craft or batch production; from local to national markets—*circa* 1770–1875); hierarchical capitalism (mass production; from national to international markets—*circa* 1875–1980); and alliance capitalism (towards flexible production; from an international to a regional and global economy—*circa* 1980 and beyond). Many of the features of the age of alliance capitalism have been discussed above, at least as regards the characteristics and operations of enterprises. What needs to be added to complete the picture is the changing role of governments: thus the need to replace bureaucratic and authoritarian regimes of hierarchical governance applies as much to governments as it does to enterprises. And relationships between the public and private sectors require to change from confrontation to cooperation and partnerships. In addition, since the locational options of firms are widened, action by governments to ensure that the economic environment is conducive to promoting competitiveness becomes critical. Investment in education and training, in transportation and telecommunications, in research and development, etc. are major components of this. Yet overall the scope for independent action at national level has undoubtedly narrowed; and, therefore, the increasing internationalization of domestic policy issues has the potential to exacerbate 'system friction' (Ostry, 1992) between separate but linked national economies and social systems. As will be discussed fully in later chapters, the continuing liberalization of cross-border trade and investment markets is not necessarily assured, with protectionist responses and destructive policy competition still on the horizon. *International rules would be helpful both in locking in the liberalization that has taken place and in reducing conflicts between governments over FDI issues.*

The changing role of emerging economies

In the 1990s, the developing world became a major player in the world FDI scene. The change was a reflection of a more liberalized regulatory framework, growing markets and a recognition of the potential for incorporating developing states within global production systems. The major contributor to the improved developing country situation was China, consequent on internal market liberalization, with the Asia Pacific region as a whole representing over 70 per cent of the total developing country FDI stock in the mid-1990s (UNCTAD, 1996*a*). The importance of technology transfer from abroad (via MNEs or other modes) in the emergence of the Tiger economies of Hong Kong, Korea, Singapore, and Taiwan is well known. And there is every indication of a replication of this development process in countries such as Indonesia, Malaysia, and Thailand, with a major role for FDI. The liberalization policy in India is also beginning to be reflected in significant inflows of investment.

There are a variety of implications of these trends and especially the focus of FDI flows on Asia Pacific developing nations. First, as the fastest growing region in the world and as a source of low-cost production labour, the area will grow in importance as an integral element of MNEs' global strategies. Second, as a consequence of economic development in the region, there is likely to be increasing competition between, say, Europe and Asia Pacific for global investment projects and, therefore, a potential for rising tensions. Third, the evolution from recipients of inward investment to sources of outward investment, which is already evident among the newly industrialized countries (NICs) (and indeed China), will begin to reveal itself in other countries in the region. *As countries and their firms become sources of outward FDI, they become more interested participants in negotiations on global FDI issues as well as trade liberalization. Thus interest in multilateral rules on FDI becomes more widespread, including in countries which were previously only hosts to inward FDI.*

1.4 The Present International Framework for Foreign Direct Investment and the Multinational Enterprise

The previous sections have presented a rationale for multilateral FDI policies in terms of improvements in economic efficiency and world welfare; and contrasted these with national FDI policies which may generate some net advantages for particular countries or firms, but in the process generate inefficiencies and lead to a misallocation of resources on a worldwide basis. Recognition of the need to address these issues has led to a range of efforts to develop international rules and institutions for investment.

Reality is complicated by the fact that there have been a variety of approaches to international rule-making, which are commonly partial in their country coverage, certainly partial in their coverage of issues, and may deal with trade and other topics as well as FDI. Alongside multilateral and national rules, moreover, are about 1,400 bilateral investment treaties (BITs) and the investment-related provisions of regional economic blocs, most notably the EU and NAFTA. The overall investment policy scene is, therefore, characterized by fragmentation, confusion, and conflict. The purpose of this section is thus to provide an overview of the different *levels* of FDI policy, i.e. whether policies are national, bilateral, regional, or multilateral, and to highlight their major distinguishing characteristics and review in broad terms their evolution over time.

National

Many, but by no means all, countries have specific policies directed at inward direct investment and the MNE. The larger the role that FDI plays or is designed to play within the national economy, the greater the likelihood of such explicit policies. For about twenty years to the beginning of the 1990s, for example, the attraction of inward FDI, linked to incentives such as investment grants and export profits tax relief, was a key platform in industrial policy in the Republic of Ireland. And as will be shown in later chapters the regulation of inward investment was, in the past especially, an important constituent of government policies in the developing countries of the south; they reflected the desire to ensure that MNE impacts matched the economic and social objectives of the countries concerned.

While the emphasis at the national level is on host nation policies, home countries may also formulate rules relating to outward FDI. In the main, however, such rules have been focused upon the balance of payments as a macroeconomic issue, and relate to capital flows as a whole and not exclusively to direct investment flows. An exception to this is the outward FDI political risk programmes, by which some countries encourage their firms to invest in developing countries in particular.

The issue of the role of host national government policies in a world in which MNEs have an increasingly important position is an unsettled one. In general, government intervention may be justified on a number of grounds: to redistribute income in accordance with some equity goal; to remedy imperfections in the market economy; and to remedy stabilization problems. In respect of the second of these goals, the case for policies to improve the functioning of markets is very strong. Such policies may include, for instance, after-care services for foreign investors to assist with companies' manpower and training needs, assistance in identifying suppliers and upgrading supplier capabilities, investment in education and training, transport and communications, etc. The objective of such policies is to improve the competitiveness of the particular country as a location for inward FDI and to help build clusters and agglomerations to assist the anchoring of projects within the national economy.

The objectives of host nation rules will also include national economic welfare—for example, economic growth subject to an equity constraint relating to income distribution at personal or regional levels. FDI will not be neutral in its effects between and within countries, and governments must make judgements on their equity (as opposed to efficiency) goals. There are also developmental issues to be considered in the poorer countries (see Chapter 10). The problem is that legitimate and necessary discussion of these issues has been replaced on occasions by politically charged demands for sovereignty and national independence. As will be shown in Chapter 4, equity and sovereignty were key issues in many developing countries in the 1960s and 1970s; but they were also high on the political agenda in the United States in the late 1980s in respect of Japanese ownership of American industry (although attempts to legislate against inward acquisitions, for instance, did not succeed). By contrast, for most of the 1990s, debate was submerged by the tide sweeping in favour of liberalization. The need for balance is, however, recognized in some policy instruments: for example, the OECD Guidelines for Multinational Enterprises (1976) indicate that MNEs should take account of countries' aims and priorities, such as industrial and regional development, environmental protection, employment creation, and technology transfer. If a comprehensive multilateral investment agreement is to be accepted by all countries, the efficiency/equity balance and the rights of countries will need to be tackled within the framework of rules.

Despite the above, policy orientation at national level has tended in the past to focus upon methods of extracting rents from MNEs, which in turn is a function of bargaining power. In their model of the determinants of a country's strategy to attract and control foreign investors (i.e. national FDI policy), Guisinger and associates (1985) identified key national constraints as follows:

- population size;
- level of economic development;
- social and economic objectives;
- negotiating experience;
- government organization;
- international trade and investment agreements (i.e. the constraints imposed upon a country because it is a signatory to international agreements).

These factors, which mainly distinguish between small and large, and developed and developing nations, determine the bargaining power of the country. But they have also to be considered alongside the strategies and bargaining strength of the multinational itself. Guisinger and associates (1985) argued that this depended principally upon the market orientation of the firm, as between domestic markets, regional markets (free trade areas, customs unions, or common markets), and global markets. Where the MNE was seeking to enter, say, a large, closed domestic market (India or Nigeria might be illustrations from the past), the bargaining power of the host country government would be high. By contrast, the existence of alternative sites for regionally or globally oriented investments provides much greater bargaining strength for the enterprise. As suggested earlier, globalization has had an important influence on the worldwide trend towards liberalization of FDI rules.

In categorizing country-level FDI rules, different authors have developed different classifications. In describing the policy measures that governments use to attract and control foreign investors, Guisinger and associates (1985) distinguished between instruments which provided *incentives* to the MNE and those which acted as *disincentives*. A further listing by UNCTAD (1996*a*) highlights the key concepts and issues covered in investment rules, as follows.

1. *Investment measures that affect the entry and operations of foreign investors.*
   - admission and establishment (Table 1.1);
   - ownership and control (Table 1.2);
   - operational and other measures including trade-related investment measures (TRIMs) (Table 1.3);
   - incentives (Table 1.4);
   - investment-related trade measures (Table 1.5).

Table 1.1 Selected Government Impediments to Admission and Establishment[a]

- Closing certain sectors, industries, or activities to FDI.
- Quantitative restrictions on the number of foreign companies admitted in specific sectors, industries, or activities.
- Minimum capital requirements.
- Screening, authorization, and registration of investment.
- Conditional entry upon investment meeting certain development or other criteria (e.g. environmental responsibility).
- Restrictions on forms of entry (e.g. mergers and acquisitions may not be allowed, or must meet certain additional requirements).
- Special requirements for non-equity forms of investment (e.g. build–operate–transfer (BOT) agreements, licensing of foreign technology).
- Investment not allowed in certain zones or regions within a country.
- Restrictions on import of capital goods needed to set up an investment (e.g. machinery, software).
- Admission to privatization bids restricted or conditional on additional guarantees, for foreign investors.
- Investors required to comply with norms related to national security, policy, customs, public morals requirements as conditions to entry.

Note: [a]These measures may apply to all FDI or to investment in specific sectors, industries, or activities, or to investors of a certain nationality. Some measures listed in this table could also be relevant to ownership and control and operations of MNEs (Tables 1.2 and 1.3).

Source: Shortened from UNCTAD, 1996*a*: table VI.1, p. 176.

2. *Standards of treatment* (see Box 1.1).
   - national treatment, according to which the foreign investor should be treated in a manner no less favourable than that accorded to local nationals;
   - most favoured nation (MFN) treatment, by which foreign investors should be treated in a manner no less favourable than that accorded to other third country investors;
   - fair and equitable treatment, aiming to provide a basic standard detached from the host country's law.

Table 1.2 Selected Government Impediments to Foreign Ownership and Control[a]

- Restrictions on foreign ownership (e.g. no more than 50 per cent of foreign-owned capital allowed).
- Compulsory joint ventures, either with state participation or with local private investors.
- Mandatory transfers of ownership to local firms, usually over a period of time (fade-out requirements).
- Nationality restrictions on the ownership of the company or shares thereof.
- Restrictions on foreign shareholders' rights (e.g. on payments of dividends, reimbursement of capital upon liquidation; on voting rights; denial of information disclosure on certain aspects of the running of the investment).
- 'Golden' shares to be held by the host government, e.g. allowing it to prevent the foreign investor holding more than a certain percentage of the investment.
- Government reserves the right to appoint one or more members to the board of directors.
- Restrictions on the nationality of directors, or limitations on the number of expatriates in top managerial positions.
- Management restrictions on foreign-controlled monopolies or upon privatization of public companies.
- Restrictions on land or immoveable property ownership and transfers thereof.
- Restrictions on industrial or intellectual property ownership or protection.
- Restrictions on the licensing of foreign technology.

Note: [a]These measures may apply to all FDI or, more often, to investment in specific sectors, industries, or activities. Some measures listed in this table could also be relevant to admission and establishment and operation of MNEs (Tables 1.1 and 1.3).

Source: Shortened from UNCTAD, 1996*a*: table VI.2, p. 177

3. *Measures addressing broader concerns.*

- restrictive business practices, relating to anti-competitive practices by firms, and usually dealt with through forms of competition policy;
- transfer pricing;
- transfer of technology;
- employment, which may cover a wide range of issues including wages and working conditions, safety and health, equality of opportunity, security of employment, information disclosure, consultation, collective bargaining;
- environmental issues;
- illicit payments.

Table 1.3 Selected Government Impediments to Operations[a]

- Restrictions on employment of foreign key professional or technical personnel.
- Performance requirements, such as sourcing/local content requirements, manufacturing requirements; technology transfer requirements, employment requirements, regional and/or global product mandates, training requirements, export requirements, trade-balancing requirements, import restrictions.
- Public procurement restrictions (e.g. foreign investors excluded as government suppliers or subject to providing special guarantees).
- Restrictions on imports of capital goods, spare parts, manufacturing inputs.
- Restrictions on long-term leases of land and real property.
- Restrictions to relocate operations within the country.
- Restrictions on access to telecommunications networks.
- Restrictions on access to local credit facilities or to foreign exchange.
- Restrictions on repatriation of capital and profits (case-by-case approval, additional taxation or remittances, phase-out of transfers over a number of years).
- 'Cultural' restrictions, mainly in relation to educational or media services.
- Disclosure of information requirements (e.g. on the foreign operations of an MNE).
- Special operational requirements on foreign firms in certain sectors/activities (e.g. on branches of foreign banks).
- Operational permits and licences (e.g. to transfer funds).
- Special requirements on professional qualifications, technical standards.
- Advertising restrictions for foreign firms.
- Ceilings on royalties and technical assistance fees or special taxes.
- Limits on the use of certain technologies (e.g. territorial restrictions), brand names, etc. or case-by-case approval and conditions.
- Rules of origin, tracing requirements.
- Operational restrictions related to national security, public order, public morals, etc.

Note: [a]These measures may apply to all FDI or, more often, to investment in specific sectors, industries, or activities. Some measures listed in this table could also be relevant to admission and establishment, and to ownership and control (Tables 1.1 and 1.2).

Source: Shortened from UNCTAD, 1996*a*: table VI.3, p. 179.

4. *Investment protection and dispute settlement*.

- expropriation and nationalization of property;
- transfer of funds;
- other protection issues, e.g. the ability of MNEs to employ foreign key personnel of their choice;
- dispute settlement.

Table 1.4 Main Types of Incentive Measures Offered to Foreign Investors

1. Fiscal incentives, including:
   - Reduction of the standard corporate income-tax rate.
   - Tax holidays.
   - Accelerated depreciation allowances on capital taxes.
   - Investment and reinvestment allowances.
   - Reductions in social security contributions.
   - Corporate income-tax deductions based on, for example, expenditures relating to marketing and promotional activities.
   - Value-added based incentives, e.g. corporate income-tax reductions or credits based on the net local content of outputs.
   - Import-based incentives, including exemption from import duties on capital equipment or inputs related to the production process; tax credits for duties paid on imported materials or supplies.
   - Export-based incentives, including exemptions from export duties; preferential tax treatment of income from exports; income-tax reduction for special foreign-exchange-earning activities or for manufactured exports.
2. Financial incentives, including:
   - 'Direct subsidies' to cover (part of) capital, production, or marketing costs in relation to an investment project.
   - Subsidized loans.
   - Loan guarantees.
   - Guaranteed export credits.
   - Publicly funded venture capital in high-risk investments.
   - Government insurance at preferential rates.
3. Other incentives, including:
   - Subsidized dedicated infrastructure.
   - Subsidized services, including assistance in identifying sources of finance, carrying out pre-investment studies, information on markets, availability of raw inputs, advice on production processes and marketing techniques, assistance with training and retraining.
   - Preferential government contracts.
   - Closing the market to further entry or the granting of monopoly rights.
   - Protection from import competition.

Source: Shortened from UNCTAD, 1996*a*: table VI.4, p. 180.

Table 1.5 Investment-Related Trade Measures (IRTMs)

Trade measure	Possible impact on FDI
Tariffs and quantitative restrictions on imports	Induces import-substituting FDI
Sectorally managed trade, including voluntary export restraints	Induces import-substituting FDI
Regional free trade agreements	Promotes FDI in the member countries
Rules-of-origin policies	Induces FDI in component production
Export-processing zones	Induces export-oriented FDI
Export controls (security and foreign policy)	Induces export-replacing FDI
Export financing	Increases export-oriented FDI
Non-monetary trade agreements (co-production; buy-back)	Depends on the nature of specific arrangements
Safety, health, environment, privacy, and other national standards	Induces import-substituting FDI

Source: UNCTAD, 1996*a*: table VI.5, p. 181.

Examples of the application of these incentive and disincentive measures at country/region and sectoral level are contained throughout the book. As an illustration at this point, however, the case of the USA is presented in Box 1.2, and Box 1.3 highlights the issue of subsidy competition.

Bilateral

Bilateral investment treaties (BITs) concerned exclusively with investment have been in existence since the late 1950s; and their numbers have grown very rapidly, especially in the 1980s and 1990s. For the capital exporting country, the major objective is to obtain legal protection for FDI under international law, and so the provisions in BITs are designed to supplement the laws of the host country in respect of protection standards. For the capital importing country, BITs are used as one means of attracting inward FDI, and they provide important signals concerning a country's investment climate. Initially the major participants in these BITs were Western countries, on the one hand, and Central and Eastern European countries, on the other; more recently, however, treaties involving NICs and developing countries have also been concluded.

As a means of improving the investment climate, BITs guarantee non-discriminatory treatment for foreign investors through provisions concerning national treatment, MFN, and fair and equitable treatment; they provide protection in the form of standards of treatment concerning expropriation and international transfer of funds; and they establish dispute settlement procedures.

Separately from BITs but developed on a bilateral basis are large numbers of

Box 1.1

National Treatment and Other Standards of Treatment

National treatment is a central neutrality or non-discrimination standard in investment agreements. The provision is deceptively simple, specifying that *MNEs receive treatment that is no less favourable than that given to their domestic competitors*. It goes to the heart of perhaps the most significant problem facing foreign investors, namely the lack of comparable treatment to that applying to indigenous enterprises. It would thus prohibit, for instance, local content requirements, since domestic firms do not face restrictions on their choice of inputs; it would prevent preferential access for domestic firms to government contracts; it would prohibit preferential treatment in the form of aids and subsidies to government-owned enterprises; preferential aids provided by the state to domestic firms in the form of grants, low-interest loans, interest subsidies, and guarantees would be banned, and so on. On the other hand, the terminology of 'no less favourable than' means that discrimination in favour of foreign enterprises is not excluded; and investment incentives in many developed countries might well favour MNEs in reality, even if the subsidies are in theory available to all enterprises.

The national treatment standard was first applied to the general treatment of aliens, then found its way into commercial treaty practice, subsequently into bilateral and regional investment agreements, and now into multilateral investment instruments.

A national treatment provision was included within the 1976 OECD Declaration and Decisions on International Investment and Multinational Enterprises. Initially applying only to the operations of established foreign investors, in 1984 it was extended to new establishments also. Under Article 1, however, member countries are permitted to notify exceptions to national treatment, and a wide range of these exist, especially sectoral exceptions. In the case of Japan, for example, investment by foreign firms is restricted in agriculture, forestry and fisheries, mining, oil, and leather products; reciprocity provisions apply in respect of financial services and the acquisition of land; and there are limitations on voting rights and board membership for foreigners in air transport. A national treatment provision is contained in other multilateral instruments, e.g. General Agreement on Trade in Services (GATS) Article XVII in the World Trade Organization. For significant progress to be made in investment liberalization in future, new rules will need to be agreed on limiting the exceptions to national treatment (recognizing that there are legitimate exceptions on grounds of national security, defence, and public order); including a standstill on exceptions (no new exceptions to be introduced); and providing for rollback (elimination over time) of existing exceptions. Furthermore, it will be necessary to provide a consistent definition across instruments so as to avoid a confusing and contradictory patchwork. Other problems concern the distinction between foreign and domestic firms which begins to blur when MNEs operate integrated international production systems.

The second fundamental standard is that of *most favoured nation (MFN) treatment*. According to this standard, foreign investors are to be treated in a manner not less favourable than that in which other third country investors are treated. The MFN principle has also been fundamental to multilateral trade negotiations through the GATT/WTO: thus a tariff rate applying to imports of a specific product from a trading partner must be applied immediately and unconditionally to the imports of this same good from all WTO members.

The third standard is that of *fair and equitable treatment*. Its aim is to provide a basic standard separate from the host country's law which a foreign investor (or the home nation) may invoke.

Source: UNCTAD, 1996*a*; BIAC Committee on International Investment and Multinational Enterprises, 1982; OECD 1994*a*.

Box 1.2

United States Impediments to Inward FDI

Although the United States has more open FDI policies than most countries, it nevertheless has in place a variety of impediments to inward FDI. The list below summarizes the principal legislative and regulatory impediments to FDI. The list is not exhaustive; nor are most of the details of the definitions, conditions, exceptions, or applications of the impediments included here. For instance, although, under the potentially wide-ranging terms of the Exon-Florio Amendment, the President could perhaps deny foreign investments relatively easily, in fact, of the almost 800 transactions that had been registered as of April 1993, there had been investigations of only fifteen and only one had been blocked. Also note, however, that this list pertains only to US federal government legislation and regulations; it does not include any sub-national-level impediments, which are numerous for instance in the form of state-level restrictions in banking, insurance, and real estate and in the form of *de facto* local-level restrictions on government purchasing practices.

National security

Exon-Florio Amendment to the Defense Production Act: President can block or suspend mergers, acquisitions, or takeovers of US firms by foreign investors if the transaction poses a threat to national security or if other laws and regulations are not adequate to protect national security. Defense Authorization Act of 1993 requires a report to the Congress on each investigation, including an analysis of the effects on US technological leadership related to national security.

Industrial Security Program: security clearances for facilities and individuals in US firms with foreign ownership, control, or influence can be denied for contracts involving classified information.

Arms Export Control Act/International Traffic in Arms Regulations: transfer of ownership of US firm to foreign investor can be denied.

Helms–Burton Act of 1995: provides for private claims, with the potential for substantial penalties against foreign-owned corporations and individuals that purchased property in Cuba that had been confiscated by the Cuban government from US citizens.

Research and development

National Cooperative Research and Production Act of 1993: requires that a qualifying firm must be controlled by a US firm or a firm from a country that grants national treatment to US corporations concerning anti-trust policies on joint production arrangements—i.e. it imposes a conditional national treatment test.

National Competitiveness Act of 1993: requires that qualifying firms be 'United States owned' and thus be majority owned or controlled by US citizens.

Air transport

Federal Aviation Act of 1958: foreign ownership and management are restricted for airlines that receive licences to provide domestic services between points in the United States.

Communications

Communications Act of 1934: a foreign-controlled firm (e.g. one with more than 25 per cent foreign ownership) can be denied a licence to operate a radio station.

Communications Satellite Act of 1962: not more than 20 per cent of the shares of stock offered for sale to the public can be owned by foreign investors.

Shipping

Merchant Marine Act of 1920 (Jones Act): corporations involved in coastal or inland waterway transportation, including territories and possessions, must be at least 75 per cent American owned. US-owned vessels may not be transferred to a non-American owner without the approval of the Secretary of Transportation. Firms that are more than 50 per cent foreign owned may not receive various government subsidies.

Also, numerous laws and regulations require partial or complete US ownership of ships carrying shipments under various government procurement or assistance programmes.

Fishing

Commercial Fishing Industry Vessel Anti-Reflagging Act of 1987: foreign-flag vessels may not fish in the exclusive economic zone.

Energy sector

Geothermal Steam Act: in order for a corporation to construct, own, or operate an ocean thermal energy conversion facility in US territorial waters, its executives and board of directors must meet certain nationality requirements.

Atomic Energy Act of 1954: foreign-controlled firms are not allowed licences for many activities in the nuclear energy industry.

Financial services

Primary Dealers Act: US Federal Reserve can deny primary dealer status to a foreign-controlled bank—and thus not deal with it directly in transactions involving US government securities—if the bank's government does not grant reciprocal rights to US banks.

Mining

Minerals Land Leasing Act of 1920: a foreign-controlled firm may not acquire rights of way for oil pipelines or interests in mining in coal, oil, or some other minerals on US government land unless the foreign firm's government grants reciprocal rights to US-owned firms. (Otherwise, however, the Mining Law of 1872 allows foreign investment—either directly or indirectly—in minerals.)

Agriculture

Agricultural Foreign Investment Disclosure Act of 1978: foreign investors in agricultural land must report their transactions and holdings to the Agriculture Department for periodic US reports on the effects of foreign ownership on family farms and rural communities.

Sources: APEC, 1994; European Commission, 1996*a*; Warner and Rugman, 1994.

Box 1.3

Example of Investment Subsidy Competition: BMW in the UK

'The British government . . . offered a last-minute increase in state aid to ensure that a $650m engine plant for German vehicle manufacturer BMW and its Rover offshoot [would] be built in England rather than Austria. Mr. Ian Lang, Britain's chief industry minister, said the government had offered £22.5m ($37.12m) in regional selective assistance for the factory, which will produce new generation four-cylinder engines for BMW and Rover cars after 2000. This, combined with unspecified additional funds for training and infrastructure, is believed to have taken the total to the £45m–£50m sought by BMW. Mr. Lang said he was confident the British government's "substantial package" would be approved by the European Commission's competition directorate.

The deal was concluded . . . after a meeting between Mr. Lang, Mr. Bernd Pischetsrieder, BMW's chairman, and Mr. Walter Hasselkus, Rover's chief executive. Mr. Hasselkus said . . . that although the government had not offered any additional element in aid, it had raised its regional selective assistance and added "a little bit here, a little bit there". Mr. Lang said: "I had a little bit more money than before".

BMW [had] said . . . that it would prefer to build the plant in the UK. However, Mr. Pischetsrieder said the company needed to consider Austria, where it has substantial engine facilities built partly with state assistance. Delays in signing what appeared to be an almost certain investment in the UK led to speculation that the Austrian government had indicated that it would offer BMW another substantial package of assistance. By contrast, the original British proposal was "on the wrong side of £40m", according to a Rover official.

The engine plant is the latest in a string of investments which have boosted confidence in the UK motor industry. Rover has announced plans to spend £400m for a smaller Land Rover model and associated investments in nearby Solihull. The Vauxhall subsidiary of General Motors of the US announced last month that it would spend £300m on upgrading and expanding its Ellesmere Port car plant in north-west England while Nissan of Japan is to invest £70m to build an estate car version of its Primera in the north-east.

Mr. Hasselkus said the engine plant would secure 1,500 jobs at Longbridge as well as about 5,000 positions in the UK motor components industry. The new 1.6–2 litre power plants will be used in mid-sized Rover and BMW vehicles. A joint Rover–BMW engineering team is already working on the project.'

Source: *Financial Times*, 1996*b*.

double taxation agreements, and, on a much smaller scale involving a few developed countries, are cooperation, notification, and information exchange agreements in the area of competition policy.

Regional

From 1947 to 1994, 109 regional integration agreements (RIAs) were notified to the GATT (WTO, 1995*a*), with the main periods of growth being the 1970s and the years since 1990. Not all of these agreements include FDI rules but many do. In respect of investment, regional agreements may be considered from two points of view. First, regional blocs could be regarded as larger 'countries', in which case the major attribute of the bloc is its greater bargaining power, providing the member states act collectively (this was the rationale behind Decision 24 of the Andean Common Market—see Chapter 4). Failure to agree on common rules, by contrast, will lead to competitive bidding for investment, as MNEs could have a choice of country locations amongst which they are relatively indifferent (this is broadly the position of the EU at present at least in respect of FDI issues *per se*; in other regards it has many features of category two below). A second category of regional integration agreements would be those designed to replicate multilateral agreements with rules aimed at facilitating liberalization and overcoming market distortions and market failure. In regard to FDI rules, NAFTA is viewed as state-of-the-art in many respects but it has no parallels to the EU's Single Market programme or its competition policy, for example.

As these illustrations indicate, there are many types of regional integration agreements. UNCTAD (1996*a*) suggest a number of characteristics of regional level rules:

- Most regional investments are legally binding, although there are exceptions such as the Asia-Pacific Economic Cooperation (APEC) group principles.
- The definition of investment varies considerably.
- Right of entry and establishment are increasingly being granted. Nevertheless, signatory nations have commonly exempted a number of industries or activities.
- Incentives within the EU are controlled in respect of regional aid and otherwise may be subject to competition policy rules; but are excluded from most other agreements. Performance requirements have received limited attention except in the case of NAFTA. In respect of other operational conditions, admission of foreign senior personnel is often addressed.
- Standards of treatment and protection after entry follow closely the content and structure of BITs.

The expansion of regionalization is highly controversial. To cite Kobrin (1995: 15): 'Much of the discussion on regional integration is framed in terms of "building blocks" or "stumbling blocks"; will regional economic agreements . . . facilitate the development of an open and liberal international economy, or do they portend the devolution of the world economy into closed, competing economic areas?'

Multilateral

Progress with rule-making at the multilateral level has been very intermittent, partial and fragmented in respect of:

- The organizations involved, which include the World Trade Organization, the World Bank, the United Nations (ILO and UNCTAD), and the OECD.
- Issue coverage, where there is at least some reference to liberalization of capital movements and of invisible transactions (OECD), incentives (OECD

Declaration on International Investment and Multinational Enterprises), and performance requirements (TRIMs agreement in the WTO), intellectual property rights (TRIPs agreement in the WTO), insurance coverage for political risks in developing countries (World Bank), settlement of disputes (World Bank), employment and labour relations (ILO), and operational aspects of MNE activities (OECD Guidelines on Multinational Enterprises). Services are covered specifically in the General Agreement on Trade in Services (GATS—World Trade Organization).

- Depth of coverage. This is highly variable. For example, the Declaration on Incentives in the OECD has had little effect in constraining competitive bidding. The TRIMs agreement is quite limited in terms of the range of performance requirements which are forbidden. The ILO rules on employment and labour relations merely set a bottom to labour standards and arguably do not refer to some of the key issues of the 1990s. By contrast, the dispute settlement mechanisms have been somewhat successful, and the insurance coverage for political risks, available through the World Bank (the Multilateral Investment Guarantee Agency), has proved valuable.
- Binding or non-binding agreements. The WTO rules, those of the World Bank on dispute settlement, and those of the OECD on liberalization of capital movements and of current invisible transactions are legally binding. The ILO principles on employment and labour relations and most of the content in the OECD's Declaration on International Investment and Multinational Enterprises are non-binding.
- Year of establishment. The OECD Liberalization Codes date from the early 1960s, the OECD Declaration on International Investment and Multinational Enterprises from 1976, and the ILO Declaration of Principles from 1977. By comparison, the WTO agreements were negotiated as part of the Uruguay Round which was completed in 1994. Even though the 1970s agreements were voluntary, it might be expected that the lengthy experience with the rules would have increased their impact. A difficulty with the non-binding OECD instruments has been that implementation procedures were weak; and, in truth, there was a lack of interest in multilateral FDI rules among developed countries through the 1980s when it became clear that the bargaining power of developing nations was weak and forces in the world economy were driving in the direction of liberalization. It might be added that it took twenty-five years from the adoption of the binding OECD Liberalization Codes until the right of establishment was confirmed.
- Country coverage. The OECD membership is no longer limited to developed nations; now includes countries such as Korea, Mexico, Poland and the Czech Republic. The OECD have also made a big point of the fact that the Dynamic Non-member Economies in Asia and Latin America were consulted on the terms of the Multilateral Agreement on Investment (MAI) being negotiated from 1995 to 1998, and that the MAI was open to accession by non-OECD members.

- Issue interrelationships. This is a critical topic for the future, concerning not only the interrelatedness of FDI issues but also the interrelations among trade, FDI, and competition rules. A major problem concerning the latter derives from the forum in which negotiations take place. Emerging from the GATT, the WTO has a much stronger trade than FDI orientation both in terms of emphasis of rules and in expertise. Thus the TRIMs agreement in the Uruguay Round dealt only with investment measures related to trade in goods, and the GATS is focused primarily on trade.

There is now a reasonable consensus on the positive contributions of foreign direct investment in the world economy and on the welfare gains from policy liberalization. There must, of course, be recognition of development policies and objectives in any comprehensive agreement involving both developed and developing countries. Some of the principles to which an effective multilateral agreement should aspire include the following (UNCTAD, 1996*a*):

- Market contestability and modal neutrality. This concept recognizes that firms can contest markets through a variety of modalities such as trade, FDI, and licensing, and that there should be no discrimination in favour of one modality over another since this will reduce competition and economic efficiency. Where modal neutrality exists, policies leave to the firm the decision as to how the market should be serviced. The notion of contestable 'markets', however, includes both product markets and factor markets. Inclusion of the latter widens the range of policy issues very significantly. As UNCTAD (1996*a*: 164) point out, 'policies that limit participation in real estate markets, or restrict visas, or restrict grants of government research-and-development contracts on the basis of nationality of ownership of firms, inhibit the contestability of factor markets, respectively in land, labour and technology'. Market contestability would also require competition policies (which would have to be multilateral, otherwise conflicting national policies would simply introduce another distortion to the functioning of markets). Not only would the potential oligopolistic practices of MNEs be included, but so too would preferential treatment of state enterprises and discriminatory procurement policies because of their adverse effects on competition.
- Policy coherence. This concerns the level of consistency between government objectives and policies across a broad range of issues, including fiscal and monetary policies. The need to consider the interrelations between trade and FDI policies has already been mentioned, but there are many more questions that need to be considered. Essentially the issue becomes one of identifying those areas of national policy which have an international business dimension, since all may have a distorting effect on MNEs' decision-making and, therefore, on worldwide efficiency. All such policies, unless regulated, could, for instance, form the basis of competitive bidding between governments, as policy competition shifts from regulated to unregulated areas of activity.

  Dunning (1992) identified a variety of structural market distortions (brought about by participants in the market or by inappropriate government intervention, e.g. oligopoly / monopoly control of output by firms, interference with the market mechanism by government in terms of price controls, health, safety and environmental regulations, etc.); and endemic market failures (brought about by the inability of unaided markets to minimize transaction costs, e.g. failure of markets to deal adequately with risk and uncertainty; failure of markets to cope with the public goods characteristics of some products). A variety of government responses were also suggested to overcome these within the context of a global economy. Such market-improving measures are important to the improvement of economic efficiency, but they need to be considered at an international level if there are international implications.

The fact is that it will never be possible to develop such a comprehensive multilateral agreement. The solution would, therefore, seem to lie in distinguishing clearly between, first, those areas of policy which are the sovereign right of national governments including security, education, transportation and communications, and regional policies, and macroeconomic policies concerning monetary, fiscal, exchange rate, and demand management matters (in a number of these areas there will be a need for nations to cooperate, nevertheless). Second, policy areas which are strongly embedded in national institutions, culture, and tradition. Safarian (1993) mentions different national approaches to shareholder laws and rights, but there will be many other issues at this level of policy-making, where the objective should be to strive for national treatment, i.e. ensuring that the policies do not discriminate between foreign and domestic enterprises. And, thirdly, policy areas to be covered by multilateral rules.

- Binding rules with wide country coverage, for reasons highlighted above.
- Comprehensive rules. The critical building blocks concern the *definition of investment*; *national treatment* and *most favoured nation treatment* with liberalization commitments and few exceptions so that the instruments are not diluted and there are possibilities for rolling back existing restrictions; and *dispute settlement mechanisms* including both state-to-state and investor-to-investor mechanisms, with the decision of the arbitration tribunals being binding upon the parties to the dispute. A comprehensive agreement would go much wider than this to cover as many as possible of the main market closing or market distorting issues listed on pages 26–30.

The problems generated by the myriad types, systems, and levels of investment instruments worldwide are well known. Even without these difficulties, it is apparent that the design of a framework of international rules which would meet the conditions for improving economic efficiency is an immensely complex task. This derives from the ubiquitous nature of the MNE and its involvement in a wide range of market servicing methods—from arm's length trade in goods, services, and technology to internalized international production in wholly owned subsidiaries.

2

Foreign Direct Investment and the World Economy

A Historical Overview

The purpose of this chapter is to present an overview of the major influences on the growth of FDI and the MNE in the post-war years. Although global drivers (in particular rates of worldwide economic expansion, but also including globalization forces) are of paramount importance, policy issues have also been significant. Given the holistic nature of the multinational firm as a mechanism for undertaking international business activities, the present chapter discusses the links with and influences of trade and trade policy, balance of payments policy, and technology policy as well as shifts in FDI policies in the post-Second World War era.

2.1 Influences on the Growth of FDI and the MNE

In reviewing the determinants of international direct investment, Figure 2.1 distinguishes among a variety of drivers which facilitate an understanding both of the overall expansion of FDI and of sectoral and home and host country patterns. Among the *global drivers* are the rate of economic growth, which influences both domestic and international investment decisions; other macroeconomic variables and particularly exchange rates and the balance of payments; forces of deregulation and privatization which have been especially important since the late 1980s, and have been linked to regulatory reform to attract FDI; regional integration, especially in the form of the Single Market programme of the European Union; and, first, the signing of the Free Trade Agreement between the United States and Canada, and then the formation of NAFTA. Mention should also be made of global 'shocks' and geopolitical factors, into which categories would come, for instance, the political and economic reforms in Central and Eastern Europe and economic liberalization in China.

Corporate strategies are also a major influence on the growth of FDI. The strategy to invest abroad is itself likely to lead subsequently to a self-sustaining growth of investment and resource flows. Recent data, for example, suggest that approximately 80 per cent of FDI is represented by reinvestment (Dunning, 1994*b*). The internationalization and globalization of the world economy is encouraging FDI by small and

Fig. 2.1 Determinants of International Direct Investment, 1985–1990s

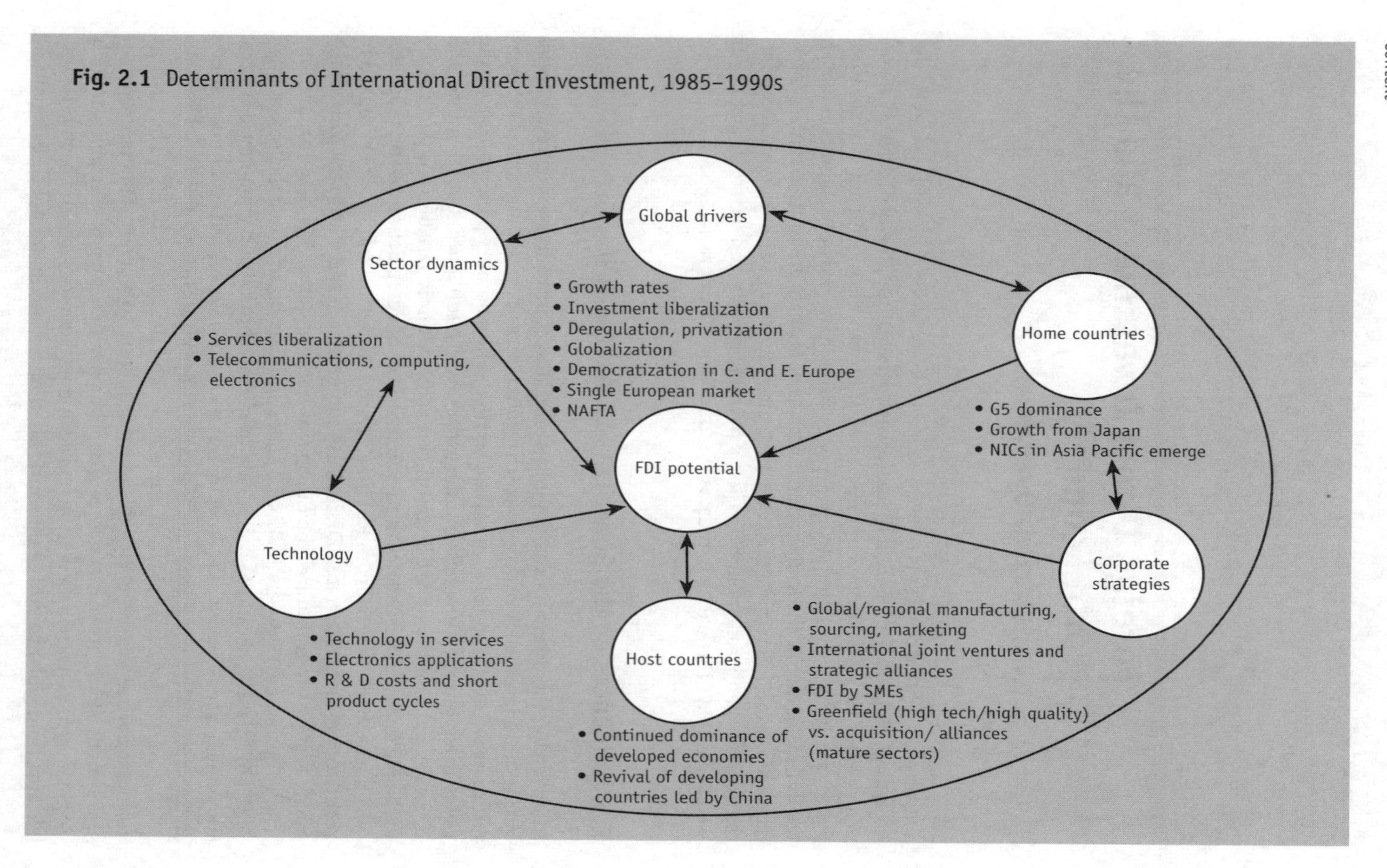

medium-sized enterprises as domestic markets are threatened by heightened competition and technological developments improve companies' capabilities to exploit opportunities abroad. Among the larger multinational firms, regional and global sourcing, manufacturing, and marketing activities are creating integrated international production systems and producing a self-sustaining momentum for FDI growth (UNCTAD, 1993). The recognition that cross-border transactions may be of many forms (see the early work of Oman, 1984), including non-equity arrangements and strategic alliances, further encourages multinational activities. Mention might also be made of changes in organizational behaviour in firms and the trend to delayering and the flattening of structures. This is at least one influence upon the early signs of moves towards heterarchies, worldwide centres of excellence, or world product mandate subsidiaries; the (usually limited) autonomy granted to foreign affiliates will stimulate a further drive to internationalization.

Figure 2.1 highlights a range of other determinants which mainly explain the patterns of FDI. For example, the level of economic development in *home nations* will be an influence upon and an indicator of the capability of the country's enterprises to generate firm-specific assets which can be exploited abroad through FDI. The outward orientation of the economy and the legislative/regulatory situation (e.g. liberalization of direct capital outflows, support programmes for outward internationalization) are further home country factors. Liberalization at *host nation* level provides a similar incentive to inward FDI, alongside market and cost variables. Finally, *sectoral dynamics* (such as factor intensity, the stage of the industry life cycle, and the industry's trade orientation) allied to *technology* (the emergence of new technologies, technological diffusion, R & D costs, and the length of life cycles for products, etc.) complete the model of determinants shown in the figure.

Further ways of categorizing determinants could be presented. For example, UNCTAD (1993) distinguish between policy variables (trade liberalization, exchange rates, etc.) and structural factors (the growth of the stock of FDI and the emergence of integrated international production). It is important, however, to recognize that short-term factors will have a significant influence on FDI flows at particular points in time (UNCTAD: 1993: 92–8). First, business cycles may have a variety of effects:

- Cyclical influences on FDI flows and capital expenditures. Since the growth of FDI outflows is closely correlated with output growth, decisions to invest abroad are affected by business cycles—both global business cycles, and cyclical conditions in home versus overseas markets.
- Sectoral differences. There are suggestions that capital spending by services' MNEs is more resilient to business cycles than that by manufacturing companies.
- Financing methods. Business cycles are likely to influence the balance of financing as between equity, reinvested earnings, and intra-company loans. For example, equity or loans to affiliates may be preferred during a cyclical upswing.

Second, mergers and acquisitions both domestically and internationally are subject to short-term influences, including interest rates and stock market valuations and (at an international level) exchange rate movements. Competitive and structural variables, such as excess capacity in low- and medium-technology industries, have also encouraged acquisition entry and expansion, with greenfield ventures predominantly in high-tech and high-growth sectors.

2.2 The Economic and Political Environment in the Post-War Years

Within the context of the above discussion, Table 2.1 summarizes some of the main highlights in the evolution of the world economy in the post-war period. In the early years, the dollar shortage in Europe at a time of accumulation of pent-up demand from the Second World War and large-scale aid from the United States under the Marshall Plan encouraged and facilitated the huge outflow of US FDI. Until the 1960s the multilateral institutional framework provided a stable and robust investment environment. It became apparent, however, that the economies of the reserve currency countries (particularly the UK, but the USA too) were incapable of sustaining their role in the face of balance of payments deficits. The devaluation of the pound and the establishment of a two-price system for gold in 1967/8 was the beginning of a period of considerable monetary volatility which culminated in 1973 in the demise of the Bretton Woods system and the introduction of floating rates. Underlying the macroeconomic instability was the overvalued dollar, the loss of competitiveness of US industry, and the growing economic strength of Germany and Japan and their respective enterprises. The substantial growth of FDI from Continental Europe and Japan has its roots in this period.

The major shocks in the 1970s were associated with the quadrupling of oil prices in 1973 and their further doubling in 1979; and the knock-on repercussions which included world recession, high rates of inflation, trade protectionism, and debt service problems in developing countries. Understandably, therefore, as later data show, FDI flows grew relatively slowly for much of the period. A surge in flows took place between 1978 and 1981, when growth averaged 11 per cent per annum (UNCTAD, 1993), before a second recession in 1982–3 curtailed international direct investment expansion. The period from the mid-1980s saw an exceptional concurrence of events

Table 2.1 Chronology of Some Major Events and Shocks in the Post-War World Economy

1944 (July)	Bretton Woods Conference and subsequent establishment of IMF and IBRD.
1945–50	Anglo-American loan agreement and Marshall Plan leading to large-scale US aid to Western Europe.
1947–48	Havana Conference and unratified Charter of the International Trade Organization. Formation of GATT.
1958 (1 Jan.)	European Economic Community (EEC) formed by Treaty of Rome. Membership comprised France, Germany, Italy, the Netherlands, Belgium, and Luxembourg.

1959–68	US balance of payments deficits, dollar glut, and overvalued dollar.
1961	OECD Codes of Liberalization of Capital Movements and of Current Invisibles agreed.
1964	UNCTAD established.
1967	GATT Kennedy Round completed.
1968–73	Two-price system of gold and creation of SDRs (1968); dollar devaluations 1971 and 1973; collapse of Bretton Woods system, and start of floating exchange rate era.
1973	Quadrupling of oil prices by OPEC.
	Enlargement of European Community (EC) to include Denmark, Ireland, and UK.
1974	Multifibre Arrangement restricting import growth in industrialized countries.
1974–early 1980s	Higher commodity prices feeding through into industrial costs. Second oil price hike 1979. High inflation rate and balance of payments problems in developing and some developed nations. Rise of the 'new protectionism' (growth of non-tariff barriers). Debt service problems in developing countries. Two major recessions in world economy.
1985	Single European Act to create Single Market in European Union (EU) by 1 Jan. 1993.
1986	Plaza Accord by G5 nations (France, Germany, Japan, UK, USA) to encourage appreciation of the yen (and DM).
1988	US Omnibus Trade and Competitiveness Act passed. Reinforced trend to protectionism and bilateralism. [a]
1989	Conference on Asia Pacific Economic Cooperation—twelve countries take first steps towards loose trade arrangement.
1990	Reunification of Germany.
1991	Opening up of Eastern and Central Europe and moves to free market economy.
1992	Signing of North American Free Trade Agreement (NAFTA) by USA, Canada and Mexico. Operational from 1 Jan. 1994.
	Establishment of Commonwealth of Independent States (CIS) among nations of former USSR.
	Treaty of Economic Union in EU established plan for economic and monetary union by 1999.
1994	GATT Uruguay Round completed.
	Commencement of negotiations in OECD for Multilateral Agreement on Investment.
1995	World Trade Organization established.
	Enlargement of EU to include Austria, Finland, and Sweden (Greece joined in 1981 and Spain and Portugal in 1986).

Note: [a]By 1987, 23% of world non-fuel trade was subject to NTBs (UN, 1989).

Source: UN, *World Economic Survey*, various issues.

in support of FDI. Figure 2.1 summarizes these factors in relation to the model of FDI determinants. Trade liberalization, through the Uruguay Round, was accompanied by extensive investment liberalization (particularly at national level and relating to both outward and inward FDI) and sectoral liberalization affecting telecommunications and other services. Liberalization in turn was driven by and also drove globalization; while in the FDI area, progress in regionalization, especially through the EU's Single Market programme and the formation of NAFTA, operated positively in support of globalization trends.

2.3 Trade and Trade Policy

The importance of the links between FDI and trade have already been pointed out. The role of trade in the international economy and the significance attached to trade in the liberalization process are, therefore, critical to an understanding of investment trends and patterns. In nearly every year in the post-war period, the growth of world merchandise trade exceeded the growth of world merchandise output (WTO, 1995*b*). During the period 1950–94, world trade increased by a little over 6 per cent annually, compared with close to 4 per cent for world output. In total during these forty-five years, world trade multiplied 14 times and world merchandise output 5½ times, both in real terms. Of course, in the decade following 1928, world trade shrank to a very low level because of the severe worldwide depression and the autarkic and beggar-my-neighbour policies pursued by many countries. The outbreak of war provided a further jolt to international trade. Therefore, it was not until 1948 that world trade reached the levels of 1928 (UN, 1956). This experience was a major driving force behind the post-war efforts to create an institutional framework to stabilize and liberalize international trade and payments.

The World Trade Organization (1995*b*) has argued that post-war trade expansion can be explained in large part by global integration with three fundamental forces behind this integration process: developments in government policies, innovations in communications and transportation, and evolving strategies of firms and individual investors. The first of these was crucial. Out of the experience of the Great Depression:

> came the conviction that the best basis - and perhaps the only basis—for establishing and maintaining a liberal world order would be a system of legal constraints on trade policies, based on the MFN principle. The innovation was to create a system based not on a system of bilateral treaties, but on a single set of multilateral rules and disciplines. The result was the creation of the GATT which . . . played a central role in the postwar global integration and accompanying prosperity. (WTO, 1995*b*: 22)

Table 2.2 provides a chronology of events in multilateral trade negotiations from the entry into force of the GATT in 1948, illustrating how it has evolved into a *de facto* world trade agreement. In terms of number of countries involved and the extent of tariff cutting, the Kennedy Round represented the greatest achievement during the first twenty years of the GATT's existence. The Kennedy Round also began to recognize an issue which has been of growing importance, namely that of non-tariff barriers (NTBs), in particular through the conclusion of an anti-dumping code. In both the Tokyo Round and the Uruguay Round, the negotiating agenda was widened, and with a significant increase in the number of countries involved, the time taken to conclude the agreements was lengthened significantly. In the context of this volume, of

Table 2.2 Chronology of Events in Trade Agreements and Multilateral Trade Negotiations

Year	Event	Outcome
1947	GATT drawn up and Geneva Round trade negotiations completed (23 countries).	Concessions on 45,000 tariff lines.
1948	Provisional entry into force of GATT.	
1949	Annecy Round negotiations completed (29 countries).	Modest tariff reductions.
1951	Torquay Round negotiations completed (1950–1, 32 countries). Germany (Fed. Rep) accedes to GATT.	8,700 tariff concessions.
1955	Numerous GATT provisions modified. Move to transform GATT into Organization for Trade Cooperation (OTC) fails. Japan accedes.	
1956	Geneva Round negotiations completed (1955–6, 33 countries).	Modest tariff reductions.
1961	Dillon Round negotiations completed (1960–1, 39 countries).	4,400 tariff concessions exchanged;tariff adjustments following creation of EEC in 1957.
	Short Term Agreement on Cotton Textiles (1961–2)	
1962	Long Term Agreement on Cotton Textiles negotiated (renegotiated in 1967 and extended for three years in 1970).	
1964	Formation of UNCTAD to press for trade measures in favour of developing countries.	
1965	Role of GATT widened to include Part IV on Trade and Development, establishing guidelines for trade policies of and towards developing countries.	
1967	Kennedy Round negotiations (1963–7, 74 countries).	Average tariff reduction of 35% by developed countries; 30,000 tariff lines included. Agreement on anti-dumping and customs valuation.
	Poland is first centrally planned economy to accede.	
1974	Multifibre Arrangement (MFA) restricts import growth to 6% per year. Renegotiated in 1977 and 1982 and extended in 1986, 1991, and 1992.	

Table 2.2 *cont.*

Year	Event	Outcome
1979	Tokyo Round negotiations completed (1973–9, 99 countries).	Average tariffs of developed countries reduced by one-third (to reach 6% on average for manufactures). Codes of conduct established on specific non-tariff barriers (NTBs).
1982	GATT ministerial meeting fails to set agenda for a new round.	
1994	Uruguay Round negotiations completed (1986–94, 128 countries by early 1995).	Tariffs of developed countries reduced by one-third. Agriculture and textiles brought into GATT. Creation of WTO, and agreements on GATS and TRIPs.
1995	World Trade Organization (WTO) established on 1 Jan.	

Source: Adapted from Hoekman and Kostecki, 1995: tables 1.1 and 1.2.

especial importance in the Uruguay Round was the inclusion not only of trade in goods, but also of measures affecting FDI, trade in services, and intellectual property. The World Trade Organization (WTO) was thus formed with a much wider remit than the GATT which it replaced.

The inclusion of foreign direct investment in the GATT / WTO negotiations was a belated recognition of the interrelatedness of trade and FDI in the global economy. Curiously, for much of the post-war period, direct international capital investments were largely ignored by international economists. Yet as early as the 1960s and early 1970s, a variety of studies (reported in Hood and Young, 1979: ch. 4) showed complementarities between trade and FDI as well as substitution effects: exports might result from additional sales of finished goods, components, raw materials, or capital equipment from the parent to subsidiaries; or they could consist of additional exports from independent suppliers in the home country to subsidiaries. In turn, the latter might export components or finished products back to the market of the parent company (as predicted by the product cycle theory) or to third countries. It is now accepted that trade, international production, subcontracting, licensing and franchising, etc. represent a range of methods aimed at ensuring access to markets for goods and services or for tangible or intangible factors of production (UNCTAD, 1995).

Although official statistics are poor, the importance of MNEs in international trade is clear. Data for 1989 for the USA show that 80 per cent of the country's external trade (exports plus imports) was undertaken by MNEs, represented by US parent companies, foreign affiliates of US MNEs, and US affiliates of foreign MNEs; one-third of exports and over two-fifths of imports took the form of intra-firm, as opposed to arm's length, transactions. For Japan and the UK, intra-firm trade accounted for one-third of the total value of their international trade in the early 1980s (UN/TCMD, 1992). This topic is discussed more fully in Chapter 8 of this book.

The multilateral GATT negotiations designed to liberalize trade in the post-war years have stimulated FDI in a variety of different ways. Most obviously trade liberalization has encouraged trade-oriented FDI, enabling MNEs to establish production and service operations in low-cost sites from which their output can be exported; by allowing MNEs to outsource inputs; and by facilitating the formation of regional and global networks and hence integrated international production. At the same time, the GATT framework has been a factor in generating a stable investment climate at a multilateral level and thereby encouraging FDI. And MNEs also have a potential role as 'an agent of growth through trade' (UN/TCMD, 1992: 216), in turn stimulating further direct investment flows.

Alongside tariff liberalization in the post-war years has been the growth of non-tariff barriers (NTBs), which have been used by some countries to restrict imports and shelter domestic industries. Such NTBs, allied to threats of other trade restrictions, have encouraged Japanese and neighbouring Asia Pacific producers to undertake foreign direct investment designed to preserve market access. In these circumstances FDI has had the beneficial effect of circumventing trade restrictive measures. On the other hand, the induced FDI might be oriented towards host country markets only, thus reducing the beneficial impacts associated with trade-oriented FDI; when NTBs have been linked to local content requirements, moreover, resources are misallocated through the replacement of efficient overseas sourcing by less efficient host country sourcing.

The belated recognition of the importance of FDI explains the need for improved coordination between trade and FDI policies, and justifies the increasing attention being paid to national, regional, and multilateral agreements for FDI. There is still an imbalance for some countries between the degree of liberalization of trade and FDI regimes; and at a multilateral level particularly trade liberalization has progressed much further than FDI liberalization.

2.4 Capital Controls, Foreign Exchange Controls, and the Balance of Payments

National governments' continuing concerns over the issue of international capital flows derive from their potential influence on macroeconomic stability and national sovereignty. In addition to trade policies that affect FDI, therefore, there are also a diverse array of international financial policies in the form of capital controls and foreign exchange controls that affect FDI flows. Such controls can be imposed by governments on either inflows or outflows of funds associated with FDI. All governments have some restrictions on international financial flows in place at all times. However, there is enormous variability across countries and over time in the nature, extent, and consequences for firms of these restrictions. Furthermore, some of the restrictions—such as limitations on currency conversions for affiliates' remittances of dividends to their foreign parent firms—are specifically targeted on FDI projects and MNEs; other restrictions are adopted for other reasons—perhaps for balance of payments (BOP) reasons or a national security emergency—but nevertheless directly affect an MNE's operations.

To illustrate the recurring nature of the issues, the President of the European Commission called for regulation of destabilizing capital movements in the wake of 1992–3 crises in the European Monetary System (EMS). Twenty years earlier the Governor of the Bank of England had alleged that 'transfers of liquid balances by multinational companies did account for an important part of the transfers which eventually led to the floating of the £, the devaluation of the $, the floating of the yen' (Hood and Young, 1979: 211). And among some developing and transition countries there were concerns in the late 1990s because of the potential effects of large foreign capital inflows on macroeconomic stability, the competitiveness of the export sector, and external viability; the main risks related to increased inflationary pressures and a rising real effective exchange rate (Ul Haque et al., 1997). The two basic premisses that freedom of capital movements exert a disciplining influence on macroeconomic policies and that capital controls are ineffective (Bakker, 1996) are hotly contested; and, therefore, there has been an extreme reluctance by national governments to permit total freedom of capital movements.

Governments' capital and foreign exchange controls can affect firms' basic strategic decisions concerning initial investments, reinvestments, and divestments; and they can also affect decisions concerning the remittances of profits, dividends, royalties, management fees, interest, and other payments between foreign affiliates and parent corporations. Such restrictions are therefore wide-ranging in their effects on FDI—as deterrents to potential FDI and as constraints on the operations of FDI projects.

Because the capital controls and foreign exchange controls of its members have been monitored by the International Monetary Fund (IMF) since shortly after its inception, it is possible to determine trends in those policies for individual countries and for the world as a whole. Thus, Quinn (1997) has coded the annual reports of all members of the IMF for the period from 1958 to 1990 on a scale of 0 to 14, where 0 represents fully closed and 14 represents fully open policies.[1] The results are displayed in Figure 2.2, where the worldwide liberalization trend since the early 1980s is evident. The generally greater degree of openness of the OECD countries for the past several decades, as compared with the developing countries, is also evident. The trend of the Latin American countries, however, is also particularly noteworthy: although the well-known and increasing restrictiveness of those countries during the period from the early 1960s until the early 1980s is apparent, their less well-known relative and increasing openness during the decade of the 1950s is also evident. Indeed, it was only

Fig. 2.2 Trend of Financial Openness: medians by year for each group of countries

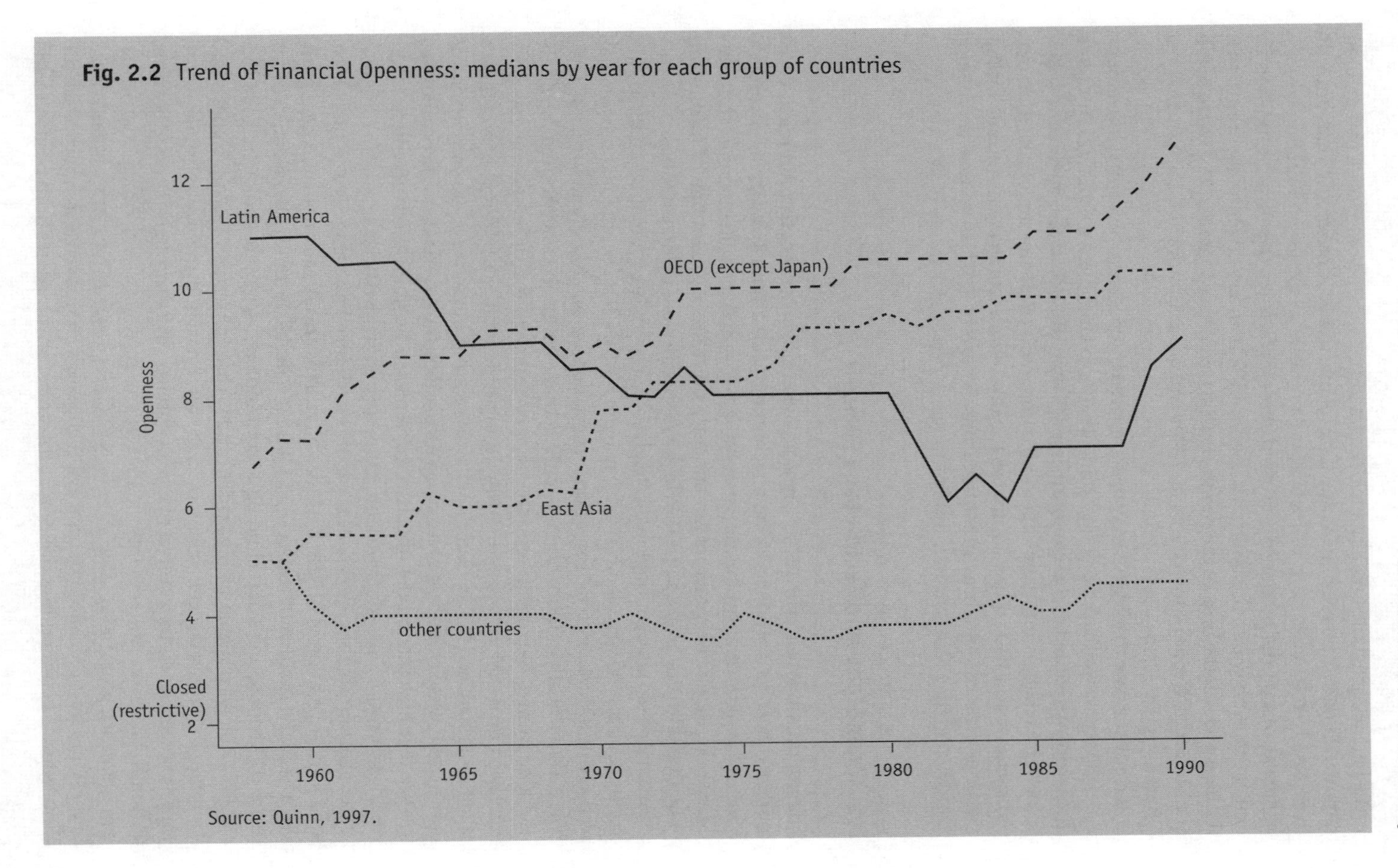

Source: Quinn, 1997.

in the late 1960s that the OECD countries as a group became more open in their international financial policies than the Latin American countries. At that time the increasingly restrictive path of the Latin American countries and the increasingly open path of the OECD countries crossed. A major factor in the OECD countries' liberalization path was their adoption of two complementary codes of liberalization in the early 1960s at the time of the creation of the OECD itself, namely, the Code of Liberalization of Capital Movements and Code of Liberalization of Current Invisible Operations.

It is still the case that MNEs may be hampered by controls over capital movements in developed as well as developing countries. For example, it was not until April 1998 that Japan abandoned exchange controls: until that time corporate buyers and sellers of foreign exchange (e.g. general trading companies) could not undertake their own transactions and had to use commercial banks; while companies without foreign exchange licences—such as manufacturing exporters—had to obtain permission from the Finance Ministry to transact foreign currency (*Financial Times*, 1997*a*).

2.5 Technology and Technology Policy

The multinational enterprise has a major role in the process of technological development—both as a producer of new technology and a vehicle for its initial application, and as a mechanism for the international transfer and diffusion of technology (Mansfield, 1974; Caves, 1996). Consequently there are a wide range of technology policies at different levels, some of which are specifically targeted at MNEs.

Around 75–80 per cent of global civilian R & D spending is undertaken by MNEs, and the world's 700 largest industrial firms (mostly MNEs) account for about one-half of the world's commercial inventions (measured by patents granted) (UNCTAD, 1995). Traditionally multinational R & D activity has been concentrated in MNEs' home countries, but the decentralization of research and development has been increasing over time: in 1992, for example, 13 per cent of US MNE R & D was undertaken at affiliate level. The traditional sequence has been one of innovation in the home country followed by a phased product launch into overseas markets following the product life cycle model; this is being replaced by innovation anywhere in the world and product introduction simultaneously in many markets.

Recognizing that the internalization of proprietary knowledge is a principal reason for the formation of MNEs, multinational firms are also an important (and probably the major) source of technology for host nations. From the perspective of the latter, the main sources of technology acquisition are scientific and technical publications (widely available at low cost); trade (through imports of machinery and equipment); foreign direct investment in the form of wholly owned subsidiaries and joint ventures; and non-equity links with foreign firms through patents, licences, technical assistance agreements, management contracts, and other contractual arrangements, plus strategic alliances (UN/TCMD, 1992). MNEs play a major role in all these modes of technology transfer. Technology in this sense is regarded as 'the knowledge of getting things done' and, therefore, encompasses both hardware and software, including the training of management and labour, organizational and marketing innovation, etc.

As discussed more fully in Chapter 8, a form of international technology policy has been in existence since 1883 as represented by the Paris Convention on international patent rights (Young et al., 1989). The principle underlying this and related Conventions (the Berne Convention—copyright; the Rome Convention—copyright and neighbouring rights; the Madrid Protocol—trademarks, etc.) is that of protecting intellectual property rights for a specified period so as to facilitate a return for companies' investment in research and development. In fact, the Paris Convention, for example, provides only that a company which files a patent application in one member country has a right of priority in filing in other countries for a period of twelve months. The existence of and coverage of rules on intellectual property varies widely among individual countries, as do degrees of enforcement. Therefore, the international position on technology policy is characterized by the same patchwork of rules that is evident in other investment-related regulations which confront the multinational enterprise.

The assumption that patents or trademarks should provide legally sanctioned monopolies was (and in some countries still is) rejected by developing nations; and hence for much of the post-war period there was confrontation between technology promoters and technology receivers. Technology recipients in developing countries were concerned about the alleged abusive practices of technology suppliers (including cartel arrangements, volume restrictions, tied purchases, and excessive cost and pricing of technology transferred) and about export restrictions (global bans on export, restrictions on products and/or markets, and requirements for prior approval to export from technology suppliers) (Bautista, 1990).

From the technology providers' perspective, complaints have focused upon the limited availability and scope of legal protection, weak commitment to enforcement of intellectual property rights, and large-scale counterfeiting and piracy. Within the first of these areas, some countries exclude particular categories of products or have no rules (China did not enact patent legislation until 1984, for example); other countries offered patent terms that were too short to permit a meaningful return (e.g. as at the end of the 1980s, India's patent term for the *process* used in making an agricultural chemical was *up* to five years); and legislation on compulsory licensing could be enacted if the patented invention was not available to the public at a reasonable price. Time scales for obtaining intellectual property protection also limit its effectiveness: Malott (1989) cites a period of six years for the granting of a patent in Japan compared with about nineteen months in the USA.

Western (mainly US) corporations and governments have pursued a multi-pronged approach to improving intellectual property protection. This has involved, first, corporate action through the formation of the International Anti-counterfeiting Coalition and other initiatives; second, home government action through bilateral trade negotiations—in the American case a more aggressive approach to enforcement was mandated by the 1988 Omnibus Trade Act; and, third, at international level shifting the forum for negotiations from the ineffective (from a developed country perspective) World Intellectual Property Organization (WIPO) to the WTO. As discussed at various points in this volume, the subject of intellectual property was included in the agenda of the Uruguay Round negotiations which began in September 1986 where the long-standing developed/developing country conflicts resurfaced. It is arguable, nevertheless, that the outcome of the Uruguay Round in the form of the TRIPs agreement will increase intellectual property protection for technology suppliers and thereby provide the security to encourage greater international transfer. Developing countries, conversely, will give up a significant amount of freedom in respect of their own ability to enact national measures aimed at technology acquisition (O'Connor, 1995). Therefore, if there is to be further progress in future in respect of harmonization of intellectual property laws internationally and a raising of standards and levels of protection, it is important that developing nations see benefits from the TRIPs agreement.

2.6 Foreign Direct Investment Policies

As will be shown in more detail in Chapters 3–6, there have been major swings in the FDI policy pendulum during the half-century since the end of the Second World War. In the immediate post-war period, with the rejection of the proposal to establish an International Trade Organization (ITO), foreign direct investment issues were temporarily left out of the efforts to develop a new framework of rules and institutions for international economic relations. During the 1960s, interest in FDI policies was dominated by concern with investment protection, especially through bilateral investment treaties, and the development of codes of liberalization among OECD countries. In the 1970s, interest in controlling MNEs and their FDI projects increased significantly, within the context of the interest in the development of a New International Economic Order (NIEO) in the United Nations; and the incidence of expropriation concomitantly increased, reaching its peak in the mid-1970s. In the 1980s and 1990s, the emphasis shifted first to the unilateral adoption of national liberalization measures by large numbers of countries and then to the development of new multilateral rules for FDI, along with the emergence of regional integration schemes that included FDI policy elements. At the same time there was a surge in the number of bilateral investment treaties, as many more developing countries became interested in attracting FDI.

The breadth and depth of the swings of the policy pendulum can be shown in various ways. In Table 2.3, the increasing number of expropriations in the 1960s and early 1970s and then the subsequent decline in their incidence since the late 1970s are shown clearly; expropriations have been virtually unheard of since the mid-1980s. The converse trend has been a marked increase in the incidence of privatizations from the 1980s, well before the demise of central planning in the economies of Central and Eastern Europe during the early 1990s.

Table 2.4 provides further specific information on worldwide trends in FDI policy changes at the national level in the 1990s, particularly policies concerning liberalization. It is evident that there were a large number of countries that undertook policy liberalization steps of various types during the first half of the 1990s. These changes

Table 2.3 Worldwide Trends in Expropriation

Indicator	Mean number per year						
	1960–4	1965–9	1970–4	1975–9	1980–4	1985–9	1990–2
Acts of expropriation	11	16	51	34	3	0.4	0.0
Countries involved in expropriation	6	9	23	15	2	0.4	0.0

Source: Computed from Minor, 1994: table 1, p. 180.

Table 2.4 The Swing of the Policy Pendulum in the 1990s

	1991	1992	1993	1994	1995
Number of countries that changed policy	35	43	57	49	64
Number of changes	82	79	102	110	112
Ownership/sectoral restrictions liberalized	21	29	n/a	n/a	17
Approval procedures liberalized	16	22	n/a	n/a	11
Operational conditions liberalized	[12]	12	n/a	n/a	34
Liberalization—subtotal	49	63	n/a	n/a	62
Guarantees increased	17	15	n/a	n/a	10
Incentives increased	14	24	n/a	n/a	36
Total- liberalization, guarantees, and incentives	80	79[a]	101	108	106[b]
Controls more restrictive	2	0	1	2	6

Notes: [a]Subtotal differs from sum of components due to double counting among components.
[b]Subtotal differs from sum of components due to rounding error.

Sources: Computed by the authors from data contained in UN/TCMD 1992: table III.3, pp. 80–1; UNCTAD,1993: table I.13, pp. 32–3; UNCTAD, 1995: Box VI.1, pp. 272–4; UNTCAD, 1996*a*: table V.1, p. 132, figure V.1, p. 132.

included the lifting of foreign ownership restrictions in many economic sectors, including reductions in the maximum shares of foreign ownership allowed in many instances. Moreover, FDI approval procedures were streamlined and otherwise liberalized, or even virtually eliminated in some instances. Restrictions on foreign-owned firms' operations—such as restrictions on the nationalities or movement of personnel or restrictions on imports or exports or the use of foreign exchange—were also significantly reduced by many countries. There were also changes in the guarantees and the subsidies offered to foreign investors—guarantees such as freedom to remit profits to parent corporations, and subsidies such as infrastructure development and employee training programmes. At the same time, during this period there were very few changes in the direction of increased controls on foreign-owned firms. The swing of the policy pendulum during this period, therefore, was strongly in the direction of greater liberalization of government policies and less regulation of firms.

Policy evolution at the *international* level paralleled national developments. It was mainly in the OECD forum that there was consistent interest in international investment policy in the years up to the 1990s.[2] But even here, as Table 2.5 shows, progress was partial and technical; standards and rules were commonly voluntary; and there was no overriding vision and strategy for an international agreement on investment.

Table 2.5 Progress of International Investment Rules at the OECD

Year	Event	Comment
1961	Code of Liberalization of Capital Movements [a b c]	Since 1964 signatories obligated progressively to liberalize inward and outward direct investment. Proceeds of liquidated investments liberalized.
	Code of Liberalization of Current Invisible Operations[a b c]	Introduced notiőn of equivalent treatment concerning FDI by insurance companies. Current transfers (profits, interest payments, etc.) liberalized.
1967	Draft Convention on the Protection of Private Property	Not formally an 'instrument' as never signed but used as a model for bilateral investment treaties.
1976	Declaration and Decisions on International Investment and Multinational Enterprises	
	• Guidelines for Multinational Enterprises	Established voluntary standards of conduct for behaviour of MNEs.
	• National Treatment[a c]	Provided that OECD members treat foreign-controlled enterprises in their territory no less favourably than domestic enterprises. Excludes monopolies.
	• International Investment Incentives and Disincentives	Encouraged transparency and provided for consultation and review.
	• Conflicting Requirements	Designed to avoid or minimize imposition of conflicting requirements on MNEs and to provide a consultation forum.

Year	Event	Comment
1984		Expanded definition of inward direct investment adopted, including main features of the *right of establishment*: national treatment principle applies when considering applications for licences or authorizations to conduct business.
1986		Code of Capital Movements extended to permit *reciprocity* requirements.
1988		Agreement to principle of *standstill* on national treatment measures; and to avoid introduction of new measures which constitute *exceptions* to national treatment.
1994	Possible Multilateral Agreement on Investment (MAI)	Since 1991 work on an MAI undertaken by CIME and CMIT. Mandate for negotiating an MAI agreed at June 1994 OECD Ministerial Council. Objective to conclude agreement by 1998.

Notes: [a]The OECD Codes of Liberalization are Decisions of the Council and are thus legally binding. Achievement of liberalization objectives conceived as being 'progressive'. Member states not in a position to remove all restrictions may lodge *reservations* in the case of the Codes of Liberalization, and *exceptions* in the case of the National Treatment Instrument.

[b]Codes provide for *derogations* applicable to member countries experiencing temporary difficulties e.g. balance of payments. Capital Movements Code also provides for suspension of obligation to liberalize in exceptional situations.

[c]Procedures. Implementation is undertaken by the Committee on Capital Movements and Invisible Transactions (CMIT) in the case of the Codes of Liberalization, and to the Committee on International Investment and Multinational Enterprises (CIME) in the case of the national treatment instrument.

Source: OECD, various publications.

2.7 Patterns of Foreign Direct Investment

Foreign investment has played an important role in the international economy since the latter part of the nineteenth century. In the pre-1914 period, capital movements were associated with large-scale population movements out of Europe. The majority of these were fixed interest, portfolio investments, with the UK being the most important creditor nation, accounting for over half of the total international capital outstanding in 1914. Indeed, in the half-century up to 1914, the UK invested abroad an annual average of 4 per cent of its national income, and as much as 7 per cent in the ten years immediately preceding the First World War. The UK was the major investor for a variety of reasons, including domestic prosperity; a desire to secure imports of primary products; and a highly developed institutional framework which successfully channelled available funds overseas. Geographically around 60 per cent of this investment was in the Americas and Australasia. Its sectoral distribution also reflected underlying motivations: 40 per cent of the investment was in railways, while 30 per cent was in government or municipal securities. Both the volume and direction of portfolio investment flows during this period were strongly influenced by the attractive interest rates obtainable in foreign locations.

The First World War and its aftermath had a dramatic effect on the relative wealth of the major European nations. As a result of loss or repudiation of investments, war debts, and reconstruction costs, Continental Europe had changed from net creditor to net debtor status by the 1920s, while the United States' position was reversed from that of a debtor to a creditor country. By 1929, the United Kingdom was still the principal creditor nation, but the USA made considerable investment abroad in these years; and, partly associated with the increasing importance of America, the pattern of investment was changing. Thus direct investment in overseas subsidiaries expanded to account for around 25 per cent of total overseas lending.

US outward direct investment in manufacturing had commenced in the middle of the nineteenth century, with Singer Sewing Machine probably the first modern multinational enterprise. It established its first overseas operation in Scotland in 1867 as part of an expansion process whose objective was 'peacefully working to conquer the world' (Wilkins, 1970: 325). Aside from being host to the initial overseas investments in manufacturing, including that of Siemens from Germany in 1858 (Schröter, 1993), the UK was also the pioneer manufacturing investor in the United States, in the form of J. & P. Coats (Wilkins, 1989). There were many European-owned MNEs by 1914, with the small economies of Europe producing a disproportionately large number of multinational enterprises (Hertner and Jones, 1986). However, Germany lost effectively all its foreign direct investments after the two world wars, and the British network of affiliates was concentrated in its colonies and former colonies and was thus out of the growth mainstream.

The years after the Second World War were, therefore, particularly favourable for US outward FDI. The period from the beginning of Marshall Aid in 1948 to the end of the 1960s was one of heavy United States involvement in both European and international economic reconstruction. US corporations, with major ownership advantages in technology and management, were aided in their access to foreign countries by the Marshall Plan operations and subsequently by the gradual liberalization of trade and payments. The convertibility of the dollar and the establishment of international organizations aimed at providing liberalization and stability were all part of this new situation. In addition, certain tax policies of the US government favoured foreign operations; in particular the reinvestment of foreign earnings was encouraged since tax was only payable on profits when they were repatriated to the USA. Thus FDI became the major component of capital flows, with the United States the principal source and Europe and Canada the major recipients. UN Economic and Social Council data indicate that in 1967 the United States accounted for 54 per cent of the total stock of FDI abroad of developed market economies.

Figures from UNCTAD (1993) show that, during the 1970s and 1980s decades, flows of FDI increased at an annual rate of 13 per cent. There were significant year-on-year fluctuations but two surges followed by falls were evident: between 1978 and 1981 growth averaged 11 per cent per year, and from 1986 to 1990 it averaged 28 per cent annually. FDI flows were associated fairly closely with the growth of output: the recession conditions of the early 1970s and 1980s were matched by declines in FDI inflows, most noticeably into developed nations. FDI flows in the late 1980s, however, continued to rise despite the downturn in output; the explanation was in part at least the response of MNEs to the announcement in 1986 of the EU's Single Market programme and the desire by third country multinationals in particular to establish a presence in the market; the rise of Japanese outward FDI was also important in the late 1980s consequent on the strong yen (coupled with rising labour costs and a shortage of skilled labour) which stimulated greenfield and acquisition-based investment into the United States (in particular). International mergers and acquisitions (M & As) in general paralleled the domestic merger boom of the second half of the 1980s linked to the economic upturn, and stronger international competition which generated substantial excess capacity in many low- and medium-technology industries; other positive factors included easier credit, the valuation of many companies below their break-up values, and the use of leveraged buyouts.

Table 2.6 confirms the influence of world growth rates on FDI flows and accompanying measures such as sales of foreign affiliates. Policy developments continued to be favourable in the 1990s including the influence of trade liberalization with the successful completion of the Uruguay Round of negotiations; the liberalization of FDI policies complemented by privatization programmes; and the completion of

Table 2.6 FDI and International Production, and Comparisons with World GDP and Exports (annual compound growth rates in US$ value)

	1981–5 (%)	1986–90 (%)	1991–4 (%)
FDI inflows	−0.1	24.7	12.7
FDI outward stock	5.4	19.8	8.8
Sales of foreign affiliates	1.3	17.4	5.4[a]
Royalties and fees receipts	n/a	21.8	10.1
World GDP at factor cost	2.1	10.8	4.3
World exports of goods and non-factor services	−0.1	14.3	3.8[a]

Note: [a]1991–3.

Source: UNCTAD, 1995: table I.1; 1996*a*: table I.2.

Table 2.7 FDI Outward Stock by Region and Major Country for Selected Years (per cent share of US$ totals)

Region/country	1967[a] (%)	1980 (%)	1985 (%)	1990 (%)	1995[b] (%)
North America	57.3	47.3	42.6	30.3	29.9
Canada	3.5	9.3	6.0	4.5	4.1
USA	53.8	38.0	36.6	25.8	25.8
European Union	n/a	41.5	41.8	46.1	44.3
France	5.7	4.6	5.4	6.5	7.3
Germany	2.8	8.4	8.7	9.0	8.6
UK	16.6	15.7	14.6	13.7	11.7
Other Western Europe	n/a	4.6	3.8	4.6	4.5
Switzerland	4.8	4.2	3.1	3.9	4.0
Other developed countries	n/a	5.5	8.7	14.6	13.4
Australia	n/a	0.4	1.0	1.8	1.5
Japan	1.4	3.7	6.4	12.2	11.2
Developing and newly industrialized countries	n/a	1.2	3.1	4.1	7.9
China	n/a	..	..	0.1	0.6
Hong Kong	n/a	..	0.3	0.8	3.1
Singapore	n/a	0.1	0.2	0.3	0.5
Taiwan	n/a	..	..	0.8	0.9
Total (%)	100.0	100.0	100.0	100.0	100.0
Total (US$ bn.)	105.3	513.7	685.5	1,684.1	2,730.1

Note: .. means less than 0.1%.

[a]The 1967 data are not directly comparable with later years. They have been included to provide an indication of the FDI position in the earlier post-war years. The figures relate to the outward FDI stock of developed market economies.

[b]Preliminary.

Source: UN Economic and Social Council, 1978: table III-32 (for 1967); UNCTAD, 1996*a:* annex table 4.

NAFTA, the further enlargement of the EU, and prospects for regional integration in the Asia Pacific region. But these were not sufficient to offset the adverse effects of slow economic growth on investment decisions.

Tables 2.7–2.9 record some of the major characteristics of FDI over the recent past. The emergence of Japan, the newly industrialized countries, and China as outward investors is shown clearly in Table 2.7. The inward stock position (Table 2.8) highlights the growing attractiveness of the United States as a host country, so that it became both the largest source and the largest recipient of FDI. Overall the significance of the Triad members and their clusters has grown, the 1993 position being shown in Figure 2.3. Ohmae (1985) had foreseen the importance of regionalization/globalization ten years earlier when he recommended that aspiring global

Table 2.8 FDI Inward Stock by Region and Major Country for Selected Years (per cent share of US$ totals)

Region/country	1967[a] (%)	1980 (%)	1985 (%)	1990 (%)	1995[b] (%)
North America	27.0	28.4	33.9	29.6	25.6
Canada	18.0	11.2	8.8	6.6	4.4
USA	9.0	17.2	25.1	23.0	21.2
European Union	n/a	38.4	30.8	41.5	38.7
France	n/a	4.7	4.5	5.0	6.1
Germany	3.0	7.6	5.0	6.5	5.0
UK	8.0	13.0	8.7	12.7	9.2
Other Western Europe	n/a	3.2	2.5	2.7	2.2
Other developed countries	n/a	7.5	6.0	6.2	6.2
Developing countries	31.0	22.5	26.8	19.9	26.1
Africa	n/a	4.3	3.7	2.4	2.2
Latin America and Caribbean	n/a	10.0	10.4	7.1	8.5
Asia	n/a	7.9	12.5	10.2	15.2
Total (%)	100.0	100.0	100.0	100.0	100.0
Total (US$ bn.)	105.0	481.9	734.9	1,716.9	2,657.9

Notes: [a]Not comparable to later years.
[b]Preliminary.

Source: UN Economic and Social Council, 1978: table III-33 (for 1967); UNCTAD, 1996*a:* annex table 3.

Table 2.9 Sectoral Distribution of FDI Stock for Largest Developed Home Countries, 1970–1990[a] (annual growth rate in per cent; and percentage share)

Sector	Annual growth rate				Share of total	
	1971–5 (%)	1976–80 (%)	1981–5 (%)	1986–90 (%)	1970 (%)	1990 (%)
Primary	14.0	8.7	5.5	6.8	22.7	11.2
Secondary	11.7	15.1	2.9	18.3	45.2	38.7
Tertiary	10.4	21.4	8.2	22.1	31.4	50.1
Total	11.7	15.7	5.5	18.3	100.0	100.0

Note: [a]Australia, Canada, France, Germany, Italy, the Netherlands, UK, and USA.

Source: UNCTAD, 1993: table III.1.

companies should establish development, manufacturing, and marketing operations in each of the Triad areas. Intra-Triad international business is also highly significant, especially for the European Union. The expansion of FDI from developing countries is concentrated among firms from the Asian region and most of this is represented by intra-regional flows in Asia: for example, nearly three-quarters of FDI into China during the years 1990–3 originated in Hong Kong, Singapore, and Taiwan. The region is

Fig. 2.3 FDI Stock among Triad Members and their Clusters, 1993 (billions of dollars)

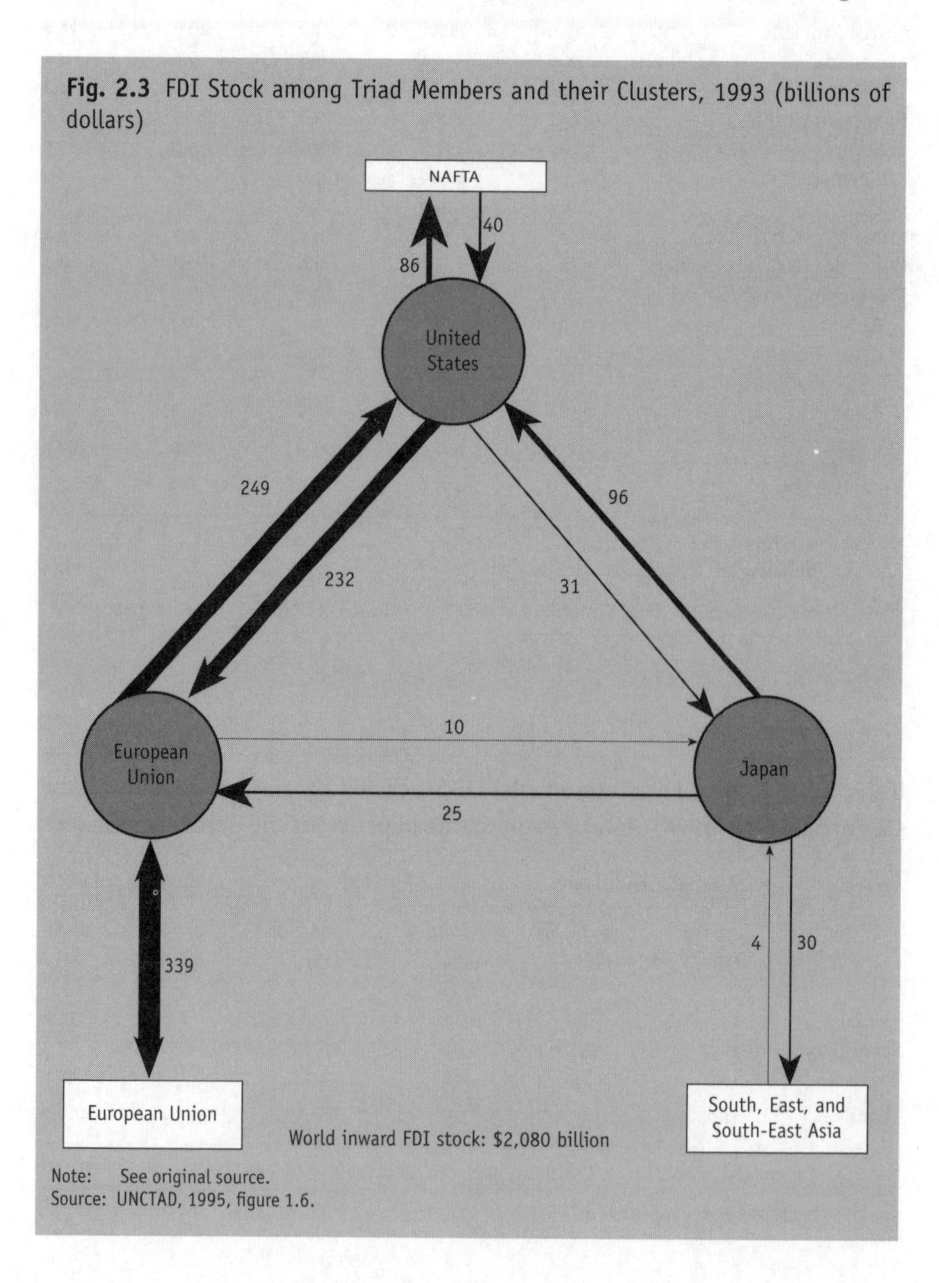

Note: See original source.
Source: UNCTAD, 1995, figure 1.6.

thus set to grow significantly into the twenty-first century as both source of and host to FDI. And shifts in source and host country patterns across the world as a whole are principally reflective of relative country growth rates and corporate competitiveness.

In a like manner, the rapid growth of FDI has been accompanied by marked shifts in its sectoral composition. In the early post-war years, FDI was concentrated in the primary sector and resource-based manufacturing. At the present time, technology-intensive manufacturing and services are the major growth sectors. FDI in services lagged behind the emergence of service economies domestically, in large part due to the slow pace of liberalization in the sector. The expansion of services which has taken place has, therefore, been driven by deregulation alongside technological change in subsectors such as financial services and telecommunications services. Initially the services MNEs were 'internationalizing' to follow their domestic customers abroad whereas the largest enterprises of the 1990s have global objectives and serve global markets. Table 2.9 records the changes in terms of a switch from the primary (mainly) and secondary sectors into the tertiary sector. In the 1990s, services flows accounted for over 60 per cent of worldwide flows for the major economies.

This chapter has shown the interrelationships which exist among FDI, capital, trade and technology flows and the significance of government policies in each of these areas. Implicitly, it highlights the need for an all-embracing, coordinated approach to multinational policy.

Notes

1. Each country's restrictions on current account and capital account transactions were recorded separately and then aggregated into a single summary measure for each country. The restrictions concerned payments or receipts. Thus, the aggregated score is an overall index of restrictiveness / openness covering a broad gamut of transactions related to FDI. For data on the more specific types of controls contributing to the summary scores as well as data on individual countries, see Quinn (1997). It should further be noted that this extensive data set has been developed through careful coding rules by two coders, whose scores have been subjected to extensive reliability tests; see Quinn (1997) for further information about the data collection process.
2. The OECD was officially established in 1961. It evolved from the Organization for European Economic Cooperation (OEEC), which itself had evolved from the Marshall Plan of economic assistance in the immediate post-Second World War era and had become a transitional institution in the European economic integration process.

Part II

Evolution of the System

3

Inauguration

The Demise of the ITO and the Rise of Bilateral Treaties (Mid-1940s–Late 1960s)

This chapter focuses on the early post-Second World War period, when the ultimately unsuccessful efforts to create the International Trade Organization (ITO) were undertaken and when the General Agreement on Tariffs and Trade (GATT) was established. It also analyses other developments during the period from the mid-1940s to the late 1960s—including in particular the liberalization of foreign exchange controls within the International Monetary Fund (IMF) and the liberalization of capital movements within the Organization for Economic Cooperation and Development (OECD). This is the first in a series of four chapters that analyse key developments in the evolution of the multilateral investment system over the entire second half of the twentieth century. It includes common elements that are present in the subsequent chapters in this section of the book. It thus describes the main agreements and other developments during the period; additionally it considers the principal factors that influenced those events and the implications of the agreements for the evolution of the international regime for investment in later years.

The early years of this period were dominated by the creation of the GATT, the International Bank for Reconstruction and Development (IBRD), and the IMF—the latter two often referred to as the Bretton Woods agreements, from the resort town in the north-eastern part of the United States where a key conference was held in 1944. As a result, three major multilateral institutions—whose principal responsibilities concerned, respectively, trade, development, and finance—came into being during the 1940s. Although each of these institutions became relevant to the investment issues that are central to this book, as is discussed later in the present chapter, they were not in fact the central focus of attention for investment issues at the time. Instead, it was the abortive attempt to create the ITO that preoccupied policymakers concerned with investment issues and this is discussed below.

3.1 International Trade Organization (ITO)

Beginning in early 1943, there was a sustained international effort to create a new system that would have included investment along with trade and competition policy in an integrated package. The record of the negotiations to create the ITO reveals that there were already important conflicts emerging on key issues, as well as a consensus on some topics. Provisions concerning investment were among the most important and controversial issues in the negotiations on the ITO. It is therefore instructive to consider the evolution of investment issues through several phases in the development and demise of the ITO because many key and perennial issues about international investment agreements were addressed. However, it is also important to recognize that investment was only one among a cluster of issues that were tackled in the context of the ITO initiative; others were tariffs, quotas, export subsidies, restrictive business practices, employment, exchange controls, and commodity agreements. All of these topics, including restrictive business practices in particular, were, of course, related to investment, even though investment was often treated as a distinct agenda item; however, when investment emerged on the public agenda in the negotiations, it was in the context of economic development matters, especially industrialization in countries outside Western Europe and North America, and in the context of post-war reconstruction in Europe.

Official governmental initiatives had begun by the spring of 1943 in the United States, in consultation with the British and Canadian governments, to create the ITO (Wilcox, 1949). During the preliminary period of development of the US 'Proposals for the Expansion of World Trade and Employment', the US preference for bilateral arrangements dominated the American approach to investment issues.[1] The USA was afraid that 'investment provisions negotiated at a multilateral conference might express the lowest common denominator of protection to which any of the participants would be willing to agree. And such a watering down of the standards obtainable in commercial [bilateral] treaties would scarcely be acceptable to the United States' (Wilcox, 1949: 145–64).[2] As a result there were no provisions whatsoever concerning investment in the initial public version of the US proposal. Thus, a strong US bias toward bilateralism—at least on investment protection issues—was already evident. The British government, which was in effect co-sponsor of the proposals, announced that it was in 'full agreement on all important points' (UK, Anglo-American Financial Agreement, 1945; cited in Wilcox, 1949: 39) and seven other governments also expressed their support for the proposals through notes exchanged with the USA.[3] These proposals thus provided the beginning point for public discussions in many countries for the next several years.

At the first meeting of the Economic and Social Council of the UN in early 1946, the diplomatic momentum gathered for the development of the ITO, and a Preparatory Committee for an International Conference on Trade and Employment was therefore created. The USA then elaborated its proposals into a *Suggested Charter for an International Trade Organization of the United Nations* (US Department of State, 1946). However, none of its seventy-nine articles referred to investment. This document became the basis of discussions at the London conference of the Preparatory Committee in late 1946—at which the eighteen participating countries agreed on a new draft.[4] A major addition at the London conference was a chapter on economic development—which was the outcome of a debate that 'was occasionally stormy, often confused, and always critical for the Charter as a whole' (Brown, 1950: 97).

Investment issues emerged in this debate in the context of questions concerning governments' rights and obligations associated with the role of foreign capital in economic development and whether there should be special provisions for developing countries. As for private foreign capital in particular, the issues concerned national treatment generally, as well as expropriation and compensation. Some developing countries, out of fear of foreign domination, wanted exceptions to national treatment when it would have been 'prejudicial to the national interest' (Brown, 1950: 100); in addition, they did not want limitations on the right of expropriation. Neither of these proposals, however, was acceptable to the USA or other industrial countries. There was also a broader question of whether the industrialized countries were obligated to ensure that developing countries would have access to capital that was essential to the development process. The resulting compromise was 'a short and general formula pledging observance of international obligations in this field, including those to be worked out by the ITO itself, and abstention from unreasonable action injurious to the interest of members supplying capital' (Brown, 1950: 100).

Investment issues were addressed more specifically at the second meeting of the Preparatory Committee in Geneva in 1947.[5] The USA introduced an entirely new article on private foreign investment. It provided for:

- national treatment for foreign investments (unless a country gave advance formal notice otherwise);
- unqualified most favoured nation treatment;
- prompt, adequate, and effective compensation in the event of expropriation;
- the creation of an ITO Economic Development and Investment Commission to develop recommendations for governments on other investment issues;
- explicit recognition of the importance of foreign investment in development;
- a statement that one purpose of the Charter was 'to encourage the international flow of capital for productive investment through measures designed to assure fair and equitable treatment of the legitimate interests of investments' (Brown, 1950: 102).

The Czech government, however, objected to unconditional MFN because it did not want to give German investors equal status with investors from other countries, and India objected to the provision for national treatment because it did not want to be bound by rules about the treatment of foreign investors implied by this principle. On the other hand, Australia, Belgium, France, and the Netherlands supported the US desire for strong statements of the principles of national treatment and MFN. The resulting compromise provided for highly qualified statements of national treatment and MFN, and a statement that 'just compensation' in the event of expropriation was required, that this could be in the local currency, and that transferability into a foreign currency could be limited to the extent that would be consistent with the country's general foreign exchange policy (Brown, 1950).

As a result of the negotiations in Geneva, only Article 12 (of the 100 articles) focused on investment. (Eight other articles focused on restrictive business practices, which were to become more explicitly related to investment issues in later discussions in the UN, especially in the 1970s, as the next chapter indicates.) The provisions of Article 12 on investment became highly controversial at the Havana conference at which agreement was finally reached on a charter for the ITO. Among the fifty-six governments in attendance, several European governments and Canada supported a US attempt to remove the restrictive notion of 'just compensation' and the qualifications of national treatment and MFN. However, when India, several Latin American countries, and Australia opposed this attempt to undo the Geneva compromise on investment, the Australian government developed a new package of investment provisions (Brown, 1950).

Finally, in March 1948 the conference published the Havana Charter for the ITO. (Excerpts from the provisions concerning investment are presented in Appendix 3.1 of this chapter.) An Interim Commission published a series of reports during 1948 in order to prepare for implementation of the ITO Charter. However, the Charter and the ITO never entered into force because the US Congress failed to ratify it. The congressional opposition focused on the ITO's investment provisions, in particular, as well as more generally the wide-ranging authority of the ITO, which was perceived as a threat to US national sovereignty and the interests of American corporations. Many members of the Congress saw the ITO as potentially too powerful, especially with regard to its mandate on international cartel issues. In December 1950 the US administration announced that it would not try again to achieve congressional ratification and no other governments were then willing to deposit ratification documents.

Despite the fact that the ITO was defeated, the lengthy period of discussions and negotiations had important consequences for the development of the investment agenda within multilateral and other international fora in subsequent years:

- The consideration of investment issues was frequently undertaken in relationship to economic development issues.
- Lines of conflict between developing and developed countries over a series of issues were drawn.
- There was a recognition that investment issues and trade issues were linked.
- There was a recognition that investment policy and competition policy, including policies on restrictive business practices, were linked.
- The issue of whether to seek international cooperation through multilateral or bilateral agreements was 'resolved' (at least temporarily) in favour of the US preference for a bilateral emphasis.

3.2 General Agreement on Tariffs and Trade (GATT)

In the aftermath of the defeat of the ITO by the USA, the GATT emerged as the principal multilateral forum for the consideration of *trade* issues. *Investment* issues did not receive attention as GATT was being created, or in its early years; yet the formative years of the GATT are nevertheless important to an understanding of the evolution of the international investment regime—precisely because investment issues received so little attention within the GATT for so long. *The resulting institutionalized separation of investment issues from trade issues within the world's principal negotiating forum for trade became an important feature of the international trade regime as well as the international investment regime until the 1980s.*

Because the GATT was conceived in narrow terms as a forum for reducing tariffs on goods, investment questions were not included on its agenda at the outset. In fact, the initial planning for the creation of GATT was based on an assumption that it would be a temporary, interim arrangement that would become superfluous and be phased out once the ITO became operational. Prior to the defeat of the ITO, therefore, the mandate of the GATT was to be quite limited in duration and in the scope of its activities. It was to focus specifically on tariff levels in manufactured goods because they had escalated so dramatically during the earlier pre-war period and thereby contributed to the worldwide depression preceding the Second World War. Thus, there were no GATT provisions concerning any of the core issues of international investment policy, such as the right of establishment, restrictions on operations, investment protection, or dispute settlement—though provisions in the GATT concerning the national treatment of goods after they entered the territory of the importing country could be construed as being related to investment. Further, the fact that the investment provisions of the Havana Charter had been among the reasons for its defeat by the US Congress suggested that it would be politically difficult for any country to place investment issues on the GATT agenda. For both legal and political reasons, therefore, investment questions did not arise in the GATT for several years following its creation in 1948.

During the mid- and late 1950s, investment issues did emerge briefly, albeit somewhat obscurely, on the GATT agenda. In 1955 there was a general statement referring to the role of investment in development (GATT, 1955: 49–50); and during 1958–9, restrictive business practices were considered by a Group of Experts, but without a specific focus on investment-related questions (GATT, 1959: 29). Neither of these events led to further consideration of investment issues in the GATT. In fact, it was not until the 1980s that the topic of investment was explicitly taken up—first within the context of a dispute case involving Canada's Foreign Investment Review Agency (FIRA) and then in the Uruguay Round negotiations (both of which are discussed in Chapter 5). Meanwhile, with the creation of the IBRD and the IMF, there were tangible developments bearing on investment policies.

3.3 The International Monetary Fund (IMF)

Another of the international organizations that was created in the 1940s was the International Monetary Fund, one of the so-called Bretton Woods organizations. Like the GATT, the IMF was created in reaction to the pre-war depression; and like the GATT, the IMF was designed to be an instrument of liberalization. Its activities were specifically and directly focused on the liberalization of government policies that inhibited international financial transactions, but these efforts had wide-ranging consequences for both trade and FDI. For there were, of course, already many interdependencies among finance, trade, and FDI, and the recognition of these interdependencies was evident in the planning for the IMF, just as it was in the planning for the ITO. Thus one specific purpose of the IMF was to establish a liberalized system for international payments that would facilitate *trade* (Hooke, 1983; Southard, 1979). Furthermore, even though none of the IMF's initial principal concerns were explicitly focused on capital transfers and payments associated with FDI flows, its mission was (and is) of direct relevance and importance to FDI. The IMF was created to establish a regime that would include: a foreign exchange rate regime that would be stable, avoid the competitive devaluations that contributed to the monetary turbulence of the pre-war period, and allow for periodic changes under the supervision of an international institution; an international payments regime that would restrict the use of foreign exchange controls, especially on current account transactions; and an international institution that would help to finance countries' balance of payments adjustment processes. All three of these original IMF functions are related to FDI because they affect a variety of macroeconomic conditions and policies of countries and thus the economic environments of FDI projects:

- *Exchange rate fluctuations*—and uncertainties about them in the future—affect MNEs' initial decisions about whether to undertake FDI projects, their country location, the structure of the financing packages, and subsequent decisions about sourcing and reinvestment. (With the collapse of the gold-exchange standard in the early 1970s, when the USA announced that it would no longer guarantee the convertibility of dollars into gold, the IMF's function as monitor of the fixed exchange rate system was of course transformed.)
- *Foreign exchange controls* that impede funds transfers related to current account transactions affect MNEs' decisions about imports and exports associated with FDI projects, as well as their remittances of profits, dividends, licensing fees and management fees, and other forms of payments among the parent firms and their affiliates.
- The mixture of domestic monetary and fiscal policies, as well as foreign exchange policies, trade policies, and external borrowing policies, and their internal income and price effects in the *balance of payments adjustment process* are all important features of the macroeconomic environment for FDI projects.

The initial goals of the IMF with regard to *capital* controls on *investment* transactions in the balance of payments capital accounts were less ambitious. The Articles of

Agreement of the IMF specifically treated capital controls differently from exchange controls on current account transactions. Articles VIII and XIV specified that members were obligated (after a transition period) not to impede foreign exchange transfers related to current account transactions; whereas Article VI stated that their obligations did not include the elimination of capital controls on transfers related to capital account transactions. Article VI provides in particular that members can impose controls on capital transfers if they 'are necessary to regulate international capital movements', but that 'no member may exercise these controls in a manner which will restrict payments for current transactions or which will delay transfers of funds in settlement of commitments' (except during the transition period or in the event of a currency scarcity declared by the Fund). Furthermore, the omission of limits on capital controls reflected in Article VI was a conscious decision, not an oversight; and it was restated in 1956 by an Executive Board decision that interpreted Article VI. The rationale for not limiting countries' capital controls was that they would be necessary in the event of capital flight during a crisis (De Vries and Horsefield, 1969; also Gold, 1965).[6] In any case, however, many industrialized countries liberalized their controls on capital account transactions as well as current account transactions, within the context of the two OECD Codes of Liberalization to be discussed below.

It is evident that in the IMF's formative years, and thus during the period of the emergence of the international investment regime in the 1940s and 1950s, the IMF was not explicitly a central institutional component of an FDI regime; yet, its core concerns were relevant to FDI from the outset. The impact of IMF policies on FDI expanded in later years, particularly in developing countries and countries in transition, through its policies of *conditionality* and its role in privatization and liberalization in the 1980s and 1990s. Furthermore, in spring 1997 a plan was approved to amend the IMF's Articles of Agreement to extend its jurisdiction to cover capital movements. The Managing Director of the IMF commented that 'this achievement incorporated into the IMF's mandate the "unwritten chapter" of the work of Bretton Woods' (IMF Survey, 1997: 129).

3.4 **World Bank**

The World Bank was also a post-war Bretton Woods international agency, but its mission was not so much a reaction to the protectionism and the depression of the pre-war period as it was a reaction to post-war economic conditions, particularly in Europe. The Bank's specific mission was to help finance large public projects, such as the construction or reconstruction of infrastructure facilities, and to do so through loans to governments. The World Bank in its initial manifestation as the International Bank for Reconstruction and Development was, therefore, not directly concerned with the private FDI policies of either the capital exporting or capital importing countries. Even so, its relevance to FDI increased significantly over time—particularly as several associated agencies were eventually created and added to its core lending programmes, and as lending to governments in developing countries in

Africa, Asia, and South America replaced post-war loans to European governments as its principal activity.

The Articles of Agreement of the IBRD envisioned that the Bank would facilitate private capital flows as well as finance projects itself; Article I notes that the purposes of the Bank are:

(i) To assist in the reconstruction and development of territories of members by facilitating the investment of capital for productive purposes, . . .
(ii) To promote private foreign invesment by means of guarantees or participations in loans and other investments made by private investors . . .
(iii) To promote the long-range balanced growth of international trade and the maintenance of equilibrium in balances of payments by encouraging international investment for the development of the productive resources of members.

Over time, additional programmes of direct relevance to FDI were added to the Bank's core lending operations—the International Finance Corporation (IFC) in 1956, the International Centre for the Settlement of Investment Disputes (ICSID) in 1966, and the Multilateral Investment Guarantee Agency (MIGA) in 1988. Because the IFC specializes in taking equity positions and putting together project finance packages for private investments in developing countries, it has a direct interest in the FDI policies of host developing countries. It thus created the Foreign Investment Advisory Service (FIAS), which advises governments in developing countries on their inward FDI policies.

ICSID is focused on a specific aspect of FDI projects, namely the disputes that sometimes arise between host governments and private investors. It represents an important element of the World Bank's overall involvement in FDI policy issues, and it is also a central element in the broad array of legal and institutional arrangements for the arbitration of investment disputes.

A third specialized component of the World Bank Group that is concerned with FDI is MIGA. Although it did not actually come into being until 1988, there were earlier attempts to create an investment guarantee programme for private projects at the Bank. As a multilateral version of the political risk insurance programmes that have been undertaken by nearly all of the industrial countries and some developing countries for the outward investments of their own nationals, MIGA reviews the FDI policies of prospective host governments as well as the features of specific projects before issuing guarantees. Thus, MIGA is directly involved in FDI policy issues at both the macro country level and the micro project level.

Altogether, these several programmes of the World Bank group have established its presence in several important aspects of the multilateral regime for FDI—albeit in selective, specialized, and often inconspicuous ways. Nevertheless, given the importance of the Bank's core lending programmes to the governments of developing countries and thus its implicit leverage in policy discussions with borrowing governments, its significance in FDI policy issues is probably greater than the low profiles of many of its activities would otherwise suggest. Furthermore, as with the IMF, the imposition of conditions on borrowing governments and the well-funded policy adjustment programmes—including in particular industry privatization and the liberalization of other economic policies—give the totality of the Bank's activities on FDI-related matters much importance in developing countries.

3.5 Organization for Economic Cooperation and Development (OECD)

Although the membership of the Organization for Economic Cooperation and Development (OECD) has never been either as large or as geographically diverse as the GATT, IMF, or World Bank, since its establishment in the early 1960s it has, nevertheless, played important roles in the evolution of the international investment regime. Furthermore, even though some of the OECD's activities still exhibit its original European orientation, as an institutional extension of the Organization for European Economic Cooperation (OEEC) that had administered Marshall Plan assistance in the early post-war period, its investment-related activities continue to be pertinent to the wider efforts to develop a more encompassing multilateral investment regime. The relevance of the OECD to the evolution of the multilateral investment regime stems in part from its work on the liberalization of capital controls. The liberalization of capital movements was, in fact, a principal concern of the OECD at its inception in the early 1960s (Ley, 1989). Among its first actions were the agreements on Codes for the Liberalization of Capital Movements (OECD, 1993*a*) and Current Invisible Operations (OECD, 1993*b*), which were adopted in 1961. Thus, in the early 1960s, the OECD countries wanted to seek greater degrees of liberalization of capital movements than had been achieved within the context of the IMF. The reason was that there were still residual forms of many of the highly restrictive controls on international financial transactions that had been put in place years earlier as emergency wartime measures.

Both codes are binding on their signatories, and acceptance of both is a precondition for membership in the OECD; however, the mechanism for enforcement is the OECD committee system, not an independent and formalized arbitration or other dispute settlement process. The Capital Movements Code required that its signatories progressively liberalize their policies concerning both inward and outward FDI, and it also required them to allow the transfer of capital for long-term loans and for liquidating investments. The code pertained to investments for establishing or expanding wholly owned or partly owned subsidiaries or branches and to loans with terms of five years or longer. The Current Invisibles Code required the signatories to allow the transfer of profits, dividends, interest payments, and other remittances associated with FDI projects through liberalized current account controls (see Appendix 3.2 for brief excerpts from these two codes).

These liberalization measures were phased in over a period of many years. Although it is difficult to say with much certainty how much effect these international OECD agreements had on the policies of its individual member countries—apart from the countries' own domestically based, unilateral policy changes—it is clear that there were significant liberalization tendencies in the OECD countries' capital control policies as the OECD codes were put into place. After the initial liberalization period in the early 1960s, however, there followed a period of many years of little further liberalization before episodic liberalization in the 1980s and beyond (see Figure 2.2 in Chapter 2 for further details of the history of the OECD countries' capital control liberalization trend).

In subsequent actions—during the 1970s and 1980s—the OECD broadened the concept of FDI, established reciprocity requirements, promulgated a national treatment instrument, developed guidelines for MNEs, and—during the 1990s—began to negotiate a Multilateral Agreement on Investment. Because all of these developments occurred later in the history of the OECD and because they can be better understood in the broader context of the evolution of the multilateral regime for FDI in those periods, the discussion of them is deferred to subsequent chapters; in the next chapter, for instance, the OECD Guidelines on MNEs are considered.

In the context of the present chapter, it is important to understand that the development of the Codes of Liberalization was undertaken by an OECD whose membership was limited to the industrialized countries of Western Europe and North America, plus Australia, New Zealand, and eventually Japan (which joined in 1964). Thus, although the codes were surely more encompassing than purely European or transatlantic agreements, they were far from multilateral agreements in the normal sense of the term. Yet, they were important instruments of liberalization among the industrialized countries, and, along with other subsequent OECD agreements, they became important building blocks during the concerted efforts of the 1990s to develop more encompassing multilateral agreements on investment issues.

3.6 Bilateral Treaties

Despite the FDI-related activities of the IMF and IBRD, and in the absence of a multilateral regime for investment, bilateral treaties emerged as the principal form of international agreements for FDI issues. Developments in the treatment of FDI issues at the bilateral level established several key features of the international regime for FDI that persist today and that underlie a series of basic issues about the future evolution of the regime. Initially, bilateral agreements were treaties of friendship, commerce, and navigation (FCN), which had already been widely used by the United States since the eighteenth century. Subsequently, bilateral investment treaties (BITs) came to be the favoured legal instrument, beginning with agreements signed in 1959 by Germany with the Dominican Republic and Pakistan. Together, FCN treaties and BITs represent a formidable body of international law with a long and extensive history of scholarly legal analysis (see, for instance, Sornarajah, 1994). In the present chapter, discussion is centred on the emergence of bilateral agreements as the primary means of addressing issues of liberalization and protection associated with FDI, and their key features are indicated.

Treaties of friendship, commerce, and navigation had traditionally been used by the United States as a means of providing a legal framework for trading, maritime, and consular relations, beginning with the first such agreement between the USA and France in 1788; they were thus not investment agreements *per se*. Investment became a more central element of FCN treaties after the Second World War; this new interest was a consequence of the joint American-European effort in facilitating private foreign investment for the post-war reconstruction effort in Europe—in addition to official economic assistance through the Marshall Plan. There were thus several new FCN treaties signed between the USA and European governments during the late 1940s and early 1950s. Their provisions concerning investment, however, were limited to the right of establishment as well as the protection of investors.

A more expansive treatment of investment issues was subsequently incorporated in the bilateral investment treaties, following the European introduction of that new mode of bilateral agreement; they were generally concluded between industrial and developing countries. During the 1960s and 1970s, Germany, Switzerland, France, the UK, the Netherlands and Benelux each concluded many bilateral investment treaties, including some with their own former colonies. A 1967 Draft Convention on the Protection of Foreign Property that was developed by the OECD, but never opened for signature, was used as a model for many BITs.[7] Over time, a 'European' version BIT evolved with many common elements despite the variations in the individual national legal traditions of the signatories. Although there were some variations among individual BITs, the common features of the 'European' BIT established a substantial degree of uniformity in the bilateral treatment of investment issues.

Some of the characteristics of BITs identified by UNCTAD (1996*a*) are as follows:

- National treatment, MFN and fair and equitable treatment, and treatment according to international law are usually prescribed. MFN is prescribed more often than national treatment, and the latter in any event tends to be stated in broad and general terms, while being qualified by a number of exceptions.
- Right of establishment is often not included, thereby implicitly recognizing the right of governments to regulate entry of FDI. An exception to this approach is found in the BITs signed by the United States.
- Most BITs do not address ownership and control issues explicitly. But some operational issues are covered, such as the admission of senior foreign personnel involved in an investment project.
- Only some BITs—those signed by the USA and some French and Canadian treaties—prohibit performance requirements.
- Specific standards of investment protection are included in respect of funds transfers, expropriation and nationalization, and the settlement of disputes.
- In BITs involving developing nations, a number of developmental issues are recognized, e.g. the importance of FDI for economic development, and exceptions for balance of payments considerations in relation to the principle of free transfer of funds.
- BITs do not address investment–trade interrelations, with the major exception of provisions that deal with performance requirements.

The US government developed its own network of BITs, with the first one being signed in 1982 with Panama. The resulting 'American model' BIT differed in at least one important respect from the European model: the typical American BIT includes a more expansive notion of the right of establishment than the typical European BIT. A conventional European BIT provides that any right of establishment that is granted to foreign investors by the host government is based on the domestic laws of the host country; foreign investment can therefore be prohibited in any sector of the economy through domestic legislation by the host country. This potential restriction on FDI is addressed in a typical US BIT by a provision for national treatment in the right of establishment; that is, the host government cannot preclude private foreign investment from any sector that is not also closed to private domestic investors. However, it is possible to designate specific sectors that are excluded from national treatment in the right of establishment in an annex to a BIT—as the USA itself does with some sectors. The list of excluded sectors cannot be expanded after the entry into force of the treaty. Furthermore, the provision for MFN treatment with regard to the right of establishment in the typical US BIT means that a host country cannot exclude US-based investors from a sector that is open to foreign investors from other countries.

Thus, whereas European BITs typically provide for national treatment only after establishment, US BITs provide for national treatment in the pre-establishment phase as well as the post-establishment phase. The provision for national treatment in the right of establishment for US-based investors, furthermore, does not extend to non-US investors through the MFN provisions in many other countries' BITs; this is because their MFN clauses pertain only to the post-establishment phase of investments. Differences between the standard US BIT and the standard BITs of many European countries thus became a contributing element to the 'patchwork problem' mentioned in Chapter 1. Brief comparative summaries of the varying provisions of BITs are presented in Box 3.1.

Therefore, one dimension of variability in the current array of BITs lies in the nationality of the developed country signatory, with variation between the typical US and European versions. Any given developing country that is a signatory to treaties with both a European country and the United States has therefore committed itself to different international agreements, and thus potentially different degrees of openness for investors from different countries. Furthermore, bilateral agreements concerning political risks and dispute settlement became a closely related and supplementary method of establishing a legal framework for FDI; and they contribute an additional element of variability in the existing array of bilateral arrangements concerning FDI.

Over time, the number of BITs increased significantly. Although the periods of most rapid growth are outside the time frame of the present chapter, it is useful to note here the increased use of BITs over several decades. During the 1980s and 1990s, many countries unilaterally undertook liberalization programmes that made FDI in them easier and more attractive to investors. They simultaneously became more interested in using BITs to increase their attractiveness as host countries, and MNEs and their home governments also became more interested in extending the networks of BITs to additional host countries for greater investment protection. Further, BITs were recognized as one way to lock in—through international agreements—the more liberalized national policies that had already been unilaterally adopted.

Box 3.1

Variability in the Terms of Bilateral Investment Treaties: Examples of The 'Patchwork Problem'

Definition of investment/property

Most BITs define investments to include a broad range of intangible and tangible property: moveable and immoveable property; claims such as mortgages and liens; shares and debentures in firms; claims to money or contracts having financial value; intellectual property rights; concessions, including natural resources concessions. However, US BITs typically include, in addition, licences, permits, and rights concerning the manufacture and sale of products, which are often granted by domestic administrative and regulatory agencies, but which are not included in the BITs of other countries.

Right of establishment (admission)

Most BITs provide for admission in accordance with the domestic laws and regulations of the host country; but some BITs, especially those of the United States, provide for national treatment. Some, including those of many West European countries, have no provisions concerning admission.

Non-discriminatory treatment

Most BITs provide for fair and equitable treatment as well as national treatment and most favoured nation treatment; but a few, particularly some German BITs, provide only for fair and equitable treatment without any provisions for national treatment or most favoured nation treatment.

Transfers of capital and returns

Most BITs provide for transfers without delay, but some (including many of the UK's) provide for transfer instalments.

Compensation for expropriation

Most BITs provide for 'prompt, adequate and effective' compensation in the event of expropriation; but some provide for 'just', 'full', 'reasonable', or 'fair and equitable' compensation, particularly some of the BITs of France and the Netherlands.

Performance requirements

Most BITs do not prohibit performance requirements, but some BITs of Canada, France, and the United States do.

Admission of personnel

Many BITs provide for the admission into the host country of senior personnel associated with FDI projects, but many others do not.

Dispute settlement

Most BITs refer to the use of the conciliation and arbitration procedures of the Centre for the Settlement of Investment Disputes (ICSID) at the World Bank for the resolution of disputes between governments and investors; but many do not, including many of those of Germany and Switzerland.

Source: Khalil, 1992; Sornarajah, 1994: 239–74; UNCTAD, 1996*a*: 134, 144–6.

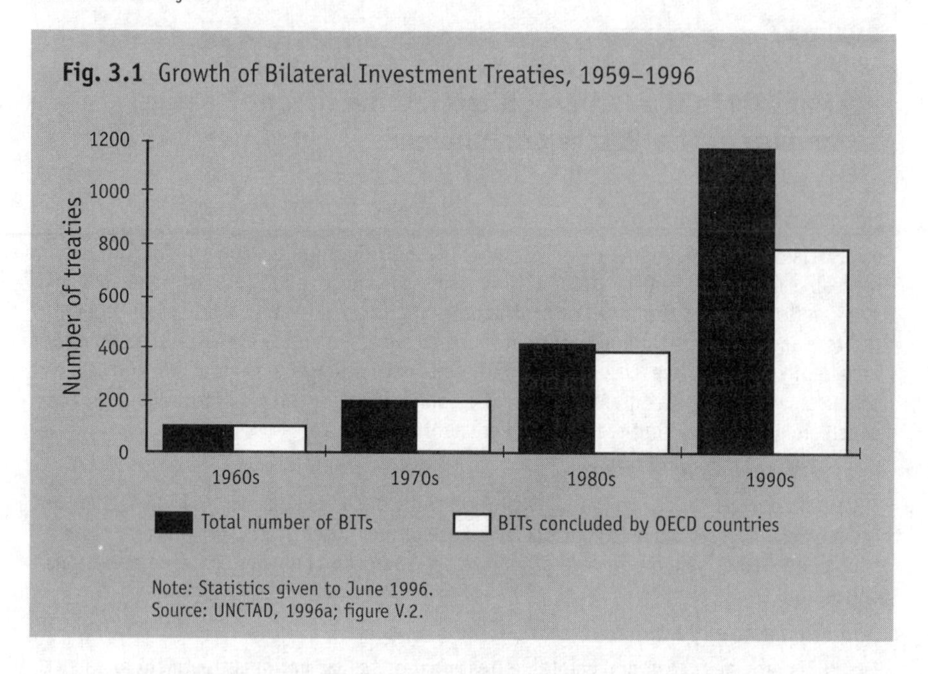

Fig. 3.1 Growth of Bilateral Investment Treaties, 1959–1996

Note: Statistics given to June 1996.
Source: UNCTAD, 1996a; figure V.2.

As a result, there was a proliferation of BITs beginning in the 1980s when the reform programmes of many developing countries were being implemented. Then, in the 1990s, with the collapse of the former Soviet Union and the revolutionary changes in the policies of the successor states and the changes in the other political economies of Central and Eastern Europe as well, there were numerous additional BITs involving countries in that region. The net result was that the total number of BITs worldwide increased from less than 200 in 1979 to more than 1,400 in 1996 (see Figure 3.1).

3.7 **Other Agreements**

There were also a large number of other international agreements among governments affecting FDI during the 1950s and 1960s (see Table 3.1). However, several of these were agreements concerning arbitration and other dispute settlement matters; while an important part of the total regime for FDI, they do not provide for liberalization measures or other forms of inter-governmental cooperation. In addition, some of the others were non-governmental agreements. Yet they are evidence of the continuing interest in developing international arrangements for selected aspects of investment issues during this period—despite the collapse of the ITO and despite the development of the IMF and IBRD as international financial institutions without FDI as one of their principal concerns. Indeed, the agreements reached in the OECD and UN were harbingers of the evolution of investment issues as central concerns of those organizations during the 1960s and 1970s (see next chapter).

Table 3.1 Other International Investment Agreements, 1943–1968

Agreement	Organization	Year
Draft Statutes, Arbitral Tribunal for Foreign Investment	Foreign Investments Court (International Law Association)	1948
International Code of Fair Treatment for Foreign Investment	International Chamber of Commerce	1949
Treaty establishing European Community		1957
Agreement on Arab Economic Unity		1958
Convention on Recognition and Enforcement of Arbitral Awards	UN	1958
General Assembly Resolution 1803: Permanent Sovereignty of Natural Resources	UN	1962
Model Tax Convention on Income and on Capital	OECD	1963
Convention on Investments, Customs, and Economic Union of Central Africa		1965
Draft Convention on the Protection of Foreign Property	OECD	1967

Source: UNCTAD, 1996*a*, table III.1.

3.8 Conclusion

Five key features of the international regime for FDI emerged from this early period:

- The primary instrument for the development of international rules on FDI was bilateral investment treaties. Bilateralism prevailed over multilateralism after the collapse of the efforts to create the ITO.
- Investment issues became largely isolated from trade issues in multilateral fora because the GATT was conceived in narrow terms as a forum for negotiating tariff reductions for trade in manufactured goods. Investment issues were not considered to be within GATT's domain.
- Although both the IMF and the IBRD became significant fora for the development and implementation of international policies, with important and direct consequences for FDI, neither institution initially embraced FDI as a central concern. Yet, as their resources grew and the purview of their policies expanded, their activities became increasingly pertinent to FDI; the Bank, in particular, developed specialized programmes and agencies whose missions specifically concern FDI.
- Investment issues were addressed in a variety of regional and non-governmental fora as well as in the United Nations.

- FDI issues were on the agenda of the OECD from the outset, but particularly in the context of capital account and current account liberalization efforts.

Altogether, these diverse organizations kept investment issues on the international economic agenda, though typically in low profile in comparison with the trade, payments, and development activities, respectively, of the GATT, IMF, and IBRD—which were the international agencies at the centre of attention. Furthermore, there were some tangible results in the non-governmental, regional, and multilateral UN fora which became building blocks for subsequent efforts to address investment issues at the multilateral level in particular.

The period of the 1950s and 1960s was to a great extent a 'honeymoon' period for FDI and MNEs, on the one hand, and governments on the other. It was a period of rapidly increasing FDI in Western Europe and in some developing countries, and it was a period when many of the larger MNEs undertook new international expansion efforts—first in the aftermath of the Second World War and then during the period of rapid economic growth in many countries during the early 1960s. There was neither much concern about regulating MNEs nor much sense of urgency about liberalizing government FDI policies. Private foreign capital in the form of inward FDI was often welcomed in host countries, and there was not much worry in home countries about the effects on trade, employment, or technology of outward FDI. Post-war reconstruction and the establishment of liberalized international trade and payments regimes preoccupied policy-makers. FDI and MNEs were typically seen as marginally relevant to the wider development and liberalization concerns, and investment policy was usually noted (if at all) as an element of international trade policy and/or an element of international financial policy. The distinctive nature of FDI and the increasing importance of MNEs in international trade, finance, and technology were hardly noted. All of this began to change in the late 1960s, as will be seen in the next chapter.

Notes

1. The structure and content of the US proposals were in fact partly the result of the (wartime) structure of the US government at the time (Brown, 1950). Other useful references on this period include: Diebold, 1952; Bronz, 1969; Horsefield, 1969; Oliver, 1971; Helleiner, 1983.
2. Claire Wilcox was a central participant in the US policy process for several years—as the Director of the Office of International Trade Policy in the US Department of State, which had principal responsibility for development of key elements of the US proposals during the war, and as the chair of the US delegation to the London conference and vice chair of the US delegations to the Geneva and Havana conferences.
3. The seven were Belgium, Czechoslovakia, France, Greece, the Netherlands, Poland, and Turkey.
4. The eighteen countries were Australia, Belgium, Brazil, Canada, Chile, China, Cuba, Czechoslovakia, France, India, Lebanon, Luxembourg, the Netherlands, New Zealand, Norway, South Africa, United Kingdom, United States. The Soviet Union had been previously invited to partic-

ipate in the discussions, but did not attend. Only an analysis of the internal documentary evidence and the relevant diplomatic histories of all of the other countries would reveal whether any of these governments explicitly favoured or opposed the absence of provisions on investment and US bilateralism on the issue. Such multi-country archival research, however, is beyond the scope of the present study.

5. A Drafting Committee met in Lake Success, New York, between the London and Geneva conferences to work on ITO voting procedures, investment protection, and the language of the London draft.
6. The thinking at the time has been summarized as follows: 'As the Fund's Articles were drafted against the background of the disturbing capital movements that had taken place during the 1930s, there was an understandable desire to prevent movements of "hot" money and to minimize the risk that inadequate foreign exchange reserves would be depleted by more or less panic-inspired capital transfers. Hence, it was thought that control over capital movements might be necessary and beneficial' (De Vries and Horsefield, 1969: 224).
7. The convention was commonly known as the Abs–Shawcross Convention, after Hermann Abs, former head of Deutsche Bank, and Lord Shawcross, former President of the UK Board of Trade, who were its principal proponents.

Appendix 3.1

Excerpts from the Havana Charter for an International Trade Organization

[The Havana Charter for an International Trade Organization was drawn up at the International Conference on Trade and Employment, which met at Havana from 21 November 1947 to 24 March 1948, for submission to the governments represented. The Final Act of the International Conference on Trade and Employment was signed by the representatives of Afghanistan, Australia, Austria, Belgium, Bolivia, Brazil, Burma, Canada, Ceylon, Chile, China, Colombia, Costa Rica, Cuba, Czechoslovakia, Denmark, Dominican Republic, Ecuador, Egypt, El Salvador, France, Greece, Guatemala, Haiti, India, Indonesia, Iran, Iraq, Ireland, Italy, Lebanon, Liberia, Luxembourg, Mexico, the Netherlands, New Zealand, Nicaragua, Norway, Pakistan, Panama, Peru, Philippines, Portugal, South Africa, Southern Rhodesia, Sweden, Switzerland, Syria, Transjordan, United Kingdom, United States of America, Uruguay, Venezuela, the United Nations and the United Nations Conference on Trade and Employment. The Charter never entered into force.]

Chapter III
Economic Development and Reconstruction

Article 11

Means of Promoting Economic Development and Reconstruction

1. Progressive industrial and general economic development, as well as reconstruction, requires among other things adequate supplies of capital funds, materials, modern equipment and technology and technical and managerial skills. Accordingly, in order to stimulate and assist in the provision and exchange of these facilities:

(a) Members shall co-operate, in accordance with Article 10, in providing or arranging for the provision of such facilities within the limits of their power, and Members shall not impose unreasonable or unjustifiable impediments that would prevent other Members from obtaining on equitable terms any such facilities for their economic development or, in the case of Member countries whose economies have been devastated by war for their reconstruction;

(b) No Member shall take unreasonable or unjustifiable action within its territory injurious to the rights or interests of nationals of other Members in the enterprise, skills, capital, arts or technology which they have supplied.

2. The Organization may, in such collaboration with other intergovernmental organizations as may be appropriate:

(a) make recommendations for and promote bilateral or multilateral agreements on measures designed:

(i) to assure just and equitable treatment for the enterprise, skills, capital, arts and technology brought from one Member country to another;

(ii) to avoid international double taxation in order to stimulate foreign private investment;

(iii) to enlarge to the greatest possible extent the benefits to Members from the fulfillment of the obligations under this Article;

(b) make recommendations and promote agreements designed to facilitate an equitable distribution of skills, arts, technology, materials and equipment, with due regard to the needs of all Members;

(c) formulate and promote the adoption of a general agreement or statement of principles regarding the conduct, practices and treatment of foreign investment.

Article 12

International Investment for Economic Development and Reconstruction

1. The Members recognize that:

(a) international investment, both public and private, can be of great value in promoting economic development and reconstruction, and consequent social progress;

(b) the international flow of capital will be stimulated to the extent that Members afford nationals of other countries opportunities for investment and security for existing and future investments;

(c) without prejudice to existing international agreements to which Members are parties, a Member has the right:

(i) to take any appropriate safeguards necessary to ensure that foreign investment is not used as a basis for interference in its internal affairs or national policies;

(ii) to determine whether and to what extent and upon what terms it will allow future foreign investment;

(iii) to prescribe and give effect on just terms to requirements as to the ownership of existing and future investments;

(iv) to prescribe and give effect to other reasonable requirements with respect to existing and future investments;

(d) the interests of Members whose nationals are in a position to provide capital for international investment and of Members who desire to obtain the use of such capital to promote their economic development or reconstruction may be promoted if such Members enter into bilateral or multilateral agreements relating to the opportunities and security for investment which the Members are prepared to offer and any limitations which they are prepared to accept of the rights referred to in sub-paragraph (c).

2. Members therefore undertake:
   (a) subject to the provisions of paragraph l(c) and to any agreements entered into under paragraph l (d).
      (i) to provide reasonable opportunities for investment acceptable to them and adequate security for existing and future investments, and
      (ii) to give due regard to the desirability of avoiding discrimination as between foreign investments;
   (b) upon the request of any Member and without prejudice to existing international agreements to which Members are parties to enter into consultation or to participate in negotiations directed to the conclusion, if mutually acceptable, of an agreement of the kind referred to in paragraph l (d).
3. Members shall promote co-operation between national and foreign enterprises or investors for the purpose of fostering economic development or reconstruction in cases where such co-operation appears to the Members concerned to be appropriate.

Source: UNCTAD, 1996c; from United Nations Conference on Trade and Employment, *Final Act and Related Documents* (New York: United Nations), Sales No. 1948.H.D.4.1 [Note added by the editor].

Appendix 3.2

Excerpts from the OECD Codes of Liberalization of Capital Movements and Current Invisible Operations

[The outlines, part names, and article names are virtually identical in the two codes; this appendix, therefore, lists the part and article titles from the Capital Movements Code only. However, there are, of course, important differences in the types of international transactions that each covers; therefore, excerpts of the texts of the two codes reflect the different types of transactions that they cover.]

Part I—Undertakings with regard to capital movements

Article 1. General undertakings
2. Measures of liberalization
3. Public order and security
4. Obligations in existing multilateral international agreements
5. Controls and formalities
6. Execution of transfers
7. Clauses of derogation
8. Right to benefit from measures of liberalization
9. Non-discrimination
10. Exceptions to the principle of non-discrimination. Special customs or monetary systems

Part II—Procedure

11. Notification and information from Members
12. Notification and examination of reservations lodged under article 2 (b)
13. Notification and examination of derogations made under article 7
14. Examination of derogations made under article 7. Members in process of economic development
15. Special report and examination concerning derogations made under article 7
16. Reference to the Organization. Internal arrangements
17. Reference to the Organization. Retention, introduction or reintroduction of restrictions

Part III—Terms of reference

18. Committee on Capital Movements and Invisible Transactions. General tasks
19. Committee on Capital Movements and Invisible Transactions. Special tasks
20. Payments Committee

Part IV—Miscellaneous

21. Definitions
22. Title of Decision
23. Withdrawal

Annex A

Liberalization Lists of Capital Movements
List A
List B

Annex B

Reservations to the Code of Liberalization of Capital Movements

Annex C

Decision of the Council Regarding the Application of the Provisions of the Code of Liberalization of Capital Movements to action taken by States of the United States

Annex D

General List of International Capital Movements and Certain Related Operations

Annex E

Decision of the Council Regarding Measures and Practices Concerning Reciprocity and/or Involving Discrimination among Investors Originating in various OECD Member Countries in the area of Inward Direct Investment and Establishment

Notes: Code of Liberalization of Capital Movements. Annex A, List A, I. Direct Investment, reads in part as follows: 'The authorities of Members shall not maintain or introduce: Regulations or practices applying to the granting of licenses, concessions, or similar authorisations, including conditions or requirements attaching to such authorisations and affecting the operations of enterprises, that raise special barriers or limitations with respect to non-resident (as compared to resident) investors, and that have the intent or the effect of preventing or significantly impeding inward direct investment by non-residents.'

Code of Liberalization of Current Invisible Operations. Annex A, List of Current Invisible Operations, includes the following items of specific relevance to foreign direct investment:

'F. Income from Capital
F/1. Profits from business activity.
F/2. Dividends and shares in profits.'

Source: OECD, 1993*a*.

4

Control

Codes and the Obligations of Multinational Enterprises (Late 1960s–Early 1980s)

4.1 Overview of the Period

Background and the new international economic order

In the early post-war years, the expansion of FDI was largely welcomed as multinationals enjoyed a honeymoon in their relations with governments. It is difficult, therefore, to define the beginning of the 'period of regulation and control'. According to data from the Harvard Multinational Enterprise project (Vaupel and Curhan, 1973; Curhan et al., 1977), the number of new manufacturing affiliates formed by their sample of the largest 180 American MNEs peaked in 1968. Scholars at the time placed very different interpretations on this expansionism: Raymond Vernon's *Sovereignty at Bay* (1971) highlighed the importance of MNEs as independent forces constraining the actions of all states with which they were involved, while stressing their positive influence on the promotion of global welfare and political harmony. By contrast, Barnet and Müller (1974) in *Global Reach* laid emphasis on the effects of multinationals in stifling competition, cartelizing world markets, worsening income distribution, and creating poverty in both home and host countries. Claims were made about the export of jobs from the United States, and about the destruction of jobs in host nations consequent on the use of capital-intensive technologies in labour-rich developing economies. In Europe Jean-Jacques Servan-Schreiber's *Le Défi Américain*—a polemical attack on American business abroad—was published in 1967.

By the late 1960s and early 1970s, therefore, it was becoming clear that the honeymoon period for multinationals was over. In 1972, Salvadore Allende, the democratically elected Marxist leader of Chile, made a considered but virulent attack on multinationals in a speech to the UN General Assembly (in Allende, 1975); subsequently, the Allende government was toppled by a military coup in which the US MNE ITT and the Central Intelligence Agency were allegedly involved (Hood and Young, 1979). Ways of curbing multinational power became top of the developing country agenda.

At the end of the 1960s, over 10,000 multinational enterprises had an estimated 70,000 foreign affiliates, with a book value of around $160 billion (with one-half of this being accounted for by 150 corporations) (Sauvant, 1977). Most of these enterprises were headquartered in only five countries—the USA, the UK, Germany, France, and Switzerland—which together represented four-fifths of the total of foreign direct investment; the USA alone accounted for more than half of the world stock of FDI at this time, with the number of US affiliates more than trebling, from 7,000 to 23,000, between 1950 and 1966 (Sauvant and Lavipour, 1976). The bulk of MNE activities (over two-thirds of estimated book value) were located in the developed market economies, linked to market opportunities and cost differentials but also to their predominantly oligopolistic character (Knickerbocker, 1973). On the other hand, the remaining one-third of the stock in developing countries was of greater relative significance, and the concentration by country and sector undoubtedly had a pronounced negative influence on attitudes towards the incoming MNEs. The major host developing nations at the time were Argentina, Brazil, India, Mexico, Nigeria, Venezuela, and some Caribbean islands, which represented 43 per cent of the total stock of FDI in developing countries (UN, 1973; Sauvant and Lavipour, 1976).

The interest and concern about multinationals for the first half of this period was driven by developing nations through the United Nations system, and was integrally related to broader questions of economic development and north–south relations. In May 1974 two General Assembly resolutions, sponsored by developing countries, affirmed the principle of permanent national sovereignty over natural resources and called for the industrialized world to assist in financing Third World economic development (Black et al., 1978). The first resolution was the 'Declaration on the Establishment of a New International Economic Order (NIEO)', which asserted the requirement for a new international economic order in order to bridge the economic gap between developed and developing nations. The second resolution and other meetings of the UN General Assembly and of UNCTAD set out the necessary actions to achieve the goals of the NIEO, including:

- Integrated programme for commodities, with mechanisms for price stabilization and protection of the real value of export earnings.
- International monetary reform, including debt relief, increased levels of assistance, and improved access to the capital markets of developed countries.
- Strengthening the technological base of developing countries through technical assistance from developed states, greater access to developed nation technologies, and the establishment of an international code of conduct for the transfer of technology corresponding to the needs of the developing countries.
- Strengthening trade and cooperation among developing nations, reference being made to the ultimate objective of the negotiation of a revised Havana Charter (UNCTAD, 1976).
- Regulation of multinational corporations, to ensure that foreign capital operated to advance national development, including limits on the repatriation of profits by MNEs. The sovereignty of states over their natural resources and the right of nations to nationalize foreign property in order to regain control of these resources was asserted. In addition, the Calvo doctrine was upheld in respect of disputes that might arise over compensation: this required recourse to the jurisdiction of the nationalizing state's own courts (Black et al., 1978).

While these resolutions and declarations had no real force in international law, they were very revealing in terms of highlighting the attitudes of developing nations, and signalled their intention to claim a leadership role in the management and development of the world economy. The increased Third World assertiveness was linked to the assumption of greater bargaining power consequent on the success of the Organization of Petroleum Exporting Countries (OPEC) and a (misplaced) belief that this could be replicated by other producers' associations (Bergsten and Krasner, 1976).

Controlling the multinational enterprise

It is interesting that some of the first proposals for international investment agreements during this period reflected a fairly balanced approach towards the relative interests of MNEs and governments. Goldberg and Kindleberger (1970) advocated the establishment of a General Agreement for the International Corporation, which was to be based on a number of universally accepted principles, with an agency being established to operate and administer the agreement. This agency would recommend action on the basis of issues submitted to it by companies or countries. Emphasis would be upon five key problem areas existing between MNEs and home and host governments, namely, taxation, anti-trust policy, balance of payments controls, export controls, and securities regulation. Each had a common denominator: the MNE was either unregulated or its operations were influenced by the overlapping rules of different countries.

However, United Nations influence was paramount at this time. Attention within the UN system on the MNE as a global economic and political phenomenon was most clearly apparent within the UN Economic and Social Council (ECOSOC). In July 1972 Resolution 1721 of ECOSOC requested the Secretary-General to establish a 'Group of Eminent Persons' for the purpose of formulating recommendations for appropriate international action concerning MNEs. The Group of twenty members[1] submitted their report in June 1974 (Hellmann, 1977; Schwamm and Germidis, 1977; Black et al., 1978). The main study was severely critical of multinationals, although about half of the report comprised comments by individual members dissenting from the principal findings and providing individual interpretations. The Group of Eminent Persons report contained two recommendations. The first of these concerned the establishment of a new and permanent commission on transnational corporations (the term 'transnational' instead of 'multinational' was used for the first time to underline the extent of the cross-border activities involved, and has been incorporated ever since into UN terminology). The commission was to be composed of twenty-five persons having in-depth knowledge of MNEs as nominated by the Secretary-General.[2] The second recommendation related to the establishment of an information and research centre on transnational corporations within the UN secretariat to provide technical assistance to developing countries on issues relating to MNEs and to undertake preliminary work on the formulation of a code of conduct.

In December 1974, ECOSOC in its resolution 1913 established the Commission and the Centre on Transnational Corporations. At the behest of the developing countries, the Commission on Transnational Corporations had forty-eight members selected by governments and appointed by the UN Economic and Social Council, and developing countries had a majority on the Commission. Although separate entities with different lines of authority within the UN system, the Commission and the Centre had the same objectives, namely:

- To enhance the understanding of the nature and impact of MNC activities in political, social and economic spheres of the international and domestic relations of home and host countries, developed and developing;
- To obtain effective international arrangements for MNC operations which promote their contribution to national goals while minimizing their costs:
- To strengthen negotiating capacity of host governments (especially of developing nations) in their dealings with multinational firms. (Black et al., 1978: 221)

The five main tasks assigned to the Centre by the Commission were:

- To formulate a Code of Conduct (taking into account the work of UNCTAD and ILO);
- To develop a comprehensive information system;
- To research into the political, economic and social effects of the activities and practices of MNEs;
- At the request of governments, to organize and coordinate technical cooperation programmes on MNCs;
- To undertake studies with view to defining the concept of MNCs. (Schwamm and Germidis, 1977: 6)

Highest priority was given to the formulation of a code of conduct dealing with multinational enterprises. The Group of Eminent Persons intended that such a code would be a 'Consistent set of recommendations which are gradually evolved and which may be revised as experience or circumstances require. Although they are not compulsory in character, they act as an instrument of moral persuasion strengthened by the authority of international organizations and the support of public opinion' (UN Economic and Social Council, 1974: 55). Comment at the time highlighted some of the basic issues facing the Commission in formulating the code, and these are worth reviewing given their continued relevance to the present day (Black et al., 1978):

- What were the purposes of a code—were they to establish rules for MNE behaviour or help ensure a favourable investment climate?
- Were the addressees of a code governments and MNEs, or MNEs alone?
- What was its geographic coverage? Were, for example, socialist regimes to be excluded, and were the least developed nations to receive special treatment?
- Was the code to be voluntary or legally binding, in whole or in part?
- Was a surveillance mechanism desirable or not, and what power and sanctions would be involved?
- Would the code present general principles or specific provisions; and in which substantive areas?
- Would the substantive coverage of the code relate to issues such as socio-economic goals, or to political affairs such as interference in domestic policy-

making; or to specific economic and commercial matters such as transfer pricing, taxation, restrictive business practices, technology transfer, labour practices, and so on?
- What would be the role of non-governmental groups in formulating a code?

As will be shown, the conflicts between different interest groups meant that negotiations continued intermittently for a large part of the next twenty years without an acceptable draft code being agreed.

During the first half of the 1970s, criticisms of MNEs became increasingly global, radical, and political. The views of the countries of Latin America and the Caribbean with respect to a code of conduct are outlined in Appendix 4.1. These submissions from the developing countries were very hostile to MNEs and included virtually no reference, even indirectly, to the potential benefits of multinational activities. In addition, there was no recognition of the stable investment climate needed for FDI, or for MNEs to have guarantees on the security of their investments. Despite these views, however, and despite their voting majority in the UN, it became obvious that agreement would not be reached on any form of a code of conduct (let alone a legally binding code) without some compromises being reached with the industrialized countries.

In the end the developing countries themselves could not support a binding agreement. As Hellmann (1977: 66) notes: 'Especially the developing countries are not willing at this point to renounce part of their newly gained sovereignty to promote control over multinational corporations.' Similarly, the labour unions (important actors at both national and international levels during this period of time—Weinberg, 1978) supported the international supervision of corporate conduct but did not want to commit themselves to any regulation of their own unions.

The emergence of the OECD instruments (including the *Guidelines for Multinational Enterprises*, 1976) and the ILO's *Tripartite Declaration of Principles Concerning Multinational Enterprises and Social Policy* (1977), which are discussed later in this chapter, need to be seen in part within the context of the discussions relating to the UN code of conduct. Hamilton (1983) argued that the OECD Guidelines were strongly promoted by the USA to counteract the moves of Third World countries at the UN to curb multinational power. The USA thus sought an agreement at the OECD which would protect US investments overseas; which promoted a liberal investment climate; and which accepted that all OECD governments had responsibilities to treat foreign enterprises no less favourably than their own national enterprises. Not all countries within the OECD supported the concept of a voluntary code. Thus, Sweden and the Netherlands sought a binding code on MNEs and at least insisted on follow-up machinery to ensure compliance. In an early draft of the Guidelines, a governing body was to be established to police infringements of the Guidelines. The USA rejected even this proposal, with the Committee on International Investment and Multinational Enterprises (CIME) being given responsibility to implement the Guidelines but with weak powers. In essence the CIME had the role of reviewing national experience with the investment package and for holding consultations with TUAC and BIAC, the OECD trade union and employer bodies respectively.

The ILO's Declaration of Principles is also understandable in the context of discussions taking place at the UN.[3] The International Labour Organization is a tripartite body representing the world's employers, trades unions, and governments. Thus, the focus of discussions covered the themes of employment, training, conditions of work life, and industrial relations. The trade unions, together with developing countries and socialist states, lobbied the ILO to produce binding rules for MNEs. Although employers were concerned about their participation in the negotiations (in the sense that it signified that multinationals had a case to answer), their involvement persuaded most governments of the need to keep the Declaration of Principles voluntary. The end results of the ILO negotiations were therefore moderate and balanced statements which recognized the beneficial effects of MNEs and which included principles preventing discrimination between foreign-owned and national enterprises in host economies.

The Commission on Transnational Corporations established the Intergovernmental Working Group on a Code of Conduct (IWGCC) to prepare the draft. But their efforts to create a code did not make substantive progress because of disarray among the various interest groups. By the early 1980s, moreover, the international economic situation had changed dramatically. Not only had demands for a mandatory code been dropped, but the argument of the developed states for a code applying to nations as well as to companies had gained ground. In 1980, at the sixth session of the Commission on Transnational Corporations in Mexico, a resolution was passed (the so-called 'Mexico Declaration') stating that any code should 'include provisions relating to the treatment of transnational corporations, jurisdiction and other related matters' (Hamilton, 1983: 6). This was a major concern, in particular to the Latin American states which were the most vocal in calling for a UN code. Since a code would apply to them as well as to companies, it would threaten their national sovereignty and also reduce their freedom of manœuvre in respect of determining their national policies on treatment of multinational enterprises.

The economic situation had also changed dramatically. The oil price hikes had a major influence on the worldwide recession conditions which emerged in the late 1970s and early 1980s, accompanied by high unemployment and strong inflationary pressures. The period of optimism surrounding a New International Economic Order for developing countries was over. The assumptions associated with the NIEO were always incorrect and the possibilities of any improved bargaining power were in any case ended with the world economic crisis and the slowdown in international direct capital flows. From the very earliest days of the discussions of a code, furthermore, there were dissensions among the developing countries themselves. These widened towards the end of the period in question with the rapid growth of the newly industrializing countries and the emergence of their own multinational firms. Discussions on the UN code continued internationally until 1990 when a revised text of the draft code was transmitted to the UN Economic and Social Council: the contents of the code were not approved by UN members (selected extracts from the draft UN code are contained in Appendix 4.2).[4]

4.2 **Policies at the International Level**

Non-governmental approaches

Although governmental organizations were particularly important in the formulation of policy at the international level, there were also a number of non-governmental efforts to create international codes or guidelines for multinational enterprises. These codes were not binding and had no force in international law. They were designed to promote the interests of particular organizations, and to provide an input to negotiations at international governmental level and serve as a model for the latter (Black et al., 1978).

The International Chamber of Commerce (ICC) published its *Guidelines for International Investment* in 1972. The voluntary ICC Guidelines attempted to provide standards for all parties concerned (investors as well as home and host governments) and covered investment policies, ownership and management, finance, fiscal policies, legal frameworks, labour policies, technology transfer, and commercial policies. The ICC Guidelines reflected the views of the international business community. On the issue of ownership, therefore, the ICC code stated that: 'the government of the host country . . . should recognise that joint ventures are most likely to be successful if they are entered into voluntarily . . . and that there may be cases where investments which deserve high priority are only possible on the basis of total foreign ownership.' And on the question of free movement of factors of production, the Guidelines took a strong free market position: 'the government of the host country should place no restrictions on the remittance of loan interest . . . license fees, royalties and similar payments.' For their part the company was obliged to 'practice fair pricing policies for goods and services in dealings with associated companies' (ICC, 1972).

The International Confederation of Free Trade Unions (ICFTU) had first proposed an international code in 1970. In 1975 it produced its own radical *Multinational Charter* for the legislative control of MNEs. Included in the charter were demands for an international convention for the suppression of restrictive practices and for the establishment of rules regarding taxation; for a drastic revision of international patent laws; for worker participation; and so on. In addition, however, the Charter included a list of 'social obligations of multinational companies' in the form of a code which could be voluntarily adopted by individual enterprises.

The ICFTU was founded in 1949 by national trade union federations and represented 119 organizations in 88 countries with over 53 million workers. The European Trade Union Confederation (ETUC) evolved from the ICFTU into a separate regional organization, and it followed the latter in presenting demands for controls over MNE activities. Its main aims were to influence the European Communities in terms of the development of European company law and European-level collective bargaining. In its executive committee paper of 1975, the ETUC demanded:

- national and international legal definition of the MNE because of the dependence of the affiliate on an externally located parent;
- labour representation on the boards of directors of the MNE parents;

- requirements for consolidated published accounts for each MNE group, including and identifying all affiliate activities.

Some of these issues are still on the agenda of the EU Commission in Brussels.

Finally, another union organization, the World Federation of Trade Unions (WFTU) headquartered in Prague, also pressed for legislative control over MNEs; and in a March 1976 statement the WFTU laid out its views on an international code. As part of a range of demands it claimed the right of workers and labour organizations to participate in the development and implementation of economic and social strategies nationally and internationally.

OECD codes

The major role of the above organizations was as pressure groups, and the most important developments were those that took place within the auspices of the Organization for Economic Cooperation and Development, simply because its member countries accounted for the bulk of both inward and outward direct investment. Hamilton (1983: 3) suggests that: 'to some extent, the OECD Guidelines could be interpreted as a type of pre-emptive strike.' But from this inauspicious beginning, the OECD has gone on to play a leading role in the area of international rule-making.

As Chapter 3 revealed, OECD involvement in international investment rules had begun in the early 1960s, with the Codes on Liberalization of Capital Movements and on Current Invisible Operations. However, since the former dealt with long-term capital movements, it was inadequate to cover many MNE-related issues. Furthermore, during this period many governments were still opposed to a true liberalization of capital movements. One delegate to the OECD Invisibles Committee is reported as saying that 'except for the United States, the Federal Republic of Germany and Switzerland, it is highly questionable whether other governments believe that capital movements should be liberalized' (Black et al., 1978: 186). Exchange controls were regarded as important instruments to ensure equilibrium in the balance of payments especially in the fixed exchange rate era. Even thereafter there was a reluctance to liberalize because of the potentially destabilizing effects of large-scale inflows and outflows, the belief that investment abroad could substitute for investment at home, and in some European countries lack of confidence in the stability of domestic currencies.

Aside from the political factors referred to earlier, the United States sought to improve the Codes on Liberalization by gaining the agreement of governments to accord national treatment to foreign affiliates. Other OECD members were reluctant to give such further commitments without a quid pro quo which was seen in terms of guidelines setting out the responsibilities of multinational enterprises. The result of the bargaining was, therefore, an agreement to work towards a package of measures on international investment and multinational enterprises.

The Committee for International Investment and Multinational Enterprise (CIME) was formed to prepare the agreements. Working speedily from a start date of January 1975, an investment package was adopted by an OECD ministerial meeting in Paris in June 1976 comprising three interrelated instruments:

- *Guidelines for Multinational Enterprises*, under which MNEs in OECD countries were encouraged to follow a set of voluntary guidelines that set standards on a range of topics including information disclosure, competition, financing, taxation, employment and industrial relations, and science and technology. Furthermore MNEs were encouraged to take into account the general policy objectives of member countries in which they operated, and to cooperate closely with the local community and local business interests, while avoiding employment discrimination, and refraining from bribes and improper political activities. Selected extracts are presented in Appendix 4.3.
- *Statement on National Treatment* obliged OECD nations to accord MNEs treatment no less favourable than that given to domestic firms.
- *Statement on International Investment Incentives and Disincentives* encouraged OECD member states to take into account the possible adverse effects on FDI flows into other members when investment incentives or disincentives are established.

What was agreed was inevitably a compromise, and until the end there were concerns about whether the package as a whole would be agreed by all governments and in particular by Canada, Australia, Japan, and New Zealand. In addition, one of the key discussion points concerned the monitoring of the Guidelines. While there was agreement that the OECD should not pass judgement on the actions of individual governments or firms, some felt that an element of accountability had to be introduced for the whole package to serve any real purpose. The Swedish government argued that the Committee should have the right to identify specific abuses by particular MNEs and to bring the enterprises involved before the Committee. The United States, on the other hand, rejected this view on the grounds that the Guidelines were voluntary. The compromise that was reached was that the Committee, after a unanimous decision, could invite enterprises to express their views although the latter were still free to accept or decline these invitations.

Two non-governmental organizations provided substantial input to the work of the CIME—the Business and Industry Advisory Committee (BIAC) and the Trade Union Advisory Committee (TUAC). The responses of the two organizations to the OECD package were as expected. The BIAC statement emphasized that the Guidelines generally reflected the recognition by OECD governments that enterprises should be treated equitably, with discrimination between public and private sector firms eliminated. By contrast, the TUAC statement noted that the Guidelines would be only a first step to further international arrangements incorporating binding rules. The widely differing views of BIAC and TUAC have continued to the present day; witness the submissions that the two organizations presented to the OECD concerning the proposed Multilateral Agreement on Investment in 1996.

Evaluation of the OECD instruments

Sauvant (1977: 388), writing at the time, notes that:

> The OECD code is important because countries that are also the major home countries of TNEs have agreed, for the first time, to elaborate certain guided principles for the behavior of 'their' TNEs. As such, the OECD Guidelines represent the response of developed market economies . . . to growing pressures from many quarters to clarify the conditions under which TNEs should conduct their activities. . . . Since the governments of the major headquarter companies stand behind the code, it has a considerable amount of moral suasion which may, in fact, persuade TNEs to volunteer information and to attempt observance.

There was, of course, considerable debate about the usefulness of voluntary rules. However, writers at the time cited the Badger case as an illustration of the way in which this type of moral suasion could operate. In 1976, employees at the Badger company in Belgium were informed that the company would close. Since the company was nearly bankrupt, full compensation, as required under Belgian law, was not paid to the employees. Badger was a subsidiary of US-based Raytheon and it refused to intervene to settle the liabilities of its subsidiary. The Belgian government, under pressure from the unions, sought OECD consideration of the case, pointing to the section on 'employment and industrial relations' in the OECD Guidelines. Demands that the parent company accept full responsibility for its subsidiary and pay employees the full compensation to which they were entitled were eventually accepted by the American multinational (for further details of the Badger case, see Vogelaar, 1977).

Schwamm and Germidis (1977) pointed to other positive aspects of the OECD codes. First, they reflected an acceptance by the industrialized countries that the activities of MNEs needed to be constrained. Second, despite their differing views, the codes did reflect real efforts at harmonization and collaboration among a range of interest groups and countries. Third, they could act as a bridge between the work of the OECD and that of the UN and its specialized agencies. Fourth, they could in time constitute part of customary international law, even for multinationals which have never accepted this.

On the other hand, many of the provisions of the codes are very general and lack precise definition. This applies, for example, to the definition of an MNE and to the borderline between direct and portfolio investment. There is vagueness, too, on the definition of an acceptable transfer price. Similarly, with respect to employment and labour relations, the Guidelines exhort the MNE to observe standards not less favourable than those observed by comparable employers in the host country. But the meaning of the qualifying word 'comparable' is by no means straightforward.

In terms of implementation, Hellmann (1977) indicates that the US government made much greater efforts than European countries to publicize the OECD codes among US MNEs both at home and abroad. On 19 August 1976, each MNE in the United States received a letter from the Secretaries of State, Treasury, and Commerce recommending observance of the voluntary Guidelines. And on 1 October 1976 the US Senate agreed to a resolution commending the voluntary Guidelines as 'reasonable standards of business practice, the observance of which will help strengthen public confidence in multinational enterprises' (US Senate, 1976). This is not, of course, the same as ensuring adherence to the codes. In the UK, requests from the Confederation of British Industry (CBI) to support the codes received positive endorsements from only 57 companies out of the total of approximately 2,000 British MNEs (Hamilton, 1983).

OECD members recognized when the Guidelines were adopted that periodic reviews would improve their effectiveness. Thus, the CIME undertook reviews in 1979, 1982, 1984, and 1991 which led to a number of actions relating to improving follow-up procedures, clarifying the Guidelines and amending the text of the Guidelines (OECD, 1994*b*).

The OECD Guidelines for Multinational Enterprises are complementary to the ILO Tripartite Declaration and do not conflict with them. The 1977 Tripartite Declaration of Principles Concerning Multinational Enterprises and Social Policy relates to principles in the fields of employment, training, working conditions, and industrial relations, whereas the OECD Guidelines cover all major aspects of corporate behaviour.

4.3 Policy at National, Bilateral, and Regional Levels

It is recognized that global policy responses represent the best solution to issues surrounding the regulation of MNEs, with a regional solution, on either a country or product basis, second best, and actions by individual host countries only a third best solution. In the early part of this period, as the discussion has revealed, there was a belief among developing countries at least in the merits of multilateral rules on the grounds of increased bargaining power.[5] As the possibilities for such controls and belief in them faded, efforts turned to the implementation of bargaining power at national or regional levels. Among developed nations, there was little unanimity of views in the early part of the period, with the United States position basically that of a home country and most others reflecting host nation interests and concerns. In the later 1970s and early 1980s, major changes occurred in the world economy, with the growth in importance of non-US countries as home nations to MNEs and the USA as a host, highly adverse macroeconomic conditions and the emergence of supply side economics. Alongside national policies which differed according to economic philosophy but generally became more liberal, was a greater (if reluctant in some cases) acceptance of the need for an international set of rules to provide a basic framework of rights and obligations for enterprises and nations.

National approaches

In respect of host developing nations, Bergsten (1974) pointed out that four features differentiated the 1970s situation from that of earlier periods. First, virtually all countries were adopting policies to regulate FDI, whereas few did before. Second, those policies were more explicit. Third, host country objectives were broader and deeper, and governments were seeking additional instruments to attain these objectives.

And, finally, host nations were in a stronger position *vis-à-vis* multinationals than before. There were also different streams of thought which influenced the approaches of developing countries, Lall (1974) distinguishing between the nationalist, the *dependencia*, and the Marxist. The nationalist approach focused upon the political and social costs of FDI and was cautious about the alleged benefits of MNEs. Controls on foreign investment were, therefore, advocated to improve the economic, political, and social position of the host state. Theorists of *dependencia*, mainly from Latin America, were highly critical of traditional theories of economic development and of the role of foreign capital (see Sunkel, 1972). Marxists' views further emphasized imperialism, class struggle, and other Marxist-Leninist concepts, within the framework of a broader attack on capitalism (Black et al., 1978).

Given such factors and economic influences on bargaining power, the patterns of foreign direct investment regulation in developing countries in the mid-1970s are shown in Table 4.1. And Box 4.1 provides one specific country illustration, namely, that of Nigeria.

Table 4.1. Patterns of Foreign Direct Investment Regulation in Selected Countries

Pattern	Pattern 1 (mostly Asia—excluding India—Africa, CACM)	Pattern 2 (mostly Middle East, North Africa)	Pattern 3 (mostly South America)
Administration	Case-by-case screening largely restricted to award of incentives (non-discriminatory).	Case-by-case screening at establishment (degree of discrimination varies).	Separate administration for foreign investment. Screening at establishment.
Investment screening criteria	Emphasis on functional contribution of investment. Little indication of extensive cost/benefit analysis. Screening largely for award of incentives.	Emphasis on functional contributions and conditions of investment. Little indication of extensive cost/benefit analysis.	Criteria formulated for cost/benefit analysis, often extensive. Includes social cost criteria in some cases.
Ownership	Few requirements. Few sectors closed to foreign investment.	Joint ventures prevalent.	Strict regulations on ownership and investment (except Brazil). Large number of closed sectors.

Table 4.1. *cont.*

Pattern	Pattern 1 (mostly Asia—excluding India—Africa, CACM)	Pattern 2 (mostly Middle East, North Africa)	Pattern 3 (mostly South America)
Finance	Few repatriation limitations.	Few repatriation limitations.	Repatriation ceilings in most areas (except Mexico). Screening of foreign loans. Special control of payments to parent company.
Employment and training	Announced indigenization policies but little headway in practice.	Local quotas for workforce. Few local quotas for management.	Specific across-the-board indigenization requirements.
Technology transfer	No controls.	No controls.	Screening and registration of all technology imported.
Investment incentives	Long-term tax incentives for establishment.	Establishment incentives limited to five years—in most cases non-renewable.	Incentives tied to specific contributions, but incentives may be curtailed for foreign-owned firms.
International dispute settlement	Adherence to international dispute regulations. Regional investment regulation: EAC, etc.	Same as Pattern 1. Regional investment regulation: Arab Economic Union.	Local adjudication and regional harmonization of investment regulation: ANCOM, CACM.

Note: CACM=Central American Common Market; EAC=East African Community; ANCOM=Andean Common Market.
Source: UN Economic and Social Council, 1976.

Among host developed nations, while different approaches were apparent, multinationals generally faced a significantly less restrictive regulatory environment than in developing states. Within Europe the position differed between, on the one hand, Germany, the Netherlands, and the UK, and, on the other, France, Sweden, and Norway. The former countries were important as capital exporters and, therefore, had a vested interest in relative ease of access for inward FDI; although in the UK a more interventionist policy was operated in respect of investment in the oil sector. Contrasting these two countries with France and the two Scandinavian states, the

Box 4.1

Nigeria

Nigeria in the 1970s had one of the world's most booming economies, based very largely on oil. Even after independence in 1960, however, the Nigerian economy was dominated by expatriate firms—especially the large British and Continental European trading companies—and this provided a major source of resentment. Within the climate of the time, therefore, there were pressures for foreign investment controls in order to ensure independence and national sovereignty.

After 1970 a number of policy measures were enacted in parallel with the rise in aggressive economic nationalism in Nigeria. While conscious of the need to maintain the inflow of foreign capital and technology, Nigerian policy was aimed at increasing local participation in ownership and management. The 'indigenization programme' had two dimensions. First, laws were passed requiring at least 55 per cent government control of certain 'strategic' industries (oil, mining, and steel, as the commanding heights of the economy) and arrangements were negotiated with foreign firms in each sector to arrange a transfer of ownership. On this basis, therefore, the government acquired a majority share in the subsidiaries of all oil-producing companies in Nigeria as well as a 60 per cent stake in petroleum distribution activities. Secondly, the government was determined to increase private Nigerian participation in the ownership of enterprises in the economy. The Nigerian Enterprise Promotion Decree of 1972 listed under Schedule 1 those enterprises reserved exclusively for Nigerian ownership and under Schedule 2 those enterprises requiring 40 per cent Nigerian ownership. This initial decree was followed by a second decree in 1976 when additional enterprises were added to Schedule 1; Schedule 2 required 60 per cent Nigerian ownership; and all other industries were placed on a new Schedule 3 requiring 40 per cent Nigerian ownership. Firms were given till December 1978 to comply.

In addition to these rules, there were also pressures for 'Nigerianization' aimed at increasing local participation in management. The firms that wished to employ expatriates had to obtain their quota from the Ministry of Internal Affairs, and these were only available for positions which were not reserved to Nigerians and if it could be proved that qualified Nigerian personnel were not available. Quotas, even then, were usually limited in duration and the government frequently reduced the number of expatriates which foreign firms could employ. Apart from this, there were also restrictions on the ability of foreign firms to dismiss Nigerian employees.

Initially foreign businesses were shocked by the government actions towards foreign firms and especially the second indigenization decree. But it seems as if they learned to live with or circumvent the rules. Thus, for example, there appears to have been widespread 'fronting' whereby Nigerians were hired principally as 'window dressing'. And the rules on Nigerian ownership led to a concentration of power as shares were acquired by family members.

Nigeria was not immune from the worldwide trend towards liberalization of FDI rules which occurred in the 1980s and 1990s. In 1995 controls on foreign investment in the non-oil sector were eased to permit MNEs to take a controlling interest in their Nigerian ventures and to take full control of their Nigerian boards. But hopes of a large inflow of FDI were not realized: Nigeria's political difficulties, poor infrastructure, high levels of crime and corruption, and low skill levels were major deterrents to investment. Companies increasing their Nigerian holdings were mainly the long-established MNEs like Unilever, Guinness, and Nestlé.

Source: Black et al., 1978; *Financial Times*, 1996*f*.

latter tended to exclude or restrict investment across wide and important sectors of their economies. French policy varied but was generally very nationalistic, and therefore bargaining would tend to take place about the terms and conditions of entry, and local equity participation was very common. In addition, takeovers were required to be entirely financed from abroad, while for new enterprises at least half of the finance had to be obtained from non-French sources. In the Scandinavian countries there was a requirement for a majority of nationals on boards of directors and in Sweden firms had the right to restrict, through their articles of association, foreign nationals acquiring shares in their countries. In reality, these differences among European countries were ones of degree, and elsewhere it was really only in Canada (see Box 4.2) that inward investors were a major focus of government economic development policy. Still, with an emphasis on industrial policy until the late 1970s, many countries were attempting to respond to *le défi américain* by the encouragement of mergers and support for 'national champions', meaning, therefore, discrimination in favour of indigenous enterprises (for details of individual developed country policies, see Boddewyn, 1974; Safarian, 1993).

Home country interests

In the United States, any policy concerns at this time related to outward FDI. In the mid- to late 1960s, two programmes (the Voluntary Credit Restraint Program, 1965, and the Mandatory Control Program, 1968) were introduced to slow the growth of outward capital flows as a means of improving the balance of payments situation.

Box 4.2

Canada

During the period under review Canada had the highest degree of foreign ownership of industry of all developed countries. The major policy instrument which is of particular interest in the present context is the Foreign Investment Review Agency (FIRA), although this was only one aspect of federal government policy in Canada.

Serious Canadian investigations into questions of foreign ownership and control date from the publication in 1957 of the Report of the Royal Commission on Canada's Economic Prospects. Subsequently, three official investigations were important in paving the way for a significant shift in Canadian policy in the early 1970s; namely, the Watkins Report (1967–8); the Wahn Report (1970), and the Gray Report (1970–2). What emerged from such studies was an expression of the required aims of Canadian policy towards foreign ownership, which stressed: the necessity to improve the overall efficiency of economy to the benefit of all firms; the necessity to retain and increase indigenous ownership and control in firms in Canada (where feasible and desirable); with regard to the foreign sector, economic benefits should be maximized and costs minimized, the ways in which US firms transmit American law and policy objectives to Canada should be ended, and the non-economic impacts of foreign firms should be minimized.

During the 1960s certain regulations were introduced in respect of foreign firms, but the various official reports brought home the need for more definitive policies, and the government responded with the 1974 Foreign Investment Review Act. This legislation established FIRA to screen proposals for foreign activity for the purpose of advising whether or not the activity would provide 'significant benefit' to Canada. For the first eighteen months after the Act was passed, the legislation applied only to takeovers of existing Canadian companies by foreign-owned firms; then from October 1975 the establishment of new foreign businesses in Canada and some expansions of existing foreign-controlled firms were also subject to review. The factors to be taken into account in determining significant benefits were: effects on the level and nature of economic activity in Canada, including employment; the degree of involvement of Canadians; the impacts on productivity, industrial efficiency, technological development, product innovation, and product variety in Canada; the effects on competition; and the compatibility of the investment with industrial and economic policies.

These criteria were extremely broad and the role of FIRA was to negotiate greater national benefits in one or more of the five areas; FIRA was in theory a bargaining agent, not merely a screening agency.

In the first two and a half years of FIRA's existence, 209 out of 293 takeover applications were approved, with a further 41 cases being withdrawn and only 43 being disallowed. FIRA also approved almost every new business investment. This led on the one hand to the accusation that the Foreign Investment Review Act was being used as a means of facilitating foreign investment rather than reviewing it—thereby undermining Canadian sovereignty. On the other hand, it was argued that FIRA's favourable attitude to foreign investment permitted Canada to continue to enjoy the benefits of international capital flows. The arguments continued in 1976 and 1977 as the Canadian economy fell into severe recession and as tensions between the federal and provincial governments increased. Other factors which influenced the debate included the significant reduction in the degree of foreign control of industry in Canada throughout the 1970s, while at the same time Canada developed into a significant home country for MNEs.

A significant change in FIRA operations took place in 1982–3, with the intention to clarify the bases for its decisions and to simplify and speed up its procedures (Safarian, 1993). Meantime, criticism from abroad had led to a reference to the GATT about the undertakings on exports and imports made by firms to FIRA. The United States argued that these trade-related investment measures were similar to tariffs, quotas, or subsidies and distorted trade. At the end of 1983 the Council of the GATT ruled that the undertakings violated Canada's national treatment obligations for imports but did not violate its obligations on quantitative restrictions; it also ruled that the export performance requirements were not inconsistent with obligations concerning subsidies.[a]

With the new Conservative government being elected in September 1984, FIRA was replaced by Investment Canada, with a mandate to encourage and facilitate investment by both Canadians and non-Canadians. The review process was no longer required in the great majority of cases. The exceptions related to the case of new businesses and acquisitions linked to Canada's cultural heritage or national identity, and other types of acquisitions. The much more welcoming attitude to FDI was characteristic of changed host country attitudes in the 1980s.

Note: [a]During the history of the GATT from 1948 to 1994, this was the only case, out of more than 200 dispute cases, directly concerned with investment issues.

Source: Hood and Young, 1979; Safarian, 1993.

The controls implemented had a significant influence on capital transfers from the USA in the late 1960s, although the impact on FDI was not substantial because many MNEs were able to raise funds abroad. In any event, into the 1970s the focus of concern in the USA shifted from the balance of payments *per se* to other macroeconomic problems, particularly unemployment and inflation. In addition there were criticisms concerning exports of technology from the USA and claims that American tax policy was subsidizing FDI. Within this environment, there were pressures from labour interests within the USA to promote legislation to control outward FDI because of claimed large-scale job losses within the USA. Although the 1972 Foreign Trade and Investment Act and subsequent bills failed, the protectionist views surrounding them continued to be heard throughout the 1970s, and into the 1980s, when the issues switched to those surrounding inward investment into the USA.

Being the world's second largest outward investor, the United Kingdom operated a regulatory system on FDI abroad which was related to the likely effects on the balance of payments. Close controls were placed on the method of financing direct investment, to ensure that the cost would not fall on the foreign exchange reserves until after equivalent benefits had accrued to the balance of payments through the repatriation of earnings. A two-tier system of foreign exchange was operated and for most of the period finance was not available for FDI at the official rate for non-sterling area investments. Controls were tightened or relaxed according to economic circumstances; then all restrictions on capital movements were abolished as one of the first acts of the incoming Thatcher government in 1979, reflecting the removal of the balance of payments constraint on economic policy-making with the advent of North Sea oil.

Japanese inward direct investment is very limited (even in 1995 Japan's share of world inward investment stock was as low as 0.7 per cent—UNCTAD, 1996*a*). This stems from an industrial policy focus from the 1950s on technology acquisition through licensing. Even with the Japanese Capital Liberalization Program, which operated from June 1967 to August 1971, inward FDI was hampered by bureaucratic delays and other hidden barriers as well as by the large number of industry exceptions. Many of these problems still remain at the end of the 1990s.

In respect of Japanese outward FDI, it was not until the end of the 1960s, when the international payments position shifted to a positive balance, that foreign exchange was available to finance significant investment, principally in manufacturing and commerce in North America, Asia, and Latin America (Sakurai, 1995). Some liberalization of foreign exchange control laws occurred in December 1980: Japanese investors were only required to notify the Ministry of Finance for some sectoral investments, but approval was still required in fisheries, leather products manufacturing, banking and securities industries, etc. The take-off period for Japanese outward FDI did not begin until the mid-1980s, subsequent to the Plaza Accords of 1985 which resulted in a sharp appreciation of the yen.

Transfer pricing

It is clear from the above that the issues of concern to home nations were significantly different from those of host countries. One area of common interest during this period, however, was that of transfer pricing. As defined by Wallace (1982: 127), transfer pricing (strictly manipulative transfer pricing) is 'that practice whereby the MNE, in its intra-enterprise transactions, can sometimes effectively modify the tax base on which its entities are assessed, or possibly avoid exchange controls by "doing business" within the MNE corporate structure itself, so as to reallocate costs and revenues in such a way that its profits are realized when the tax and exchange environment is most favourable'. This became an issue in the United States, with concerns about the avoidance of home country taxation by MNEs through transfer pricing, the operation of 'shell companies', and the sophisticated use of tax havens. A number of American states, and especially California, operated a unitary tax system whereby a company's state tax liability was determined on the basis of its worldwide—rather than its local—earnings. Disputes, involving British companies and supported by the British government, led to the rescinding of the unitary tax laws, which were designed to counteract any attempts at tax avoidance through intra-group transfer pricing.

Among host nations, especially in the developing world, concerns over transfer pricing related to the alleged manipulation of intra-firm royalties and licence fees as a mechanism for repatriating profits when controls were in place over the latter; and to overpricing of imports, especially imports associated with restrictive clauses in technology transfer contracts. Controls over transfer pricing were thus instituted in a number of countries especially in Latin America (and in regional blocs as the ANCOM case in Box 4.3 reveals).

As a postscript, it should be noted that the 1976 OECD Guidelines (Taxation, para. 2) request that 'Enterprises should refrain from making use of . . . transfer pricing which does not conform to an arm's length standard, for modifying in ways contrary to national laws the tax base on which members of the group are assessed.' The draft United Nations Code of Conduct on Transnational Corporations contains a somewhat similar clause, specifying the use of market prices or the arm's length principle. Following considerable controversy over the issue, in 1995 new guidelines on transfer pricing were agreed within the OECD forum, allowing for use of the transactional profit methods in situations of last resort and where the arm's length principle could not work.

Regional approaches and producers' groupings

Boxes 4.3 and 4.4 summarize the approaches of the Andean Common Market and the European Communities respectively to the regulation of MNEs, and highlight again the marked differences between developing and developed nations. Apart from these, a number of other regional groupings had as one of their objectives a common approach to FDI regulations. Among these were the Arab Economic Union, the Association of South East Asian Nations, the Caribbean Community, the Central American Common Market, and the East African Community. However, few of these made much progress as economic blocs during the period, and some, indeed (such as the East African Common Market) effectively broke up; hence, hardly any progress was made on the FDI front.

Box 4.3

The Andean Common Market (ANCOM)

The Andean Common Market was formed as a sub-region of the Latin American Free Trade Association (LAFTA) under the Cartagena Agreement of 1969. Initial membership comprised Bolivia, Chile, Colombia, Ecuador, and Peru, with Venezuela joining ANCOM in 1973. The agreement provided for the progressive reduction in tariffs and trade barriers between members and the establishment of a common external tariff. An equally important element of ANCOM concerned the regulation of MNEs (the body of rules and regulations commonly called Decision 24). The three key elements of control related to the ownership of MNEs; to the transfer of technology; and to the regulation of transfer prices.

Ownership

Foreign companies within the ANCOM region that wished to export to other countries in the community and thus operate community wide were required to transfer between 51 per cent and 81 per cent of their equity to national investors (the so-called 'fade-out provisions'). Foreign investors had to relinquish direct ownership rights and also a corresponding amount of effective control. Existing companies were given fifteen to twenty years to bring about the necessary changes in ownership, while new investors were subject to the terms immediately. All new investment projects had, in addition, to be approved by the competent national authority, thereby introducing a selective admission pattern. Other regulations placed restrictions on the sectors in which foreign firms might operate, and so foreign companies in banking, insurance, and the media were required to convert to indigenous ownership and no new foreign direct investment was permitted.

Technology transfer

In contracts for the transfer of technology to local firms, numerous practices were forbidden including: price-fixing of a licensed product; terms requiring the purchase of intermediate and capital goods from a specific source; restrictions on the output of licensed products; restrictions on the use of competitive technology; restrictions on exports (in most cases); and package deals in which the recipient paid for technology which would not be used, in order to obtain certain services.

Transfer pricing

The ANCOM foreign investment code also provided for a control system for transfer pricing, involving screening the price of technology, product prices, credit terms, etc. Related to this, the agreement limited profit remittances to 14 per cent of registered capital per year, and any reinvestment in excess of 5 per cent of registered capital had to be approved by the national agency. Royalty payments to the parent company were not permitted.

The actual operation of Decision 24 was left to individual countries, so that all member states had to draw up their own legislation. This was a significant weakness of the scheme, since important differences existed in implementation from country to country. This was only a subset of a more general problem which concerned a gradual divergence in the political-economic philosophies of the ANCOM member governments. In late 1976, Chile, which had joined ANCOM under the Allende regime, withdrew completely under the Pinochet government. Major disputes followed over production sharing, such as that in 1977 concerning the assignment of car and truck production between member countries.

Perspectives on success or failure

ANCOM had the improvement of bargaining power as its basic purpose. The evidence showed, however, that the package offered to foreign investors was unacceptable in terms of its trade-offs. Reported new investments after 1969 were insignificant, with the exception of investments relating to the natural resources. Even so, ANCOM interested many countries at the time: over twenty governments established accredited observers to ANCOM, and the EC Commission established a special committee to study ANCOM and its approach to regulating MNE activities.

Postscript: Decision 24 of the Andean Pact was abolished in May 1987, and replaced by Decision 220 allowing each country to adopt whatever investment regime it saw fit. In the late 1990s, the Andean Pact itself was effectively subsumed within wider South American trade cooperation and integration.

Source: Hood and Young, 1979; Sell, 1989; *Financial Times*, 1997*b*.

An alternative approach to controlling MNEs existed in the form of producers' groupings. The prototype was OPEC, the members of which implemented a range of measures to improve their control of and returns from the oil industry in the early 1970s. From a position in 1970 when hardly any crude oil facilities in OPEC were domestically controlled, foreign majority ownership was rare by the end of 1974 (Sauvant, 1977: table 2). The bargaining power of OPEC was unique, and although there were a number of efforts in 1974 and 1975 to strengthen producers' associations in other commodity areas, they were generally less successful. Sauvant (1977) cites as an exception the International Bauxite Association, and in bauxite, copper, and iron ore there were numerous nationalizations in the early 1970s.

4.4 **Conclusion**

Of the fifty-year period covered by this book, the years from the late 1960s to the early 1980s were the most negative in terms of host country (and to a lesser extent home nation) attitudes to FDI and MNEs. The explanations were partly FDI-related and partly more general environment-related. The speed of growth of FDI into host countries meant high levels of concentration in some sectors and a high degree of visibility for foreign companies. In addition the inexperience and ethnocentricity of American investors (as the dominant home nation) led to difficult relationships on occasions, thereby accentuating concepts of 'foreignness'. And the nature of organization structures and headquarter–subsidiary relationships within MNEs created fears of superordinate–subordinate relationships among states. The perceptions of and reactions to such characteristics of MNE activity and behaviour were different for developed, developing, and centrally planned economies and for individual countries and groups within these blocs.

Box 4.4

European Communities

European Commission interest in the activities of MNEs dates back to 1973 and its memorandum on *Multinational Undertakings and the Community*. This set out three principles of treatment for proposed MNE policy, namely, a legal framework and opposition to codes of conduct; non-discriminatory treatment between indigenous and foreign firms; and a comprehensive framework, implying a rejection of specific isolated measures. Proposals to the Council of Ministers involving about thirty measures were approved by the Economic and Social Committee (ESC) and European Parliament, but were then withdrawn by the Commission in 1976. Since then, there has been no attempt to propose a comprehensive, or indeed any, approach to MNEs *per se*, with the exception of the ill-fated Vredeling Directive on Procedures for Informing and Consulting the Employees in Multinational Firms, which dated from 1980 (Brewer and Young, 1995*c*).[a]

Despite the above, the European Parliament made its own views clear in discussion on the so-called *Lange–Gibbons Code* (1977) (Schwamm and Germidis, 1977). This code was prepared by Erwing Lange of the Social Democratic Party, West Germany, and Sam Gibbons of the United States Congress. The tone in both the Lange–Gibbons Code and the European Parliament comments was more critical of the role of MNEs than the European Commission and called upon the Council and Commission to establish legally binding international agreements for MNE behaviour. The documents basically reflected labour concerns and criticisms about MNEs and thus included elements relating to detailed information provision by MNEs, to social policy and labour market policy, and to capital markets and monetary policy; in addition there were calls for specific rules governing the political activity of multinational enterprises. The views were essentially those of left-wing parliamentary representatives and were not taken further.

As Van Den Bulcke (1992) notes, in the early 1970s the EC Commission did not have a clear vision about its policies towards MNEs. On the one hand, there were views that countervailing powers should be developed to restrain the monopoly position of multinationals; on the other hand, the Commission wanted to support its own multinationals in external markets. It was perhaps because of these contradictions that Commission attitudes towards multinational enterprises were very ambivalent.

Substantial progress was made during the 1970s in a range of policy areas which impacted upon the activities of multinationals, although MNEs were not singled out for special treatment reflecting EC commitments to OECD rules. The main areas in which developments took place included: harmonization of company law; harmonization of corporate tax systems; competition policy; harmonization of national and regional aids; protection of workers; and rules concerning the establishment of European MNEs in developing countries.

Note: [a]Within the agreement on social policy in the Maastricht Treaty (1992), a directive was approved in June 1994 to establish Europe-wide works councils in MNEs above a certain size as a mechanism for information and consultation.

Prevailing characteristics of the world economy reinforced the negative attitudes to MNEs. Within Third World nations, the belief in united action and increased bargaining power as part of the NIEO was a major factor in the first half of the 1970s. Attitudes in developed nations changed over the period: in the early years, there were concerns about sovereignty and about the economic contribution of MNEs; and as interests in industrial policy and support for 'national champions' grew, so there were ambivalent views about the role and position of multinational affiliates in high-tech sectors. In the late 1970s and early 1980s, concerns changed again as multinational divestment became an issue (Van Den Bulcke et al., 1979; Hood and Young, 1979) with recession conditions and deindustrialization top of the economic agenda in Europe, for example. On the trade side, the period saw the implementation of the Kennedy Round of trade negotiations and the completion of the Tokyo Round. But within an environment in which exogenous shocks (the collapse of the fixed exchange rate regime and the oil price hikes enforced by the OPEC cartel) had a major impact, the positive effects of tariff restrictions were offset by the growth of non-tariff barriers (NTBs) and the rise of the 'new protectionism'. The concerns about MNEs began to be more muted with the realization that FDI to circumvent NTBs could have a beneficial job effect in host industrialized nations where high unemployment had become a highly sensitive economic and political issue.

In summary, distinctive features of this period included:

- The emphasis in the early part of the period at least on control of the multinational corporation. The term 'control' was almost universally used to describe national, regional, and multilateral rule-making.
- Although a more balanced view emerged later in the period, in the early years the stress was upon the rights of countries and the obligations of firms.
- From a country perspective, interest in multilateral rules derived from the desire to increase bargaining power and enforce controls.
- Trade unions at national and especially international level had a significant influence on attitudes towards MNEs and on the development of codes of conduct, reflecting their strongest involvement in economic policy-making generally at this time (Weinberg, 1978).
- Curiously the critical views of labour (alongside those of developing countries and centrally planned economies) may have accelerated progress towards multilateral rules, with the USA as the main driving force in the development of the OECD Guidelines and related instruments.

Notes

1. Eight were from developing nations, two from socialist countries, and ten from industrialized states, chosen in their individual capacity rather than as official representatives of their respective countries.

2. Equal representation of business and labour interests was proposed, and while regard was to be given to geographical distribution, the members of the commission were to serve in their individual capacity.
3. The ILO Declaration was submitted to the UN Commission on Transnational Corporations in 1981 to be cross-referenced in a draft UN code of conduct.
4. The issue of what constitutes the 'final draft' of the UN code is rather hazy. The 1983 draft is the version that reflects how far negotiators actually managed to bring the Code. The 1990 draft is a compromise version which reflects the attempts by the chairman of a special session of the Commission on Transnational Corporations to resolve outstanding issues. The present authors are grateful to Michael Gestrin of UNCTAD for explaining the position.
   It should be noted that Commission and Centre on Transnational Corporations were disbanded in the early 1990s. The programme was transferred to UNCTAD in Geneva and became the Division on Transnational Corporations and Investment, and subsequently the Division on Investment, Technology and Enterprise Development.
5. This chapter has presented only some of the major developments. Others included, for example, the Draft Code of Conduct on Transfer of Technology under the auspices of the Pugwash Conferences on Science and World Affairs; and the instrument on International Accounting Standards developed by the International Coordination Committee for the Accountancy Profession. For further details, see Sauvant, 1977.

Appendix 4.1

Proposals by Countries of Latin America and the Caribbean[a]

1. MNCs shall be subject to the laws and regulations of the host country and, in case of litigation, they should be subject to the exclusive jurisdiction of the courts of the country in which they operate.
2. MNCs shall abstain from all interference in the internal affairs of the States where they operate.
3. MNCs shall abstain from interference in relations between the Government of a host country and other States, and from disrupting those relations.
4. MNCs shall not serve as an instrument of the foreign policy of another State or as a means of extending to the host country provisions of the juridical order of the country of origin.
5. MNCs shall be subject to the exercise by the host country of its permanent sovereignty over all its wealth, natural resources and economic activities.
6. MNCs shall be subject to the national policies, objectives and priorities for development, and should contribute positively to carrying them out.
7. MNCs shall supply to the Government of the host country pertinent information about their activities in order to ensure that these activities shall be in accord with the national policies, objectives and priorities of development of the host country.
8. MNCs shall conduct their operations in a manner that results in a net receipt of financial resources for the host country.
9. MNCs shall contribute to the development of the scientific and technological capacity of the host country.
10. MNCs shall refrain from restrictive business practices.
11. MNCs shall respect the socio-cultural identity of the host country.

Note: [a]Argentina, Barbados, Brazil, Colombia, Ecuador, Jamaica, Mexico, Peru, Trinidad, Tokyo, and Venezuela.
Source: Schwamm and Germidis, 1977.

Appendix 4.2

Draft United Nations Code of Conduct on Transnational Corporations (1983 version)[a]

Preamble and Objectives
Activities of Transnational Corporations
A. General and Political
Respect for national sovereignty and observance of domestic laws, regulations and administrative practices[b]
Adherence to economic goals and development objectives, policies and priorities
Review and renegotiation of contracts
Adherence to socio-cultural objectives and values[c]
Respect for human rights and fundamental freedoms[d]
Non-collaboration by transnational corporations with racist minority regimes in southern Africa
Non-interference in internal political affairs[e]
Non-interference in intergovernmental relations
Abstention from corrupt practices
B. Economic, Financial and Social
Ownership and control
Balance of payments and financing
Transfer pricing
Taxation
Competition and restrictive business practices
Transfer of technology
Consumer protection
Environmental protection
C. Disclosure of Information[f]
Treatment of Transnational Corporations
A. General treatment of transnational corporations by the countries in which they operate
B. Nationalization and compensation
C. Jurisdiction
Intergovernmental Cooperation
Implementation of the Code of Conduct
A. Action at the national level
B. International institutional machinery
C. Review procedure

Notes: [a]Certain of the economic development provisions of the UN code are reproduced in Chapter 10, Box 10.3. Other selected paragraphs are included below to illustrate some of the features of the code.
[b]Para. 6 states that: 'Transnational corporations should/shall respect the national sovereignty of the countries in which they operate and the right of each State to exercise its [full permanent sovereignty] [in accordance with international law] [in accordance with agreements reached by the countries

concerned on a bilateral and multilateral basis] over its natural resources [wealth and economic activities] within its territory.'
[c]Para. 12 states that: 'Transnational corporations should/shall respect the social and cultural objectives, values and traditions of the countries in which they operate . . . transnational corporations should/shall avoid practices, products or services which cause detrimental effects on cultural patterns and socio-cultural objectives.'
[d]Para. 13 states that: 'Transnational corporations should/shall respect human rights and fundamental freedoms in the countries in which they operate . . . In their social and industrial relations, transnational corporations should/shall not discriminate on the basis of race, colour, sex, religion, language, social, national and ethnic origin or political or other opinion.'
[e]Para. 15 states that: 'Transnational corporations should/shall not interfere [illegally] in the internal [political] affairs of the countries in which they operate.'
[f]Para. 44 states that: 'Transnational corporations should disclose to the public in the countries in which they operate, by appropriate means of communication, clear, full and comprehensible information on the structure, policies, activities and operations of the transnational corporation as a whole.'

Source: UNCTAD, 1996c: 161–80.

Appendix 4.3

Declaration on International Investment and Multinational Enterprises[a]

Annex 1 Guidelines for Multinational Enterprises

[Paras. 1–11 contain statements of the aims and philosophy of the Guidelines, e.g. para. 1 states that: 'The common aim of the Member countries is to encourage the positive contributions which multinational enterprises can make to economic and social progress and to minimise and resolve the difficulties to which their various operations may give rise.']

General Policies[b]
Disclosure of Information
Competition[c]
Financing
Taxation[d]
Employment and Industrial Relations[e]
Environmental Protection
Science and Technology

Notes: [a]The OECD framework for MNEs contained in the above was reviewed in 1979, 1984, and 1991. Selections from the Guidelines are included below.
[b]General Policies: 'Enterprises should (2) in particular, give due consideration to those countries' aims and priorities with regard to economic and social progress, including industrial and regional development, the protection of the environment, the creation of employment opportunities, the promotion of innovation and the transfer of technology;' (7) 'not render—and they should not be solicited or expected to render—any bribe or other improper benefit, direct or indirect, to any public servant or holder of public office'.
[c]Competition: 'Enterprises should while conforming to official rules and established policies of the countries in which they operate, (1) refrain from actions which would adversely affect competition in the relevant market by abusing a dominant position of market power, by means of, for example, (a)

anti-competitive acquisitions, (b) predatory behaviour toward competitors, (c) unreasonable refusal to deal, (d) anti-competitive abuse of industrial property rights, (e) discriminatory (i.e. unreasonably differentiated) pricing and using such pricing transactions between affiliated enterprises as a means of affecting adversely competition outside these enterprises.'

[d]Taxation: 'Enterprises should (2) refrain from making use of the particular facilities available to them, such as transfer pricing which does not conform to an arm's length standard, for modifying in ways contrary to national laws the tax base on which members of the group are assessed.'

Source: OECD, 1976*b*.

5

Liberalization

National and Regional Policy Changes and the Creation of the WTO (Early 1980s–Mid-1990s)

5.1 Introduction

There was a dramatic swing of the policy pendulum away from an emphasis on regulation of MNEs during the 1970s to an emphasis on liberalization of government policies during the next two decades. In fact, the era of the 1980s and 1990s was marked by significant developments at all levels—national, bilateral, regional, and multilateral—and the unifying theme in all of them was liberalization of government policies. However, the agreements at various levels were inconsistent in their coverage of sectors and in the substantive content of many of their elements. As a consequence, while the new array of international agreements created a fundamentally new and more hospitable public policy environment for investors, they also created a much more complex array of international rules. At the national level, numerous countries undertook substantial privatization and liberalization programmes that included more open FDI policies as an important element. Among individual countries, India and China were particularly notable because of the extent of the policy changes in their previously highly restrictive policy regimes and of course because of the sizes of the countries. At the bilateral level, a proliferation of BITs was the most conspicuous trend. At the regional level, the major development was the creation of NAFTA, in which the reduction of international investment barriers was a central element. At the multilateral level, investment issues emerged on the GATT agenda, especially in the Uruguay Round negotiations, culminating in the establishment of the WTO in January 1995.[1] With the WTO's implementation of the Uruguay Round agreements, several of which concerned investment, the international investment regime entered a new era in which multilateral investment rules became much more central to the international economic policy agenda.

5.2 Liberalization at the National Level

Beginning with the external debt crisis in Mexico in the summer of 1982, the difficulties of developing countries in repaying their loans led many to reconsider the role of FDI as a source of foreign capital in the economic development process. During the remainder of the 1980s and into the 1990s, as a result, scores of governments shifted from an attitude of ambivalence or hostility toward FDI to a more positive attitude, and they accordingly adopted more open and welcoming policies toward MNEs. The specific policy changes included the lifting of foreign ownership restrictions in many economic sectors, including in particular reductions in the maximum shares of foreign ownership allowed. Moreover, FDI approval procedures were streamlined and otherwise liberalized, or even virtually eliminated in some instances. Limitations on foreign-owned firms' operations—such as restrictions on the nationalities or movement of personnel or restrictions on imports or exports or the use of foreign exchange—were also significantly reduced by many countries. Not only were there

Table 5.1 Policy Change in 22 OECD Countries, 1981–1985

FDI policies	Mean policy scores[a]	
	1981	1985
1. FDI entry restrictions (scale range: 0.0, +4.0)[b]	2.05	1.80
2. FDI incentives (scale range: 0.0, +1.0)[c]	0.38	0.38
3. FDI restrictions–incentives: line 1–line 2 (scale range: −1.0, +4.0)[d]	1.67	1.42
4. Foreign exchange controls (scale range: 0.0, +1.2)[e]	0.55	0.45
5. Overall score: line 3+line 4 (scale range: −1.0, +5.2)[f]	2.22	1.87

Notes: [a]Mean scores for 22 countries as of 1981 and as of 1985.
[b]0.0=lowest restrictive possible score; +4.0=highest restrictive possible score.
[c]0.0=lowest possible incentives; +1.0=highest possible incentives.
[d]Receptiveness toward FDI=Restrictions score minus incentives score from lines above. Net scores on line 3 thus range from −1.0 (most receptive) to +4.0 (least receptive). Seemingly reversed signs are maintained for ease of interpretation of change from 1981 to 1985.
[e]0.0=least restrictive; 1.2=most restrictive.
[f]Sum of lines 3 and 4 indicates overall restrictiveness on scale ranging from lowest possible score of −1.0 to highest possible score of +5.2. Thus change from mean of 2.22 in 1981 to a mean of 1.87 in 1985 indicates a change in the direction of being less restrictive over time.

Source: Computed from Safarian, 1993: 413–15, and table 12.1, 474.

these types of liberalization measures, however, there were also increases in the guarantees and the subsidies offered to foreign investors—guarantees such as freedom to remit profits to parent corporations, and subsidies such as infrastructure development and employee training programmes. At the same time, during this period there were very few changes in the direction of increased controls on foreign-owned firms. In short, liberalization replaced regulation and control as the dominant approach to FDI, especially in developing countries.

The liberalization trend of the 1980s and 1990s, however, included developed as well as developing countries. In Table 5.1 there is summary evidence for twenty-two OECD countries, a number of which changed their FDI policies in the early 1980s (Safarian, 1993). In particular, the mean score indicating the degree of restrictiveness of their FDI entry screening policies declined from 2.05 in 1981 to 1.80 in 1985. On the other hand, there was a mix of countries that increased their subsidies and other incentives for inward FDI along with many that reduced such incentives. On balance, the climate for FDI became more attractive for foreign investors along the combined dimension of entry restrictions-and-incentives. More broadly, several of the twenty-two countries also liberalized their foreign exchange controls as part of an encompassing liberalization process, and thus the overall policy environment for FDI became more hospitable along several policy dimensions.

In the case of Japan, the changes tended to be incremental and fitful, and they extended over a long time period. After a long period of highly restrictive policies in the aftermath of the Second World War, there were modest liberalization reforms in the 1960s and 1970s, followed by much more significant changes in the 1980s and the 1990s. In 1980 a combined Foreign Exchange and Foreign Trade Law eliminated formal FDI entry restrictions in general, though several sectors (mining, petroleum, leather, agriculture, forestry, and fishing) remained closed to foreign investment. Furthermore, proposed projects were otherwise still subject to *ad hoc* approval on the basis of flexible criteria concerning national security, public order, and safety of the public. In addition, as a basis for deciding whether to accept or reject or request a modification of a proposed project, the government could consider if the foreign investment 'might adversely and seriously affect activities of [Japanese] business enterprises . . . or the smooth performance of [the Japanese] national economy' (quoted in Safarian, 1993: 252). As a formal matter, eight years after its passage, the new law had not resulted in a single denial or modification of an FDI project proposal—but, again, only in official terms.

Informally, however, a pre-notification process was widely used by investors to determine whether a project was likely to be accepted, rejected or subjected to requests for modifications, and lengthy informal negotiations about the terms of entry often ensued. Furthermore, 'administrative guidance' in the form of informal bureaucratic directives, especially by the Ministry of Trade and Industry (MITI), remained an important constraint on foreign investors as well as domestic investors, though that obstacle to FDI began to be tempered with the passage of the Administrative Procedures Law of 1993 (Tamura, 1995). For investors seeking FDI entry, therefore, the relative importance of the formal legal requirements, on the one hand, varied significantly across national business–government cultures. Thus, just as

Japanese business people might be surprised to receive outright formal rejection of proposals from the Canadian government, for instance, Canadian business people could be surprised by the lengthy informal discussions involved in FDI entry into Japan (Safarian, 1993: 256).

While the developed countries were generally moving in the direction of liberalization and away from control during the 1980s and 1990s, the trend was more pronounced for the developing countries. Indeed, among developing countries, the trend included many instances of revolutionary changes in FDI policies in the context of wide-ranging policy reform programmes involving deregulation and privatization of major segments of their economies as well as liberalization of their international economic policies. The trend, moreover, was evident in Asia and Latin America as well as Central and Eastern Europe. Among the diverse cases of unilateral liberalization programmes, one of the most significant was the one undertaken by India, which began a long series of liberalization steps in the summer of 1991 (see Table 5.2). One of the early steps, for instance, was the adoption in thirty-four industries of an automatic approval policy for projects with up to 51 per cent foreign ownership. During the next several years these and other policy changes concerning FDI were embedded in an encompassing programme of liberalization that included changes in macroeconomic policies, trade policies, technology transfer policies, and regulatory policies. Thus, the FDI policy reform process was an element of revolutionary changes that opened and liberalized India's economy for the first time since its independence nearly half a century earlier. However, the Indian experience also illustrates many of the conflicts and complexities of the liberalization process. Thus, for instance, the liberalization of civil aviation generated intra-governmental conflicts among several agencies. Liberalization in the telecommunications sector involved all of the regional-level state governments as well as diverse agencies within the central government—and complexity, conflict, and uncertainty resulted.

Of course, there were significant variations across economic sectors and industries in the extent of the liberalization of FDI policies—not only in India and China but more generally around the world. The opening of financial services to FDI, for example, was relatively slow compared with most other industries. On the other hand, there has been much liberalization in the mining and infrastructure sectors. Mining was, of course, an economic sector in which much FDI took place in earlier periods, despite widespread restrictions; many of the liberalization changes in that sector were incremental and marginal. In the infrastructure sectors of economies, on the other hand, the changes in the 1990s were revolutionary because they opened up to private ownership, including by foreign firms, large segments of economies that had previously been dominated, or even monopolized, by state-owned enterprises. This opening of the infrastructure sector to foreign ownership was widespread across industries and included telecommunications, television, airlines, railways, water systems and power generation and transmission. The geographic scope of such changes in infrastructure, moreover, was global in the sense that it included many countries from all regions of the world (see Table 5.3).

By the 1990s, the cumulative effect of all of these changes was compounded by the revolutionary political and economic changes in Central and Eastern Europe. As a

Table 5.2 FDI Policy Change in the Context of a Broad Liberalization Programme: A Chronology of India's Changes [a]

1991

- Reduction in industrial policy protection of state economic enterprises.
- Automatic approval of FDI projects with up to 51 per cent foreign equity in 34 industries.
- Reduction of local content requirements.
- Abolition of technology transfer requirement for FDI projects.
- Adoption of automatic approval of licensing agreements with royalty rates and lump sum payments below threshold amounts.
- Reduction of capital goods tariff rates.

1992

- Opening of energy sector to foreign investors.
- Elimination of restrictions on the use of foreign brand names.
- Reduction of restriction on foreign ownership in mining operations for 13 minerals.
- Removal of capital goods imports from negative list.
- Reduction of government monopoly on imports to eight product lines.
- Reduction of maximum import duty on raw materials and components.
- Acceptance of membership in Multilateral Investment Guarantee Agency (MIGA) for investment protection agreements.

1993

- Establishment of national treatment for foreign-owned enterprises.
- Provision for foreign ownership in mining sector.
- Additional reduction of maximum import duty on raw materials and components.
- Provision for potential 100 per cent foreign ownership on case-by-case basis.
- Provision for foreign participation in building, maintaining and operating selected highways and bridges—and telephone service networks—on toll-collection basis.
- Deregulation of financial sector, including elimination of interest rate restrictions on loans above threshold amount.

1994

- Removal of restrictions on repatriation of earnings and divested capital.
- Reduction of maximum tariff levels on most items.
- Provision for foreign ownership in basic, cellular, and paging telecommunications services.
- Relaxation on import restrictions on second-hand capital goods.
- Reduction of negative list of imports.
- Strengthening of copyright law for satellite broadcasting, computer software, and digital technology.

1995

- Further reduction of maximum tariff levels.
- Inauguration of programme of 'tariffication' of non-tariff barriers to imports.

1996

- Reduction of barriers to trade and investment in consumer goods sector.

1997

- Foreign ownership up to 51 per cent receives automatic approval in 51 industries—and up to 74 per cent in nine industries.

Note: [a]This is a selective listing of changes during the period 1991–7.
Sources: UNCTAD, 1994*a*: box II.6, pp. 81–3; Georgetown University, 1995; Bhattacharyya, 1994, 1995*a*, 1995*b*.

result, during the first half of the 1990s, there was an overwhelming liberalization trend extending to all regions of the world.

5.3 Regional Integration and Investment Issues

At the regional level, the most significant development of the period was the creation of NAFTA, which entered into force in 1994 (see especially Graham and Wilkie, 1994; Hufbauer and Schott, 1993; Gestrin and Rugman, 1994). The origins of the NAFTA, however, were partly in the USA–Canada Free Trade Agreement (FTA), which entered into force in 1989. A core provision of the FTA concerned national treatment such that neither government would impose on foreign investors from the other country limits on the percentage of ownership, or forced divestiture requirements, or performance requirements concerning exports, local content, local sourcing, or import substitution. These provisions pertained to the establishment of new firms, the acquisition of existing firms, and the operations of foreign-owned firms. However, these provisions were substantially constrained because they did not apply to existing laws, and furthermore there were several important sectoral exceptions, including financial services, cultural industries, and gas and oil. Finally, although the project value threshold for screening by Investment Canada was raised, reviews of proposed investments over US$150 million were continued (Safarian, 1993: 140–1).

Although the investment provisions of the FTA were thus modest, they nevertheless provided a precedent for the inclusion of investment in the NAFTA a few years later. NAFTA's provisions concerning investment are in fact wide-ranging. The most germane portion of the NAFTA agreement is chapter 11, which includes fourteen articles concerning such items as the following:

- national treatment;
- most favoured nation treatment;
- performance requirements;
- nationalities of senior management and boards of directors;
- transfers of funds internationally;
- expropriation and compensation;
- environmental measures.

Table 5.3 The Liberalization of FDI in Infrastructure Projects in the 1990s[a]

Asia	
China	Opens construction of airports and aircraft to FDI (1993).
India	Allows FDI in road projects on build-operate-transfer (BOT) basis; FDI in telephone services and television broadcasting companies also permitted (1994).
Indonesia	Opens ports, shipping, airlines, railways, mass media, water distribution and sanitation, and production, transmission, and distribution of energy to FDI (1994).
Philippines	Authorizes the financing, construction, operation, and maintenance of infrastructure projects in the private sector (1994).
Vietnam	Promulgates and streamlines BOT regulations for FDI in infrastructure projects (1993–4).
Central and Eastern Europe	
Albania	Opens power sector, water supply, transport, electrical energy, telecommunications, waste material disposal, and industrial zones and parks to FDI (1995).
Bulgaria	Opens postal and telecommunication networks, roads, harbours, civil airports, water supply and irrigation, electric power supply and distribution to FDI (1995).
Czech Republic	Opens the energy sector to FDI (1994).
Hungary	Opens roads, railways, ports, public airports, and telecommunications to FDI and sets the framework for granting concessions (1994).
Latin America and the Caribbean	
Argentina	Allows FDI in the privatization of the state gas company (1992).
Bolivia	Opens the privatization process to FDI including in infrastructure projects (1994).
Brazil	Authorizes public sector concessions to foreign (and domestic) investors in electric power and supply, telecommunications, sanitation, sewerage and water supply, transport, highway construction, ports and airports, and national gas distribution (1995).
Colombia	Opens television broadcasting to FDI (1995).
Mexico	Opens land transportation of passengers and cargo to FDI (1995).
Peru	Allows FDI in the electric power industry through concessions (1991).
Venezuela	Allows FDI in public works and services through concessions (1994).
Middle East	
Turkey	Authorizes and organizes the use of foreign BOT financing and investments in major infrastructure projects (1993).
Republic of Yemen	Opens the electricity, water, and telecommunications projects to FDI (1994).
Developed countries	
Japan	Allows FDI up to 20 per cent in Nippon Telegraph and Telecom (1991).
Portugal	Opens the water production and distribution and basic sanitation services sector to FDI (1993).

Note: [a]Table does not reflect existing policies of countries where the infrastructure sector had already been open to FDI prior to 1991, or where FDI is encouraged, but without specific legislative measures applicable to infrastructure. This table does not include privatization laws, even though a number of countries have included state-owned enterprises in infrastructure among those to be privatized, opening them in the process to foreign investors. As of 1996, about 129 such privatization laws had been passed worldwide.

Also note that this is not an exhaustive list. Several items in the original source table have been omitted because of incomplete information about their precise nature.

Source: Adapted from UNCTAD, 1996*a*: table I.11, pp. 27–8; UNCTAD, 1993: annex table 6; and various official gazettes and official publications.

The national treatment provisions apply to subnational governmental entities (though with long phase-in periods) as well as the central governments. The provisions on performance requirements are particularly extensive; they include requirements concerning export performance, domestic content, domestic sourcing, trade balancing, product mandating, and technology transfer. There are also measures concerning nationality requirements for senior managers and members of boards. An innovation of the NAFTA is its provisions on environmental protection; although there are no provisions for sanctions for non-compliance, there is a provision for consultation if any of the governments thinks another is using relaxed environmental, safety, or health standards to entice investors (see Box 5.1).

In addition, there are extensive provisions concerning investment dispute settlement procedures—for both government–government and investor–government disputes. The inclusion of both types of disputes in NAFTA marks a significant difference from the WTO dispute settlement procedures, which concern only government–government disputes.

Numerous sector-specific provisions of the NAFTA agreement also include provisions affecting investment, either directly or indirectly:

Box 5.1

NAFTA Provision on Using Domestic Environmental, Health and Safety Measures to Attract Investments

'The parties recognize that it is inappropriate to encourage investment by relaxing domestic health, safety or environmental measures. Accordingly, a Party should not waive or otherwise derogate from, or offer to waive or otherwise derogate from, such measures as an encouragement for the establishment, acquisition, expansion or retention in its territory of an investment of an investor. If a party considers that another Party has offered such an encouragement, it may request consultations with the other Party and the two Parties shall consult with a view to avoiding any such encouragement' (Chapter 11, Article 1114, Environmental Measures).

- textiles;
- energy and basic petrochemicals;
- agriculture and sanitary and phytosanitary measures;
- telecommunications;
- financial services;
- motor vehicles.

These sector-specific agreements, though, contain numerous important sectoral exceptions to the general rules—cultural industries in Canada, the primary energy sector in Mexico, and airlines in the USA. In addition, both the financial services and motor vehicles' industries involve significantly less liberal elements.

Although NAFTA contains significant elements of the liberalization of investment policies as well as trade policies within the region, it also includes significant *discriminatory* elements *vis-à-vis* firms with substantial portions of their production processes outside the region. As with any regional economic arrangement, NAFTA's rules of origin put firms that are located outside the region at a competitive disadvantage compared with firms that are located within the region, when they try to compete in the regional market. For instance, a Japanese parent firm such as Toyota that has an affiliate in the USA that assembles motor vehicles must use a production process that produces vehicles with 62.5 per cent regional content in order to export the vehicles to other NAFTA countries duty-free. Traditional US-based manufacturers such as General Motors must meet the same regional content requirements, but because the US-based firms have traditionally sourced more of their parts from within the three-country NAFTA region, it is easier for them than for their Japanese competitors to meet the 62.5 per cent regional content requirement, particularly in the early years after the regional scheme was established.

The same point can be made with regard to firms in other industries and other countries. For instance, Japanese firms that assemble television sets in Mexico for sale in the USA may have to source more of the parts from firms within NAFTA rather than their traditional suppliers in Japan (including their own parent firms) than they would prefer. This is in order to qualify for zero-level, intra-regional tariffs as they export televisions from Mexico to the USA. Furthermore, there can be a discriminatory effect against firms even though they may qualify for other regionally based preferential treatment; for instance, NAFTA discriminates against textile firms in Jamaica that are entitled to preferential access to the US market through the regional Caribbean Basin Initiative because firms in Mexico face even lower tariffs for their exports to the USA.

It is not surprising, therefore, that many firms and their governments outside the region consider NAFTA to be protectionist and discriminatory, especially in some industries. Elements of protectionism and discrimination, however, are inherent in all regional economic agreements; they are in that sense inherently incompatible with the principle of most favoured nation treatment since they treat outsider nations (and firms) less favourably than they treat insider nations (and firms). Furthermore, regional agreements therefore have investment-distorting effects as well as investment-creating effects, as discussed in more detail in Chapter 7 on the interactions between regional and multilateral agreements. Technology transfer issues in NAFTA are discussed in Chapter 8. For excerpts of the actual text of the NAFTA agreement, see Appendix 5.1 of the present chapter.

5.4 GATT Uruguay Round Negotiations and the Establishment of the WTO

Until the Uruguay Round, the only notable instance in which FDI issues were on the GATT agenda was a dispute case concerning the Canadian Foreign Investment Review Agency (FIRA). During the history of the GATT from 1948 to 1994, of the more than 200 dispute cases, the FIRA case was in fact the only one that directly concerned investment issues. Yet the case was principally treated as a case about import restrictions, and its investment issues were accordingly relegated to a secondary status (Christy, 1991; McCulloch and Owen, 1983; GATT, 1994*a*: 151–61).

The case was prompted by a US complaint against the Canadian government that its agreements with foreign investors imposed conditions whereby foreign investment projects in Canada would give preferences to domestic Canadian suppliers and Canadian products over foreign suppliers and foreign products, and would also meet export performance requirements. The dispute panel report found that the domestic purchasing conditions violated Canada's national treatment obligations on imports under the GATT but did not violate its obligations on quantitative restrictions. It also ruled that the export performance requirements were not inconsistent with obligations concerning subsidies. The panel, therefore, in effect was making recommendations concerning what were later to be called trade-related investment measures (TRIMs).

More broadly, however, the panel noted that it only addressed issues concerning *trade* in products, that it did not address questions concerning the effects on foreign investors because *investment* issues were not within GATT's legal competence. Thus, although the GATT dispute panel concluded that some provisions of FIRA were inconsistent with GATT trade rules, the report also explicitly eschewed the panel's willingness or GATT's legal competence to reach formal decisions on investment issues. The panel also suggested that future consideration of any similar cases involving a developing country should take into account the special circumstances of that country. This became the basis for an often-made argument that developing countries were not necessarily subject to GATT restrictions on export performance requirements, domestic content requirements, or related types of trade restrictions on foreign investors. Later, during the Uruguay Round negotiations, the removal of any ambiguity about the applicability to developing countries as well as developed countries of limitations on such trade-related investment measures was one of the motivating factors in some developed countries' desire for a TRIMs agreement.

The USA, in particular, had been trying to get TRIMs and other investment-related issues on the GATT agenda for many years (Croom, 1995). The US government had a special interest in using the GATT to help liberalize other countries' investment policies, partly because of the already extensive FDI of US-based MNEs and the desire to make it easier for them to operate in less restrictive policy environments. More importantly, however, US firms in service industries were especially competitive in international business; but they faced many highly protectionist measures in those industries, which had been neglected by GATT as a consequence of its focus on trade in goods and hence the manufacturing sector. Furthermore, FDI tends to be especially important in service industries as a way for firms to enter and serve foreign markets because FDI offers the physical presence in the market and the proximity to customers which are essential to being competitive in those industries.

Despite its efforts, however, the USA was not successful in getting investment issues on the agenda of the GATT Tokyo Round negotiations (1973–9). Developing countries had been particularly resistant to having investment and services issues on the agenda, and many developed countries were only lukewarm about the prospect. There was much concern about opening their vulnerable service industries to increased competition from US firms. There was also much hostility towards MNEs during that period (see Chapter 4), and there was still relatively little understanding of many of the issues involved in investment policy liberalization and in international investment and trade in the services sector. By the early 1980s, however, these political and analytical conditions that had deterred GATT from addressing investment issues in the past were much less problematic. Interests, ideology, and understanding of the issues had all become more propitious for the inclusion of investment issues in the next round of GATT negotiations. US MNEs also became even more active in lobbying the US government for it to push for investment policy liberalization and for services industries to be on the GATT agenda. As a result, during the early 1980s, when planning for the next GATT negotiating round began, the prospects for agreements on investment and services were much more favourable. Discussion thus turns to the Uruguay Round negotiations and the creation of the WTO.

The negotiations that led to the inauguration of the WTO in 1995 began formally in 1986 in Punta del Este, Uruguay, after a period of several years of preparations and preliminary negotiations. The results of the negotiations included fifty legal instruments in thirty-three volumes containing over 20,000 pages. The agreements were signed initially by 124 countries—and subsequently by an additional 7 countries as of mid-1997.[2] Most of the agreements and their implementation procedures are relevant to investment because they influence the totality of the investment climate in each of the signatory countries. Yet only a few of them are explicitly concerned with multilateral rules and institutional processes that directly affect investment. The Uruguay Round negotiations were therefore predominantly about trade issues such as tariffs and non-tariff barriers to trade, and about changes in institutional structure and procedures concerning trade (see Table 5.4). Indeed, most of the thirty-three volumes of agreements are schedules of commitments on tariff levels on traded goods as part of the 'GATT 1994' agreement, which provides for phased-in lower tariff levels over a ten-year period.[3]

On the other hand, a full understanding of the negotiations of the investment-related agreements requires a recognition that there were trade-offs across issues in the negotiations; the 'investment' agreements and the 'trade' agreements were in that sense politically linked. For instance, the initial objective of some governments,

Table 5.4 Uruguay Round Agreements

Agreements with explicit investment content
Trade Related Investment Measures (TRIMs)—Limits FDI performance requirements
General Agreement on Trade in Services (GATS)—Includes FDI in services
Agreements with continuous and direct relevance to investment
Trade Related Intellectual Property Rights (TRIPs)—Establishes standards and enforcement procedures
Subsidies and Countervailing Measures (SCMs)—Limits subsidies and retaliatory actions
Dispute Settlement Understanding (DSU)—Includes government-to-government disputes on investment issues
Trade Policy Review Mechanism (TPRM)—Includes review of countries' investment policies
Other agreements with some relevance to investment
Agriculture—GATT 1994 agreement on Tariffs and Other Trade Issues (e.g. anti-dumping)—Import Licensing Procedures—Pre-shipment Inspection—Rules of Origin—Safeguards—Sanitary and Phytosanitary Measures—Textiles—Technical Barriers—Plurilateral Agreements (civil aircraft, government procurement, dairy, bovine meat)

including the USA in particular, to reach a wide-ranging agreement on trade-related investment measures was eventually sacrificed in order to achieve a strong agreement on trade-related intellectual property rights, partly because the latter were of greater interest to politically powerful MNEs. In addition, some of the Uruguay Round agreements that are not generally regarded as investment agreements *per se* are nevertheless so directly related to investment issues that they need to be considered, at least in their basic provisions; this is especially true of the agreements on Subsidies and Countervailing Measures as well as the TRIPs agreement. There are also Uruguay Round agreements that establish institutional processes that are important to investment issues, even though they are predominantly concerned with trade issues; the agreements establishing the WTO and its dispute settlement process are particularly important in this regard. Thus, these various other agreements and their relationship to investment issues are considered in this chapter. However, the two agreements that are emphasized are those which are most directly relevant to investment and which explicitly include provisions concerning FDI, namely the TRIMs agreement and the General Agreement on Trade in Services (GATS). The latter is in fact a significant investment agreement, as well as trade agreement, despite the limitations of its name.

It should also be noted that some of the agreements, such as those on agriculture and textiles, are industry-specific and that the applicability of many provisions of the other agreements varies a great deal across industries. However, mention is made of only a few of the industry-specific issues in relationship to investment. Further, there are many country-specific exceptions and qualifications, only some of which can be highlighted. The discussion below should therefore be understood to be an explanation of only the basic provisions, concepts, and principles of the agreements—and not a detailed guide to the rules for particular industries or the policies of particular countries.

Trade Related Investment Measures (TRIMs)

The TRIMs agreement is sometimes perceived to be tangible evidence of the failure of the Uruguay Round to make significant progress on FDI in manufacturing, since its core provisions were already embodied in previous GATT agreements concerning trade in goods. Because the TRIMs agreement provides for the phased elimination of practices that were arguably already disallowed under the GATT, it is sometimes suggested that the TRIMs agreement is actually retrogressive. On the other hand, it can also be argued that the TRIMs agreement is important because it unambiguously and explicitly put investment policies on the multilateral agenda—something which the panel report in the FIRA dispute case had specifically not done. The TRIMs agreement provides an 'Illustrative List' of measures that are inconsistent with national treatment (i.e. domestic content requirements) or that reflect quantitative trade restrictions (i.e. import–export balancing requirements, foreign exchange balancing requirements, and export restrictions). The agreement provides for notification, national treatment, and the phased elimination of such TRIMs.

Furthermore, and potentially most importantly for the longer term, there is a provision for a review of the agreement by the year 2000—with a specific mandate to determine whether it should be complemented with provisions on investment policy and/or competition policy. The prospective inclusion of competition issues on the agenda reflected a frequently expressed desire by many developing countries that there be a Uruguay Round agreement on the restrictive business practices of MNEs—a desire which was generally opposed by the developed countries. At the same time, many developing countries opposed an agreement on TRIMs, because they are widely used in FDI entry negotiations with MNEs as one way to offset MNEs' restrictive business practices and because they are often considered an element of 'domestic' economic development strategies, often in the context of 'industrial policies' that target selected industries for export promotion and others for import protection. The provision for a review of the TRIMs agreement, including a consideration of competition policy issues, was part of a compromise between developing and developed countries.

Another principal issue in the negotiations on the TRIMs agreement was the list of measures that would be covered, and this issue also divided to some extent along developing country–developed country lines. The developing countries wanted a relatively short list—if there was going to be an agreement at all—while the developed countries wanted a longer list. But there was not merely an issue of length; there was also an issue of type. Whereas developing countries tend to employ 'negative' TRIMs that impose requirements on investors, for instance to export, developed countries often use 'positive' TRIMs in the form of subsidies to encourage investors to export. Part of the difference in emphasis can be attributed to differences in macro-policy contexts and ideology, but part of the difference can also be attributed to the greater wealth and hence more substantial coffers for government subsidies in the developed countries.

However, there were also divisions of opinion among the developed countries on the issues of the length and emphasis of the list of prohibited measures. Thus, whereas the USA initially proposed a list of fourteen types of TRIMs to be limited and although the Japanese government was supportive of an encompassing list, the EU preferred a shorter list of only eight measures. In particular, the EU did not want provisions concerning incentives, technology transfer, or licensing, because of the importance of such measures in many European industrial policies and regional development policies at both the national level and the EU level. As a result of these differing preferences and the dynamics of the negotiating process, the list of proscribed TRIMs is 'illustrative' and thus presumably not necessarily exhaustive, on the one hand; however, it is limited to a relatively small number, on the other hand (see Box 5.2). In addition, as is typical of the Uruguay Round agreements, there is a graduated schedule for meeting the requirements of the agreement—two years for developed countries, five years for developing countries, and seven years for least developed countries.

In any case, there is much doubt about the actual impact of TRIMs on investors—particularly in light of the tendency of some host governments to waive them or to offset them with subsidies on a case-by-case basis, and the ability of MNEs to circumvent them or otherwise mitigate their effects on operations. Thus, studies (see EIU, 1994, for a summary) at various points in time have found, for instance, that as few as 6 per cent of the foreign affiliates of US-based MNEs are affected by TRIMs; that most firms would have done what was required by TRIMs even in their absence; and that most firms were compensated by other host government measures to offset the effects of the TRIMs. Further, there is much variation across industries in the incidence of TRIMs, with motor vehicle and chemical firms commonly being targets while computer firms are not.

In sum, the TRIMs agreement represented for investment issues a modest incremental expansion beyond the GATT—or even a degree of backsliding in the view of some critics, because the agreement allowed a long phase-out period for measures that had long ago been prohibited by the GATT. Further, of course, the TRIMs agreement only pertains to manufacturing industries because it is limited to goods.

Box 5.2

Highlights of the TRIMs Agreement

- Explicitly establishes linkage between trade policy and investment policy.
- Applies only to investment in manufacturing and trade in goods.
- Prohibits domestic content, import–export balancing, and foreign exchange balancing requirements that could otherwise be imposed on FDI facilities.
- Provides for phase-in periods of 2 years (for developed countries), 5 years (for developing countries), and 7 years (for least developed countries).

General Agreement on Trade in Services (GATS)

In contrast, the General Agreement on Trade in Services not only obviously pertains to services, it not so obviously also contains important and unprecedented provisions concerning investment. A standardized list of service industries prepared by the GATT / WTO secretariat as a potential basis for the individual governments' schedules of commitments is presented in Appendix 5.2. The significance of the GATS to FDI is due in part to the fact that FDI in the services sector has been growing more rapidly in recent years than FDI in other sectors (UNCTAD / World Bank, 1994: tables 1.8 and 1.9, pp. 16–17).

Trade is defined in the GATS to include *investment*. For 'trade' includes the supply of services 'by a service supplier of one Member, through commercial presence in the territory of any other Member', and *commercial presence* is defined to be 'any type of business or professional establishment, including through (i) the constitution, acquisition or maintenance of a juridical person, or (ii) the creation or maintenance of a branch or a representative office, within the territory of a Member for the purpose of supplying a service'. Thus, FDI is one of the international 'modes of supply' of services covered by the GATS. In addition, the provisions in the GATS on market access refer specifically to joint ventures and to limitations on the percentage of foreign ownership, and they therefore also incorporate FDI in the agreement (see Box 5.3).

In the GATS, governments have undertaken 'general obligations' and 'specific commitments'; general obligations apply to all parties and sectors, while specific commitments apply only as individual countries establish them for specified sectors and specified modes of supply. The general obligations for all countries include notification, transparency, subsidies, domestic regulations, safeguards, foreign exchange restrictions, and MFN. However, MFN is substantially qualified by an Annex which lists individual countries' exemptions from MFN and thus imposes 'conditional MFN' or 'reciprocity'. Individual countries' agreements to provide national treatment and market access on a sector-by-sector basis are provided in Schedules of Specific Commitments. These specific commitments combine 'positive' lists and 'negative' lists. In the positive lists, each government indicates those service industries for which it is making liberalization commitments; in the negative lists, each government itemizes for each of the modes of supply and for national treatment and market access the exceptions to its commitments in the listed industries (see Table 5.5 for an example). In addition, there are provisions for institutional arrangements that include dispute settlement procedures and sectoral annexes that cover financial services and other sectors.

Trade Related Intellectual Property Rights (TRIPs)

The TRIPs agreement is relevant to investment because FDI projects usually involve international technology transfer between parent firms and their foreign affiliates, and much of the technology is actually or potentially protected by copyrights, trademarks, or patents. Licensing agreements concerning the intellectual property rights of parent firms and their use by foreign affiliates are thus widely used by MNEs. The

Table 5.5 Excerpts from India's Schedules of Specific Commitments to National Treatment and Market Access in the GATS[a]

(a) Horizontal commitments: all sectors included in schedule[b]

Mode of supply[c]	Limitations on market access[d]	Limitations on national treatment[e]
1. Cross-border supply		
2. Consumption abroad		
3. Commercial presence (FDI)		In case of collaboration[f] with public sector enterprises or government undertakings as joint-venture partners, preference in access will be given to foreign service suppliers/entities which offer the best terms for transfer of technology
4. Presence of natural persons	Unbound[g] except for measures affecting the entry and temporary stay of natural persons who fall in any of the following categories: business visitors, . . . intra-corporate transferees, . . . professionals	Unbound except for measures referred to under Market access

(b) Sector-specific commitments [e.g. telecommunications services][h]

Mode of supply	Limitations on market access	Limitations on national treatment
1. Cross-border supply	None	None
2. Consumption abroad	Unbound	Unbound
3. Commercial presence (FDI)	Only through incorporation with a foreign equity ceiling of 51 per cent[i]	None
4. Presence of natural persons	Unbound except as indicated in the horizontal section	Unbound except as indicated in the horizontal section

Notes: [a]Each country filed its own schedule of commitments, which are arranged by industry sectors, by modes of supply (e.g. investment and cross-border trade), and by types of limitations on market access (e.g. quantitative restrictions on licences) and on national treatment (e.g. restrictions on percentage of foreign ownership).

[b]Horizontal commitments are made *across* industries (as opposed to vertical commitments, which pertain only to individual industries).

[c]There are four modes of supply, and each country's commitments are specific to one or more of the modes.

Table 5.5 *cont.*

[d]Market access is not defined explicitly in the agreements. However, government measures such as restrictions on the numbers of licences granted in a given service industry or limitations on the numbers of firms or individuals are examples of government policies that impede market access.
[e]National treatment here has the same meaning as elsewhere, namely the principle of not treating foreign-produced products or foreign-owned firms less favourably than their domestic counterparts.
[f]This entry means, for instance, that the Indian government is registering an *exception* to its commitment to provide national treatment to foreign investors in India in all those industries that are listed in its schedule. The exception to national treatment of FDI projects is that it will discriminate in some instances on the basis of the terms of technology transfer that are offered.
[g]Unbound means the country has not committed itself to any particular policy.
[h]This is one among many sector-specific items in India's schedule of commitments. Thus this particular combination of limitations on market access and national treatment for the modes of supply pertains to telecommunications.
[i]This means that market access in telecommunications in India through FDI is limited to 51 per cent or less equity.

provisions of the TRIPs agreement that result in more stringent enforcement of those rights by host governments make technology transfers through international licensing and other arrangements more secure and attractive and thereby make FDI more attractive as well.

Intellectual property is defined broadly in the TRIPs agreement to include copyrights, trademarks, industrial designs, patents, and layout designs of integrated circuits. Although such intellectual property and associated legal rights are especially important in 'high-tech' industries such as pharmaceuticals, informatics, and telecommunications, they are also important in some 'traditional' heavy manufac-

Box 5.3

Highlights of the GATS

- Establishes framework agreement for all service industries.
- Includes separately negotiated agreements for several sectors - telecommunications, transportation (air and maritime), and financial services.
- Provides for many industry-specific and country-specific exceptions to the application of most favoured nation and national treatment principles.
- Covers all modes of supply—investment as well as cross-border trade, movement of consumers, and movement of persons as service suppliers.
- Limits restrictions on joint ventures and percentages of foreign ownership.
- Opens previously protected domestic services sectors to foreign competition through investment and/or trade.

turing industries, e.g. chemicals and motor vehicles (see Box 5.4 for the highlights of the TRIPs agreement).

Box 5.4

Highlights of the TRIPs Agreement

- Establishes uniform standards for national laws for the protection of intellectual property rights.
- Includes copyrights, trademarks, industrial designs, patents, designs of integrated circuits.
- Mandates transparent and equitable domestic judicial procedures for the enforcement of intellectual property rights.
- Provides for interception at borders of counterfeit trademark or pirated copyright goods in international trade.
- Establishes phase-in periods of 1 year (developed countries), 5 years (developing countries), and 10 years (least developed countries).

Subsidies and Countervailing Measures (SCMs)

The SCMs agreement evolved as the most recent stage in a long GATT history of concern with export subsidies in manufacturing; during the 1980s this concern was expanded to include domestic subsidies as well. Since a variety of types of subsidies are often offered to foreign investors—and increasingly so in recent years—the SCMs agreement is relevant to FDI. In short, if a government grants a specific subsidy to a particular FDI project, and if the subsidy is more than 15 per cent of the total investment at the time of start-up or more than 5 per cent of the sales (if it is a tax-related subsidy), then the government has the burden of demonstrating that the subsidy is allowable under the SCMs agreement.

However, there is much complexity in the provisions concerning the types of subsidies that are covered, are not covered, or may be covered. In the first place, the SCMs agreement concerns only goods; it does not cover services.[4] Further, only 'specific' subsidies that are 'limited to certain enterprises' are covered; more generalized, non-specific subsidies are not covered.

In addition, a 'traffic light' classification scheme establishes three categories of subsidies, according to which 'red light' subsidies are prohibited, 'green light' subsidies are permissible and non-actionable, while 'amber light' subsidies are actionable. The prohibited subsidies include subsidies that are contingent on the use of domestic over imported goods or export performance. The latter include: currency retention schemes with bonuses for exports; favourable transportation rates for exports; tax remissions, export credits, and guarantees; and others. 'Permissible' subsidies include all non-specific subsidies and any 'specific' subsidies for pre-competitive R & D, assistance to disadvantaged regions, and adaptation of existing facilities to new environmental regulations. The 'actionable' category includes subsidies that have 'adverse effects to the interests of other members'—that is, 'injury to domestic industry', nullification or impairment, or serious prejudice (each of which is further specified).

Dispute settlement

The Uruguay Round Dispute Settlement Understanding (DSU) is important to investment because FDI-related disputes under the GATS, TRIMs, TRIPs, and SCMs agreements can be brought into the WTO dispute settlement process (see Box 5.5). Moreover, there is a provision for cross-retaliation in the DSU that can affect FDI; cross-retaliation involves retaliation outside the policy area and agreement of the initiating dispute. Thus, trade disputes under the various trade agreements could spill over into investment-related issues under the GATS or the TRIMs agreement. Cross-retaliation can also occur in the opposite direction as a withdrawal of a concession concerning trade in goods as a retaliation in an FDI dispute. However, a particularly important limitation of the dispute settlement process is that only government–government disputes can be brought into the process; disputes between firms and governments cannot be taken to the WTO. Thus, the traditional concern of international investment agreements with investor–government disputes is not included within the purview of the WTO. The Textiles and Clothing agreement provides for dispute settlement through a special Textile Surveillance Body, and the Trade Policy Review Mechanism (TPRM)—though technically not a dispute settlement procedure—can affect investment issues by reporting and clarifying members' FDI policies. Particular cases that arose in the implementation of the new WTO dispute settlement procedures are considered in the next chapter. For excerpts from the texts of some of the Uruguay Round agreements, see Appendix 5.3 at the end of the present chapter.

Box 5.5

Dispute Settlement Procedures in the WTO

- Dispute cases can include government–government disputes concerning investment, trade, technology transfer, and other policies affecting FDI projects and MNEs' other international business activities.
- Specially formed, case-specific dispute panels conduct investigations and file reports, which can be appealed by a (losing) government.
- Unanimous agreement of members is needed to overrule dispute case reports.

5.5 Conclusion

The 1980s and 1990s were obviously marked by widespread liberalization of investment policies at all levels. At the national level, scores of countries undertook significant liberalization programmes. At the bilateral level, the number of BITs increased from a couple of hundred to well over a thousand. At the regional level, the NAFTA included significant investment policy liberalization measures. At the multilateral level, investment issues entered the GATT/WTO agenda through several Uruguay Round agreements.

Yet, despite—or because of—the numerous and diverse liberalization agreements in the 1980s and 1990s, the 'patchwork problem' became worse. Thus, although MNEs faced a much more open and hospitable investment climate in most of the world by the mid-1990s than at any time during the preceding half-century, they also faced a much more complex array of international agreements. There was, therefore, increasing uncertainty about the future of investment policies at the regional and multilateral levels in particular in the mid- to late 1990s. These tendencies, furthermore, were compounded as the OECD initiated negotiations on a Multilateral Agreement on Investment, and as regional integration schemes in Latin America and elsewhere evolved. The relationship of such developments to the roles of the newly created WTO and the relationship of investment policies to trade policies became central issues in the late 1990s, as is discussed in the next chapter.

Notes

1. Portions of this chapter draw from Brewer and Young (1995*a*, 1995*b*, 1995*c*, 1996, 1997). Also, on the positions of countries in the Uruguay Round negotiations and the resulting compromises, see especially Croom (1995) and Economist Intelligence Unit (1994).
2. The four agreements on civil aircraft, dairy, bovine meat, and government procurement have much smaller numbers of signatories and are thus designated 'plurilateral' agreements to distinguish them from the 'multilateral' agreements signed by all member countries.
3. The legal instruments vary from the lengthy, complex, and detailed GATS in three volumes (including each of the signatories' national schedules of specific commitments) to the simple one-paragraph ministerial decision on timing of notifications for the textile agreement. The legal instruments are technically in two groupings based on whether they require national ratification or not. The former are twenty-two core instruments (technically 'agreements' and in one case an 'understanding') that establish the rules and institutional procedures for trade, intellectual property, and investment. The latter are twenty-eight supplementary instruments ('ministerial decisions' and 'declarations' and one 'understanding') that amplify one or more of the core instruments. Some of the latter are potentially politically important and expansive (e.g. the establishment of a committee on trade and the environment), while others are technical clarifications of specific points (e.g. the classification system to be used in conjunction with the International Standards Organization).
4. The general framework provisions of the General Agreement on Trade in Services (GATS) do

not cover subsidies. Three particularly problematic sectors—agriculture, civil aircraft, and textiles—are covered in separate agreements. Agriculture and civil aviation are explicitly excluded from some provisions of the SCMs agreement, while the textiles agreement suggests that the SCMs agreement does apply to that industry.

Appendix 5.1

NAFTA's Provisions Concerning Investment: Titles of Selected Chapters and Articles

Chapter 11

[The most germane portion of the NAFTA is Chapter 11, 'Investment', which includes 14 articles in Section A on 'Investment', 15 articles in Section B on 'Settlement of Disputes between a Party and an Investor of Another Party', and four brief annexes concerning dispute settlement procedures.]

Section A—Investment
Scope and Coverage (Article 1101)
National Treatment (Article 1102)
Most-Favored-Nation Treatment (Article 1103)
Standard of Treatment (Article 1104)
Minimum Standard of Treatment (Article 1105)
Performance Requirements (Article 1106)[a]
Senior Management and Boards of Directors (Article 1107)
Reservations and Exceptions (Article 1108)
Transfers [of funds internationally] (Article 1109)
Expropriation and Compensation (Article 1110)
Special Formalities and Information Requirements (Article 1111)
Relation to Other Chapters (Article 1112)
Denial of Benefits (Article 1113)
Environmental Measures (Article 1114)

Section B—Settlement of Disputes between a Party and an Investor of Another Party
[Twenty-four articles]

Section C—Definitions
Definitions (Article 1139)

Other Chapters: Investment in Specific Sectors

Trade and Investment in the Automotive Sector (Chapter 3, Annex 300–A)
Textile and Apparel Goods (Chapter 3, Annex 300–B)
Energy and Basic Petrochemicals (Chapter 6)
Agriculture and Sanitary and Phytosanitary Measures (Chapter 7)
Telecommunications (Chapter 13)
Financial Services, including Investment Disputes in Financial Services (Chapter 14)

Note: [a]The first paragraph of Article 1106, Performance Requirements, reads as follows:

'No Party may impose or enforce any of the following requirements, or enforce any commitment or undertaking, in connection with the establishment, acquisition, expansion, management, conduct or operation of an investment of an investor of a Party or of a non-Party in its territory:

(a) to export a given level or percentage of goods or services;
(b) to achieve a given level or percentage of domestic content;
(c) to purchase, use or accord a preference to goods produced or services provided in its territory, or to purchase goods or services from persons in its territory;
(d) to relate in any way the volume or value of imports to the volume or value of exports or to the amount of foreign exchange inflows associated with such investment;
(e) to restrict sales of goods or services in its territory that such investment produces or provides by relating such sales in any way to the volume or value of its exports or foreign exchange earnings;
(f) to transfer technology, a production process or other proprietary knowledge to a person in its territory, except when the requirement is imposed or the commitment or undertaking is enforced by a court, administrative tribunal or competition authority to remedy an alleged violation of competition laws or to act in a manner not inconsistent with other provisions of this Agreement; or
(g) to act as the exclusive supplier of the goods it produces or services it provides to a specific region or world market.'

Appendix 5.2

Services Industries: Classification List

I. Business Services

Professional services
Computer and related services
Research-and-development services
Real estate services
Rental/leasing services without operators
Other business services

II. Communication Services

Postal services
Courier services
Telecommunications services
Audiovisual services
Other

III. Construction and Related Engineering Services

General construction work for buildings
General construction work for civil engineering
Installation and assembly work
Building completion and finishing work
Other

IV. Distribution Services

Commission-agents services
Wholesale-trade services
Retailing services
Franchising
Other

V. Education Services

- Primary education
- Secondary education
- Higher education
- Adult education
- Other

VI. Environmental Services

- Sewage services
- Refuse disposal services
- Sanitation and similar services
- Other

VII. Financial Services

- Insurance and insurance-related services
- Banking and other financial services
- Other

VIII. Health Related and Social Services

- Hospital services
- Other human-health services
- Social services
- Other

IX. Tourism and Travel Related Services

- Hotels and restaurants
- Travel agencies and tour operators services
- Tourist guide services
- Other

X. Recreational, Cultural and Sporting Services

- Entertainment services
- News agency services
- Libraries, archives, museums and other cultural services
- Sporting and other recreational services
- Other

XI. Transport Services

- Maritime transport
- Internal waterways transport
- Air transport
- Space transport
- Rail transport
- Road transport
- Pipeline transport
- Services auxiliary to all modes of transport
- Other

XII. Other Services not Included Elsewhere

Source: UNCTAD/World Bank, 1994: table A-1, pp. 169–72; adapted from GATT Secretariat, *Services Sectoral Classification List* (Geneva: GATT, 1991).

Appendix 5.3

Uruguay Round Agreements

MARRAKESH AGREEMENT ESTABLISHING THE WORLD TRADE ORGANIZATION
Annex 1
Annex 1A: Multilateral Agreements on Trade in Goods
General Agreement on Tariffs and Trade 1994
Understanding on the Interpretation of Article II:1(b) of the General Agreement on Tariffs and Trade 1994
Understanding on the Interpretation of Article XVII of the General Agreement on Tariffs and Trade 1994
Understanding on Balance-of-Payments Provisions of the General Agreement on Tariffs and Trade 1994
Understanding on the Interpretation of Article XXIV of the General Agreement on Tariffs and Trade 1994
Understanding in Respect of Waivers of Obligations under the General Agreement on Tariffs and Trade 1994
Understanding on the Interpretation of Article XXVIII of the General Agreement on Tariffs and Trade 1994
Marrakesh Protocol to the General Agreement on Tariffs and Trade 1994
Agreement on Agriculture
Agreement on the Application of Sanitary and Phytosanitary Measures
Agreement on Textiles and Clothing
Agreement on Technical Barriers to Trade
Agreement on Trade-Related Investment Measures[a]
Agreement on Implementation of Article VI of the General Agreement on Tariffs and Trade 1994
Agreement on Implementation of Article VII of the General Agreement on Tariffs and Trade 1994
Agreement on Preshipment Inspection
Agreement on Rules of Origin
Agreement on Import Licensing Procedures
Agreement on Subsidies and Countervailing Measures
Agreement on Safeguards
Annex 1B: General Agreement on Trade in Services[b]
Annex 1C: Agreement on Trade-Related Aspects of Intellectual Property Rights
Annex 2: Understanding on Rules and Procedures Governing the Settlement of Disputes
Annex 3: Trade Policy Review Mechanism
Annex 4: Plurilateral Trade Agreements
Agreement on Trade in Civil Aircraft
Agreement on Government Procurement
International Dairy Agreement
International Bovine Meat Agreement

Notes: [a]Excerpts from the TRIMs agreement:

'ARTICLE 1

1. Without prejudice to other rights and obligations under GATT 1994, no Member shall apply any TRIM that is inconsistent with the provisions of Article II or Article XI of GATT 1994.
2. An illustrative list of TRIMs that are inconsistent with the obligation of national treatment provided

for in paragraph 4 or Article III of GATT 1994 and the obligation of general elimination of quantitative restrictions provided for in paragraph 1 of Article I of GATT 1994 is contained in the Annex to this Agreement.

ANNEX–ILLUSTRATIVE LIST

1. TRIMs that are inconsistent with the obligation of national treatment provided for in paragraph 4 of Article III of GATT 1994 include those which are mandatory or enforceable under domestic law or under administrative rulings, or compliance with which is necessary to obtain an advantage, and which require:
   (b) the purchase or use by an enterprise of products of domestic origin or from any domestic source, whether specified in terms of particular products, in terms of volume or value of products, or in terms of a proportion of volume or value of its local production; or
   (c) that an enterprise's purchases or use of imported products be limited to an amount related to the volume or value of local products that it exports.
4. TRIMs that are inconsistent with the obligation of general elimination of quantitative restrictions provided for in paragraph 1 of Article XI of GATT 1994 include those which are mandatory or enforceable under domestic law or under administrative rulings, or compliance with which is necessary to obtain an advantage, and which restrict:
   (e) the importation by an enterprise of products used in or related to its local production, generally or to an amount related to the volume or value of local production that it exports;
   (f) the importation by an enterprise of products used in or related to its local production by restricting its access to foreign exchange to an amount related to the foreign exchange inflows attributable to the enterprise; or
   (g) the exportation or sale for export by an enterprise of products, whether specified in terms of particular products, in terms of volume or value of products, or in terms of a proportion of volume or value of its production.'

[b]General Agreement on Trade in Services (GATS) and Related Ministerial Decisions

'PART I SCOPE AND DEFINITION

Article I	Scope and Definition

PART II GENERAL OBLIGATIONS AND DISCIPLINES

Article II	Most-Favoured-Nation Treatment
Article III	Transparency
Article III *bis*	Disclosure of Confidential Information
Article IV	Increasing Participation of Developing Countries
Article V	Economic Integration
Article V *bis*	Labour Markets Integration Agreements
Article VI	Domestic Regulation
Article VII	Recognition
Article VIII	Monopolies and Exclusive Service Suppliers Business Practices
Article IX	Business Practices
Article X	Emergency Safeguard Measures
Article XI	Payments and Transfers
Article XII	Restrictions to Safeguard the Balance of Payments
Article XIII	Government Procurement
Article XIV	General Exceptions
Article XIV *bis*	Security Exceptions
Article XV	Subsidies

PART III SPECIFIC COMMITMENTS

Article XVI	Market Access
Article XVII	National Treatment
Article XVIII	Additional Commitments

PART IV PROGRESSIVE LIBERALIZATION

Article XIX	Negotiation of Specific Commitments

6

Expansion

Multilateral, Regional, and Sectoral Developments (Late 1990s)

6.1 Introduction

The entry into force of the Uruguay Round agreements and the inauguration of the WTO on 1 January 1995 marked the beginning of a new era. During the second half of the 1990s, there was a significant intensification of interest in the evolution of international rules and institutions affecting investment. While there was increased interest within the WTO on investment issues, there were also significant developments in a variety of other arenas as well. The OECD undertook a major initiative by beginning formal negotiations on a Multilateral Agreement on Investment (MAI) in 1995—negotiations that were still in progress in mid-1997 as this book was being written. Furthermore, there were new sectoral agreements that included investment provisions as well as trade provisions—among them an agreement on basic telecommunications within the framework of the GATS at the WTO, and another sector-specific agreement, the Energy Charter Treaty, which is a free-standing agreement with a regional emphasis on the energy industry of Central and Eastern Europe. In addition, there were important developments in other regional arenas—including in particular the formation of the Mercosur in Latin America. Meanwhile, the number of bilateral treaties continued to increase, and many governments continued with their liberalization programmes. One theme of the present chapter, then, is the expansion of the international investment regime to include significant new agreements that were added to the already existing array of bilateral, regional, and multilateral agreements. The result was a much more complex system, in which overlaps, gaps, and inconsistencies became more problematic.

At the same time there was also evidence of increasing ambivalence and doubts—and in some instances, resistance—in the midst of the liberalization trends. There were conspicuous differences in the attitudes and approaches to liberalization—differences not only between developed and developing countries but also among developed countries and among developing countries. In particular, differences between the United States, on the one hand, and the EU and its member governments, on the other, became more evident. In Latin America, differences became more evident between those developing countries that had undergone the most extensive liberalization programmes such as Argentina and Chile, and those that had moved more slowly such as Brazil. Similarly in Asia, although both China and India had undertaken revolutionary changes in their previously highly restrictive systems, they and some other Asian countries such as Malaysia and Indonesia resisted some liberalization measures in regional and multilateral fora as well as in their own national policies. Questions about the scope and pace of liberalization of investment policy were among the core issues in China's accession to membership in the WTO, and negotiations about the terms of China's entry were among the most consequential developments affecting the evolution of the international investment regime.

These differences, moreover, concerned not only the pace and nature of liberalization, but also the balance between liberalization and regulation. Thus, differences on issues concerning MNEs' environmental practices, their labour relations, and their competitive practices (i.e. restrictive business practices) became more salient, and revealed continuing differences among developing countries and among developed countries. Among developed countries, the WTO dispute case concerning US policy on investors in Cuba (the Helms–Burton Act) revealed differences in approaches to issues concerning the control of MNEs and the interpretation of national security exemptions in international agreements. The emergence of investment issues on the active agendas of both the WTO and the OECD also brought to the fore a series of differences—not only about substantive provisions concerning liberalization, investment protection, and other issues, but also 'forum' issues about the appropriate arena(s) for negotiating further investment agreements.

6.2 Investment Issues at the WTO

Provisions in the Uruguay Round agreements for subsequent negotiations and reviews in the GATS and TRIMs were especially important to the future of investment issues at the WTO (Sauvé, 1994, 1995). A list of the negotiations scheduled for the early years of the WTO is presented in Table 6.1. Some of the negotiations pertained to a variety of trade issues that had been on the agenda of the GATT for many years. But many of them—even most of them—also concerned investment issues as well, and several of them had the potential for significant expansion of the WTO's coverage of investment matters. The items that were particularly important in this regard were: (1) review of the TRIMs agreement, with the possibility of including additional investment issues and competition policy issues, and (2) review of the GATS, particularly individual countries' exceptions to MFN and individual countries' lists of specific commitments (and thus exceptions to national treatment). Even if neither of these two review processes concerning agreements with explicit investment provisions in fact produced significant progress in the liberalization process, other negotiations on more narrowly defined issues could, *in toto*, expand the scope of investment issues within the WTO's purview. This included, for instance, further negotiations—as well as analytical work and implementation—concerning anti-dumping, the environment, subsidies, and agriculture. Finally, reviews of the

Table 6.1 WTO Negotiations Scheduled for 1998–2000[a]

1998 (1 January)

Examine standard of review for anti-dumping disputes, and consider its application to countervail cases (ministerial agreement)

First review of operation and implementation of technical barriers to trade provisions (reviews are to be held every three years thereafter) (Article 15.4 of agreement on Technical Barriers to Trade)

Deadline for report with recommendation from Working Party on Trade in Services and the Environment on modifications of GATS Article XIV (general exceptions) (ministerial agreement)

Review of operation and implementation of sanitary and phytosanitary provisions (further reviews to be held as need arises) (Article 12.7 of Sanitary and Phytosanitary agreement)

1999 (1 January)

Start negotiations on further improvement of the GPA (extension of coverage) (GPA Article XXIV.7)

Deadline for review of provision on patent or *sui generis* protection of plant varieties (TRIPs agreement Article 27.3.b)

Deadline for review of dispute settlement rules and procedures (ministerial decision)

1999 (30 June)

Start review of provisions on serious prejudice and non-actionable subsidies (Article 31 of Subsidies agreement)

2000 (January)

Start first round of negotiations on progressive liberalization of services (new negotiations to increase the general level of specific commitments) (GATS Article XIX)

Review of Article II (MFN) (GATS Annex) exemptions

Launch new negotiations to continue reform process in agriculture (Article 20 of Agriculture agreement)

First review of TRIPs agreement; reviews to be held every two years thereafter (TRIPs agreement Article 71.1)

Deadline for review of TRIMs agreement and consideration of whether to complement it with provisions on investment and competition policy (TRIMs agreement Article 9)

Review of interpretation of the rules on modification and withdrawal of concessions (Understanding on interpretation of GATT Article XXVIII)

First review of grandfathering of US Jones Act (and like provisions); reviews to be held every two years thereafter (paragraph 2 of GATT 1994)

Deadline for appraisal of TPRM (TPRM agreement section F)

2000 (unspecified date)

Negotiations on increased protection for geographical indications for wines and spirits (TRIPs agreement Articles 23 and 24.1)

Subsidies in services (GATS Article XV)

Note: [a]The dates are deadlines for completion in some instances, and deadlines for commencement in other instances.

Source: Adapted from Schott, 1994: table 6, pp. 35–6.

agreements on intellectual property, dispute settlement procedures, and the policy review mechanism each had the potential to affect the place of investment issues in the WTO in many ways. Finally, there were provisions for negotiations in specific sectors, especially in services, that contained significant investment issues. In fact, already by mid-1997, there had been significant progress—as well as notable failures—in several sectoral negotiations.

Sectoral agreements

Early failures to reach agreement, temporarily at least, in maritime services and financial services created doubts about the political will of the members to extend (or complete, depending on one's perspective) the Uruguay Round agreements, but eventual agreement on telecommunications and financial services gave substance to the GATS framework in these important service sectors (see Box 6.1 on GATS sectoral annexes). These were in addition to sector-specific provisions of NAFTA (noted in the previous chapter) and a free-standing agreement in the form of the Energy Charter Treaty (discussed below). The development of such sectoral agreements added to the complexity of the investment system as a whole and also in at least some instances for the individual sectors as well. The complexity is particularly evident in the telecommunications sector, a service industry with total worldwide revenues of more than $600 billion per year.

Box 6.1

Sector-Specific Annexes in the GATS

A group of annexes, decisions and an understanding associated with the GATS establishes special sectoral provisions concerning:

- *Air transport*: the air transport annex excludes traffic rights covered by bilateral agreements under the Chicago Convention from the GATS.
- *Financial services*: two annexes, a decision, and an understanding on financial services identify the specific types of services included, establish the validity and potential recognition of prudential regulations, and provide for subsequent listing of specific commitments concerning national treatment and market access, as well as exemptions from MFN, through continuing negotiations.
- *Maritime transport*: the annex on maritime transport provides for further negotiations, to be concluded by June 1996 (though they were subsequently extended beyond that initial deadline).
- *Telecommunications*: an annex on telecommunications includes definitions, obligations, and rights concerning users' access to communications services. It excludes radio and television broadcasting and cable distribution. A basic telecommunications annex and decision clarify a variety of terms and provisions in the main text of the GATS and provide for continuing negotiations (which reached an agreement in early 1997) to open countries' telecommunications sectors to foreign service providers.

Telecommunications

Two of the GATS sector-specific annexes concern telecommunications. One, called simply the 'telecommunications' agreement, was completed by the time the Uruguay Round agreements were formally agreed in April 1994, and is sometimes referred to as the 'value-added telecommunications' agreement. It provides assurances, for instance, that foreign-owned banks and foreign-owned firms in other services industries that use telecommunications services can have access to the telecommunications services within a country without being discriminated against. The 'basic telecommunications agreement', which was not concluded until early 1997, grants foreign firms market access and national treatment as providers of telecommunications services, whether through cross-border trade transactions or through foreign-owned affiliates or joint-venture partners in the country.

In addition, the TRIMs and TRIPs agreements are also germane to the telecommunications industry. The TRIMs agreement is germane because it affects the manufacturing of telecommunications equipment; for instance, under the terms of the TRIMs a foreign-owned manufacturer that produces telecommunications equipment cannot be required to meet export performance or domestic content requirements. The TRIPs agreement is germane because it affects the transfer of telecommunications technology; under the terms of the TRIPs, licensing agreements with local firms concerning the manufacture of telecommunications equipment, for instance, have to be enforced.

Furthermore, there is an Information Technology Agreement (ITA), which was agreed in early 1997 and which includes many goods such as telephone sets, telephone answering machines, and facsimile machines—all of which are of course directly involved in providing telecommunications services. The ITA in its initial version, however, is only a trade agreement in the narrow sense, and it only directly concerns tariffs. Further, although the ITA was negotiated within the WTO system and is administered by the WTO, it is a 'plurilateral' agreement among only 28 countries (the 15 countries of the EU plus 13 other countries). Yet the ITA has important implications for foreign investment, for instance, by allowing FDI projects to import equipment and other goods tariff-free. Thus, an agreement that is explicitly neither a telecommunications agreement nor an investment agreement is nevertheless related to firms' strategic and operational decisions about telecommunications investment projects. Analogously, government tariff rates in one industry are implicitly an element of its investment policy in another industry.

Thus, within the WTO there are at least five different agreements that directly concern telecommunications (to which one could add the SCMs and other WTO agreements as well, not to mention regional and bilateral agreements). In order to understand the 'investment climate' in the 'telecommunications industry' in any one country, therefore, one needs to understand the provisions of all five agreements, plus the precise nature of the specific commitments made by that particular country under the terms of each of the five agreements. A comparative analysis of the coverage of the five agreements is provided in Table 6.2.

Table 6.2 Comparisons of Five WTO Agreements in Telecommunications: Types of Government Policies and International Business Transactions Covered

Agreements and key provisions	Sector in which agreement is directly applied	
	Services	Manufacturing
GATS Telecommunications Annex		
Provides for market access and national treatment for foreign-owned *users* of telecommunications . . .	yes	no
GATS Basic Telecommunications Annex		
Provides for market access and national treatment for *providers* of telecommunications . . .	yes	no
TRIMs		
Limits performance requirements for FDI projects in . . .	no	yes
TRIPs		
Establishes intellectual property rights standards and enforcement procedures in . . .	yes	yes
Information Technology Agreement (ITA)		
Reduces tariffs on . . .	no	yes

Sources: WTO, 1996*a*, 1997*a*, 1997*b*, 1977*c*.

TRIMs

There were many delays in the individual countries' notifications of their non-conforming TRIMs. An example of the issues that emerged in the implementation of the TRIMs agreement is given in Box 6.2, where the issues raised by Brazil's request for a waiver for its TRIMs and tariffs in the motor vehicle industry are discussed.

Dispute settlement

One of the most important developments of the late 1990s was the much greater use of WTO dispute settlement procedures than had been the case with the GATT (see Box 6.3 for a summary as of early 1997, two years after the new WTO procedures had been put in place). One apparent trend was that a much greater proportion of the cases were being brought by developing countries than in the past; previously, EU–US cases dominated the agenda. It remained to be seen, however, whether investment disputes would become common in the process, for the early cases continued to arise mostly from the implementation of the Uruguay Round provisions on trade. Complaints by Japan and the USA against the Brazilian TRIMs noted above in Box 6.2, however, put investment issues squarely into the dispute settlement process.

Box 6.2

Implementing the WTO TRIMs Agreement: Brazil's Automotive Regime Waiver and Its Differential Implications for MNEs

In March 1996, Brazil requested a WTO waiver for its system of dual tariff rates for imported parts, raw materials, and capital goods that were used in motor vehicle production as well as for assembled vehicles. Firms that met Brazil's domestic content and export criteria would pay 35 per cent tariffs on imported parts and assembled vehicles, while firms that did not meet those criteria would pay 70 per cent tariffs. The criteria meant, for instance, that exports had to match imports by approximately a 1 : 1 ratio. Because these restrictions violated the TRIMs agreement, it was necessary for Brazil to ask the WTO Council for Trade in Goods, which administers the agreement, for a waiver until 31 December 1999.

Exports from Korea were being substantially reduced by the high tariff rate because they could not qualify for the lower rates available to firms with substantial facilities in Brazil. Within the USA, both Chrysler and Honda of the USA objected and put pressure on the US government to resist the Brazilian request for a waiver in the WTO because they both exported assembled vehicles and parts to Brazil from the USA. Honda noted that its exports from the USA to Brazil during the nine-month period in 1995 just before the Brazilian regime went into effect exceeded 4,000 vehicles, but that during the comparable nine-month period in 1996 after the regime went into effect they exported only about 800 vehicles, a decline of approximately 80 per cent.

Not all automotive manufacturers were unhappy, however. In fact, both Ford and General Motors actually favoured the waiver for Brazil since both firms had large facilities in Brazil, and the dual tariff scheme protected their positions in the Brazilian market against imports from their Korean, Japanese, and US competitors. Thus, General Motors advised the US government not to oppose the waiver in the WTO (and also not to proceed with a parallel unilateral US investigation under its section 301 legislation). General Motors observed that it would 'continue to oppose any action on the part of the U.S. to challenge Brazil's auto policies in the WTO. . . . [It believed that] the U.S. should judge the Brazilian auto policies according to their impact on U.S. trade. . . . [T]he beneficiaries of any U.S. trade action against Brazil would not be U.S.-based companies, but our Japanese and Korean competitors.'

Source: *Inside US Trade*, 1996*b*.

China's membership in the WTO

Although China had undertaken revolutionary changes in its economic policies, including its FDI policies in particular, there were still many respects in which its policies were fundamentally at odds with WTO rules during the negotiations for Chinese membership. There were still significant elements of centralized economic planning, and several sectors of the economy were still dominated by state-owned enterprises. In addition, its international economic policies, including its policies on inward FDI, contained many restrictions.[1]

The USA–China Business Council surveyed its members to determine their preferences for the US government priorities in the negotiations with the Chinese government on admission to the WTO. The executives from fifty-five firms that responded nearly unanimously favoured China's admission to the WTO, and many preferred a multilateral to a bilateral approach to China's relations with the USA. Many thought that a multilateral arena was more advantageous to their firms' interests because multilateral commitments would be more effective in gaining the liberalization and investment protection goals of their firms, without endangering their commercial interests as much as a bilateral approach would. They also expressed their opinions on the specific types of problems they encountered in their business activities in China and therefore their priorities for the US negotiators. Aside from their desire that China have permanent MFN status, which is an inherent and overarching element of membership in the WTO, the executives focused on the following types of problems:

- transparency—opaque policies, abrupt changes in them, and an absence of opportunities for appealing administrative rulings;
- trading rights—restrictions on the ability of foreign-invested enterprises (FIEs) to import products of their choosing (without using authorized foreign trade companies);

Box 6.3

Dispute Settlement Cases in the Early Years of the WTO

Two years after their entry into force, the new WTO dispute settlement procedures had done the following:

- Adopted two appellate reports—one that decided against US standards for reformulated and conventional gasoline on the basis of a complaint by Brazil and Venezuela, and another that decided against Japanese taxes on liquor on the basis of a complaint by Canada, the EU, and the USA.
- Noted that as many as fifteen disputes had been settled by the parties without a formal panel report after a request for the establishment of a panel had been made - including US duties on imported motor vehicles from Japan, EU policies on agricultural trade, and Japanese policies on telecommunications equipment.
- Established or was considering establishing sixteen additional panels—concerning, for instance, Pakistan's compliance with TRIPs, and the US Cuban Liberty and Democratic Solidarity Act (also known as the Helms–Burton Act), which was subsequently settled without a formal dispute panel report.
- Had fourteen cases under consultation, prior to the possible formation of a dispute panel - including cases involving Turkey's policies on textiles, Korea's telecommunications policies, and Indonesia's policies on motor vehicles (including possible violation of the TRIMs, SCMs, and TRIPs agreements).

Source: WTO, 1997*d*; *Inside US Trade*, website, Feb. 1997.

- trade-related investment measures—widely used for FDI projects in manufacturing;
- trade-related intellectual property rights—weak enforcement;
- liberalization in services—especially banking, telecommunications, and insurance (*Inside US Trade*, 1997*a*).

At the same time, there were, of course, a variety of major liberalization measures in progress, including: establishment of trial sites for foreign-owned insurance companies in Shanghai and Guangdong; a plan to begin to open the market for transfers of mining rights (for exploration and excavation) to foreign-owned firms by allowing them to purchase rights from domestic firms, which had had exclusive rights; a plan to begin to allow build-operate-and-transfer (BOT) agreements with foreign firms for infrastructure projects; and a programme to make the domestic currency convertible for current account transactions, including foreign firms' profit remittances.

In Box 6.4 are excerpts from a US government assessment of China's policies at the time that negotiations over the terms of China's admission to the WTO were a major

Box 6.4

Excerpts from a US Government Assessment of China's FDI Policies

'In June 1995, Chinese authorities issued investment "guidelines" detailing sectors in which investment [was to be] encouraged, restricted or prohibited. The new guidelines were a positive step toward clarifying China's policies on foreign investment. However, a continued general lack of transparency in the foreign investment approval process and inconsistency in the implementation of regulations continue to hinder investors that meet the substantive requirements of the "guidelines".

There are many areas in which, although foreign investment is technically allowed, it is severely restricted. Restricted categories generally reflect: (1) the protection of domestic industries, such as the services sector, in which China fears that its domestic market and companies would be quickly dominated by foreign firms; (2) the aim of limiting luxuries or requiring large imports of components or raw materials; and (3) the avoidance of redundancy (i.e. excess capacity).

China also—

- bans investment in the management and operation of basic telecommunications, all aspects of value-added telecommunications as well as in the news media, broadcast and television sectors.
- severely restricts investment in the rest of the services sector, including distribution, trade, construction, tourism and travel services, shipping, advertising, insurance and education.
- hinders foreign investment . . . by insisting on fulfillment of contract-specific local content, foreign exchange balancing, and technology transfer requirements.'

Source: US Office of the Trade Representative, 1997.

item on the agendas of several governments. It is important to recognize that the central issue about China's accession to the WTO was not *whether* it would meet WTO rules (which it had to do in order to become a member) but rather the length of the *transition periods* during which it would make changes in its policies so that they would meet WTO standards by the end of the period. Furthermore, of course, the extent to which the Chinese government actually implemented any new stated policies in accordance with the WTO accession agreement would be a matter to be determined during the WTO's policy review and consultation processes, as well as dispute settlement cases; in these respects China would technically be no different from any other subsequent member of the WTO. However, as the policies listed above and the assessments in Box 6.4 make clear, the amount of change in China's policies needed to meet WTO rules was unusual. Moreover, the associated challenge to the WTO to include such a large and previously isolated national economy in the multilateral investment–trade system was also unusual.

6.3 The Multilateral Agreement on Investment (MAI) at the OECD

The work at the OECD during the 1990s to create a Multilateral Agreement on Investment built on earlier OECD investment-related agreements, including the Code of Liberalization of Capital Movements and the Code of Liberalization of Current Invisible Operations (Ley, 1996; OECD, 1996*a*; Smith, 1996; Witherell, 1996; also Houde, 1996; and Poret, 1992).[2] The Capital Movements Code explicitly included foreign direct investment as well as other kinds of capital movements such as securities, money market transactions and trade credits (OECD, 1993*a*). Because FDI is a so-called List A item in the agreement, governments cannot add reservations beyond those they have already recorded, and there is thus a standstill on restrictions on FDI. However, the listed reservations are extensive for some countries, including for instance Canada, France, and Japan. In any case, it was only an agreement to 'endeavour to avoid introducing any new exchange restrictions on the movements of capital or the use of non-resident-owned funds' and to 'endeavour to avoid making existing regulations more restrictive' (Article 1(e)). These obligations in the code were technically binding. Though there were provisions for transparency, reporting and examination, there were no formalized dispute settlement or enforcement procedures; there was only 'enforcement' through consensus in a committee process.

The Current Invisible Operations Code (OECD, 1993*b*) is precisely parallel to the Capital Movements Code, even to the degree that most of the articles have identical titles. Thus, the provisions concerning undertakings, measures of liberalization, transparency, examination, derogations, and reservations are all quite similar. The principal difference between the two codes is in the types of international transactions that are covered by them. Income from capital in the form of profits and dividends is explicitly covered, and the payments of subsidiaries and branches to foreign parents for overhead expenses are also explicitly covered. Like the Capital Movements Code, the Invisible Operations Code pertains to many types of transactions that are not directly related to FDI, for instance, the international movement of bank-

Table 6.3 Illustrative Industry Exceptions to National Treatment among OECD Countries

	Australia	Canada	Japan	Mexico	New Zealand	USA
I. *Investment by established foreign-controlled enterprises*						
Trans-sectoral	Y	Y		Y	Y	
Agriculture			Y			
Air transport	Y	Y	Y	Y	Y	Y
Atomic energy						Y
Auto parts				Y		
Book publishing	Y					
Construction				Y		
Education services				Y		
Film		Y				
Financial services: banking	Y		Y			
Financial services: life ins.	Y					
Financial services: securities			Y	Y		Y
Fishing		Y	Y	Y	Y	Y
Forestry			Y			
Leather			Y			
Legal services				Y		
Marine transport	Y	Y		Y		Y
Mining			Y			Y
Newspapers	Y			Y		
Oil and gas		Y	Y	Y		Y
Radio and television	Y	Y		Y		
Real Estate (land)				Y	Y	
Road transport		Y		Y		
Telecommunications	Y	Y		Y	Y	Y
Uranium		Y				
II. *Official aids and subsidies*			N			
Trans-sectoral		Y				Y
Agriculture		Y				Y
Films, audio-visual		Y			Y	
Foreign aid	Y					
Credits for small-scale enterprises				Y		
III. *Tax obligations*	N		N	N		N
Trans-sectoral		Y			Y	
Mining					Y	
IV. *Government purchasing*	N		N	N	N	
Air transport						Y
Consultancy		Y				
Technical services contracting						Y
V. *Access to local finance*	N	N	N	N	N	N

Note: Y=yes; N=no.
Source: Compiled from OECD 1994*a*.

notes and travellers' cheques, exchange of means of payment by travellers, and use of cash cards and credit cards abroad.

Another pair of OECD agreements concerning FDI are in the 1976 Declaration on International Investment and Multinational Enterprises, which includes the Guidelines for Multinational Enterprises (OECD, 1994*b*) as discussed in Chapter 4, and the National Treatment Instrument (OECD, 1994*a*). The signatories to the national treatment instrument registered sectoral exceptions, and the industries where there are exceptions are numerous and diverse. They include natural resources, agriculture, transportation, financial services, telecommunications, real estate, and others. In addition, there are exceptions imposed by regional governmental units in federal systems, i.e. Australia, Canada, the United States (see Table 6.3 for details). Such industry exceptions became significant issues as the MAI negotiations progressed.

As of mid-1997 there had been agreement in the MAI negotiations on many of its principal provisions (see outline in Table 6.4). Thus, in particular, it would include the usual commitments to both MFN and national treatment, standard investment protection provisions already embodied in BITs, and liberalization measures pertaining to right of entry, performance requirements, movement of personnel, and the transparency of policies. However, disagreement on a wide range of issues was also evident: the scope of the definition of the types of investment covered; the possibility of restricting investment incentives; the applicability of the dispute settlement process to investor–government disputes, especially in advance of an actual investment; the particular industries that each country would exclude from its national treatment and right of entry commitments.

In view of the prospect of rather limited liberalization measures and no apparent need for extensive investment protection or dispute settlement procedures beyond those already in force through other multilateral and bilateral agreements, the potential value of the MAI became increasingly controversial. Further, it had the potential of exacerbating an already difficult patchwork problem. Moreover, although non-OECD countries were kept informed about the status of the negotiations and afforded opportunities in a series of workshops to voice their concerns, the fact that the MAI was being negotiated without the direct participation of non-members rekindled old resentments on the part of some developing countries. Yet there was also serious interest in becoming signatories to an MAI, if it eventually materialized, on the part of a few Latin American countries in particular. As a free-standing agreement open to non-members to sign, it would provide countries a way to signal—and to have ratified—their new liberalized investment policies. As of the writing of this book in mid-1997, therefore, the eventual existence, content, and significance of the MAI were all very much in doubt.

6.4 Regional Developments

The 1990s was a period of intense activity on investment issues at the regional level, especially in the western hemisphere. Preliminary steps were undertaken to expand

Table 6.4 Outline of the Preliminary Draft of OECD Multilateral Agreement on Investment (MAI)

I. General Provisions
II. Scope and Application
  Definitions
  Geographical Scope of Applications
    Application to Overseas Territories
III. Treatment of Investors and Investments
  National Treatment and Most Favoured Nation Treatment
  Prudential Measures
  Transparency
  Special Topics
    Key Personnel
    Performance Requirements
    Privatization
    Investment Incentives
    Monopolies / State Enterprises
    Corporate Practices and Senior Management and Board of Directors
IV. Investment Protection
  General Treatment
  Expropriation and Compensation
  Transfers
  Subrogation
  Protecting Existing Investments
  Protecting Investor Rights from Other Agreements
V. Dispute Settlement
  State–State Procedures
  Investor–State Procedures
VI. Exceptions
  General Exceptions
VII. Relationship to Other International Agreements
VIII. Implementation and Operation
  The Preparatory Group
  The Parties Group
IX. Final Provisions
  Signature
  Ratification and Entry into Force
  Accession
  Review and Amendment
  Withdrawal
  Authentic Texts
  Denial of Benefits
X. Other Provisions
  Taxation
  Financial Services

Source: *Inside US Trade*, 1997b.

NAFTA by bringing in Chile; the four countries in Mercosur (Argentina, Brazil, Paraguay, Uruguay) added Bolivia and Chile as associate members; and thirty-four countries in the western hemisphere (i.e. all of them except Cuba) agreed to the establishment of a Free Trade Area of the Americas by the year 2005. These developments, furthermore, were in addition to the continued existence of three smaller regional organizations in the western hemisphere—the Caribbean Community (CARICOM), the Central American Common Market (CACM), and the Andean Pact. Beyond the common element of tariff reduction within each grouping, there were significant differences in the degree of policy liberalization and the extent to which investment policies were included in them. Although each reflected ambitious goals for the future, each was also experiencing difficulties in progressing toward more liberalized and uniform investment policies. Within Mercosur, for instance, Argentina and Brazil were at odds over investment incentives, which were widely used at both the central and state level by Brazil but which were opposed by Argentina.

The relatively intense activity on regional agreements involving investment issues in the western hemisphere was in great contrast to the relative quiescence in Asia. Along with the continuation of modest arrangements concerning FDI in the ASEAN, the only development was the incremental advancement of investment issues within the Asia Pacific Economic Cooperation (APEC) forum (Bora, 1995; Graham, 1995*b*; Green and Brewer, 1995; Guisinger, 1995). The non-binding principles agreed at the end of 1994 and the subsequent annual summit meetings of the leaders of the APEC economies reflected—and contributed to—greater salience for international investment issues in the region. But there was little interest—at least among the Asian members—in developing extensive, formal binding rules on investment.

Within Europe there was a significant sectoral agreement in the form of the Energy Charter Treaty, which was signed by forty-one countries and the EU. The treaty liberalizes trade and investment policies in the countries of Central Europe and the former Soviet Union, and it includes extensive provisions on investment protection and other post-investment issues. An additional treaty concerning pre-investment issues was being negotiated as of 1997. Although many countries outside Europe also signed the ECT, the USA did not because it considered the investment protection provisions to be lower than US BIT standards and therefore unacceptable. Meanwhile, the EU expanded its membership to include Austria, Finland, and Sweden, continued to implement the Single European Act, progressed toward monetary union, and became an advocate for progress on investment issues in the WTO. Investment issues continued to be central in the regional integration process within the EU, and at the same time they were becoming more salient and contentious in its external relations, especially in its relations with the USA.

6.5 Investment Protection: Political Risk Insurance Programmes

As FDI continued to increase in all parts of the world during the late 1990s, and at an especially rapid rate in a few large developing countries, MNEs' home governments expanded their political risk insurance programmes that protected investors against losses from contract repudiation, currency transfer restrictions, war, expropriation, and other 'political risks'. Many of these programmes had begun as early as the 1950s and had grown over the years, but they became more prominent and extensive during the 1990s, particularly for investments in the countries of Central and Eastern Europe. In many instances, the programmes were complemented by loan guarantee programmes and other subsidies to encourage outward investment. At the multilateral level, the Multilateral Investment Guarantee Agency (MIGA) at the World Bank provided an additional facility for investment projects that would not otherwise be able to obtain coverage against political risks because of gaps in the national programmes.

6.6 Conclusion

The period of the second half of the 1990s, therefore, was marked by several key features:

- Though the period was fundamentally different from earlier periods because of the investment agreements in place in the WTO, many of the basic concepts and underlying issues that had been at the centre of efforts to create a multilateral regime for investment during the previous half-century remained highly pertinent—for instance, application of the principles of most favoured nation and national treatment and conflicts over exceptions to them.
- The potential impact on investment of many of the Uruguay Round agreements became increasingly apparent as they were implemented in the WTO.
- International agencies in addition to the WTO became increasingly involved in the development of the investment regime; this included the OECD.
- The combination of sectoral agreements in telecommunications and information technology significantly liberalized two of the most economically important (and closely related) industries in nearly all parts of the world.
- The continuing proliferation of initiatives and agreements at the regional level added more layers and overlapping relationships across the bilateral and multilateral levels as well as the regional level.
- There was increasing conflict about specific, tangible issues of investment liberalization and protection, as the entire international regime became more salient at all levels.
- Reaching new international agreements that were responsive to the multiple linkages among investment, trade, and technology transfer posed formidable analytic and diplomatic challenges.
- There was increasing interest in the regulatory issues that had been at the centre of the FDI-MNE agenda in the 1940s and 1970s but that had been largely ignored in the 1980s and early 1990s.
- There was continuing reticence to address technically complex but economi-

cally significant issues that would be of central importance to a comprehensive investment regime—issues such as competition policy, investment incentives (subsidies), and transfer pricing and other tax issues that had been shunted off the agenda in the past.

- Further efforts to address investment issues in the WTO encountered many obstacles, including the periodic opposition of key countries such as India, a division of opinion among the EU and its member countries, caution about assuming a leadership role on the part of Japan, and the continuation of substantial elements of unilateralism, bilateralism, and regionalism in the policies of the USA.

As the nearly worldwide liberalization trends of the 1980s and early 1990s were reflected in the tangible institutional developments of the late 1990s, the terms of the discussions about the development of the system shifted. Thus, there was not only an expansion of the geographic scope and policy coverage of the international investment system during the 1990s, there was also an expansion of the analytic and diplomatic discussions of the substantive issues about the future evolution of the system. In those discussions, 'architectural' issues often became more salient than ideological issues; questions about design replaced questions about assumptions. For instance, at the multilateral level, there were issues about the relationship between the MFN provisions of the GATS at the WTO and the provisions on services industries in the MAI negotiations at the OECD. At the regional level, there were issues about the conflicting provisions of the NAFTA and the Mercosur for Chile, which signed agreements with both. Many of the basic institutional design questions of the early 1990s, when the institutions were being created, continued into the late 1990s; but they were joined by a variety of additional questions about the implementation of earlier agreements and about the proliferation of yet more institutional arrangements.

There was not only a proliferation of multilateral, regional, and bilateral agreements, there were also 'plurilateral' sectoral agreements (the Energy Charter Treaty) and 'minilateral' sub-regional agreements (the G3 of Colombia, Mexico, and Venezuela). Thus, relationships across *levels of agreements* became increasingly complex and added to the 'patchwork' problem—issues that receive more detailed attention in Chapter 7. An additional element of complexity that contributed to an exacerbation of the patchwork problem was the increasingly apparent overlaps, gaps, and inconsistencies across types of agreements—that is, the linkages among investment policies, trade policies, competition policies, and other types of policies—issues that are considered more fully in Chapters 8 and 9.

Beyond the specific architectural issues about the design of the system and the relationships among its elements, however, there were still significant unresolved questions about the basic nature of the new regime. The policy pendulum had clearly swung far enough in the direction of government policy liberalization and away from control of MNEs so that specific and binding new liberalization measures could be adopted and implemented; but there were at least two sets of important issues about the scope of the new system that remained to be resolved. Those issues concerned, first, the increasing use of government FDI subsidies to attract investors; and, second, the competition policies of governments and anti-competitive practices of firms. These two sets of issues had been largely ignored in international investment agreements at all levels; yet both would be central to a regime that was truly 'liberal' in the classic meaning of the term. Whether and how these issues would receive serious attention in further efforts to expand the international investment system became central issues at the turn of the century. These and other questions about linkages across policy areas and relationships across levels of international agreements are the focus of the chapters in the next section of the book.

The political context in which these issues were being addressed at the end of the millennium was significantly different from any other period in the previous half-century; the differences reflected changes in the configuration of interests, the lines of conflict–cooperation, the distribution of power, and the leadership roles of key countries. All of these changes were evident among both developing and developed countries. Many developing countries (for instance, several countries in South-East Asia) had become source countries as well as recipient countries for FDI, and they consequently experienced a transformation of their interests in relation to investment issues. Many developing countries that had had restrictive policies in the past became some of the world's most open, liberalized economies on investment issues (for instance, Argentina and Chile). At the same time, as major developing countries in Asia and Latin America grew economically, their political influence also increased. So, although Brazil and India, in particular, continued to be important leaders, and sometime obstacles to liberalization measures, their influence was more widely shared with other developing countries than in the past—and their own preferences had become less consistently opposed to those of countries that advocated further liberalization.

The combination of shifts in the ideological tendencies—and the economic and political position of many developing countries—altered the international political landscape on investment issues, at the same time as there were important shifts occurring among the developed countries. The USA had become the world's principal host country as well as home country, and its commitment to open investment policies became increasingly ambiguous. Its ability and willingness to assume a leadership position on multilateral issues, furthermore, were more widely doubted. The 'hegemon' that had periodically led multilateral efforts to liberalize international economic relations seemed no longer so committed or so focused as it had been during much of the previous half-century. In fact, its position was in some respects akin to its position at the time of the efforts to create the ITO—with an executive branch inclined to support multilateral efforts and a legislative branch of divided opinions, with much hostility toward multilateral institutions. There was a remarkably parallel set of circumstances separated by half a century: three US administrations assumed a significant leadership role from the early to late 1940s in international negotiations and domestic politicking to create the ITO but then conceded defeat by the US Congress; subsequently, three US administrations spent a decade in the 1980s and 1990s to reach an agreement to create the WTO and then witnessed a congressional attempt to limit the strengthened dispute settlement procedures that were at the core of the WTO (and this from a Congress that had itself specifically instructed the US administration to achieve such a strengthening in the Uruguay Round negotiations). More generally, the US pursuit of a 'plurilateral' approach to international economic issues, which persisted and even gained strength in the late 1990s, tended to undermine its traditional commitment to multilateralism and consequently often confuse other countries.

As a result of these tendencies in the USA, there was room for other countries to exert a greater leadership role than in the past. Although the EU in fact began to take a more assertive and public role on investment issues in the WTO, the fact that representation in the OECD was still in the hands of the individual member countries (who disagreed on some key issues) limited the EU's ability to fill some of the vacuum left by the USA. Japan, meanwhile, continued to be cautious in both the WTO and OECD. Occasionally, however, other countries such as Canada, Australia, and the Nordic countries took the initiative.

In any case, the political leadership roles, policy preferences, and patterns of conflict and cooperation were all rather fluid among developed and developing countries at the end of the 1990s. Yet the increased salience of investment issues as a result of the dramatic increases in FDI flows during the 1990s ensured that they would become both more contentious and more complex in political terms. While the economic conditions of the late 1990s were therefore tending to raise the political profile of investment issues, political conditions were making it less clear how they would be addressed and resolved. These economic and political conditions will be important determinants of the resolution of the substantive policy problems that are addressed in more detail in the next section of the book.

Notes

1. There was a significant exaggeration in the common estimates of inward FDI in China because of data problems associated with the widespread practice of domestic Chinese investors first moving funds out of China, especially to Hong Kong, and then bringing them back in as 'FDI' to qualify for FDI subsidies; at least until the reversion of Hong Kong to China in June 1997, therefore, the estimates of inward FDI in China in a meaningful sense probably should have been about two-thirds to three-quarters of the nominal estimates.
2. A Draft Convention on the Protection of Foreign Property was completed by the OECD in the mid-1960s, and a related set of principles was accepted by the OECD in 1967. However, the Convention was never formally adopted, nor would the principles have been binding on member governments in any case.

Notes

Part III

Policy Problems

7

Policy Interactions
Regional and Multilateral Arrangements

This section of the book comprises a series of chapters focusing upon issues which have major multinational corporate and FDI dimensions but which are not tackled adequately within the existing framework of rules. The present chapter is designed to review the state of play with regard to regional integration agreements especially in respect of foreign direct investment, to assess their compatability with developing multilateral arrangements, and to make suggestions to facilitate greater integration in the future. Agreements at regional levels (in the latter case not focused specifically on FDI) have grown rapidly in the past and seem likely to continue to do so in future as part of the whole process of liberalization of the world economy. There has been considerable concern aroused by regional integration agreements, such as the European Union (EU) or the North American Free Trade Agreement (NAFTA), because of fears that they will act as 'stumbling blocks' rather than 'building blocks' in the development of an integrated and liberal world economy (Lawrence, 1995; Kobrin, 1995).

7.1 An Overview of Regional-Level Arrangements

It is important to recognize initially that regional integration agreements do not usually have as their sole or prime purpose the liberalization (or indeed regulation) of foreign direct investment. Most of the focus of analysis of free trade areas, customs unions, or common markets, which are included within the generic term 'regional integration agreements' (RIAs), is trade liberalization.

In total 109 agreements were notified to the GATT between 1948 and 1994, although a number of these have ceased to be operative and others have been modified or superseded. An overview of recent developments is presented in Box 7.1. The WTO (1995*a*) highlighted three main features of post-war regional integration agreements. First, integration has chiefly been centred in Western Europe, with these countries accounting for 76 of the 109 post-war RIAs; and 24 of the 33 agreements notified to GATT in the years 1990–4 (the main growth period) were represented by trade agreements concluded with Central and East European countries. Nevertheless, at the beginning of 1995, with the exception of Hong Kong and Japan, virtually all WTO

Box 7.1

Worldwide Activity in Regional Integration Agreements[a]

During the early 1990s, significant developments occurred among regional integration agreements (RIAs) worldwide.

Europe

Developments in Europe were among the most numerous and rapid. Implementation of the Single Market programme within the EU progressed quickly; the European Economic Area (EEA) was formed between Austria, Finland, Iceland, Liechtenstein, Norway, Sweden, and the EU (Austria, Finland, and Sweden have acceded to the EU); several Central and East European countries formed association agreements with the EU (Hungary and Poland have applied for EU membership); and the EU entered into free trade agreements with the Baltic states, a customs union with Turkey, and cooperation and partnership agreements with several states of the former USSR.

Western hemisphere

The trend toward regional blocs accelerated. NAFTA was accompanied by formation of the Southern Cone Common Market (Mercosur), and of numerous, overlapping RIAs between several Latin American countries, such as Colombia and Venezuela. Among existing RIAs, the Andean Pact and the Central American Common Market (CACM) agreed on common external tariffs, and the Caribbean Community (CARICOM) became more active.

Africa

There were some moves toward greater integration. With the recent devaluation of the CFA franc, the Economic and Customs Union of Central African States (UDEAC) moved forward on a number of fronts, including carrying out a common external tariff, replacing quantitative restrictions with tariffs, and phasing out intra-UDEAC duties. In eastern and southern Africa, a Cross-Border Initiative—co-sponsored by the African Development Bank, the Commission of the European Communities, the IMF, and the World Bank—was launched as a pragmatic step toward economically integrating thirteen countries in the sub-region.

East Asia

Economic integration mainly reflected private market forces. The Association of South-East Asian Nations (ASEAN) signed a pact (the ASEAN Free Trade Agreement, or AFTA); the South Asian Association for Regional Cooperation (SAARC) agreed to draft a preferential trading arrangement; and the Asia Pacific Economic Cooperation forum (APEC), as part of its increased activity, agreed to include Chile, Mexico, and Papua New Guinea as members, and announced plans to lower trade and investment barriers by the year 2020.

Middle East

The Gulf Cooperation Council (GCC) liberalized movements of capital and labour, worked toward setting up a common external tariff, and held talks with the EU about a possible economic cooperation agreement. The Economic Cooperation Organization signed on several former states of the USSR as members. There was little movement on ambitious plans for integration within the Arab Common Market (ACM) and the Arab Maghreb Union (AMU), which were established in the 1960s.

Note: [a]A list of RIAs in force as of January 1995 is contained in Appendix 7.1.

Source: Shiells, 1995.

member countries were parties to at least one preferential agreement. In fact all countries will be included if APEC is formalized as a free trade area by the year 2020.

A second feature of regional integration has been the small number of agreements established by developing countries that have met their timetables for the creation of a free trade area or customs union. Explanations relate to the differing policy objectives of member states, the incompatibility of inward-oriented development policies and regional integration, and the unfavourable external environment of the 1970s and early 1980s.

Third, the level of regional integration achieved and the coverage of the agreements has varied widely. Free trade areas are the commonest form of agreement, with a distinction between reciprocal and non-reciprocal agreements; in the former each member agrees to reduce or eliminate barriers to trade whereas non-reciprocal agreements have been designed to assist the trade expansion of developing countries without a requirement for reciprocity. More advanced forms of regional integration, such as customs unions, are limited to very few agreements, such as the EU, CARICOM, and Mercosur (see Box 7.2). Reflecting this, most agreements are simply concerned with tariff elimination rather than the removal of non-tariff barriers. Product coverage focuses upon industrial products and generally excludes agricultural, fishing, forest, and mining products. Some agreements have been extended or superseded by later arrangements which have extended the scope of liberalization; and, paralleling the widening of the multilateral agenda to cover services and the protection of intellectual property, RIAs have also begun to include these areas of activity.

As is evident from the definitions of types of agreement, FDI has generally been a less important objective than trade in RIAs: as has been shown in Chapter 4, the EU does not have an FDI policy *per se* and most measures with implications for FDI and MNEs have other major objectives (Box 4.4); there were exceptions, of course, such as the (now superseded) Decision 24 of the Cartagena Agreement within the Andean Sub-regional Economic Group (Box 4.3) which specified common regulations governing foreign capital movements, trademarks, patents, and licences.

International provisions on regional integration agreements

As many authors have noted, RIAs are, in a trade sense, discriminatory by definition since they contravene Article I of the GATT on MFN treatment (Hoekman and Kostecki, 1995; Thorstensen, 1996). However, Article XXIV permits departure from MFN treatment for free trade areas and customs unions provided that (see Box 7.3):

- the integration arrangements do not raise trade barriers against other members;
- agreements eliminate tariffs and other trade restrictions on 'substantially all' exchanges between partners within a 'reasonable' length of time;
- other members are notified of the details of the arrangements, and the GATT may establish a Working Party to ascertain if these conditions are met.

In practice, the provisions of Article XXIV have not been strictly observed since 1957 when the GATT decided not to issue a formal ruling on the compatibility of the

Box 7.2

Mercosur

Mercosur—*Mercosul* in Portuguese—is an acronym for the Common Market of the South, created under the Treaty of Asunción by the governments of Argentina, Brazil, Paraguay, and Uruguay in 1991.

Despite its name, it is still a long way from being a common market, because free movement of labour remains a distant and difficult prospect. But it has come a long way. Most trade within Mercosur is already tariff-free, although free trade in all products will not be realized until 2000. By then, agreements on cars and sugar should have been concluded.

A common external tariff has also been adopted on most products. But the group will not become a full customs union until 2006. Then Paraguay and Uruguay should adopt for all products the common external tariff, which ranges from zero to 20 per cent, five years after the target date for Brazil and Argentina to do the same.

Mercosur has also widened. Chile acceded in October 1996 as an associate member, meaning it will become part of the group's free trade zone without adopting the common external tariff. Bolivia, a member of the Andean Pact trade area, negotiated a similar association in December.

Negotiations for a free trade association with other members of the Andean group - Colombia, Ecuador, Peru, and Venezuela—could start this year. Talks with Mexico may follow soon after.

The group is also in talks—going slowly—to establish a trade area with the European Union.

Since its members started reducing tariffs on one another's products in 1991, trade within Mercosur has grown rapidly—at an average 27 per cent a year from 1990 to 1995, at a time when members' trade with the rest of the world expanded an annual 7.5 per cent. One-fifth of the four countries' foreign trade is now conducted with the other three Mercosur members, compared with 9 per cent in 1990.

Trade between Brazil and Argentina has quadrupled since 1990 to more than $15bn. last year and is forecast to double again in the next six years.

Some critics have seen this growth as a sign that the group may be a stumbling block to free trade, rather than a building block. Supporters retorted that the growth of intra-Mercosur trade reflected rapid growth in the region's imports from all sources since the economies were opened at the turn of the decade.

As Mercosur has progressed, the difficulties of integration have become more apparent. The region's infrastructure is ill-equipped to deal with the growth of trade that has already taken place. More fundamentally, perhaps, integration has reached the stage where a range of coordinated policies is now widely seen as necessary. These include a unified competition code, a common anti-dumping policy, and the need to incorporate services into the Mercosur agreement. Tax harmonization is another issue.

Source: Adapted from *Financial Times*, 1997c.

Box 7.3

WTO Provisions on Regional Integration Agreements

Article XXIV. This Article is the principal one dealing with customs unions and free trade areas. It provides a number of rules governing such agreements, including notification and review by the contracting parties acting jointly. Agreements must meet the 'substantially-all-trade' requirement, and members of a regional integration agreement must have a trade policy with respect to third countries that is not on the whole higher or more restrictive than the individual policies prior to the agreement.

Grandfathering. Certain then existing preferential trade arrangements were exempted from the MFN requirement at the time of GATT's inception, including British Imperial Preferences, and preferences granted by the Benelux customs union and the French Union (Article 1:2). However, these preferences were capped and their significance reduced in the course of multilateral tariff-cutting exercises. If agreed by the contracting parties acting jointly, pre-existing regional integration agreements may be so exempted (grandfathered) at the request of new members at the time of their accession (for example, the customs union between Switzerland and Liechtenstein is provided for in Switzerland's GATT accession protocol).

Part IV on 'Trade and Development', added to the GATT in 1965, provides for special measures intended to promote the trade and development of developing contracting parties. Prior to the 1979 Enabling Clause, Part IV was invoked by developing country participants with respect to preferential trade arrangements which did not meet the 'substantially all trade' requirement of Article XXIV.

In some instances, parties to agreements with developing countries have invoked Part IV in Article XXIV working parties to justify preferential, non-reciprocal access for developing country members (for example, the European Community in the context of the First, Second, and Third Lomé Conventions). Views among contracting parties differ regarding the merits of linking Article XXIV with Part IV.

The Enabling Clause, agreed in 1979 during the Tokyo Round of negotiations, includes a legal cover for preferential trade agreements between developing countries, subject to certain conditions, including transparency. Among contracting parties, views differ as to whether the Enabling Clause covers regional integration agreements (customs unions and free trade areas) for which provision is also made in Article XXIV.

Article XXV. The contracting parties acting jointly have occasionally granted waivers for sectoral free trade agreements (for example, the European Coal and Steel Community in 1952 and the 1965 Canada–United States Auto Pact). In one early instance, a waiver was obtained by France for its proposed customs union with Italy, not then a GATT member.

Source: WTO, 1995*a*: box 2.

Treaty of Rome with the GATT provisions. (The explanation was political: a finding of incompatibility could have led to withdrawal of the EEC six member states from the GATT.) Of the 70 regional agreements examined by the GATT, 4 were deemed to be compatible with Article XXIV but no arrangement was formally declared to be incompatible with it (reflecting the need to reach unanimous conclusions). As Box 7.3 shows, special arrangements apply to developing country RIAs, which, under the Enabling Clause of 1979, may allow member states to apply lower tariffs to each other's trade than are applied to imports originating from non-members. Like the GATT, the General Agreement on Trade in Services allows for regional integration agreements subject to conditions and surveillance. Hoekman and Kostecki (1995) observe that the 'substantially all trade' criterion of the GATT Article XXIV is stronger than the 'substantial sectoral coverage' in the GATS, and so too are the rules applying to the magnitude of liberalization required. In both the GATT and the GATS, compensation of non-members for the raising of external barriers is foreseen; but the GATS allows affected states to seek binding arbitration if there is no agreement on compensation.

In their evaluation of the WTO rules, Hoekman and Kostecki (1995: 231) conclude that:

> WTO disciplines are relatively weak. An example is the absence of any disciplines with respect to preferential rules of origin in the WTO . . . Another is the lack of a requirement that RIAs be open to new members that are willing to satisfy their obligations . . . Multilateral surveillance is limited—the WTO Secretariat has no mandate to monitor the trade effects of RIAs. WTO consistency is not sufficient to ensure that RIAs are a complement to the multilateral trading system . . . developing countries may be able to opt out of GATT's disciplines on RIAs altogether by invoking the enabling clause, and negotiate preferential tariff reduction agreements for a limited number of products. Such agreements can greatly distort trade flows, generating substantial welfare-reducing trade diversion.
>
> Notwithstanding these comments, RIAs may embody many good practices and some go far beyond the WTO in terms of liberalizing markets.

The authors go on to comment that, in respect of trade policies, the challenge was to pursue multilaterally what the more advanced RIAs were implementing internally. The latter could, therefore, act as 'experimental laboratories' (Hoekman and Kostecki, 1995: 231) and as drivers for further multilateral trade liberalization.

The WTO rules on regional integration agreements are clearly trade focused, although since the GATS' rules extend to the coverage of FDI, there is an investment component in them. In respect of FDI specifically, the OECD instruments include some reference to regional agreements. The non-discrimination principle of the binding Codes of Liberalization of Capital Movements applies to the pre-establishment phase of direct investment (but not to the post-establishment phase which is covered by the non-binding National Treatment Instrument). Under Article 10 of the Code there is exemption from the principle of non-discrimination for countries which belong to a special customs or monetary system. The consequence is that non-discrimination applies to FDI in non-EU OECD member states but not to investment in European Union countries: therefore, the latter are able to maintain preferential arrangements among themselves (Smith, 1996). In general, however, the absence of multilateral rules and of terms for foreign direct investment in regional agreements means that the characteristics of FDI rules in such agreements are determined by the members themselves. The possibility of widely varying rules arises and of inconsistencies and discrimination. Before considering these, the chapter reviews the different types of regional integration agreements and their trade and investment effects in theory and practice.

Types of regional integration agreements

Traditionally a distinction has been made between four main types of regional integration agreements, namely, the free trade area, where member countries remove trade restrictions among themselves while maintaining their own trade policies against third countries; the customs union, where, in addition, a common external tariff is adopted against third countries; the common market, which also permits free movement of factors of production among member countries; and the economic union which extends the integration process to include some economic policy harmonization in the macroeconomic and regulatory spheres.

Laird (1996) has developed a more refined categorization which takes account of the realities of regional agreements in the post-war world and which suggests some areas where FDI liberalization would occur. For instance, free trade areas may include provisions to liberalize investment rules (at a minimum permitting repatriation of capital, profits, and royalties). With full economic integration and economic and monetary union, common policies will exist in areas such as competition and government procurement and a supra-national legal framework pertaining to technical barriers, intellectual property, etc. These clearly impact upon FDI and require national treatment if discrimination is not to exist between foreign- and locally owned enterprises.

It is important to consider more fully *how FDI liberalization might evolve in an RIA*, especially now that the attraction of inward investment and the facilitation of outward investment are much higher on the policy agenda than formerly. Table 7.1 presents a possible evolution of FDI liberalization measures, linked to the form of regional integration agreements. In the *free trade area*, countries might offer on a multilateral basis similar terms to those included in their existing bilateral investment treaties. There is an assumption that this would be coordinated across the member states and hence organizational arrangements would be necessary to implement these measures (just as the internal tariff elimination programme is coordinated).

Right of entry and establishment with exemption could follow in the *customs union*, with, in addition, the harmonization of national treatment exceptions among the member states. The main deepening of liberalization measures would, however, occur at the *common market* stage. Measures to permit the free movement of capital internally and externally are a prerequisite for the development of RIA's own multinational enterprises. It is arguable that in future this might occur earlier in the life of an RIA given the importance of non-trade modes in market servicing in the 1990s, although the experience of countries like the USA and UK was that existing MNEs at least were not particularly hampered by exchange controls, given their ability to

Table 7.1 FDI Liberalization Within Forms of Regional Integration Arrangements

Regional integration agreement	FDI liberalization measure [a]
Free trade area	• Definitions of investment. • National treatment subject to a number of exceptions; most favoured nation treatment; fair and equitable treatment. • Minimum international standards of protection; recourse to international means for settlement of investment disputes. • Ability to transfer funds (capital, profits, royalties).
Customs union	• Right of entry and establishment, with exemption for particular industries or activities. • Harmonization of national treatment exceptions across member countries.
Common market	• Free movement of capital and ending of all exchange controls. • Abolition of or common rules on inward acquisitions. • Common rules on FDI in privatizations. • Limitation on investment incentives and prohibition of a range of performance requirements. • Admission of foreign senior personnel permitted. • Rollback of exemptions on right of entry and establishment, and of national treatment exceptions.
Economic and monetary union	• Focus upon market contestability, modal neutrality, and policy coherence in respect of: – Continued use of NTBs such as anti-dumping duties. – Competition policy, including application to joint ventures and strategic alliances. – Service industries. – Government procurement. – Participation in R & D programmes. – Harmonization of company law.

Note: [a]A critical issue which arises at stages 3 and 4 is the extent to which RIA members will be prepared to liberalize unilaterally, as opposed to requiring reciprocity in return for liberalization.

Source: Authors.

borrow abroad. At this stage, a start would be made on strengthening rules in respect of national treatment and MFN—the ultimate objective would be an unqualified national treatment and MFN—to offer international investors strong protection from discrimination and allow them to compete on an equal footing with other foreign investors in the market. Again moves would be initiated to ensure modal neutrality through, for example, freedom to undertake inward acquisitions (or at least common rules since there might be national security reasons for some restrictions) and common rules on FDI in privatizations. Finally, limitations on investment incentives to prevent beggar-thy-neighbour competitive bidding and the prohibition of a range of trade-related investment measures would be important.

At the stage of *economic and monetary union*, the main emphasis would be on trying to ensure market contestability, modal neutrality, and policy coherence (UNCTAD, 1996*a*) to avoid discrimination between, for example, trade and FDI; between greenfield projects, acquisitions, joint ventures, and strategic alliances; and between state-owned and private enterprises whether foreign or domestic. Ensuring foreign and domestic firms have equal access to government procurement contracts and R & D contracts and programmes is also critical to ensure competition and economic efficiency. The deeper this integration proceeds, however, the more it will run into very deep-rooted cultural barriers and resistance. A focus upon consistency of government objectives and policies across a broad range of issues should be a further aim.

The FDI liberalization programme in Table 7.1 is ahead of the market in a number of respects. The European Union is by far the most advanced regional grouping, but, as will be shown later in this chapter, it has failed in many ways to recognize the importance of FDI. The background studies for the Single Market programme, for instance, scarcely mentioned the international investment dimension, either inward or outward. Of course, the era in which the Treaty of Rome was written was very different from that forty years later. The consequence is that national treatment exceptions have not yet been harmonized across countries (an objective for the customs union stage in Table 7.1); and little progress has been made on a number of the common market liberalization measures. On the other hand, continuing attempts are being made to tackle discriminatory government procurement; competition policy was included in the Treaty of Rome itself; foreign companies are in theory permitted to participate in Community R & D programmes alongside indigenous partners and subject to certain safeguards on technology transfer; and a programme is in place to liberalize service industries. The different degrees of emphasis as compared with Table 7.1 essentially reflect the priority upon internal liberalization.

It is important not to take the parallels between trade and investment liberalization too far. External liberalization in a trade sense is determined through multilateral trade negotiation and not by the RIA unilaterally, and the limited progress in dealing with NTBs is a reflection of this. The question that arises in respect of FDI liberalization, similarly, is why foreign MNEs should get unconditional access to the internal market of the RIA, if the liberalization is not reciprocated in the multinational's home market. The OECD has noted a rise in such reciprocity conditions at the same time as investment liberalization is occurring internationally. This is one area where regional integration agreements may act as a stumbling block to multilateral liberalization in investment.

Trade and investment effects of regional integration agreements

As with theoretical contributions (from the classic work of Viner, 1950, onwards), most of the empirical work on RIAs has been trade focused. The obvious question is whether the growing role of trade in the world economy has been accompanied by an increasing share of trade conducted on a regional basis; and the related question of whether regional integration (which in effect means EU integration) has expanded intra-regional trade. In Western Europe, the share of intra-regional trade in total trade rose from 53 per cent to 70 per cent between 1958 and 1993. Most of this rise occurred up to 1973; the limited further increase between 1973 and 1993 is explained largely by the accession of the UK and the reorientation of its trade from outside to inside the EU. In other areas the changes in shares of intra-regional trade were minor compared with those in Europe (see WTO, 1995*a*: tables 3 and 4). Prima facie, therefore, the data lend support to the theoretical conclusion that regional integration increases the share of trade carried out among participants. By contrast with the intra-regional trade position, Western Europe's extra-regional trade share declined somewhat over the years since 1958; this was in contrast to the rising extra-regional trade share of North America. It starts to draw attention to a problem which has been identified by policy-makers in the EU. In a global era, it is arguable that there is a further type of trade diversion which is of great practical significance. This concerns the diversion of member country exports from countries outside the RIA to countries inside the RIA where competition is less severe and their high-cost production is not disadvantaged. In the context of the EU it is suggested that integration has meant that companies have failed to capitalize upon the fastest growing markets in the world, namely, those in the Asia Pacific area.

There have been numerous *ex ante* and *ex post* attempts to estimate formally the trade effects of RIAs. Considering the customs union between the original six members of the EEC, empirical research indicates that trade creation exceeded trade diversion in the case of manufactures, while the opposite was true for trade in agricultural products (because of the protectionist Common Agricultural Policy) (Young, 1975). *Ex ante* studies on the effects of the EU's Single Market programme on third countries suggest a decline in extra-EU imports in virtually every product category: these losses were magnified when account was taken of efficiency gains at the level of EU firms.

In the case of the Canada–United States Free Trade Agreement (FTA), *ex ante* estimates suggest positive welfare effects for Canada, but negligible impacts for the USA because of its larger size. A decline in trade with third countries as a whole is also indicated, the magnitude being greater if economies of scale were realized in Canada. Studies of NAFTA show welfare gains for all three countries, and small trade effects for third countries, with some estimates, indeed, suggesting net trade creation.

In most of this work the stimulus to third country exports from a higher rate of growth (dynamic effects) in RIA member countries has been ignored. In reality, except for agricultural products, absolute declines in imports from third countries have been rare.

By comparison with work in the trade area, the theory of FDI and RIAs is much less advanced (WTO, 1995*a*). Firms based outside the RIA will have a variety of incentives to locate within the regional area. First, there is a marketing reason concerning improved service to customers, where production is viewed as a marketing tool. In this respect it is interesting to note that the market shares of US motor vehicle producers in the EU are positively correlated with the establishment of an assembly plant in particular countries. Second, when there are increasing returns to scale, the formation of a larger integrated market together with an increase in competition will lower unit production costs, and improve the attractiveness of locating within the RIA. Third, the dynamic effects of internal liberalization on per capita income growth will further increase the market potential and the possibilities for unit cost reduction. Fourth, local producers may argue for protection to enable them to rationalize and exploit the benefits from the RIA (the equivalent of the infant industry argument). Foreign companies may jump the tariff or non-tariff wall by locating production inside the RIA. Fifth, FDI may be undertaken by foreign exporters with the aim of creating local employment and thus heading off arguments by labour interests lobbying for import protection.

There are also issues relating to the nature of the inward investment, with acquisition entry being the preferred route in mature industries characterized by slow growth and excess capacity.

Assuming that the increased investment is not financed from a higher internal or external rate of savings, it will direct FDI flows away from one or more locations outside the regional integration agreement.

A further set of effects concern the rationalization and relocation of existing production consequent on the removal of internal tariff barriers (in a free trade area) and non-tariff barriers (in a common market / economic union). Companies may respond by a variety of strategies, including centralization of production in one or a smaller number of optimally sized manufacturing facilities (horizontal integration); or location of different parts of the production process in different countries according to their relative labour / capital intensity and the comparative advantage of member states (vertical integration). The relocation costs will, of course, be high and the net effects on FDI are unknown. It should be noted that both third country MNEs and host RIA MNEs will be affected somewhat similarly. However, the point has been made that indigenous MNEs are at a disadvantage in that the political and cultural pressures upon them to retain existing facilities are much greater than for non-member multinational enterprises (Young et al., 1991).[1]

Most of the empirical evidence relates to the experience of the European Union, although the results are not always clear-cut. The studies tend to agree that there was a structural increase in FDI inflows into the EEC in the 1960s, but there is less agreement as to whether this occurred because of the creation of the customs union. The increase in tariff discrimination had a weak positive impact on inflows; on the other hand, variables such as market size and market growth were much more significant. It has been suggested (WTO, 1995*a*) that the Single Market programme could cause greater investment diversion since it involves the whole or partial removal of NTBs and market access restrictions in service sectors. And the statistics on inflows of FDI in the second half of the 1980s tend to support this view. Clegg (1996) re-examines the facts and empirical findings on US FDI into the EU over the period 1950–91.

In respect of the specific effects of non-tariff barriers on outsider firms, there is some survey evidence relating to the EU. This shows for Japanese and other Asian firms a switch from exporting to FDI as a result of the announcement of anti-dumping investigations or the imposition of anti-dumping duties. (Some authors have argued that such import restrictions merely accelerated the timing of the investments.) The EU actually also imposed anti-dumping duties on imports to the so-called screwdriver assembly facilities which were established to circumvent the anti-dumping duties on the imported finished product; these duties operated unless the assembly plant achieved 40 per cent local content, but the EU regulation concerned was abolished because it contravened GATT rules.

Evidence on relocations and rationalization within the EU is extensive but mainly case study or survey based.

7.2 Regional Agreements: Building Blocks or Stumbling Blocks?

The theory and evidence above, combined with arguments derived from political economy, have stimulated an active and vociferous debate on whether regional integration agreements and the WTO system are complementary or competing in efforts to achieve a more integrated world economy.

Focusing upon trade issues, the arguments have been summarized as follows (*Financial Times*, 1996*c*). The proponents of RIAs argue that:

- Rules can be more easily negotiated in a closed group of relatively homogeneous or at least like-minded countries than in the heterogeneous WTO (the same argument has been made for basing negotiations on a multilateral investment agreement in the OECD rather than the WTO).
- Regional trade agreements are the best alternative if global liberalization is not feasible. And the nine years of negotiations to reach an agreement in the Uruguay Round suggest that multilateralism has been taken to its limits.
- Regional trade agreements provide a stimulus to liberalization at the global level.
- Regional trade liberalization is beneficial since proximity determines whether countries are natural partners in an RIA.
- Trade liberalization (regarded as preferential) between natural trading partners is economically beneficial.

Wolf (*Financial Times*, 1996*c*) rejects these arguments, suggesting that, first, the Uruguay Round has to be regarded as a success and bodes well for future negotiations at a multilateral level. Second, rather than stimulating global liberalization, RIAs may actually raise obstacles to further liberalization by diverting time and effort and creating vested interests. Third, the idea that there is a link between proximity and natural trading relationships is not accepted; and in any event, rather than determining membership in advance, it would be preferable to open membership to any country which was interested in developing rules in areas not covered by the WTO. Fourth, following Bhagwati and Panagariya (1996), trade gains may be small if two partner countries already trade a great deal with each other, since the potential for beneficial additional trade is clearly limited. Alternatively, if trade is diverted towards a high-cost member country away from lower-cost third country suppliers, the losses may be large. A further negative perspective has been added by Krugman (1992), who argued that the idea of open RIAs was almost a contradiction in terms. Since insiders would always have a stronger voice than outsiders, the result could be a world of regions which were more restrictive against trade from the outside.

A balanced perspective on this debate has been presented by the WTO (1995*a*: 56), which concludes that

> regional and multilateral integration initiatives are complements rather than alternatives in the pursuit of more liberal and open trade. Regional integration agreements contain both higher and lower levels of obligation than the WTO. In the latter case, the WTO complements the liberalization achieved at the regional level, while the converse is true in the former case.

It may be concluded, therefore, that both sets of organizations may have a contribution to make to liberalization of the world economy. Some RIAs, particularly the EU, go well beyond the WTO in that there are no tariffs, no safeguard mechanisms, and full binding of policies (Hoekman and Kostecki, 1995). Improvements in WTO rules with respect to regional integration agreements are accepted as being necessary, nevertheless. Although there is still a good deal of debate on the subject, a number of suggestions for improvement have been made (Bhagwati, 1993; WTO, 1995*a*; Hoekman and Kostecki, 1995):

First, Article XXIV of the GATT, which provides legitimacy for RIAs, requires to be strengthened and the process of examining agreements (currently effectively *ex post*) needs to be improved. As the WTO (1995*a*: 64) comments: 'The perceived neglect of the rules and procedures for regional integration agreements not only continues to set questionable precedents, but also has an adverse effect on the credibility of the WTO rules and procedures in other areas.' Associated with this, there is a need to reform the 1979 Enabling Clause which exempts regional agreements among developing countries from the terms laid down in Article XXIV. There is fairly general agreement on this although the proposed reforms differ (see De Melo et al., 1992). Second, the 'substantially all trade' requirement within Article XXIV should be clarified to avoid 'a mass of protectionist-oriented *à la carte* agreements that exclude broad ranges of "sensitive" sectors'. Third, 'hub and spoke' systems (i.e. where two or more third countries are given associate status in an existing RIA, or a third country concludes an agreement with a member of an existing RIA) create dangers of protectionism since there are risks that the hub country will negotiate free trade agreements with the spokes to deal with sensitive trade issues in each case. Multilateral rules concerning the nature of accession clauses in RIAs would satisfy Bhagwati's (1993) proposal that regional agreements be open to new members that are willing to satisfy their obligations. Fourth, there appears to be a case for strengthening multilateral disciplines in respect of rules of origin for regional agreements, particularly free trade areas (see Box 7.4 on rules of origin in free trade areas).

Although a number of the topics discussed above clearly have their parallels on the FDI side, the emphasis in the literature is very much on trade. The linkages, however, stem from the coverage of investment-related issues in the WTO through the Subsidies Code and the Government Procurement agreement, and from the Uruguay

Box 7.4

Rules of Origin

Free trade areas are distinguished by the fact that the members retain their own external tariffs. Because tariff rates generally differ among members, third country exporters would have an incentive to access the market of the higher-tariff members through the market of the lowest-tariff member. To avoid such 'trade deflection', members of a free trade area adopt procedures to determine whether a good entering a member country has been produced within the area and is therefore eligible for duty-free entry.

These procedures are based on *rules of origin*. If all of the inputs and value added in a product have come from one country, there is no difficulty in determining a product's origin. When a product incorporates inputs imported from other countries, or undergoes processing in at least one country in the area and at least one outside the area, one or more of three tests may be used to determine its 'nationality': (1) whether there has been a *change in tariff heading* (CTH) between stages of production (for example, from steel to bicycles); (2) whether the *value of the materials* utilized in transforming the product exceeds a specified percentage of the value of the transformed product, or the *value added* in the country of processing reaches a specified level; and (3) whether there is a list of *specific processing operations* which confer (or do not confer), upon the products involved, the origin of the country in which the operations were carried out.

Such rules are an integral part of all free trade areas. While the basic purpose of rules of origin is to prevent trade deflection, rules of origin in and of themselves may also lead to trade diversion. For example, under NAFTA rules of origin, clothing produced in Mexico gains tariff-free access to the United States market, provided it meets the 'yarn forward' rule, which for many products requires virtually 100 per cent sourcing of inputs in North America. Mexican clothing manufacturers face a choice between sourcing all inputs beyond the fibre stage in North America and obtaining free trade area treatment, or sourcing inputs outside the free trade area at potentially lower cost, but forgoing duty-free access to the United States and Canada. If profits are higher under the first option, Mexican clothing manufacturers will opt for 'North American' status and stop buying from lower-cost third country suppliers. Alternatively, there can be situations in which it is more profitable to select the second option. Generally speaking, the more restrictive the rule of origin, the greater the scope for trade diversion involving intermediate products—up to the point where the origin rule becomes so restrictive that producers opt for the second option.

The potentially restrictive effects of the rules of origin first became an issue in the GATT in the working party examination of the 1960 European Free Trade Area (EFTA). Third countries pointed out that the highly technical process criteria and the requirements of the origin rules could lead to practical difficulties which could adversely affect the trade of third countries. In addition, rules of origin could also discourage the importation of semi-finished inputs or partly processed raw materials. More recently, rules of origin have been recognized as being more susceptible than other, more transparent, measures to influence by domestic protectionist interests. Moreover, the administration of rules of origin imposes additional transaction costs on traders seeking to document whether they satisfy rules of origin. These factors not only tend to restrict imports from third countries, but also diminish the benefits to be gained from preferential trade liberalization for members. There has been a growing debate over the design of rules of origin, especially in the period since the NAFTA negotiations began.

Until recently, origin was an issue confined to merchandise trade, but it is now recognized as being relevant to services trade too. The key issue in service trade is deciding which 'countries' obtain the benefits of an RIA and thus ascertaining the nationality of service providers for the purposes of establishment.

Rules of origin may have investment as well as trade effects. Thus they may be used to 'force' MNEs to invest in the target market in order to avoid the risks associated with change of origin rules. For example, the US multinational Intel complained that changes in the EC's definition of rules of origin for integrated circuits 'forced' it to set up a plant in Ireland.

Source: Adapted from WTO, 1995*a*: 48–9; Woolcock, 1996.

Round TRIMs and TRIPs agreements and the GATS. More generally, the question that requires to be answered is the same one posed at a trade level, namely, *are RIAs from an investment perspective complementary or competing in facilitating the achievement of a more integrated world economy*? In one sense this is easier to answer than on the trade side because of the absence of a comprehensive multilateral investment agreement and the rather preliminary nature of some of the existing accords. Therefore, 'state-of-the-art' elements in existing regional agreements (and the emphasis must be upon the EU and NAFTA) could act as a model for a multilateral accord. But to do this alone would be over-simplistic since it is also necessary to ascertain how far existing regional agreements have been distortionary.

In some industries, the 'natural scale' is no greater than the size of EU or NAFTA markets. MNEs in food or consumer products, previously operating on a country-by-country basis within regional blocs, could reorganize successfully and implement effective regional strategies. In industries where globalization is the norm (e.g. electronics, pharmaceuticals, aerospace) or globalization is emerging (e.g. semiconductors, vehicles), by contrast, regionalism is a significant barrier to optimal scale operations (Kobrin, 1995).

It was shown above that the EU may also have had a distortionary investment-diversion effect (such as in the second half of the 1980s) in encouraging Asian companies in particular to replace or complement exports by production inside the Union market. Such operations are inherently insecure in a global era if motivated by market imperfections.

European Union policies in respect of FDI are presented in Appendix 7.2. Comparing Table 7.2 with this Appendix, it is very clear that the failure to implement a considered and structured FDI policy poses some difficulties for multilateralism, as well, of course, as being substantially ahead in some fields of whatever could possibly emerge from multilateral rule-making in the foreseeable future. The EU presents a classic illustration of the problems that arise in 'patchwork rule-making', that is where policy imperfections might distort market mechanisms in respect of corporate decision-making. With the range of interests in FDI matters in different directorates in the EU, there is inevitably the possibility of overlap, contradictions, and gaps in policy coverage. And when the division of competences between the EU and member states is added, such difficulties not only exist among the EU directorates but between the EU and multilateral organizations, between the EU and member states, and among member states themselves.

Some of the same comments could be made about the NAFTA provisions. Gestrin and Rugman (1996: 63) assert that 'no other multilateral or bilateral investment agreement goes as far as the NAFTA in terms of the scope of the coverage, the depth of coverage or the enforcement of rules'. This is true in respect of FDI rules *per se* and also in its consideration of the interrelatedness of investment, trade, intellectual property protection, and services; but it cannot be compared with the EU which has evolved so much further with its overall integration process. A further important issue concerning the NAFTA derives from the drafting of FDI rules for developed plus a developing country participant (Mexico). The authors (Gestrin and Rugman, 1994) claim that it will both stimulate FDI and also give rise to (second-best) efficiency gains as MNEs rationalize their operations across the three economies.

Table 7.2 presents a summary of the 'strong' and 'weak' investment-related provisions of the NAFTA. The former illustrate areas, for example, where NAFTA instruments go beyond the multilateral rule-making of the Uruguay Round. In this regard,

Table 7.2 Strengths and Weaknesses of the NAFTA's Investment-Related Provisions

Investment-related provisions that are:	Investment-related provisions that can be characterized as:	
	Procedural	Sectoral
Strong	• Dispute-settlement mechanisms • Coverage / definition • Performance requirements • Intellectual property • Negative lists • Accession clause • Promotion of standards harmonization • Temporary entry of business people	• Government procurement • Services (including financial services) • Mexican manufacturing • Land transportation
Weak	• Rules of origin • Subsidies • Competition policy • Anti-dumping	• Energy (Mexico) • Cultural industries (Canada) • Maritime transport (USA) • Air transport (all 3 parties) • Rail transport (Mexico) • Agriculture (all 3 parties)

Source: Gestrin and Rugman, 1996: figure 1.

the restrictions on the use of performance requirements go further than the WTO, first, in prohibiting not only trade balancing and local content requirements (as in the Uruguay Round), but also technology and exclusive supplier requirements with respect to establishment; and, second, in allowing developing countries a five-year phase-out period. The dispute settlement mechanisms, too, have enhanced the role of international rules and administrative structures in governing FDI regimes in the region.

By contrast, NAFTA totally ignores subsidies (reflecting the US position which has prevailed in other fora) and is weak on anti-dumping rules and competition policy. The NAFTA rules of origin too are in some respects *discriminatory*. Thus several NAFTA industries have been granted considerable competitive advantage against non-NAFTA producers through tighter regional content requirements (combined generally with restrictions on duty drawback and related programmes). These include motor vehicles, electronics, textiles and apparel, home appliances, and measuring and testing equipment. In the motor vehicle industry, because of the extensive procedures for determining rules of origin and the relatively high regional content requirements (basically 62.5 per cent), it is difficult for parent firms based outside the region to compete with firms based inside the region. Thus even though many Japanese and German auto firms have affiliates within NAFTA for vehicle assembly, they naturally rely more than their US-based competitors on parts that are supplied through imports from their own affiliates and other firms located outside the region. The NAFTA rules of origin could similarly disadvantage new producers in the region whose traditional supplier networks were based in other regions. It is perhaps these rules more than any other (while necessary for the functioning of free trade agreements) that are potentially protectionist and could encourage beggar-thy-neighbour responses. To cite Gestrin and Rugman (1994: 93), NAFTA 'sets a dangerous example for future regional trade agreements in its limited, but obvious, use of rules of origin to support particular industries'.

The negotiations in the OECD on the Multilateral Agreement on Investment were not complete at time of writing, but in any event it is doubtful if they will deal substantively with regional integration agreements *per se* (as compared with issues which happen to be considered by RIAs, e.g. performance requirements). It would seem, therefore, that improvements could be implemented through the WTO forum which would complement an MAI and also ensure that both the trade and FDI aspects of RIAs were considered concurrently.

Earlier in this section mention was made of necessary changes in WTO rules on RIAs from a trade perspective. If these were to occur, it would be obvious to incorporate an FDI element into Article XXIV of the GATT as well. Certainly the fundamental issue for a multilateral agreement in respect of FDI concerns the inclusion of an RIA clause which would allow regional blocs to continue with internal investment liberalization at a faster pace than external liberalization (Karl, 1996). The argument for this is that it prevents free-riding, that is an automatic extension of the benefits of RIAs to third countries without the latter acceding to the obligations of the agreement. Opponents argue that such a clause would be contrary to a core principle of any international agreement, namely the establishment of equal rights and obligations between all partner countries.

Examining the EU situation, Karl (1996: 46–7) concludes that an RIA clause was needed:

> where, otherwise, MFN treatment would result (a) in a better treatment than national treatment, or (b) would introduce the principles of precedence and direct applicability of European law to non-European investors, or (c) where the treatment of a foreign investor is based on the concept of mutual recognition.

However, the author proposes that such an RIA clause should be defined as narrowly as possible. While referring specifically to the EU situation, there may be ideas here which could be applied more generally.

In redrafting the 'substantially all trade' provision in Article XXIV of the GATT to avoid protectionist *à la carte* agreements, the wording might also include foreign direct investment where the exclusion of sensitive sectors is equally an issue (as NAFTA showed). Again, the necessary reform of the rules of origin provisions should reflect the FDI dimensions too.

7.3 Conclusion

This chapter has attempted to answer three questions. First, whether regional integration agreements are good or bad for foreign direct investment as well as for trade. Second, what lessons can be learned from existing FDI rules for RIAs? And third, how can these FDI rules be improved to ensure their compatibility with multilateral rules and the multilateral agenda. Essentially at present the EU and NAFTA are the two significant blocs which incorporate FDI rules of one form or another; they are a reality and a driving force for multilateral trade and investment liberalization. Therefore, a mechanism has to be found to support the latter while preventing discrimination against the rest of the world. Some suggestions have been made above to facilitate this.

Regionalism represents one of the more important issues on the multilateral investment rules agenda alongside issues such as control over subsidies, efforts to limit anti-dumping actions, and competition policy. This chapter has revealed the potential for discrimination and distortions which could increase as RIAs expand in future, and hence the need for RIA-specific rules in multilateral agreements. As has been shown, the eighteen APEC members are committed to freeing all trade and investment in the Pacific Rim region by 2010 in industrialized countries and by 2020 in developing nations; the APEC agreement is still at an early stage of development (the principles of APEC are presented in Appendix 7.3) and even if there is still a large gap between words and deeds, relationships between members and non-members will raise serious issues. The same potential problems arise with the negotiations to create a Free Trade Area of the Americas (FTAA) by 2005, and more speculatively a transatlantic free trade area. Meantime, the EU will be expanding to encompass many of the countries of Central and Eastern Europe.

Notes

1. Strange (1997) has conceptualized the effects of liberalization measures on flows of FDI into a trading bloc/common market. He identifies six motivations for FDI and distinguishes separately the effects of a relaxation in ownership and entry requirements; liberalization of intra-bloc labour movements; liberalization of intra-bloc capital movements; and reduction of intra-bloc trade barriers.

Appendix 7.1

Regional Integration Agreements Notified to WTO and in Force as of January 1995

Reciprocal Regional Integration Agreements

Europe

European Community (EC)

Austria	Germany	Netherlands
Belgium	Greece	Portugal
Denmark	Ireland	Spain
Finland	Italy	Sweden
France	Luxembourg	United Kingdom

EC free trade agreements with

Estonia	Latvia	Norway
Iceland	Liechtenstein	Switzerland
Israel	Lithuania	

EC association agreements with

Bulgaria	Hungary	Romania
Cyprus	Malta	Slovak Rep.
Czech Rep.	Poland	Turkey

European Free Trade Association (EFTA)

Iceland	Norway	Switzerland
Liechtenstein		

EFTA free trade agreements with

Bulgaria	Israel	Slovak Rep.
Czech Rep.	Poland	Turkey
Hungary	Romania	

Norway free trade agreements with

Estonia	Latvia	Lithuania

Switzerland free trade agreements with

Estonia Latvia Lithuania

Czech Republic and Slovak Republic Customs Union

Central European Free Trade Area

Czech Rep. Poland Slovak Rep.
Hungary

Czech Republic and Slovenia Free Trade Agreement

Slovak Republic and Slovenia Free Trade Agreement

North America

Canada–United States Free Trade Agreement (CUFTA)

North American Free Trade Agreement (NAFTA)

Latin America and the Caribbean

Caribbean Community and Common Market (CARICOM)

Central American Common Market (CACM)

Latin American Integration Association (LAIA)

Andean Pact

Southern Common Market (Mercosur)

Middle East

Economic Cooperation Organization (ECO)

Gulf Cooperation Council (GCC)

Asia

Australia–New Zealand Closer Economic Relations Trade Agreement (CER)

Bangkok Agreement

Common Effective Preferential Scheme for the ASEAN Free Trade Area

Lao People's Dem. Rep. and Thailand Trade Agreement

Other

Israel–United States Free Trade Agreement

Non-Reciprocal Regional Integration Agreements

Europe

EEC-Association of certain non-European countries and territories (EEC-PTOM II)

EEC Cooperation Agreements with

Algeria Lebanon Syria
Egypt Morocco Tunisia
Jordan

ACP-EEC Fourth Lomé Convention

Asia

Australia–Papua New Guinea Agreement

South Pacific Regional Trade Cooperation Agreement (SPARTECA)

Source: WTO, 1995*a*: table 1.

Appendix 7.2

European Union Policies and Foreign Direct Investment

As Chapter 4 showed, European Commission interest in the activities of MNEs dates back to 1973 and its memorandum on *Multinational Undertakings and the Community*. Proposals to the Council of Ministers for rules on MNEs were, however, then withdrawn by the Commission in 1976. Since then there have been few attempts to propose measures focusing specifically on MNEs; although within the agreement on social policy in the Maastricht Treaty (1992), a Directive requires Europe-wide works councils in MNEs above a certain size.

While there is no 'FDI Policy' as such, aspects of many existing policies have applicability to FDI, and these are summarized in Table A7.1.

1. Foreign exchange controls: the Capital Movements Directive (1988) and Article 73 of the Maastricht Treaty prohibit any restrictions on the movement of capital between member states and between member states and third countries. Some member states were granted extensions to enable them to abolish exchange controls as required, with Greece being the last country to liberalize on 16 May 1994. However, member states still have a variety of controls, principally on inward investment. These controls represent permissible exemptions to the OECD Code of Liberalization of Capital Movements and chiefly relate either to takeovers from outside the country or the EU or to sectoral measures in regulated or sensitive industries (where in addition reciprocity requirements may prevail). The Commission has for some time attempted to persuade member states to remove the most blatant or discriminatory of these: examples relate to the authorization procedures for FDI in France and to the 29.5 per cent equity limitations on foreign ownership in British Aerospace plc and Rolls-Royce plc imposed by the UK. The applicability of Article 73 to these national rules is clearly a test case for EU policy in the FDI area, and this Article might, indeed, provide the basis for a legal code on FDI or policy harmonization.

2. Other FDI-related policies: within the broad area of *internal trade and factor movements*, there are a wide range of policy matters which impinge upon the activities of MNEs—most obviously the ongoing internal market programme with its implications for new greenfield investment, mergers, acquisitions, and alliances (MAAs), and corporate restructuring, but also policies concerning government procurement, liberalization in service sectors, privatization, and corporate taxation. Of great potential importance to MNEs too are the rules on European works councils, which require MNEs without an existing agreement to establish works councils representing the labour force in their subsidiaries in different member states as a mechanism for information and consultation; and the proposed European Company Statute encompassing rules on takeover bids, company law, and transfers of headquarters from one country to another. Other policy areas listed in Table A7.1 concern Competition Policy, Trade and Commercial Policy, Regional and Social Policy, Industrial Policy, and Research and Technology Policy, which in their various ways may impact upon MNEs.

Table A7.1 Selected EU and Member State Policies and Their Interaction with MNEs

Allocation of powers	MNE issues
Internal trade and factor movements: free movement of goods, services, persons, capital; government procurement; intellectual and industrial property; taxation; company law	
EU competence widespread derived from Treaty and Single European Act, but implementation still ongoing.	Single Market measures gave large stimulus to inward FDI pre-1993; and acting as major factor in MNE reorganization within EU in 1990s.
Limited progress on services liberalization.	Predominance of national rules preventing inward and outward FDI and free competition.
Government procurement: number of directives passed.	Discrimination in favour of national producers still present in public purchasing.
Liberalization of capital movements and removal of exchange controls (exemptions ended on 30 June 1994).	Variety of FDI controls still present in member states (see below).
Privatization: national government competence, but some issues within 1988 Capital Movements Directive.	Restrictions on foreign shareholdings, 'golden shares' for government, etc.
Company law: European Company Statute still under discussion: also Directive on European Works Councils.	Without Statute, problems posed for international mergers and takeovers.
Taxation mainly national competence, but 1993 directives on elimination of double taxation.	Some taxation assistance to cross-border flows.
Competition policy	
EU competence under Articles 85 and 86 of the Treaty (restrictive business practices, cartels, and abuse of dominant position), plus Council Merger Regulation adopted in 1989 (concentrative joint ventures and oligopolies). Under Articles 85 and 86, EU competence limited to operations affecting intra-EU trade; in area of concentrations EC effects across states.	Slow pace of decision-making under Articles 85 and 86. Uncertainty over which rules apply to joint ventures. Competition policy and need to open up closed sectors, e.g. telecommunications. Extraterritoriality issues. Merger Regulation procedures speedy and efficient administratively but lacking transparency.
EC competence under Article 92 (1) on state aids above a certain threshold which affect intra-EU trade, where notification and approval required. Various industry schemes in steel, shipbuilding, motor vehicles, synthetic fibres, air transport.	Aid in some sectors subject to political bargaining and favours indigenous producers.

Allocation of powers	MNE issues
Trade and commercial policy	
EU competence under Treaty of Rome (Articles 110–15 to establish common commercial policy. Includes bilateral, multilateral and sectoral agreements, rules of origin, anti-dumping rules. But EU competence debated in discussions over ratification of GATT Uruguay Round as regards 'new issues' (IT, Services, TRIMs). Within the framework of the common commercial policy, member states are entitled to maintain existing bilateral agreements on trade and to conclude cooperation agreements.	Wide range of trade-related investment measures (TRIMs). Anti-dumping rules have variety of consequences for MNEs of different nationalities concerning trade and location of production.
Regional and social policy	
Member states have own national regional policies, under terms of Rome Treaty, modified by Maastricht Treaty, to emphasize goal of economic and social cohesion (Articles 130a and 130c). Commission can vet member states' regional aids taking account of different types of regions. EU also part finances existing schemes through the Community Support Frameworks.	Support from member states (and co-financing from EU) for FDI; ability to play off countries and regions against one another. Difficulties of establishing level of aid to be offered. Interface problems between competition policy (state aids), industrial policy and cohesion policy could create confusion but also offer potential for manipulation.
Industrial policy and research and technology policy	
No EU competence for industrial policy outside coal and steel industries. Attempts to take initiative through Commission White Paper on competitiveness, growth, and employment. Discussions on need for wider view of industrial policy than that derived from competition policy. Some sectoral programmes considered within industrial policy framework.	Difficulty in understanding EU views on future policy directions for individual sectors.
EU competence for research and technological development (R & TD) under Article 130f–p of Maastricht Treaty aimed at avoiding duplication and encouraging coordination among member states. EU funds represent 3–4% of total spending at member state level.	Participation of non-EU companies in EU programmes possible where an objective is the transfer of results or technology to member states ('Common Position of Council . . . Concerning Rules for the Participation . . . in Research, Technological Development and Demonstration Activities of the European Community', 18 July 1994).

Table A7.1 *cont.*

Allocation of powers	MNE issues
Foreign direct investment policy	
Uncertainty as regards EU competence on FDI matters (subject debated in the framework of Uruguay Round implementation). Article 73 of Maastricht Treaty grandfathers existing direct (mainly inward) investment restrictions and allows new common regimes to be established or existing regimes to be modified.	No notification procedures on inward FDI at EU level (except where state aid/regional aid involved).
EU represented in OECD discussions on FDI by member states.	
At member state level virtually no restrictions on outward FDI; in regard to inward FDI, some sectoral restrictions, rules on takeovers from outside EU, and reciprocity provisions in sectors like banking.	Inward investing MNEs must comply with national rules, especially significant in area of takeovers.

Source: Adapted from Brewer and Young, 1995c.

Appendix 7.3

APEC Principles[a]

In the spirit of APEC's underlying approach of open regionalism; recognizing the importance of investment to economic development, the stimulation of growth, the creation of jobs, and the flow of technology in the Asia Pacific region; emphasizing the importance of promoting domestic environments that are conducive to attracting foreign investment, such as stable growth with low inflation, adequate infrastructure, adequately developed human resources, and protection of intellectual property rights; reflecting that most APEC economies are both sources and recipients of foreign investment; aiming to increase investment, including investment in small and medium enterprises, and to develop supporting industries; acknowledging the diversity in the level and pace of development of member economies as may be reflected in their investment regimes, and committed to ongoing efforts towards the improvement and further liberalization of their investment regimes; without prejudice to applicable bilateral and multilateral treaties and other international instruments; and recognizing the importance of fully implementing the Uruguay Round TRIMs Agreement, APEC members aspire to the following nonbinding principles:

Transparency. Member economies will make all laws, regulations, administrative guidelines and policies pertaining to investment in their economies publicly available in a prompt, transparent, and readily accessible manner.

Nondiscrimination between Source Economies. Member economies will extend to investors from any economy treatment—in relation to the establishment, expansion, and operation of their investments—that is no less favourable than that accorded to investors from any other economy in like situations, without prejudice to relevant international obligations and principles.

National Treatment. With exceptions as provided for in domestic laws, regulations, and policies, member economies will accord to foreign investors—in relation to the establishment, expansion, operation, and protection of their investments—treatment no less favourable than that accorded in like situations to domestic investors.

Investment Incentives. Member economies will not relax health, safety, and environmental regulations as an incentive to encourage foreign investment.

Performance Requirements. Member economies will minimize the use of performance requirements that distort or limit expansion of trade and investment.

Expropriation and Compensation. Member economies will not expropriate foreign investments or take measures that have a similar effect, except for a public purpose and on a nondiscriminatory basis, in accordance with the laws of each economy and principles of international law, and against the prompt payment of adequate and effective compensation.

Repatriation and Convertibility. Member economies will further liberalize towards the goal of the free and prompt transfer of funds related to foreign investment, such as profits, dividends, royalties, loan payments and liquidations, in freely convertible currency.

Entry and Sojourn of Personnel. Member economies will permit the temporary entry and sojourn of key foreign technical and managerial personnel for the purpose of engaging in activities connected with foreign investment, subject to relevant laws and regulations.

Removal of Barriers to Capital Exports. Member economies accept that regulatory and institutional barriers to the outflow of investment will be minimized.

Avoidance of Double Taxation. Member economies will endeavour to avoid double taxation related to foreign investment.

Investor Behavior. Acceptance of foreign investment is facilitated when foreign investors abide by the host economy's laws, regulations, administrative guidelines and policies, just as domestic investors should.

Settlement of Disputes. Member economies accept that disputes arising in connection with a foreign investment will be settled promptly through consultations and negotiations between the parties to the dispute or, failing this, through procedures for arbitration in accordance with members' international commitments or through other arbitration procedures acceptable to both parties.

Note: [a]As agreed by APEC Ministers, Jakarta, November 1994.
Source: Bora and Graham, 1995.

8

Policy Linkages

Investment, Trade, and Technology Transfer

8.1 Introduction

An investment regime, as a set of international rules and institutions, cannot be understood or evaluated in isolation from international trade rules and institutions. Nor can investment, as a type of international business transaction for a firm, be understood in isolation from other types of transactions. This chapter, therefore, places FDI in the context of the broader array of international business transactions that MNEs engage in, including technology transfer as well as trade, and it analyses the relationships among investment, trade, and intellectual property rules, particularly within the context of the World Trade Organization. It is followed by Chapter 9 which also concerns linkage issues—in that case linkages between competition policy and investment policy.

Relationships between investment and trade were on the agenda of international regime formation as early as the discussions concerning the ITO in the 1940s (see Chapter 3). Because the ITO did not come into existence, however, and because the GATT was specifically focused on trade (and, at least initially, even more narrowly on tariffs in particular), issues concerning linkages between investment and trade did not receive sustained attention in the early period. Furthermore, over time, investment and trade came to be substantially separated from one another in disparate policy fora. Within the UN system, while investment issues received much attention within the Centre on Transnational Corporations (CTC) in New York, trade issues were mostly the domain of UNCTAD in Geneva. Even within the much smaller OECD, investment and trade issues were substantially separated from one another in different committee systems.

Several changes during the 1980s and 1990s, however, created new pressures for more careful consideration of the relationships between investment and trade—and hence the linkages between investment and trade policies. One set of changes was the unprecedented increases in the amounts of FDI and the associated expansion of related international business transactions, as FDI and trade became increasingly complementary forms of international business, rather than substitutes. As FDI–trade relationships became more intense and more thoroughly integrated into firms' strategies and operations, it became increasingly arbitrary and ineffective to treat them in isolation in public policy-making.

Another set of changes was the inclusion of provisions concerning investment in the Uruguay Round agreements. In particular, the TRIMs agreement and the GATS explicitly established linkages—for goods and services, respectively—between selected aspects of investment policy and trade policy; and those agreements institutionalized subsequent reconsideration of the linkages, with provisions for reviews of the functioning of the agreements within set time schedules. Similarly, the TRIPs agreement also places intellectual property and related technology transfer issues within the wider WTO institutional framework—though there is no explicit, formal linkage with investment in the provisions of the TRIPs agreement itself.

Yet another development fostering more focus on investment–trade relationships has been the proliferation of regional integration agreements (see Chapter 7). The NAFTA, in particular, is more than a *trade* agreement; it is in fact a *trade-and-investment* agreement. Experience at the regional level thus reinforces the recognition that investment and trade cannot be treated in isolation in international policy-making fora.

8.2 **Investment–Trade Relationships**

An understanding of the issues about policy linkages between investment and trade and associated issues about incorporating both in multilateral negotiations requires an understanding of issues about their empirical relationships. Consideration is thus given, in order, to empirical relationships, multilateral negotiations, and policy linkages.

Empirical relationships

The empirical questions about relationships between investment and trade as international economic transactions are often stated in terms of whether investment and trade are substitutes or complements. At the macroeconomic level, the emphasis is typically on the net effects of investment on home and host countries' balance of payments. This issue often enters public policy discussions about whether or how to limit outward investment from home countries in view of its effects on trade and hence employment; for instance, it sometimes emerges in the context of home country outward FDI political risk insurance schemes, which may screen projects for their effects on the home country's trade (and employment). In host countries, the issue emerges at the micro-level in respect of negotiations between investors and host governments about the effects of particular FDI projects on host country imports and exports, and more generally there are frequently questions about the net impacts of inward FDI on trade.

One way to begin to understand the extent to which trade and investment have become complements is to consider intra-firm trade examples at the level of individual firms. Thus, in Box 8.1 there are highlights of the intra-firm trade of Toyota in South-East Asia for the production of automobiles and the intra-firm trade of Honda

Box 8.1

Examples of Intra-firm Trade by Two Japanese-based Firms

A. Toyota's intra-firm trade in South-East Asia for automotive production

- There are 10 Toyota affiliates in 6 countries in South-East Asia: Indonesia, Malaysia, Philippines, Taiwan, Thailand, Singapore (regional headquarters).
- Their intra-firm trade in parts and components totalled $100 million in 1995 for the assembly of 371,000 vehicles.
- Intra-firm traded goods included exports of diesel engines from Thailand; transmissions from the Philippines; steering gears from Malaysia; and engines from Indonesia.

B. Honda's intra-firm trade in Europe for motorcycles, mopeds, and scooters

- Small-sized engines are exported from France by Honda for assembly of scooters and mopeds by Honda in Italy.
- Medium-sized engines are exported from Honda's affiliate in Italy for assembly of motorcycles in Spain by Honda's affiliate in that country.
- Large-sized engines are exported from Honda of Japan for assembly of motorcycles by Honda in Italy.
- Honda's R & D centre and their headquarters for Europe are in Germany.

Source: UNCTAD, 1996*a*: 100–2.

Table 8.1 Intra-firm Trade by Parent Corporations in Japan and the United States

	1982/3	1992
A. *Intra-firm trade as percentage of total national trade*		
Japan exports	22.5	26.9
Japan imports	15.1	14.8
US exports	34.2	37.2
US imports	36.8	42.5
B. *Intra-firm trade as percentage of parent firms' total trade*		
Japan exports	28.3	32.1
Japan imports	20.8	28.7
US exports	30.6	42.4
US imports	36.2	45.7

Note: Data for Japan are for 1983 and 1992, and for the United States 1982 and 1992.

Source: UNCTAD, 1995: tables IV.1 and IV.2, pp. 194–5.

in Europe for the production of motorcycles, mopeds, and scooters. It is evident that even within the limits of these regionalized production processes there is much intra-firm trade. The firms not only exploit their firm-specific advantages by transferring their production know-how outside their home countries, they also exploit the comparative advantages of different foreign countries in the production of different components and the assembly of final products. Though these examples are from an industry that has had substantially internationalized production processes, involving high levels of both FDI and trade for many years, they are not the only examples of industries exhibiting such tendencies. Other sectors include, for instance, integrated circuit manufacture, and, among service industries, computer programmes and systems design and development (UNCTAD, 1996*a*: 106).

In addition to firm-level examples, aggregated intra-firm trade data for countries and for industry sectors also reveal the extent to which trade is linked to FDI. Although information on intra-firm trade is not available for many individual countries, there are generally consistent patterns and trends in the data that are available. At the global level, total worldwide intra-firm trade was estimated at $1.6 trillion in 1993—or one-third of world trade and one-half of the total trade of MNEs (UNCTAD, 1995: 193). In Table 8.1, the data for Japan and the United States indicate that exports by parent firms to their own foreign affiliates were, respectively, about one-quarter and slightly more than one-third of those countries' total exports; the parallel proportions for imports were somewhat smaller for Japan but larger for the USA. The intensity of intra-firm trade is particularly pronounced in some industries, including some of the most important ones in international commerce as the data in Table 8.2 for US-based MNEs reveal. There is also significant intra-firm trade in service industries (Table 8.3).

Another way to examine the relationship between trade and investment is to consider the results of empirical studies that focus on the statistical association of trade and FDI across countries, industries, and time. A review by the WTO (1996*b*) of the

Table 8.2 Intra-firm Trade of US Parent Firms and Their Foreign Affiliates by Industry (as a percentage of total firm trade, 1993)

Industry	*Parent firms*		*Foreign affiliates*	
	Exports	Imports	Exports	Imports
Petroleum	32.1	30.5	47.3	75.8
General machinery	74.9	75.8	84.3	87.0
Electronics	39.2	45.2	76.6	93.2
Transport equipment	45.9	77.0	87.9	76.1
All manufacturing	48.5	63.4	74.2	82.5
All industries	44.4	48.6	64.0	85.5

Source: UNCTAD, 1996*a*: table IV.2, p. 104.

Table 8.3 US Intra-Firm Trade in Goods and Services, 1994

Type of intra-firm transactions	US dollars (intra-firm)	Per cent (intra-firm / total)
Goods—exports	186.0	36.3
US parents—foreign affiliates	134.3	26.2
US affiliates—foreign parents	51.7	10.1
Goods—imports	283.5	42.7
US parents—foreign affiliates	119.4	18.0
US affiliates—foreign parents	164.1	24.7
Services—exports (receipts)	34.6	18.9
US parents—foreign affiliates	28.0	15.3
US affiliates—foreign parents	6.6	3.6
Services—imports (payments)	15.6	15.9
US parents—foreign affiliates	6.0	5.0
US affiliates—foreign parents	9.6	10.9

Source: US Department of Commerce, *Survey of Current Business* (Nov. 1996), 90–3.

results of studies of the association of FDI with exports and imports in both home countries and host countries finds a generally positive correlation between FDI and trade. In particular, studies of MNEs' outward FDI from Austria, Germany, Japan, Sweden, and the United States found positive correlations with exports. As for imports into the home countries of MNEs, the evidence is less extensive but suggests a weak positive relationship. As for host countries,

> the available evidence suggests that FDI and host country exports are complementary, and that a weaker but still positive relationship holds between FDI and host country imports. Except for the apparently stronger complementarity between FDI and host country exports (than between FDI and home country exports), these results are very similar to those reported for the relationship between FDI and home country trade. (WTO, 1996*b*: 15–16)

The overall picture, then, is that the linkage between FDI and trade is substantial—not only in absolute terms, but also in relation to trade among unrelated firms. Trade and investment tend to co-vary at the level of national economies as well as industries and projects. Thus, trade and investment have become inextricably intertwined in the internationalized production processes of MNEs. Furthermore, the generally positive associations that have been evident in empirical studies to date are likely to strengthen as government trade policy liberalization allows firms more easily to adopt more internationally diversified and integrated production processes. In a liberalized trade environment, firms can more fully exploit countries' comparative advantages in different stages of the value-adding process; they can shift from multidomestic strategies adapted to countries' import-substitution policies to more globalized production strategies to capture economies of scale. In any case, as a WTO (1996*b*: 8–9) report indicates,

> When the focus is on interlinkages, the question of whether FDI and trade are substitutes or complements is of secondary importance. A substitute relationship can create just as strong an interlinkage as a complementary one. And if they are interlinked, it means that trade policy affects FDI flows, and FDI policies affect trade flows, and therefore that both sets of policies would benefit from being treated in an integrated manner.

It is clear that the liberalization of investment policies becomes an essential complement to trade policy liberalization. Just as trade and investment often go hand in hand as modalities for the conduct of international business, trade policy and investment policy are similarly complementary in their effects.

Investment and trade in multilateral negotiations

There is another set of questions about trade–investment relationships; they concern the negotiations of multilateral investment agreements and trade agreements. These questions reflect the similarities and differences between the two and therefore questions about whether investment and trade agreements should be negotiated in the same fora and/or using the same *modus operandi*. Such issues became particularly salient with the advent of negotiations on the Multilateral Agreement on Investment at the OECD and the implementation of the investment agreements of the Uruguay Round at the WTO. Questions and comparisons concern normative implications (principles) for policy-making as well as substantive differences in the interests, conflicts, trade-offs, and other aspects of the economics and politics of the actors involved. The question of whether and how investment and trade are different is at the core of the forum issue, for instance, in which advocates of the OECD as the preferred forum contend that because investment is fundamentally different from trade it is desirable to negotiate an investment agreement in an organization with extensive experience with investment issues (i.e. the OECD) and not in an organization that will tend to treat investment issues like trade issues (i.e. the WTO).

It is sometimes suggested that investment negotiations are more difficult than trade negotiations, both analytically and politically. Compromises may be easier to negotiate in trade negotiations than in investment negotiations, it can be argued, for several reasons. Because tariffs are numerical gradients, they can be easily negotiated, whereas investment entry for instance tends to be more nearly an all-or-nothing matter (though percentage foreign ownership restrictions represent an important qualification for such an absolutist notion). In negotiations, investment policy offers are inherently more 'lumpy' or more often of an 'either/or' nature, as compared with the more graduated/incremental nature of trade offers. Investment alternatives tend to be more qualitative, while trade alternatives can more easily be conceived in quantitative terms. This is obvious for instance in the case of right of entry (either/or, yes or no) for investment, versus the level of tariffs (whether *ad valorem* percentage or specific money amount) or quotas for trade. However, many non-tariff barriers to trade and many barriers to investment have much in common in this regard—for they both tend to be qualitative rather than quantitative in nature. Furthermore, various investment barrier issues are also inherently quantitative, at least in part—for instance, limits on the percentage of foreign ownership, or domestic content or export performance requirements (both of which can be expressed in percentage terms). Of course, there is also some 'lumpiness' in the increments—for instance, the implications for control of a difference between 49 per cent and 50 per cent in the limit on foreign ownership.

Because investment intrudes more into domestic regulatory regimes, it involves a greater number of government agencies which protect their regulatory turf and make liberalization difficult. There are also more agencies with interests at stake in investment negotiations because of the pervasive domestic consequences of investment; and there is thus more inter-agency conflict, coordination, and compromising in investment negotiations.

There are greater asymmetries in negotiating strength among countries in investment negotiations because some countries are only (or overwhelmingly) recipient countries, with no (or little) outward investment, whereas other countries are both significant source (home) and recipient (host) countries.

Policy linkages

There is a third set of questions about the relationship between investment and trade, therefore, namely policy questions about the relationships between international rules concerning investment and trade. These questions concern both actual relationships among existing rules and desirable relationships for additional rule-making. Questions about policy linkages are not limited to the multilateral level; they exist as well at the regional, bilateral, and national levels. In NAFTA, for instance, there are separate sections of the agreement for the motor vehicle industry and financial services industries, and they address both investment and trade issues that are specific to those industries.

Linkages between trade and investment are particularly striking in anti-dumping policies, and that linkage was evident during the Uruguay Round negotiations. As Chapter 9 will show, the Uruguay Round, however, failed to strengthen significantly the anti-dumping agreement, leaving these measures as a means of inducing firms to switch from trade to investment as a strategic alternative for serving foreign markets.

Policy linkage issues are central to discussions about the future of investment issues at the WTO and about the nature of the MAI at the OECD. At the WTO, the GATS includes both trade and investment, but the opportunities in the schedules of specific commitments to treat trade policies and investment policies independently of one another tend to negate the inclusion of both in the overall agreement. There are thus numerous exceptions to market access commitments and national treatment commitments for particular modes of supply for specific industries.

In contrast, the Information Technology Agreement (ITA) is an example of an agreement that is limited to trade, even more specifically only to tariffs on goods, and ignores investment issues altogether. Yet, because several of the categories of goods that are covered by the ITA include telecommunications equipment, the ITA overlaps with the Basic Telecommunications agreement, which is actually an annex to the GATS and thus a services agreement. The existence of separate but overlapping agreements—one concerning trade in goods and the other concerning investment and trade in services—creates questions about gaps and consistencies of coverage for a particular industry, in this instance telecommunications.

The TRIMs agreement represents yet a different approach to issues concerning investment–trade linkages and thus a further complication as well. That agreement focuses rather specifically on a set of investment–trade policy linkages—namely trade performance requirements imposed on investment projects; it thus reflects an explicitly integrated approach to investment–trade linkages. However, trade performance requirements are also linked to subsidies, which themselves often involve both trade and investment policy issues. These linkages were revealed in the Uruguay Round negotiations of the Subsidies and Countervailing Measures (SCMs) agreement and the TRIMs agreement. TRIMs entered into the SCMs negotiations, and vice versa, through the distinction between trade-related investment measures that are required by law versus those that are available as a quid pro quo condition for receiving a subsidy (Croom, 1995).

Furthermore, investment incentives, such as subsidies for exports that are tied to particular FDI projects, to entice investors into host countries also link investment and trade policies. Where investors are considering alternative sites, say, in different US states or different EU countries, competitive bidding may lead to a spiralling of aid offers to levels higher than those that are economically justifiable on the grounds of externalities (UNCTAD, 1996*b*). Aside from the waste and misallocation of resources, competition may be distorted, especially when large-scale, capital-intensive projects are aided in oligopolistic markets (European Commission, 1996*b*). It is arguable that the distortions created by incentive bidding for FDI have to date largely been intra-regional (intra-EU or intra-North America) as opposed to inter-regional. The similarities in forms of incentives and the existence of aid ceilings within regions might thus limit the extent of competitive bidding. However, in an era of globalization, it would be expected that certain types of projects at least would become globally, as opposed to simply regionally, mobile. Worldwide competition for such projects could lead to greater incentive bidding because of both fewer constraints (the very limited scope of international rules at present) and more widely varying types and levels of incentives—for example, fiscal versus financial incentives (see UNCTAD, 1996*b*, for details). The numerous types of incentives available to MNEs were summarized in Table 1.4, and some recent illustrative cases are summarized in Table 8.4. Table 8.5 presents data on the incidence of investment incentives in recent years. In sum, those tables reveal that incentives are diverse, widespread, and increasing.

It would be misleading to consider investment incentives without also discussing performance requirements, because of the linkages between the two and because of the problems created for north–south agendas and negotiations on multilateral trade and investment rules. Local content, trade balancing, and export requirements are the most frequently quoted examples of performance requirements; although a much wider range of measures (fourteen in total), which are included within the general category of trade-related investment measures, were cited in the Uruguay Round discussions (UNCTC/UNCTAD, 1991). The linkages between performance requirements and investment incentives derive from the fact that the former may be negotiated as a quid pro quo for incentives. In addition, firms have reported

Table 8.4 Illustrations of FDI Incentive Packages

Location	Year	Plant	Other locations considered	State investment on behalf of company (millions of dollars)	Company's investment (millions of dollars)
Setubal, Portugal	1991	Auto Europa Ford Volkswagen	United Kingdom Spain	484	2,603
Tuscaloosa, Alabama, United States	1993	Mercedes-Benz	Alabama, Georgia, Nebraska, North Carolina, South Carolina, Tennessee	250	300
North-east England	1994/5	Samsung	France, Germany, Portugal, Spain	89	691
Spartenburg, South Carolina, United States	1994	BMW	Oklahoma Nebraska	130	450
Castle Bromwich, Birmingham, Whitley, United Kingdom	1995	Jaguar	Detroit, United States	129	767
Hambach, Lorraine, France	1995	Mercedes-Benz Swatch	Belgium, Germany	111	370

Source: UNCTAD, 1995: table VI.3, pp.296–7.

(UNCTC/UNCTAD, 1991) that developed countries used investment incentives with much the same effect as developing countries used TRIMs, e.g. cash grants in a country such as Ireland for operations larger than the Irish market had the same effect as export performance TRIMs.

The developed countries have argued that TRIMs cause distortions in patterns of trade and investment, whereas developing nations regard them as important tools to promote development objectives and strengthen trade balances. As with the analysis of incentives, under assumptions of perfect competition TRIMs are clearly distortionary. Under conditions of oligopoly, however, TRIMs may be employed to shift rents and producer surplus from firms to countries where the investment is located.

Table 8.5 Fiscal Incentives for Foreign Investors, Early 1990s (number of countries that offer each type of incentive)

Types of incentives	Developing countries		Developed countries		Central and Eastern Europe	
	Number	Proportion[a]	Number	Proportion[a]	Number	Proportion[a]
Reduction of standard income-tax rate	43	0.83	20	0.77	20	0.80
Tax holidays	37	0.71	11	0.42	19	0.76
Accelerated depreciation	26	0.50	15	0.58	6	0.24
Investment/reinvestment allowance	18	0.35	5	0.19	3	0.12
Deductions from social security contributions	5	0.10	5	0.19	2	0.08
Specific deductions on gross earnings for income-tax purposes or reductions in other taxes (e.g. VAT, sales)	32	0.62	11	0.42	2	0.08
Exemption from import duties	39	0.75	11	0.42	13	0.52
Duty drawback	28	0.54	9	0.35	12	0.48
Total number of countries	52	1.00	26	1.00	25	1.00

Note: [a]Countries with incentives, proportion having each type of incentive (not proportion of all countries).
Source: Adapted from UNCTAD, 1995: table VI.1, p. 292.

The conclusion depends upon the type of measure, and TRIMs in general represent a second best development tool. In the Uruguay Round negotiations, under pressure from the developed countries (and especially the United States), efforts focused upon means of controlling, reducing, and prohibiting TRIMs. But a balanced approach which deals both with incentives and with performance requirements is clearly an essential prerequisite for further progress on a multilateral agreement (see also the discussion in Chapter 10 on this topic).

This overview has illustrated some of the distortions and misallocation of resources which may arise both intra- and inter-regionally from government policies on FDI incentives. It provides a strong case for multilateral rules, while highlighting the need for a comprehensive agreement in the OECD and/or WTO, because of linkages between policy areas and because of the scope for shifting beggar-thy-neighbour policies into areas outside the domain of rules. The two Uruguay Round agreements that are germane to investment incentives are the agreement on Subsidies and Countervailing Measures (Box 8.2) and the agreement on Trade Related Investment Measures. The conclusion of the SCMs agreement is that if a government grants a specific subsidy to a particular FDI project, and if the subsidy is more than 15 per cent of the total investment at the time of start-up or more than 5 per cent of the sales (if it is a tax-related subsidy), then the government has the burden of demonstrating that the subsidy is allowable.

Whether the restriction would apply to subsidies granted to expansions of existing facilities is an interesting issue. In any case, the distinction between market access and market presence may limit the applicability of the SCMs to investment incentives. It has been observed, in particular, that

> although the [SCMs] Agreement considers market access problems (in both the subsidizing country market and in third market) as relevant in terms of meeting the adverse effects test, and thus allowing for a remedy, it does not consider investment access (or market presence) problems as equally relevant. Consequently, a country may not be able, for instance, to successfully complain about investment incentives which divert investment flows away from its market. Again, given the increasing complementarity between trade and investment flows, this seems a systemic anomaly worth considering. (Zampetti, 1995: 26–7)

Because investment incentives are often linked to performance requirements in national policies and in individual FDI project entry negotiations, it is important to consider at least briefly the provisions of the agreement on TRIMs from the Uruguay Round. First, the TRIMs agreement pertains to goods only, not to services or to agriculture, civil aircraft, or textiles; its scope is thus sectorally limited in the same way as the Subsidies agreement. As to the types of measures that are restricted, because it was developed from previous GATT provisions concerning national treatment (Article III) and quantitative import restrictions (Article XI), the essence of the TRIMs agreement is that it imposes discipline on those two categories of TRIMs. The list of performance requirements that violate national treatment includes domestic content and trade balancing requirements. Three types of quantitative import restrictions are listed: restrictions on imports for local production (or tying export requirements to the level of imports), restrictions on foreign exchange access for import purchases, and restrictions on the volumes or values of exports. There is

Box 8.2

Agreement on Subsidies and Countervailing Measures

The SCMs agreement evolved as the most recent stage in a long GATT history of concern with export subsidies in manufacturing; during the 1980s this concern was expanded to include domestic subsidies as well. Four key features of the SCMs agreement concern: the sectors that are covered; the nature of the subsidies that are covered; the classification of subsidies as being prohibited, actionable, or non-actionable; and the criteria for determining whether the effects of subsidies are great enough to be covered by the agreement. Thus, in order to determine whether any given subsidy is covered by the agreement, one must consider its relationship to each of these four features.

As to *sectoral* coverage, the SCMs agreement concerns only goods; it does not cover services. The general framework provisions of the General Agreement on Trade in Services (GATS) does not cover subsidies; however, several sector-specific annexes are still being negotiated and may contain provisions concerning subsidies. Further, three particularly problematic sectors—agriculture, civil aircraft, and textiles—are covered in separate agreements. Agriculture and civil aviation are explicitly excluded from some provisions of the SCMs agreement, while the textiles agreement suggests that the SCMs agreement does apply to that industry. The *nature of the subsidies* that are covered is defined in terms of three attributes. First, subsidies are defined as 'financial contributions' (e.g. grants, loans, tax credits) provided directly or indirectly by a government, or as 'price or income support' programmes. Second, only 'specific' subsidies are covered—i.e. those that are 'limited to certain enterprises'; more generalized, non-specific subsidies are not covered.

A *'traffic light' classification scheme* establishes three categories of subsidies according to which red light subsidies are prohibited, green light subsidies are permissible and non-actionable, while amber light subsidies are actionable. The prohibited subsidies include subsidies that are contingent on the use of domestic over imported goods or export performance. The latter include: currency retention schemes with bonuses for exports; favourable transportation rates for exports; tax remissions, deferrals export credits, and guarantees; and others. 'Permissible' subsidies include all non-specific subsidies and any 'specific' subsidies for pre-competitive R & D, assistance to disadvantaged regions, and adaptation of existing facilities to new environmental regulations. The 'actionable' category includes subsidies that have adverse effects on the interests of other members—that is, 'injury to domestic industry', nullification or impairment, or serious prejudice (each of which is further specified). There are also criteria for determining whether there is a presumption of serious prejudice so that a subsidizing government has the burden of demonstrating that the subsidy is allowable (Article 6). One such criterion (in Annex IV, paragraph 4) is particularly relevant to FDI incentives: 'Where the recipient firm is in a start-up situation, serious prejudice shall be deemed to exist if the overall rate of subsidization exceeds 15 per cent of the total funds invested.' Two additional criteria are also pertinent, though probably less constraining on FDI incentives. There is a 5 per cent threshold (in Article 6.1 (a) and Annex IV, paragraphs 1-3), according to which a subsidy of more than 5 per cent of the value of the product is presumed to involve serious prejudice. However, the value of the product is usually based on the sales of the preceding twelve-month period—which would seem not to apply to greenfield FDI projects because there would be no sales prior to start-up. For tax-related subsidies, though, the value of the product is the value of the firm's sales in the fiscal year when it earns the subsidy (Annex IV, paragraph 2, note 64).

some ambiguity and uncertainty in the scope of coverage of each of these two categories because the types of prohibited measures are specified in 'illustrative lists'. Variations in the interpretations of the significance of the TRIMs agreement can thus hinge on whether these illustrative lists are considered closed-ended lists that merely restate existing limitations, or are non-exhaustive lists that do not preclude other types of subsidies from being subject to restrictions.

8.3 Technology and Intellectual Property

There are parallels in the relationship of investment to trade and the relationship of investment to technology transfer. As was pointed out in Chapter 1, technology is an integral element of the bundle of factors that MNEs transfer between countries as they engage in FDI, and in that respect technology transfer and FDI are complements, just as trade and FDI are complements. On the other hand, technology transfer through an international licensing agreement is sometimes a strategic alternative to FDI as a way for a firm to serve a foreign market, and the two are therefore sometimes substitutes, just as FDI and trade are also sometimes substitutes. The relative importance of the substitute–complement relationship has not been analysed empirically for the FDI–technology relationship with the same intensity as in the studies of the FDI–trade relationship—partly because the balance of payments issues are not so controversial and partly because the data for technology transfer are much less extensive than the data for trade, especially trade in goods. Yet, balance of payments data on royalties and licensing fees make it possible to examine the magnitudes of those international transactions as indicators of the relative magnitudes of the international technology transfers that lead to the payments / receipts. The relative importance of intra-firm technology transfer within MNEs, as opposed to inter-firm, arm's length transactions, is evident in Table 8.6, which presents information from US balance of payments data. In terms of both international receipts and payments for royalties and licensing fees, intra-MNE transactions were two to four times greater than arm's length transactions among unrelated firms. Of course, such data reflect only some types of technology transfers, and not necessarily the most frequent or the most important for the firm or the host economy. For example, a major issue associated with Japanese FDI has been the transfer of 'soft' managerial know-how involving employee relations, for instance, along with production process technology. Technology transfer thus occurs in the context of MNEs' operations as information that is embodied in organizations, production processes, products, and even individual employees (Agmon and von Glinow, 1991: 1).

The effects of the transfer of these diverse types of technology and managerial know-how are often highly significant. The experience with the Toyota–General Motors joint venture, New United Motor Manufacturing, Inc. (NUMMI), in northern California is a well-known example, and it is described in Box 8.3. The effects of the transfer of technology and managerial know-how from Toyota to the former General Motors plant can be inferred from the data on performance for other Toyota and GM facilities, compared with the NUMMI facility.

Table 8.6 Relative Magnitudes of Intra-Firm (MNE) and Arm's Length Royalty and Licensing Fee Transactions: US Receipts and Payments

	1992	1993	1994	1995
Receipts				
Affiliated (MNEs) ($bn.)	15.7	15.7	17.4	21.6
Unaffiliated (arm's length) ($bn.)	4.0	4.6	4.8	5.3
Ratio (affiliated / unaffiliated)	3.9	3.4	3.6	4.1
Payments				
Affiliated (MNEs) ($bn.)	3.4	3.4	3.8	5.1
Unaffiliated (arm's length) ($bn.)	1.7	1.4	1.7	1.2
Ratio (affiliated / unaffiliated)	2.0	2.4	2.2	4.3

Source: US Department of Commerce, *Survey of Current Business* (Nov. 1996), 90–3.

Definitions and problem areas

MNEs' role in the process of technological development is multifaceted—as a producer of new technology and a vehicle for its initial application, and as a mechanism for the international transfer and diffusion of technology. In the wide range of cases in which MNEs license technology, protection of intellectual property is vital, including:

- wholly owned subsidiaries and joint ventures—licensing of know-how and / or supply of know-how free of charge;
- licensing agreements—licensing of know-how to third party licensees on an arm's length basis (in markets, for example, which are small or where barriers exist to other forms of market entry, or the technology is mature);
- management contracts and other contractual arrangements—especially where licensing agreements form part of the contract;
- strategic alliances - particularly those incorporating licensing agreements.

In all of these activities, of course, technology does not simply flow from parent to subsidiary or from home to host country; rather multi-way flows operate among subsidiaries; between subsidiaries and parents, and among and between third countries and home countries.

There are also many types of technology for which intellectual property protection does not (and will not) exist. These include scientific and technical publications, the training of management and labour, and spillovers from external linkages. Together with the dissemination of technology associated with patents etc. (and indeed trade secrets), this provides the basis for technology transfer into host economies.

It is clear from the above that a robust framework for the protection of intellectual

Box 8.3

FDI-Technology Transfer Linkages at the Project Level: The Case of the Toyota–General Motors Joint Venture

Toyota is credited with the introduction, in the 1950s, of just-in-time management practices (Womack et al., 1990), which is considered a main reason for Toyota's strong market position. Underlying the just-in-time practices is a philosophy of production that rests on three pillars: the reduction of costs by eliminating waste; the use of minimum amounts of equipment, material, parts and working time; and the full use of workers' capabilities.

In the early 1980s, Toyota, for the first time, transferred its unique managerial style to an affiliate abroad, its United States affiliate New United Motor Manufacturing, Inc. (NUMMI). NUMMI is a joint venture between General Motors Corporation (GM) and Toyota Motor Corporation (Toyota) established in 1984 at the site of a former GM plant in Fremont, California.

NUMMI adopted Toyota's philosophies and concepts and its production system, *lean production*, the team concept, which is key to the management of production in Toyota, as well as Toyota's supplier-relations methods, based on long-term and stable relationships. A key ingredient in the latter is close connection between the manufacturer and suppliers, with regular meetings between NUMMI's employees and managers and its suppliers in order to increase communications and reinforce commitment to the production philosophy of NUMMI and its goals. This results in improvement of their products. Team members do play an important role in suggesting cost-cutting measures and continuous improvement ideas (*kaizen*) to suppliers.

In order to keep their practices as close to the original as possible and to transfer directly the ideas and philosophy behind them, Toyota continued to use the same language as in the parent company in Japan. For example, *andon*, *heijunka*, *jidoka*, *kanban*, *kaizen*, *muda*, *mura*, *muri*, *poka-yoke*, etc. are terms used at NUMMI.

The actual transfer of the practices developed by Toyota to NUMMI was implemented through a series of training and teaching programmes. The adoption of Toyota's managerial practices rapidly improved NUMMI's performance. By 1986, NUMMI employed 2,500 team members (employees), about half the number at the former GM plant. In 1987, efficiency and productivity levels, by some measures, already reached those of Toyota's high-performance plants at other locations. Subsequently, GM adopted many of Toyota's practices and started using them in its other plants. The Spring Hill (Tennessee) Saturn plant started working with team management and the team concept (job rotation and reduction of job classification). Knowledge based on experiences of managers in working and associating with workers at the factory shop was transferred to the Lansing (Michigan) plant. Similar practices were introduced in other plants of GM. General Motors believes that these managerial practices provide a competitive edge to its organization.

Despite its strong performance, NUMMI is not independent of its parent firm. After one decade of operation, the parent company still assists NUMMI in implementing its production system. Several of the key posts in NUMMI, such as that of the president and those of general managers of finance and of purchasing, are held by Japanese expatriates—Toyota employees assigned to NUMMI for three to four years. In general, however, the attempt of Toyota to introduce its own management style appears to have been successful. Toyota's subsequent establishment of two fully owned plants in North America (one in Ontario, and the other in Kentucky; both established in 1988) was a reflection of Toyota's confidence in the transferability of its production system.

Source: UNCTAD, 1995: 180–1.

property is a critical component of an attractive investment climate. Foreign direct investment is considered to be a mechanism for internalizing and therefore protecting proprietary know-how when external alternatives (such as rules on intellectual property) are non-existent or inefficient. In reality, however, weak, obsolete, or absent intellectual property protection will act as a barrier to all technology-related operations abroad. It is also apparent that technology and intellectual property issues associated with FDI and the multinational enterprise are much wider than those related to trade. For example, with subsidiaries, joint ventures, licences, and franchises abroad, questions relating to remittances of royalties, licence and management fees arise (as do issues of transfer pricing).

The agreement on TRIPs addresses some—but not all—of these issues. For the purposes of defining the subject matter of intellectual property, in the TRIPs negotiations a broad approach was adopted. Thus trade in intellectual property was deemed to cover patents, copyrights, neighbouring rights, trademarks, appellations of origin, industrial design, layout designs of integrated circuits, and trade secrets. Significant industry sectors relying on each form of IP include (Keon, 1988):

- patents—a wide range of sectors including pharmaceuticals, chemicals, computers, and electronics;
- copyright—printing and publishing, film-making, audio and video recording, broadcasting, musical and other performances, computer software, cluster merchandising;
- neighbouring rights—performers, recording, and broadcasting;
- trademarks—all sectors but particularly consumer goods such as clothing, footwear, cosmetics, watches, sporting goods, wines and spirits, tobacco products;
- appellations of origin—wines and spirits, cheese, other food products;
- industrial designs—textiles, ceramics, watch-making, furniture;
- designs of integrated circuits–semiconductor chips;
- trade secrets—most high-technology sectors, especially where product life cycles are shorter than the acquisition time for IP protection.

International rules on intellectual property

The requirement for international standards for the protection of intellectual property was recognized in 1883 with the Paris Convention for the Protection of Industrial Property (covering inventions, trademarks, industrial designs, unfair competition, etc.) and the Berne Convention for the Protection of Literary and Artistic Works in 1886 (covering literary, artistic, musical, and dramatic works). These have been developed and updated over time and a number of other agreements and conventions have been added (see Table 8.7); most are administered by the World Intellectual Property Organization (WIPO).

Despite this level of activity at international level, huge losses are occurring as a consequence of patent infringement, trademark counterfeiting, copyright piracy, and misappropriation of trade secrets. A widely quoted figure for losses to US firms in the 1980s from inadequate intellectual property protection was $40–60 million per annum (Keon, 1988). Conversely, there is evidence of sharply increased R & D spending on the back of improved intellectual property protection in a sector such as pharmaceuticals where national rules have been strengthened in some major countries in the recent past (Mossinghoff, 1996). These examples highlight the benefits to be gained from stronger agreements at the international level. The Paris Convention, while incorporating the principle of national treatment, establishes only a few general guidelines for member states and there is no effective dispute settlement mechanism (see also Table 8.8).

Alongside the international framework established under WIPO, other multilateral efforts were undertaken from the 1960s to create an international regulatory system for *technology transfer*. These efforts were driven by developing countries within the context of the demands for a New International Economic Order (NIEO) (see Chapter 4). Three sets of negotiations were instituted within the UN system, namely negotiations for an international code of conduct for the transfer of technology (within the auspices of UNCTAD); for revision of the Paris Convention (WIPO); and for a Restrictive Business Practices Code of Conduct (UNCTAD) (Sell, 1989). In all these negotiations, the views of developing and developed countries were almost diametrically opposed. For example, in the case of the international code of conduct for technology transfer, developing nations sought agreement on significant government involvement in the screening and approval of technology contracts; in the Paris Convention, developing states argued for reductions in patent protection; and in the RPB Code negotiations, they advocated a definition of a restrictive business activity as any practice which would adversely affect their development goals. In the end only the Restrictive Business Practices Code was ratified and adopted in December 1980. According to Sell (1989: 181): 'The Code was vague enough to satisfy the parties at the time, but later when questions of interpretation arose it was clear that the parties had never agreed on the spirit, substance and purpose of the Code.'

The inadequacies of these attempts to formulate international rules (associated with the fora in which the negotiations were undertaken) led to US pressure to include intellectual property in the Uruguay Round of GATT negotiations (illustrations of some of the IP problems in these negotiations are listed in Table 8.8). In these endeavours, the US government was pressured by American corporations and backed by Japan and the European Community.

Until the Uruguay Round, GATT activity relating to intellectual property was limited. GATT provisions referring specifically to intellectual property rights (IPRs) are those on marks of origin (Article IX—which requires that these are not used to restrict trade); and Articles XII:3 and XVIII:10—which specify that quantitative restrictions may only be used for balance of payments purposes if they do not violate

Table 8.7 Major International Conventions on Intellectual Property

Agreement	Description	Administered by
Paris Convention (1883; 12 signatories; revised in 1967)[a]	Protection of patents, trademarks and service marks, trade names, utility models, industrial designs, indications of sources or appellations of origin and the 'repression of unfair competition'. Allows for compulsory licensing.	WIPO
Berne Convention (1886; 111 signatories; revised 1971)[a]	Basic copyright treaty based on principles of non-discrimination and national treatment (like Paris Convention).	WIPO
Madrid Agreement (1891; 31 signatories)	Allows imported goods bearing a false origin indication to be seized on importation.	WIPO
Universal Copyright Convention (1952; 57 signatories)	Copyright treaty accommodating US statutory requirements and based on principles of non-discrimination and national treatment.	UNESCO
Lisbon Agreement (1958; 17 signatories)	Protection of appellation of origin.	WIPO
Rome Convention (1961; 47 signatories)[a]	Protection of neighbouring rights (performers, producers of phonograms, broadcasting organizations).	ILO, UNESCO, and WIPO
Geneva Convention (1971; 52 signatories)	Protection of producers of phonograms against the making of duplicates in another country.	WIPO, ILO, and UNESCO
IPIC Treaty (1989; 8 signatories)[a]	Treaty on Intellectual Property in Respect of Integrated Circuits.	WIPO

Note: [a]Agreements which are explicitly referred to in the TRIPs agreement.
Source: Hoekman and Kostecki, 1995: table 6.1

Table 8.8 Illustrations of Intellectual Property Problems for TRIPs Negotiations

Enforcement of intellectual property rights

- Enforcement at the border
  - — inadequate procedures and remedies, e.g. lack of assistance from customs authorities in excluding the importation of infringing products;
  - — discriminatory procedures, e.g. legal or administrative systems or procedures that apply only to imports of goods protected by intellectual property but not to domestic products;
  - — internal enforcement, i.e.against domestic production and sale of infringing goods.

Availability and scope of intellectual property rights

- Patents:
  - — excessively wide exclusions from patentable subject matter, e.g. chemicals and pharmaceuticals;
  - — term of protection which is too short;
  - — procedural problems with obtaining patents;
  - — over-reliance on compulsory licensing.
- Copyright:
  - — no protection in some countries;
  - — terms of protection which are too short;
  - — over-reliance on compulsory licensing;
  - — no protection for computer software.
- Trademarks:
  - — difficulty in obtaining marks;
  - — difficulty in meeting use requirements because of high tariffs and / or import restrictions.
- Industrial designs:
  - — no protection in some countries.
- Integrated circuits:
  - — no protection in many countries.

Use of intellectual property

- Trade restrictions relating to aspects of licensing agreements.
- Tie-in commitments on non-patented articles.

Source: Keon, 1988.

intellectual property legislation (Hoekman and Kostecki, 1995). There is a general exception provision in the GATT (Article d) which specifies that measures necessary to protect intellectual property are not subject to GATT rules provided they are non-discriminatory. In general GATT involvement prior to the Uruguay Round was principally limited to a small number of dispute settlement cases concerning trade in counterfeit goods.

The opposing viewpoints which had bedevilled other multilateral negotiations also arose in the TRIPs discussions. However, by the late 1980s and early 1990s, the

Box 8.4

United States Bilateral Activity Against Counterfeiting and Piracy and the Evolution of National Rules

The protection of intellectual property rights by multinational corporations became a major issue on the US government agenda from the early 1980s. From that time increasing authority was conferred on the United States Trade Representative under Section 301 of the Trade and Tariff Act to link trade sanctions to the protection of intellectual property. Starting in 1982, the USA initiated bilateral consultations with countries such as Hungary, Taiwan, and Singapore which were allegedly not guaranteeing effective protection, leading to revisions in their patent, copyright, and trademark laws. With revisions to the US Trade and Tariff Act and the passing of the Omnibus Trade Act in 1988, a more aggressive approach to enforcement was mandated: eight countries (five of which were in Asia, namely, India, China, Korea, Taiwan, and Thailand) were placed on a 'priority watch list' because of failure to enforce IPRs, with a further five Asian nations (Indonesia, Japan, Malaysia, Pakistan, and the Philippines) being placed on a lower priority 'watch list'. For such countries, failure to improve the protection of IPRs within a specified time period could be followed by countervailing US trade restrictions.

China first introduced trademark and patent laws in 1983 and 1985 respectively, but because of slow progress in intellectual property protection, in recent years China has been the major target of US bilateral actions. Following an ineffective 1992 Sino-US copyright agreement, in 1994 the United States initiated a sanctions process under Section 301 of the US Trade Act threatening sanctions unless China agreed to specific measures to curb piracy; the latter was estimated to be costing the US information and entertainment industry around $1bn. per year. US officials identified twenty-nine plants in south China producing counterfeit compact and laser discs, principally for export. The computer software sector was also badly affected. Resolution of the dispute (which was in part linked to agreement to resume negotiations on China's WTO entry) was reached in July 1995, with China agreeing to the following:

- carrying out over three/five years an enforcement policy on intellectual property rights;
- setting up task forces in various cities and provinces to curb infringements;
- raiding factories involved in illegal manufacturing and retailers selling pirated goods;
- revoking factories' operating licences for repeated offences;
- giving greater authority to customs officials to halt exports of pirated products;
- opening up Chinese markets to imports of software and audio-visual products and making its censorship policy on imports more transparent;
- inviting US software and audio-visual companies to establish a commercial presence in China.

As of 1997, Vietnam was added to the list of countries succumbing to US action. Thus agreement was reached on an IPR deal protecting a range of products, including computer software, from copyright infringement. It created for the first time in Vietnam a legal framework for the protection of artistic, musical, literary, cinematic, choreographic, and computer software works. The next step was for Vietnam to respond to US proposals for an all-embracing trade pact, which in turn would pave the way for Vietnam to be granted most favoured nation status.

Source: Malott, 1989; Sell, 1989; *Financial Times*, 1995*a*, 1997*d*.

developing countries were not a unity: some of the East Asian NICs had strengthened their rules on intellectual property in response to threats of US action and to attract technology and MNE investment; and they were concerned at being undercut by other developing country competitors. The history of US activity at a bilateral level especially in the area of counterfeiting and piracy is described in Box 8.4.

The Agreement on Trade Related Aspects of Intellectual Property Rights, Including Trade in Counterfeit Goods (TRIPs agreement)

The TRIPs agreement in the Uruguay Round covers copyrights and related rights, layout designs of integrated circuits, geographical origin indications, trademarks, industrial designs, and patents in a complex agreement containing seventy-three articles. Hoekman and Kostecki (1995: 153) comment that the agreement:

(1) establishes minimum substantive standards of protection of the above rights;
(2) prescribes procedures and remedies which should be available in Member States to enforce rights;
(3) makes the general dispute settlement mechanism of WTO available to address TRIPs-related conflicts; and
(4) extends basic GATT principles such as transparency, national treatment and MFN to IPRs.

Some exceptions are, however, permitted on non-discrimination given that certain international agreements permit discrimination in particular circumstances.

Some of the features and implications of the TRIPs deal in respect of *patents* are as follows (the same basic principles apply to copyright and trademarks etc.) (Kent, 1993). First, the scope of patent protection is defined for the first time in an international agreement to include 'any invention, whether products or processes, in *all fields* of technology, provided that they are new, involve an inventive step and are capable of industrial application' (emphasis added). Permitted exemptions concern inventions, 'the prevention . . . of which is necessary to protect ordre public or morality' (Article 27 (2)) as well as diagnostic, therapeutic, and surgical methods for the treatment of humans or animals, and plants; these exemptions were designed to address the most pressing concerns of developing countries, namely access to food and medicine. There is reasonable agreement that the wider scope of patentability provides increased control over technology and its transfer, with technology holders being able to set the terms of licensing agreements in certain areas instead of host government bodies; however, the vague notion of 'ordre public' could lead to more exemptions from patentability than many people would like.

Second, in regard to the patent application process, Article 29 (1) of the TRIPs specifies that the application 'may require the applicant to indicate the best mode for car-

Box 8.5

Mexico and NAFTA and Rules on Intellectual Property

Mexican rules on IP date back to 1976 when the Law on Inventions and Trademarks was passed, with the purpose of preventing foreign owners of technology from acquiring exclusivity within key industrial areas in the Mexican economy. Thus a wide range of inventions and methods of preparing them were non-patentable. From 1982, the technology transfer process was regulated by an extremely restrictive law. This situation resulted in Mexico being included in the US 301 'priority watch list' on the grounds that the unacceptably restrictive laws and regulations for the licensing of technology and IPR and the lack of suitable protection for trade secrets made it almost impossible to license modern technology to industry and commerce.

The major stimuli for change, however, were the prospects of membership of GATT and NAFTA. The legal framework for protecting IPR in Mexico was radically overhauled, culminating in the Industrial Property Law of 1 October 1994; the latter was backed up by anti-monopoly rules incorporated in the Federal Law of Economic Competition which entered into force in 1992. The IP law includes provisions to provide a first-to-file system (also operating in Canada, but not in the USA where the first-to-invent system operates); to include the one-year grace term for novelty requirements; to introduce the eighteen-months publication of patent applications; to provide for an examination petition after said publication; to include product patent protection to reverse the burden of the proof of infringement in process patents; and to change the duration of the patent term to twenty years as of filing. The only restrictions relate to a number of express provisions of non-patentability concerning essentially biological processes for plant and animal reproduction, biological and genetic materials, plant varieties, surgical, therapeutic, and diagnosis methods, etc.

The licensing environment in Mexico and NAFTA as a whole may be summarized as follows:

- No restrictive laws on technology transfer exist within NAFTA countries other than the anti-monopoly laws.
- In Mexico, pure patent or trademark licence agreements will not be subject to the provisions of the anti-monopoly law for the duration of the agreement rights.
- Licensing of know-how and other proprietary information is an entirely free process with no government intervention.
- Licence agreements of any kind do not need to be registered with any authority of the respective countries.
- Only when a licence agreement involving a patent or a trademark is to be enforced against a third party in Mexico, the agreement must be recorded with the Mexican Institute of Industrial Property; disputes are settled under Mexican law or through international arbitration procedures.
- In order to provide proof of working of patents or of use of trademarks, the licence should preferably be recorded with the appropriate authority.
- The IP laws of the three NAFTA countries provide a suitable legal framework for protecting almost all types of inventions in any technical field, with very limited exceptions permitted; grant full protection for product patents in chemistry, pharmacy, and biotechnology; and provide effective trade secret protection and enforcement.

- Although the US maintains a first-to-invent system, US law has been amended in accordance with NAFTA and TRIPs, in order to recognize the date of conception of an invention when this took place in a NAFTA (and eventually in a WTO) country and not only in the USA.

Source: Becerril, 1996.

rying out the invention known to the inventor at the filing date'. The result is that under TRIPs (and NAFTA—see Box 8.5) the USA may continue to be one of the only countries in the world to require disclosure of 'best mode' in the patent claim as a condition precedent of patentability. The US insistence on maintaining its own first-to-invent (as compared with the more common first-to-file) system represents a non-tariff barrier: investors seeking protection in America face the risk that their investments will be jeopardized by investors who can successfully establish an earlier date of invention.

Third, the TRIPs agreement permits continued compulsory licensing but with significant restrictions, e.g. (1) compulsory licensing is only permitted if the licensee has attempted for a reasonable period of time to obtain the authorization of the IP holder on reasonable commercial terms; (2) compulsory licences are required to be non-exclusive; (3) an explicit right for judicial review is given to the IP holder for decisions imposing compulsory licences or establishing the level of remuneration of such licences.

The quid pro quo for stronger protection for mainly developed country intellectual property providers is contained in the technology transfer articles of TRIPs, namely:

Article 7—Objectives
The protection and enforcement of intellectual property rights should contribute to the promotion of technology innovation and to the transfer and dissemination of technology, to the market advantage of producers and users of technological knowledge and in a manner conducive to social and economic welfare, and to a balance of rights and obligations.
Article 8—Principles
. . . 2. Appropriate measures, provided that they are consistent with the provisions of this Agreement, may be needed to prevent the abuse of intellectual property rights by right holders or the resort to practices which unreasonably restrain trade or adversely affect the international transfer of technology.

Many feel that if TRIPs is to work and encourage a raising of standards and level of intellectual property protection throughout the world, then developed nations have an obligation to ensure that Articles 7 and 8 become a reality (O'Connor, 1995). According to Rodrik (1994), as at present the impact of enhanced IPR protection will be a redistribution of wealth from developing country consumers and firms to industrial countries' enterprises. Supporting this, Hoekman and Kostecki (1995: 156) argue that 'US pharmaceutical, entertainment and informatics industries, which were largely responsible for getting TRIPs on the agenda, obtained much, if not most, of what was desired when the negotiations were launched'.

Investment–technology transfer interrelationships

It is clear from the foregoing that substantive rules on the protection of intellectual property represent an important component of the worldwide climate for international investment, influencing everything from investment in R & D to technology transfer to host countries. In respect of the latter, an UNCTAD Ad Hoc Working Group on the interrelationships between investment and technology transfer neatly summarizes the position (Astolfi, 1994):

> The relationship between foreign investment flows and the building of technological capacities runs in both directions. While investment flows present the opportunity of acquiring and absorbing technology, it has become apparent that investment is attracted most strongly to those countries that have adopted measures to strengthen their domestic technological capability and create an overall policy framework conducive to innovation, investment in infrastructure, intellectual property protection, human capital formation, and a stable macroeconomic and regulatory environment.

8.4 **Conclusion**

It is important to understand both the similarities and the differences among investment, trade, and technology. At one extreme, presuming that investment and trade are more similar than they actually are can lead to unrealistic expectations about the integration of trade, technology, and investment—and ultimately to bad policy. At the other extreme, presuming that their differences are greater than they actually are can retard efforts to integrate trade, technology, and investment—and also lead to bad policy. In fact, there are both similarities and differences. In order to be effective, international rules must of course be sensitive to these economic and strategic facts about investment, trade, and technology transfer. Integrative concepts—market contestability, modal neutrality, and policy coherence—exist to evaluate inter-policy linkages. These were reviewed in Chapter 1 and recognize that firms can contest markets through a number of modalities and have access to and compete for factors of production as well as having access to product markets. Thus policies that limit participation in real estate markets or restrict visas, or restrict grants of government R & D contracts on the basis of nationality of ownership of firms, inhibit the contestability of markets, respectively, in land, labour, and technology. The concept of modal neutrality refers to policies that leave to firms the decision as to how markets will be served: anti-dumping rules, as an illustration, clearly violate this principle. Policy coherence relates to the level of consistency between government objectives and policies across a broad spectrum of issues: an investment policy that facilitates the establishment of final assembly facilities in combination with a trade policy that discourages capital equipment imports is an example of policy incoherence.

MNEs have become principal organizational means for the conduct of international business transactions of all types, and they have much flexibility in their choice of strategic alternatives. International rules that focus on selected types of transactions and ignore others can significantly skew the calculations of MNEs as they move funds, goods, services, knowledge, and people across international boundaries and put together complex 'bundles' of such transactions for particular FDI projects. In the process, distortions are created, competition and competitiveness impeded, and, potentially, world welfare damaged. Globalization, moreover, means that policy 'mistakes' carry much higher penalties than they did when national markets were more segmented. To date, international rule-making has not fully recognized the ubiquitous role of the MNE, and, hence, trade, technology, and investment are often treated in isolation, as this chapter and others in the book have shown.

9

Policy Linkages
Competition Policy

9.1 Introduction

Competition policy represents another issue which is of major importance for the international policy agenda, but one which poses problems because of difficult interrelationships with other policy areas such as trade policy. Its significance emanates from the fact that it is a key constituent of the 'liberalization conditions' for market efficiency. The objectives of this chapter are, first, to consider the requirement for international competition policy as part of the evolving framework of international business rules; secondly, to evaluate the existing structure of national, regional, and international laws together with progress in transnational cooperation, and to highlight deficiencies which exist; and, thirdly, to review the proposals which have been made to strengthen international cooperation and rules. The importance of the latter is widely recognized: witness the WTO Director-General Renato Ruggiero's observation in November 1995 on 'the urgent need for analysis of links between competition policy and trade policy, notably to identify the problems that may require action and the options for such action' (cited in Breland and Cordell, 1996).[1] Similarly the EU Commissioner responsible for competition policy, Karel Van Miert, recently instituted a study by a group of experts into *Competition Policy in the New Trade Order* (European Commission, 1995*a*): this called for the development of a plurilateral framework to prevent anti-competitive activity in an era of economic globalization.

9.2 Competition Policy and the Problems of the Multinational Enterprise

Despite the potential influence of multinational enterprises on patterns of market competition, study of MNEs' relationships to monopoly and oligopoly and to competition policy has been somewhat limited. In part the problem derives from difficulties in analysis. It is known that where a market structure reveals high seller concentration, a significant degree of product differentiation, and high entry barriers, this confers on existing firms a degree of market power which they may exploit in various ways. Oligopolistic behaviour may result in wasteful advertising, excessive discretionary expenditure, and sub-optimal efficiency. MNEs have distinctive structural characteristics: they tend to be larger than comparable indigenous firms; they produce under conditions of imperfect oligopoly, are more capital intensive, and advertise more. Some of these features indeed generate the ownership advantages which explain why MNEs exist in the first place. But the structural characteristics of high concentration and high degree of product differentiation in host countries could have been the same without an MNE presence. The empirical challenge is to disentangle the specifically MNE characteristics and effects.

Caves' (1996) exhaustive review of the evidence revealed the following:

- While oligopoly and FDI share common structural causes, concentration has also been shown to have some effects on FDI (see, for example, Knickerbocker, 1973; Graham, 1978; Franko, 1976).
- In respect of the effects of FDI on concentration, the evidence is quite mixed.
- There have been a range of studies concerning multinationals and market behaviour. Imitative rivalry linked to loose-knit oligopolies became more common after the Second World War, but there has been little research in the post-1985 'global era' when international cartels and collusive behaviour may have begun to reappear. Most importantly, research shows that multinational firms 'earn both monopoly profits and rents to their proprietary assets' (Caves, 1996: 97).

The research undertaken to date probably substantially underestimates the potential influences of MNEs on patterns of market competition. There are several reasons for this. First, regional and global integration is associated with higher levels of intermediate and intra-firm trade. This means that it is much more problematic both to measure concentration levels meaningfully at national level and to identify anti-competitive practices. Second, and linked because of globalization, competition problems increasingly transcend national boundaries. Examples include international cartels, export cartels, restrictive practices in international services such as air or sea transport, world-scale mergers and the abuse of a dominant position in several major markets (European Commission, 1995*a*). Third, the increasing range and complexity of relationships within and between firms (quasi-internalization) means that collusive behaviour is difficult to establish and investigate, and it is thus also difficult to judge the pro-competitive versus anti-competitive effects. As discussed earlier, the large multinational enterprises will operate extensive networks of strategic alliances as well as licensing arrangements, management contracts, joint ventures, and so on. And fourth, multinationals can play off one jurisdiction's agreement against another in competition policy (as in other) matters.

Reflecting these and other arguments, there is little doubt that competition policy as currently implemented by national authorities (mainly) is inadequate. The economic arguments are straightforward. Effective competition policies implemented by individual countries may maximize national incomes taken separately. World income may not however be maximized in the presence of MNEs with global market power, and there is also the potential for conflicts when welfare is redistributed internationally.

A variety of issues arise at the practical level (European Commission, 1995*a*). First, MNEs are subject to different competition rules across countries. The transaction costs, deriving from different procedures, time scales, and criteria, can act as a barrier to the expansion of FDI and trade. One extreme example is that of the Gillette Company's acquisition of Wilkinson Sword which had to be cleared by fourteen distinct merger review offices (Scherer, 1994; see also Box 9.1). The same difficulties can actually arise within a country: so the takeover of the US-owned insurance company Eagle Star by BAT Industries of the UK had to be approved by the insurance regulators in every state in which Eagle Star operated.

The ease of transacting takeovers across frontiers varies significantly across countries, not because of competition policy (although there are, of course, major competition implications) but because of other factors. For example, limited shareholders' rights and related issues, cross-holdings of equity and interlocking directorates, and closed state or private holdings of shares make it very difficult to undertake hostile takeovers in several Continental European countries. An interesting example concerns the 1988 bid by Nestlé of Switzerland for Rowntree, the British confectionery company. This caused an outcry in British industrial circles who argued that the acquisition should be disallowed because the Swiss market structure, with its division between registered and bearer shares, stopped British companies purchasing Swiss enterprises (Montagnon, 1990). At the same time some governments appear to have used competition policy to at least delay acquisitions from abroad in sensitive sectors or where the acquiring company from abroad is state-owned (Safarian, 1993).

Second, distortions may result from the fact that competition policy is more lax (either in terms of standards or of enforcement) in one country than another. At the extreme, tolerance of anti-competitive practices could prevent market access. This is recognized as having been a problem in Japan, linked to closed distribution networks, the extent of permitted cartels under the Japanese Antimonopoly Act, bid rigging and opaqueness in public procurement, the anti-competitive role of the *keiretsu*, and weaknesses of the Fair Trade Commission (Wilks, 1994). (It should also be noted that, because of weak competition policy, Japanese firms may have used monopolistic profits generated in Japan to price at marginal costs in overseas markets.) In fact there is no requirement that countries have a competition policy at all. (For recent work on competition policies in Central and Eastern European countries, see Dyker and Barrow, 1994; European Commission, 1995*b*.)

Third, the national policies of some countries may contain extraterritorial provisions by which competition policy rules extend beyond the boundaries of the domestic market. Julius (1990) cites the decision of the New York State court to block the takeover of a UK-owned mining firm, Consolidated Goldfields, by a South African company which also had substantial gold interests. The rights of the American court derived from the fact that some of the assets of Consolidated Goldfields were located in the USA. The judgement was based on the threat to US consumers if such a high proportion of world gold production was controlled by a single firm.

The extraterritorial provisions of the anti-trust laws of the United States have also been used on numerous occasions as tools of American foreign policy, and the

Box 9.1

Gillette—Wilkinson Sword

This case concerns the competition policy consequences of an agreement which was reached for the world's number one firm in the wet-shaver market, Gillette, to acquire a stake in a principal competitor, Wilkinson Sword, on 20 December 1989.

The players

Stora Kopparbergs Berslags AB Eemland Holdings NV, which owned the wet-shaver business Wilkinson Sword (previously Eemland Management Services BV, then Swedish Match NV).

The transaction

1. The Gillette Company and other members of the Gillette group financed the purchase of Stora's consumer products division through a $630 million leveraged buyout (LBO). The consumer products division included the Wilkinson Sword wet-shaving business which had manufacturing facilities in the UK, Zimbabwe, and Brazil.
2. Having been previously advised by government officials that the competition rules of the UK, Germany, and the EC would probably prevent the buyout since Gillette and Wilkinson Sword competed directly with each other in many countries, the Gillette Company bought the entire Wilkinson Sword wet-shaving business outside the European Community from Eemland.

Investigations

1. Of the LBO where authorities in the EC and its member states were looking at the possible effect of Gillette's involvement in Eemland: European Commission, UK, Germany, France, Ireland, Spain.2. Of the non-EC acquisition where authorities were looking at the effects on competition: USA, Canada, New Zealand, Australia, Brazil, Switzerland, South Africa, Sweden.

Outcomes

1. Of the LBO and Gillette's acquired influence over Eemland within the EC: due to fierce opposition and the inevitable negative decisions, expected and later issued, from the EC, the UK, Germany, and France, Eemland sold Wilkinson Sword division to Warner-Lambert. If they had not done so, a divestiture order from all countries and the Commission would have forced a dissolution of the merger. Only Ireland and Spain did not oppose the transaction.
2. Of the non-EC acquisition of Wilkinson Sword:

- *USA*. In response to a case filed with the USDOJ, Gillette, Eemland, and Wilkinson rescinded Gillette's acquisition of Wilkinson Sword business in the US market.
- *Canada*. Before an investigation could be completed, Gillette's ownership of Wilkinson Sword's Canadian business was acquired by Warner-Lambert.
- *New Zealand*. The transaction was approved.
- *Switzerland*. The Commission conducted an investigation and found no harm.
- *South Africa*. No action was taken.
- *Sweden*. Minimal effects were found and no prohibition order was made.

Sources: OECD, 1994*c*, cited in Breland and Cordell, 1996; Commission of the European Communities, 1993.

potential for conflict between nations is clearly considerable in such circumstances. Recent problems have concerned US legislation prohibiting trade with Cuba (the Helms–Burton Act, 1996) and with Libya and Iran (the D'Amato Act, also 1996). These laws apply to US MNEs including their affiliates across the world; and the anti-Cuba law, for example, includes a provision allowing the USA to sue foreign companies 'trafficking' in former US property confiscated by the Cuban government. The EU passed 'blocking legislation' in response, whereby European companies could be prosecuted if they cooperate with US investigations or pull out of Cuba (Van Miert, 1996*a*).[2] And a major issue in the past concerned US sanctions against the sale of American goods and technology through a number of European companies (e.g. John Brown Engineering of the UK which had a licence from US General Electric to manufacture its range of industrial gas turbines) for the Siberian gas pipeline. These measures were applied unilaterally under US re-export controls in December 1981 (Rosenthal and Knighton, 1982).

By contrast with these extraterritorial cases, MNE mergers may fall outside the net of national competition policies. If firms are primarily selling into world markets, national authorities are unlikely to object to the merger. Thus, even if competition is reduced, there may be benefits occurring to the merged group which exceed the costs from any reductions in competition. Furthermore, the home country gains if most of the costs are borne by foreign consumers (Hoekman and Kostecki, 1995).

9.3 Competition Policy Interrelationships and Coverage

The case for internationalizing competition policy is unquestionably strong. There are major constraints, however, deriving from the interrelationships among trade policy, FDI policy, competition policy, and other microeconomic policies. And in a related manner there are difficulties in defining the types of agreements and restraints on business activity which should be incorporated within competition rules.

The role of trade policy is to reduce barriers to international trade and thereby secure market access, on the presumption that free and open trade maximizes world welfare. (In a like manner, FDI policy is designed to facilitate market access and market presence, where trade and FDI are largely complementary to each other.) According to Jenny (European Commission, 1995*a*) trade policy is also concerned to some extent with 'fairness' as, for example, in anti-dumping procedures (a controversial topic which will be discussed below). The implementation of trade policy occurs through '*cooperative* solutions among trading nations' (Scherer, 1994: 7). Competition policy is also designed to provide consumers with the benefits of free competition, through the existence of market structures and processes which promote economic efficiency. But the mechanism to secure these goals is very different from that of trade policy. Thus 'competition policy fosters *non cooperative* solutions among the business enterprises facing one another in the market place' (Scherer, 1994: 7). FDI policy must draw upon both trade and competition policy: MNEs trade but also behave as (oligopolistic) business enterprises and engage in anti-competitive actions.

Deriving from these divergencies are different yardsticks for judging performance (e.g. market structures and processes in the case of competition policy, trade performance measures such as levels of exports in respect of trade policy). Remedies too are different, with injunctions or penalties in respect of competition law, decisions on market access in regard to trade policy. (Generally, remedies would focus upon improving market access, but anti-dumping laws restrict market access and prevent competition.) Jenny (European Commission, 1995*a*) also points out that competition laws do not discriminate among firms according to nationality, whereas trade policy does. Furthermore, the scope of both competition policy and trade policy is restricted in various ways—of particular importance, perhaps, is the fact that competition laws do not usually apply to the behaviour of governments.

Many of the difficulties with trade policy essentially derive from the use or misuse of strategic trade theory. The assumption of imperfect competition and of economies of scale have led to the proposal that governments may justifiably intervene in certain target industries (that produce positive externalities) (Brander and Spencer, 1985; Krugman, 1986). By so doing, the nation will benefit from the externalities created by the industry and by shifting rents from foreign to domestic firms. Subsequent analysis has seriously qualified the case for using these arguments as the basis for trade policy (see Eaton and Grossman, 1986; Dixit and Grossman, 1986). However, they have been used by policy-makers to justify the erection of non-tariff barriers such as voluntary export restraints and the imposition of reciprocity requirements as a means of countering and correcting market distortions introduced by trading partners. In the process there may well be resource misallocations and serious anti-competitive effects.

Aside from the interrelationships between trade policy and competition policy, important issues also arise in the interface between competition rules and other microeconomic policies such as industrial policy. Although the term 'industrial policy' is no longer in vogue, all countries have some form of industrial or structural policy. Industrial development and international competitiveness is sought through public procurement practices; state aids for investment, innovation, R & D, and regional development; the operation of government-owned enterprises and state-sanctioned monopolies; tax policies; support for small and medium-sized enterprises, technical standards, and so on. The importance attached to these policies has varied over time and also by country depending upon policy philosophy (Jacquemin in Scherer, 1994; Moncarz, 1995).[3] The growing consensus at present leans towards the 'Anglo-Saxon model', with market competition believed to exert a key, positive influence on social welfare.

However, while interventionist industrial policies are viewed as undesirable, the role of the state in remedying market failure is still accepted as necessary. Especially important in the latter regard is the issue of cooperation in R & D. The argument for permitting R & D cooperation is based on the problem of market failure concerning the appropriability of the benefits of research and development. The dilemma arises because, on the one hand, a company will only undertake R & D if it can ensure appropriability by limiting diffusion of research output; while, on the other, the public interest demands costless spillovers of R & D results to other firms. Cooperative

R & D can be a solution which internalizes the externalities created by significant spillovers of R & D while ensuring a sharing of information among firms. However, difficult problems that arise concern the possible access of foreign producers to cooperative R & D programmes that are funded by national governments; and global strategic alliances in R & D which could lead to international monopolies and reduce competitive pressures to innovate. Warner and Rugman (1994) have strongly criticized the discriminatory use of performance requirements and reciprocity provisions in certain recent US R & D policy initiatives. For example, the National Competitiveness Act of 1993 stresses that funds provided should for the most part benefit only citizens or nationals of the United States: it therefore attempts to limit access to technology support programmes. The EU in reality may only be a little less discriminatory: the position of the Council of Ministers is that participation of non-EU companies in EU programmes is possible where an objective is the transfer of results or technology to EU member states (Brewer and Young, 1995c).

What is evident is that competition policy may be used to achieve industrial policy objectives. For example, the aim of giving indigenous enterprises an advantage in high-growth, high-tech export markets might prompt the introduction of specific competition policy exemptions; these could include export cartels and joint ventures supplying overseas markets or operating in R & D-intensive sectors. The encouragement of 'national champions' through weak competition action towards dominant firms (linked to restrictive trade and investment policies against foreign competition) could generate important problems of market access and market presence (Zampetti and Sauvé, 1995).

It is because of the range and complexities of policy interrelationships and their potential for supporting anti-competitiveness that Rosenthal and Nicolaïdes (1997), for example, have argued that: 'Merely harmonizing broad, substantive antitrust norms will not have much impact on anticompetitive behavior and practices tolerated or promoted by other national and international economic laws and policies.'

In considering the potential coverage of international competition policy, Warner (1996) distinguishes between private restraints on trade (i.e. the behaviour of firms) and public restraints on trade (i.e. the behaviour of governments). Within the former category are agreements on price-fixing, market allocations, refusals to deal, bid-rigging, etc., while public restraints include tariff and non-tariff barriers, subsidies, voluntary export restraints, and investment reviews and restrictions. Warner's (1996: 244) argument is that

> Where the harm arises from purely private conduct, traditional anti-trust laws may be most effective in removing the relevant barrier to entry. Where the harm results from governmental action in the form of regulations and laws, then traditional trade law instruments may be more fruitfully employed, so long as they are influenced by concepts of competition and contestability.

However, this distinction is less clear-cut when the FDI decisions of multinational enterprises are taken into consideration. Thus a number of the public restraints on trade have clear investment consequences which affect market access and the level and nature of competition. For example, non-tariff barriers such as product standards, labelling, certification, and accreditation are blatantly protectionist. The same is true of anti-dumping duties, which are discussed in the following section together with some suggested remedies. Subsidies may take a variety of forms, but investment incentives are especially significant in an FDI context and could be targeted directly through international investment rules.

In respect of private restraints, there are issues of debate but also of agreement as to what might be included within international competition policy. Immenga (European Commission, 1995*a*) suggests the following:

1. Horizontal agreements (among competitors)

- Hard-core export and import cartels (price-fixing, output restraints, market division, customer allocation, collusive tendering). These are anti-competitive and impede cross-border market access. In normal circumstances they should be banned.
- Other anti-competitive agreements. Arrangements such as R & D cooperation should not be excluded from competition rules, and a 'rule of reason' might be envisaged in which three points were considered, namely, the balance against pro-competitive effects, the balance against efficiencies, the requirement for cooperation as a condition to enter a new market.

2. Vertical agreements (between buyers and sellers, e.g. exclusive arrangements, vertical price-fixing, resale price maintenance, territorial restrictions). There is general agreement on the anti-competitive effects of resale price maintenance. Otherwise, the competitive effects are uncertain: the penetration of new markets is often facilitated by agreements between producers who want to break into a new market and local distributors; however, producer–distributor arrangements may also lead to the partitioning of a market and the exclusion of new entrants. One solution which has been suggested is to deal only with vertical restraints which are linked to dominance; whereas a recent European Commission Green Paper (CEC, 1997) suggested a variety of options for discussion.[4]

3. Abuse of intellectual property rights. The aim of intellectual property right (IPR) laws is to grant legal monopolies and as such there is a conflict with competition policies. Therefore, the objective of competition policy should be to define the scope of IPR rules and identify those practices which are harmful to competition.

4. Dominance. There is a presumption that dominance is detrimental to competition.

5. Merger policy. There are considerable divergencies with respect to the handling of mergers in competition law. Complex issues arise which relate both to the ability to undertake mergers and takeovers in different countries (questions of corporate governance etc.) and to their effects. In addition, merger policy is close to industrial policy when issues concerning the classic anti-trust dilemmas arise (e.g. the belief in Europe at particular points in time that large-scale mergers were to be encouraged in order to enable European companies to compete against overseas competitors).

6. The fact that public undertakings and state-approved monopolies are free from market restraints and may use their powers to impede competition. A solution might rest in either imposing a requirement on these enterprises that they behave according to market principles or eliminating all exclusive trading rights and monopolies.

The ability to introduce such solutions at an international level is, however, a very long-term objective.

9.4 Anti-dumping and Competition Policy

Amongst the issues where potential policy conflicts arise, there is little question that anti-dumping (AD) is one of the most significant and controversial (for a detailed series of analyses, see Tharaken, 1991). Anti-dumping duties are authorized by Article VI of the AD Agreement. Dumping is deemed to occur when the 'normal value' of a product is higher than its price when sold in the export market. 'Normal value' is the price of the product when traded in the home market of the exporter *or* its cost of production. When a product is dumped, *and* the dumped imports have caused or threaten to cause 'material injury' to domestic producers of a similar product, anti-dumping duties are permitted. The AD duty may be no greater than the dumping margin, namely the difference between the normal value and the export price (Hindley, 1994).

The incidence of AD activity has increased substantially in the last few years (a recent case which highlights some of the dilemmas posed by alleged dumping is presented in Box 9.2; a major criticism of AD actions, reflected in the Box, is that they are excessively tilted in favour of domestic producers). Historically the major users of AD policies were Australia, Canada, the EU, and the USA, and in the early to mid-1980s these countries accounted for virtually all formal AD actions. The investigations focused upon non-OECD nations, especially those in the Asia Pacific region and the economies in transition. And actions were concentrated in a limited number of sectors, particularly chemicals, metals, machinery, textiles, consumer electronics, and cement (Leidy, 1995). From the late 1980s, developing countries and other non-traditional users have increasingly initiated formal AD actions and at present account for about 20–30 per cent of total initiations and definitive duties.[5] In large part the explanation for the latter lies in the demonstration effect, with traditional users having shown the effectiveness of AD measures as a form of selective protection which is approved by the GATT.

Anti-dumping policies have been severely criticized by economists (for a recent review and proposals for reform, see Lipstein, 1997). As Leidy (1995: 27) points out:

> the treatment of foreign firms under anti-dumping and the treatment of domestic firms under anti-trust (competition policy) are fundamentally at odds. While anti-trust embraces competition as a means of ensuring efficient resource allocation and improving living standards, AD internationally discourages price competition. Discriminatory pricing among domestic competitors is not challenged under anti-trust when such pricing is deemed 'predatory' . . . Foreign discriminatory pricing, however, is often challenged successfully under AD laws without the least hint of predation.

These anomalies are very evident in the EU: anti-dumping duties are not applied on intra-EU trade, where, in addition, competition policy permits new entrants to break into the market through 'loss-leader' pricing. Anti-dumping duties against foreign firms have not only discriminated against foreign firms but have encouraged

Box 9.2

EU Fashions Duties From Chinese Handbags

'. . . Women who live in western Europe may end up paying more as a result of import duties imposed by the European Commission on Chinese-made handbags.

The duties of up to 39 per cent are being contested by importers and retailers, which say they will cramp consumer choice and lead to higher prices.

Nearly half the estimated 148m handbags sold in western Europe last year came from China, according to European Commission figures. In the shops, Chinese bags often cost around a quarter of the price of £70 or so of an equivalent bag made in Europe.

"We are disappointed that the Commission did not take into account the relevant issues and hope it will reconsider," said Mr Alberto Bichi, assistant director at the Brussels-based Foreign Trade Association, which represents importers and retailers of textile goods across Europe.

Marks and Spencer, the UK retailer, said the duties were "unwarranted and unnecessary" and against consumer interests. They were instituted this month on a preliminary basis after a study into the effect on manufacturers in Europe of imports of a wide range of Chinese-made luggage.

Proposals for duties on Chinese-made schoolbags and sports bags were dropped, leaving only handbags affected. A decision on whether to make the duties permanent is to be taken by the summer.

Complaints about the large volume of bags from China were made to the Commission by the Paris-based European Federation of Producers of Leathergoods and Luggage. Brussels has been swayed by the arguments of bag makers mainly in Italy and Spain that the Chinese products are being sold in Europe at below their production price, constituting "dumping".

But many European importers argue that the Chinese bags represent products that are virtually impossible to purchase from European makers. Mr Nicholas Long, chairman of the UK's Luggage and Leathergoods Association, said most Chinese products were "totally different" in design from those made by European manufacturers, which in recent years have moved up-market to relatively high price styles.

Mr David Shilton, chairman of Shilton, a UK supplier of handbags and fashion goods, said: "The Commission's action is inflationary and will do no one any good." Other handbag suppliers have warned that, as well as pushing up prices, the import duties could have the impact of threatening thousands of jobs in retail and distribution of textile products. Total retail sales of handbags across Europe last year totalled an estimated £1.5bn.

The Commission said it was still examining all factors regarding the handbag market before a final decision on the duties.'

cartel behaviour within the Union. In the 1980s about one-quarter of all cartel cases initiated by the Commission concerned firms and products that were also involved in anti-dumping cases (Montagnan, 1990).

It is also increasingly recognized that the multinationality of business may facilitate the circumvention of AD rules as well as lead to other distortions. For example, foreign MNEs may switch sourcing to third countries which are not subject to duties. Other problems arise where EU MNEs (as an illustration) locate production in Asia Pacific locations or enter into joint ventures with producers in Asia Pacific for subsequent export to Europe: anti-dumping actions against such imports may for obvious reasons be impossible.

Anti-dumping rules in the EU (again as an illustration) have encouraged FDI from Japan and other Asia Pacific countries as a means of circumventing actual or potential duties. EU anti-circumvention legislation allowed for the imposition of anti-dumping duties on imports to these assembly ('screwdriver') plants which were established to avoid the original duties and did not achieve a level of 40 per cent local content. These rules were deemed to be inconsistent with the GATT in 1989 and were withdrawn.

These examples could be generalized out to encompass the myriad alliances and global production, sourcing and marketing decisions made by multinational enterprises, and emphasize the point that in a global era AD rules are both arbitrary and meaningless (Hoekman and Kostecki, 1995).

Rugman and Gestrin (1991) have further criticized AD laws in an FDI context. Their argument is that AD cases may derive from lobbying by weak domestic producers. Unable to develop sustainable firm-specific advantages in technology, management, and/or marketing skills to facilitate international competitiveness, the firms resort to 'shelter-based' strategies (i.e. protectionism associated with anti-dumping duties). Of course, such strategies are doomed to failure if foreign exporters subsequently establish assembly or manufacturing facilities within the domestic market.

It has been argued that AD policies may be useful as a tool of reciprocity, and represent a justifiable attempt by importing countries to offset the market access restrictions existing in the home nation of the exporting firm (Hoekman and Kostecki, 1995). Such restrictions, such as weaknesses in competition policy, could underlie the ability of the exporting firms to engage in dumping activity. Tyson (1992), moreover, has focused upon anti-dumping duties as a means of offsetting 'predatory behaviour' by foreign (Japanese) firms in high-technology industries.

In the light of the above discussion, the best policy would be to deal with anti-dumping within a competition policy rather than a trade policy framework. The overriding criterion for judging anti-dumping allegations would be an assessment of actual or threatened injury to competition (Leidy, 1995). Failing this a variety of second or third best options have been suggested, including:

- fixing penalties for AD appeals that are later judged to be frivolous or anti-competitive;
- allowing a greater say for consumer groups and downstream industries which are directly hurt by AD actions;
- requiring a national benefit/cost analysis as part of AD actions;
- introducing greater transparency into AD actions;
- limiting AD measures to trade adjustment assistance, without imposing protective duties;

- giving competition policy authorities a formal role in evaluating the competitive effects of proposed AD actions.

In the context of the last of these options, Hoekman and Mavroidis (1994) have suggested that allegations of dumping should be investigated initially by the competition policy authorities of the exporter's home country (in conjunction with the importing country's competition body). If anti-competitive behaviour was found to exist, a decision would be implemented which would benefit the importing industry. Where the two competition policy bodies disagreed, the authority in the importing country could invoke WTO dispute settlement mechanisms or initiate an anti-dumping investigation.

Despite the weight of informed opinion in favour of change, the Uruguay Round negotiations largely ratified existing anti-dumping rules. This was largely because of US and EU pressure, since some industrial countries such as Japan and developing nations were in favour of strong limitations on AD use.

There was some clarification of rules, in regard to guidelines for determining injury to domestic producers. The minor changes included a 2 per cent *de minimis* dumping margin below which an AD inquiry would be terminated; a *de minimis* threshold which required the termination of an enquiry when the volume of dumped imports was considered negligible; and a five-year sunset rule for AD actions unless a review was formally requested. Hindley (1994), however, is highly critical of the failure of the Uruguay Round to handle the problem whereby anti-dumping authorities inflate dumping margins through the methodology of price calculations.

Hindley, moreover, is sceptical as to whether the *Agreement on Safeguards* in the Uruguay Round, which bans any future voluntary export restraints (VERs) and requires the phasing out of existing VERs, will actually remove the underlying protectionist pressures. As is noted, anti-dumping actions can be legally discharged under WTO rules by 'undertakings' (that is, commitments by exporters found to have dumped that they will not sell in the particular market at a price lower than an agreed non-dumping price; or on occasions that they will not sell more than a certain quantity). To quote the author (Hindley, 1994: 27): 'In the light of this, what price the ban on VERs?' While VERs secured at least some level of exports for the exporters, anti-dumping measures could result in a complete ban on exports. Furthermore, anti-dumping measures have proved in the USA, for example, to be very long lasting: one-third of the current anti-dumping measures on Japanese exports to the USA have lasted longer than ten years and those on colour TVs have been in existence for more than twenty-two years (Itoh and Nagaoka, 1997). It should also be noted that another form of discriminatory, quantity-fixing trade intervention exists through voluntary import expansions (VIEs): while supposedly trade and competition enhancing, they distort resource allocation and may actually have anti-competitive effects if shares of imports are fixed. Certainly they are a poor substitute for a strengthening of competition policy in the importing country and internationally.

Australia and New Zealand agreed to deal with dumping allegations through competition policy when they signed the Closer Economic Relations Agreement; members of the EU and the European Free Trade Area reached a similar agreement when they formed the European Economic Area. And it is important to make further multilateral efforts within a competition policy framework.

9.5 Competition Policies at National, Bilateral, and Regional Level

National level

In the period after the Second World War, the prevailing philosophy in the industrialized countries was more strongly pro-competitive than previously. Thus there was a decline in the view prevalent in Continental Europe that competitive market processes were basically unstable. The competition policies enacted have, however, been significantly different in the USA and Europe in terms both of substance and procedure. In the United States, particular violations of competition laws carry criminal penalties, while in most other countries non-compliance with competition rules is a matter of civil law only. The criteria for evaluating large mergers and acquisitions are divergent as between the USA and Europe. As Graham (1996) points out, an 'efficiency defence' (that is, significant cost savings would be achieved and passed on to consumers) can be applied to justify a merger in the United States that would significantly increase seller concentration; such an efficiency defence is not allowable in Europe. In addition, the United States and some other countries prohibit price-fixing cartels without qualification; other countries will permit the cartels but attempt to control the abuses. Again, in Europe 'block exemptions' may be granted to particular activities or industries to provide immunity from certain aspects of competition law, whereas this is generally unknown in the United States. There are also differences between the USA and Canada, particularly in terms of implementation. In the USA laws are enforced on a case-by-case basis federally and locally, whereas in Canada the Bureau of Competition Policy has the responsibility for implementing and enforcing a clearly specified set of rules concerning anti-competitive behaviour. (Among the large number of writings on competition policy in North America and Europe, see Comanor et al., 1990).

Among the industrialized countries, nevertheless, it is only Japan in present times that stands out in respect of a fundamental ambivalence towards the role of competition. There has been a strong feeling among industrialists and government officials that competition is both unproductive and un-Japanese. Wilks (1994) indeed points out that a new word had to be invented to denote the Western meaning of 'competition'. A theory of 'excessive competition' was developed and used subsequently to justify mergers, cartels, rationalization, and industrial intervention. Although the Japanese statute book contains stringent and comprehensive competition policy provisions, legal enforcement has been very weak. As an illustration, critics point to the comparison of the 350,000 practising lawyers in the USA with the 14,700 fully qualified lawyers in Japan (Wilks, 1994). The weak enforcement of competition policy has been a major influence on the closed character of the Japanese market. Therefore, pressure from the USA and Japan to improve market access has inevitably focused *inter alia* upon a strengthening of the activities of the Japanese Fair Trade Commission, more active use of and the elimination of exemptions from the Anti-Monopoly Act, and actions against the alleged anti-competitive behaviour of the *keiretsu*. An example of the problems of one company—Chrysler—in the Japanese market is contained in Goldfarb (1995.) For a review of competition regulations in other countries of the Pacific Rim, see Green and Rosenthal (1996).

Regional level

Given the failure of the Havana Charter, the European Union provides the best illustration of both the benefits and the problems of transnational competition policy. It is important to stress the centrality of competition law which is contained in Articles 85–94 of the Treaty of Rome relating to restrictive business practices, cartels, and the abuse of a dominant position; and in the more recent Merger Regulation of 1989. It is the area, therefore, where the Commission has had some of its clearest and strongest powers. The common competition rules have been designed to remove obstacles to the Europeanization of firm activity by ensuring that anti-competitive behaviour does not keep the internal market divided. They are also designed to ensure that consumers enjoy the benefits from market integration.

Community law applies to forms of conduct that prevent, restrict, or distort competition within the Union in the form of affecting trade between member states; while the Merger Regulation covers 'concentrations with a Community dimension' specified in terms of world- and Union-level turnover and the requirement that each of the parties has no more than two-thirds of its aggregate Union-wide turnover within one and the same member state (Morgan, 1997).[6] EU competition policy also covers state aids to national (usually state-owned) enterprises and preferential national procurement regulations that distort competition within the bloc.

To provide some indication of the extent of activity in 1995, there were 668 anti-trust cases (559 new cases of restrictive agreements and abuse of dominant position and 109 merger cases), and 685 state monopoly and monopoly rights as well as state aid cases (Van Miert, 1996*b*).

The EU's success in a number of high-profile cases and the size of the fines imposed indicate that competition policy has teeth. Some of the criticisms which have been made of actions under Articles 85 and 86 concern the slow pace of decision-making but this is primarily a reflection of the small number of Commission staff. There have also been areas of dispute between the Commission and member states over their respective authority in competition cases. A 1997 case concerned the proposed alliance of British Airways and American Airlines where the UK was insisting that its competition authorities should be the final arbiter of the case; at the same time the EU were investigating the case under the terms of Article 86 (*Financial Times*, 1997*f*). In respect of the Merger Regulation, the scope of the rules has been limited by the high thresholds for investigation but it seems likely that new Commission proposals to lower these will be approved (see note 6). The application of competition policy to state aids, furthermore, has brought the competition policy directorate into conflict with both national governments and other directorates, particularly those responsible for industrial policy and transport. Recent examples include state aid for the 'restructuring' of state-owned airlines in a number of Continental European countries (e.g. Air France and Olympic, the Greek national carrier); there have been instances of Commissioners buckling under the pressures of national governments and sanctioning large aid packages without adequate commitments to reorganization and rationalization.

In respect of the latter issue, recent debate has centred on the problems that the Commission acts 'too much like a prosecutor and judge rolled into one' (Graham, 1995*a*: 111); and that decisions on state aid and other issues become part of a secret and broader bargaining process within the Commission and between the Commission and member states. In the light of these difficulties, the German government has put forward a proposal for a European competition agency, separate from the Commission, to depoliticize the decision-making process in individual cases. The Commission's view is that such an agency, which would enforce the EU's anti-trust rules separately, would cut important links between competition policy and other policies, such as research and technical development, regional or environmental policy (*Financial Times*, 1995*b*; Van Miert, 1996*b*).

Study of the European Union experience is clearly highly instructive for deliberations concerning the future of competition policy on a wider, international scale. The EU is, however, very distinctive because of the degree of economic integration which is involved, the extensive supranational powers of the Commission, and the ultimate authority which rests in the European Court of Justice to settle disputes between the EU and its member states.

It has been shown in Chapter 7 that the NAFTA has made extensive progress in the development of FDI rules, but the agreement does not cover dumping, subsidies, or competition issues. There are general expressions of agreement concerning the adoption or maintenance of measures to proscribe anti-competitive behaviour, consultation on the effectiveness of each country's measures, and cooperation on enforcing their competition laws. The competition guidelines are not subject to the dispute provisions of NAFTA, and there is provision for the parties to designate a monopoly and maintain or establish state enterprises. There is agreement, finally, to set up a working group on competition and trade with a five-year mandate to make recommendations on the interrelationships between competition and trade rules. The implication is that substantive progress on the competition issue really depends upon deep economic integration allied to some political integration, which only exists within the European Union at present. As evidence of wider interest, nevertheless, a Free Trade Area of the Americas (FTAA) competition policy working group has also been established as part of the discussions to establish an FTAA by 2005 (*Inside US Trade*, 1996*a*).

Bilateral cooperation

The EU has extensive experience in cooperation internally and this has been extended to cooperation with other countries in Europe and the USA. On the other hand, the number of international bilateral anti-trust cooperation agreements and mutual legal assistance agreements concluded by the EU remains very limited in comparison with the USA. Thus the United States had bilateral agreements with West Germany (1976), Australia (1982), Canada (1984 and 1995), France and Germany (1987), and Australia and New Zealand (1990), as well as with the EU (1991).[7]

In respect of the USA–EU agreement, in the fifteen months up to June 1996, fifty-four cases were notified by the EU and forty-four by the USA (Van Miert, 1996*a*). Aside from notification of cases where the interests of the other party may be affected, the agreement covers cooperation and coordination of the enforcement actions of both parties' competition authorities; a 'traditional comity' procedure by virtue of which each party takes into account the important interests of the other when competition measures are enforced; and a 'positive comity' whereby either party can invite the other to take appropriate measures regarding anti-competitive behaviour on its territory which affect the important interests of the requesting party.

From an EU perspective, positive features of the cooperation agreement include the following (Van Miert, 1996*b*):

- Constant contact between authorities offers considerable opportunities to bring competition policy approaches closer together (despite differences in legislation).
- Cooperation on individual cases has shown considerable similarities in the economic analyses of the Commission and its US counterparts.
- One of the issues most frequently raised has been the extraterritorial application of US anti-trust law. Despite the problems with the Helms–Burton and D'Amato Acts, there has been evidence of the US authorities being prepared to forgo unilateral action in favour of close cooperation with the Commission.

However, it was also noted that cooperation had its limits:

- Differences in procedural rules can make coordination difficult.
- Each system of competition laws deals with practices which harm its own market e.g. the Commission could not assist in circumstances in which US interests were harmed by practices which have no impact in Europe, even if they were wholly or partly organized in Europe.
- For a multinational firm operating transatlantically or globally, different remedies may be devised by the US and EU authorities since the competition problems facing the two anti-trust bodies may be different. An illustration concerns the Kimberley Clark (KC)/Scott Paper (SP) case: in the Commission's decision the parties were obliged to divest the KC's Kleenex brand toilet tissue and SP's Andrex brand facial tissue and hankies in the UK and Irish markets; in the USA, divestiture of Scott's facial tissue and baby wipes was required.
- The content of the information which can be exchanged is limited by both sides' confidentiality rules.

9.6 Competition Policy Developments at the International Level

United Nations

The UN Conference on Trade and Employment in Havana in 1947 and 1948 produced an impressively wide-ranging and far-sighted scheme for reform of the world trade and investment system. The Havana Charter proposals on multilateral tariff reductions and on arbitration in trade barrier and dumping disputes were incorporated subsequently into the GATT regime. The unratified Charter, however, also included within Article 46 proposals on international competition policy (US Department of State, 1948: 86, cited in Scherer, 1994: 38):

> Each Member shall take appropriate measures and shall cooperate with the [ITO] to prevent, on the part of private or public commercial enterprises, business practices affecting international trade which restrain competition, limit access to markets, or foster monopolistic control, whenever such practices have harmful effects on the expansion of production or trade or interfere with the achievement of any of the other objectives [of the Charter].

The unfair business practices referred to included price-fixing, market-sharing, production quota-setting, discrimination against particular enterprises, collusive suppression of technology, and the abuse of patent rights; and reflected the anti-competitive behaviour of international cartels which had operated during the inter-war, depression years (Fox, 1995). In terms of implementation, the International Trade Organization was directed to consult with member states on apparent violations, encourage corrective action, and publish reports on compliance.

Although the USA did not ratify the Havana Charter, it was supportive of attempts under UN auspices to devise international competition rules. In 1953 a UN Committee produced a Draft Convention on Restrictive Practices which was endorsed by the UN Economic and Social Council and passed to member states for ratification. The Convention proposed mechanisms to control international trade practices that 'restrain competition, limit access to markets or foster monopolistic control' (Scherer, 1994: 39). An international agency would be set up to receive and investigate complaints relating to restrictive practices, with the home nation of the accused firms representing them in a formal hearing. The findings from this hearing would be considered by a Representative Body in which each signatory nation had one vote. On reaching a decision, the enterprises' home government would take appropriate action in accordance with its own system of law. With opposition from the US business community, the United States would not ratify the Convention. Their view was that companies resident in the USA would be particularly adversely affected given that country's strong anti-trust policies. Furthermore, the one-signatory, one-vote system was considered to be unfair on the small number of nations responsible for the bulk of international trade.

Efforts to formulate international competition rules continued in the 1970s within the auspices of UNCTAD. The focus, however, was restrictive business practices that could affect the trade and development of developing nations, in particular international cartels, national external trade cartels, domestic restrictive practices, and acquisition or abuse of market power (Sauvant, 1977). The provisions of this set of *Multilaterally Agreed Equitable Principles and Rules for the Control of Restrictive Business Practices* was adopted by the General Assembly in its Resolution 35/63 of 5 December 1980. They were subsequently incorporated into the Draft United Nations Code of Conduct on Transnational Corporations, which, as explained in Chapter 4, has not been ratified. As UNCTAD (1996*d*) notes, this is the only proposal in existence for a comprehensive multilateral instrument.

OECD

The developed countries continued their efforts to make progress on the competition policy front through the 1976 *Guidelines for Multinational Enterprises*. MNEs were advised to conform to the official competition rules of the countries in which they operated, and to refrain from actions which would adversely affect competition through abuse of a dominant position. Such actions would include, for example, anti-competitive acquisitions; predatory behaviour towards competitors; unreasonable refusal to deal; anti-competitive abuse of industrial property rights; discriminatory pricing including transfer pricing; and cartel behaviour. Warner (1996) points out, however, that some of the other provisions are questionable in terms of their economic justification. The guidelines on vertical practices fall into this category, because, as discussed above, they are not necessarily anti-competitive.

In the subsequent reviews of the OECD Guidelines, attempts were made to improve cooperation between member states on restrictive business practices, and to encourage member countries to draft competition policy legislation in a way which would not lead to conflicting requirements being imposed on multinational enterprises (see Appendix 9.1). As with other aspects of the non-binding guidelines and declarations, the aim in terms of competition policy has been gradually to improve cooperation between member states, share information, and encourage governments to act moderately and with self-restraint when extraterritorial issues are involved. Essentially the Guidelines on competition policy at OECD level are attempting to reflect at an international level the experience which is being gained from cooperation agreements established among countries on a bilateral basis.

Other OECD codes and instruments embody competition principles too (Warner, 1996). Thus the 1962 Code of Liberalization of Capital Movements specifies a binding obligation with respect to right of establishment unless reservations or exceptions have been established. Similarly the 1976 OECD Declaration of National Treatment has since 1988 included a standstill agreement relating to the adoption of non-conforming measures. Both agreements could be of assistance in establishing the principle of contestability as it applies to FDI.

GATT/WTO

At a very fundamental level, the core WTO principles of most favoured nation treatment, national treatment, and the elimination of quantitative restrictions establish important competition as well as trade standards. Thus they are designed to eliminate barriers to access and establish the principle of contestability of markets.

More specifically, agreements negotiated in the Uruguay Round on trade in services and intellectual property contain provisions on competition policy issues. The TRIPs agreement deals with the interface between technology transfer and restrictive business practices in Article 40.1. The Article specifies that 'some licensing practices or conditions pertaining to intellectual property rights which restrain competition may have adverse effects on trade and may impede the transfer and dissemination of technology'. Examples of anti-competitive practices quoted include 'exclusive grantback provisions, conditions preventing challenges to validity, and coercive package licensing'.

The General Agreement on Trade in Services within the Uruguay Round Final Act also includes a number of competition policy principles. In respect of monopolies and exclusive service suppliers and their business practices, Article VIII specifies that signatory nations shall ensure that such a supplier does not abuse its monopoly position by acting in a manner inconsistent with the GATS MFN principle. In Article IX, members of the agreement accept that certain 'other business practices of service suppliers . . . may restrain competition, and thereby restrict trade in services', and they consent to cooperate in eliminating such practices.

The Uruguay Round Agreements have also influenced competition policy through the maintenance (albeit with some amendments) of anti-dumping rules. According to Warner (1996), in the past these have led to more anti-competitive than pro-competitive results. More progress on competition was considered to have been made, on the other hand, through the agreement on Subsidies and Countervailing Measures. This defined three classes of subsidies: prohibited subsidies, actionable subsidies, and permitted subsidies. In the first—prohibited—category were export subsidies and local content subsidies, whereas subsidies for research and pre-competitive development were permitted. The agreement sets out a 'rule of reason' approach to actionable subsidies, which is a test to establish whether serious injury is caused to the domestic industry of another member nation.

In summary, Hoekman and Kostecki (1995) (drawing on Hoekman and Mavroidis, 1994) identify four basic weaknesses in the GATT / WTO rules as far as competition policies are concerned. First, exclusively private business practices restricting market access which are not supported by government cannot be dealt with under the GATT or GATS. A complaint may be possible only if government support can be identified, e.g. provision of subsidies or anti-trust exemptions. Second, as noted previously, there is no requirement that WTO member states have a competition policy at all. Third, WTO rules relate to national policies whereas the challenge is to devise an international competition policy. And fourth, the rules of the WTO apply to government measures affecting the conditions of competition on their territory, and do not cover anti-competitive behaviour and practices in export markets. Industrialized countries' export prohibitions or quantitative restrictions and export subsidies are banned. However, GATT rules still allow member states to impose tariffs on exports and form export cartels and monopolies.[8]

9.7 The Future for International Competition Policy

It is clear from the foregoing that there is a degree of recognition that any comprehensive multilateral agreement on investment and trade should include competition policy. There are, however, major difficulties stemming from inconsistent policies, from differing degrees and strength of legislative implementation, and, indeed, from diverse policy philosophies among nations; from knowledge limitations concerning which competitive practices should be permissible and which should be banned; and from problematic interrelationships among competition, trade, and FDI policy. The debate, therefore, concerns how to make progress to ensure that liberalization of trade and FDI rules is not compromised by corporate behaviour that restricts competition; and to guarantee that multinational corporations are subject to the same competition disciplines as enterprises operating nationally.

Probably the most ambitious set of proposals recently have been those made by F. M. Scherer (1994), which, as he states, 'recognizes individual nations' perceived needs for exceptions and respects national sovereignty while moving as far as seems feasible towards eliminating avoidable restraints upon international competition' (p. 92). The phased proposals are as follows:

Proposal 1: the establishment of an International Competition Policy Office (ICPO) within the framework of the WTO with both investigative and enforcement responsibilities.

Proposal 2: one year after the international competition policy agreement has been signed, all 'substantial' (defined quite precisely) single-nation and cross-border export and import cartels should be registered.

Proposal 3: a petition by a signatory nation or nations that international trade has been restrained or distorted by monopolistic practices would be followed by ICPO investigation and publication of results including recommendations for action.

Proposal 4: within three years from the ICPO's establishment, signatory nations would agree to supply information on the proposed mergers of substantial enterprises. This information on supply and international trading activities would then be distributed to the competition policy authorities of affected countries.

Proposal 5: within five years, all signatories would enact national laws prohibiting export cartels operating from their home territory. Each country would be allowed three exceptions from this blanket prohibition.

Proposal 6: within this same time scale, signatories would also prohibit import cartels, except those created specifically to provide countervailing power against the activities of export cartels.

Proposal 7: in its seventh year, the ICPO would accept from signatory countries complaints about alleged abuse of monopoly power by cartels or any substantial enterprise accounting for more than 40 per cent of world exports in a four-digit SITC category. The ICPO would investigate the complaint and, where an abuse existed, recommend appropriate measures. If corrective action was not taken by national authorities, the WTO would authorize sanctions.

Proposal 8: in the same time scale, the ICPO would handle merger cases, where the notified merger would account for 40 per cent or more of world trade in some four-digit SITC category. Corrective actions would be recommended in appropriate instances, with action to be undertaken within the national laws of signatory nations.

Proposal 9: if a substantial enterprise controlled 40 per cent or more of world trade for a period of more than twenty years on the basis of patents or copyrights, compulsory licensing (at reasonable royalty levels) could be required by any affected signatory nation.

Proposal 10: within a similar time frame, the ICPO would also deal with complaints concerning other monopolistic practices that distort international trade. If any problem is not remedied through national action, individual countries would be authorized to impose countermeasures against nations or industries in which the distorting practices occurred.

Proposal 11: none of these proposals would prevent any signatory nation from implementing more stringent rules with regard to restraints of competition within its national market; nor indeed weaker rules when the effects of restraints of competition occurred solely within its national market.

These proposals were presented as a basis upon which international competition policy negotiations could proceed. In reality even this phased approach probably represents a step too far at this stage. More realistic, therefore, is the approach presented in the European Commission (1995*a*) sponsored report by a group of independent experts, which was set up to consider ways of strengthening international cooperation and rules in the field of competition policy. Their conclusion was that an international competition code superimposed on national laws and including a single implementation authority was not a realistic short- or medium-term option. Rather a twin-track approach was proposed.

The first track would concentrate on assisting the introduction of competition rules into countries that did not yet have them; and, more importantly, strengthening bilateral cooperation. In the latter regard, it was recommended that the EU/USA bilateral agreement should be strengthened in ways that could serve as a model for the development of cooperation elsewhere. This would mean a commitment by the parties not to act unilaterally until all the means provided by comity had been exhausted; and the removal of current obstacles to information exchanges relating to confidential data. The establishment of a network of such arrangements, including an EU/Japan agreement, was suggested.

The second track would entail the gradual construction of a plurilateral competition policy framework based on a common set of rules and a dispute settlement procedure. The aim would be to ensure that cross-border restrictive practices were effectively monitored; and to reduce the risks of conflict derived from the heterogeneity of national and bilateral agreements. The three major issues to be tackled concern the geographical coverage of the agreement, the determination of common rules, and the establishment of a new structure:

- Geographical coverage. This should include the OECD countries, Central and East European nations, and the Asian NICs in the first instance, with extension thereafter to the most advanced countries in Latin America. It was considered that the proposed competition policy agreement could be established as a 'plurilateral agreement' under Annex 4 to the agreement establishing the WTO.

- Determination of common rules. While the establishment of a list of minimum principles would be difficult in areas such as vertical agreements, for example, the group felt that a consensus could be built on the prohibition of horizontal cartels (including export cartels) relating to the fixing of prices, restriction of supply, or market-sharing. In respect of the abuse of a dominant position, a regime similar to that of Article 86 of the EC Treaty was recommended. In the case of mergers, priority should be given to the harmonization of procedures, including time scales for investigation to allow for consultations between competition authorities. Finally, it was proposed that Article XVII of the GATT relating to national monopolies or companies with 'exclusive or special privileges' would need to be strengthened.
- Establishing a new structure with three functions was regarded as a necessary constituent of this plurilateral agreement. The functions would be: to serve as a forum for review and analysis (including all aspects of the relationships between competition and trade); to establish a register of anti-competitive practices; and to provide a structure for settling disputes between nations (where the WTO dispute settlement mechanism was regarded as an appropriate model).

These proposals were approved by the European Commission and were presented as the Union position on trade and competition in a WTO forum. An outcome was the agreement at a WTO ministerial meeting in Singapore in 1996 to set up a working group to study the interaction between trade and competition policy.

Recognition of the importance of the competition policy issue is reflected in other discussions regarding policy blueprints and principles. One possibility is to concentrate on a single sector at a time, another to negotiate one aspect of competition law at a time, e.g. restrictive business practices or merger control. An alternative approach is being pursued by the OECD, which is studying prospects for competition policy harmonization; while a draft harmonized international competition code was published by a group of exporters with a strong German representation in summer 1993 (Rosenthal and Nicolaïdes, 1997). The latter was attacked for being premature and over-ambitious; and many believe that more important issues concern the need to strengthen national constraints to competition, to reduce the exceptions to and exemptions from national competition laws, and to improve cooperation, transparency, and dispute settlement procedures (Fox, 1995; Rosenthal and Nicolaïdes, 1997).

9.8 Conclusion

It is apparent that there is a large and complex international competition policy agenda. Even if it is premature to think of an EU-style competition policy extended onto a global stage, it is important to take some initial policy steps fairly quickly. This is both because anti-competitive activity (inevitably increasingly linked to multinational enterprises given their growing importance in world investment, production, and trade) is a barrier to further progress in liberalizing market access and facilitating market presence; and because competition policy needs to have a central place on the international rule-making agenda.

There are, of course, many problems to be overcome such as the barriers which exist to cross-border mergers because of very different national laws on shareholder rights and other issues of corporate governance; and related matters pertaining to corporate and national cultures.[9] Nevertheless, as things stand at present, as little progress has probably been made in international competition policy as in any area on the multilateral rule-making agenda.

Notes

1. The original reference was web site: http//www: unicc.org/wto/Pressrel/romel.htm.
2. Reflecting the continuing nature of such problems, in 1997 the EU was again in dispute with the United States over extraterritoriality. The issue concerned a Massachusetts law which prohibits purchases by state-owned bodies from companies doing business in Burma. The state blacklisted about 150 foreign and 40 US companies (*Financial Times*, 1997e).
3. Three different policy philosophies may be identified (Moncarz, 1995):
   1. The Anglo-Saxon model, based on free trade, the decentralization of economic decision-making, and a minimal role for the state. There is an excellent statement of this philosophy in a recent UK government paper (Foreign and Commonwealth Office, Department of Trade and Industry, 1996).
   2. The European model, based on social consensus between workers and the private and public sectors. The latter provides a number of social benefits for those potentially affected by the outcomes between labour and business. Support for state-owned enterprises and 'picking winners' would be a feature of this model.
   3. The Asian model, where the state intervenes in the identification and active promotion of strategic sectors of the economy. The time frame of protection and subsidy to industry is based on the concept of infant industry, with liberalization linked to emerging international competitiveness.
4. The four options were: (1) Maintenance of the current system, which *inter alia* treats resale price maintenance and impediments to parallel trade as serious violations of competition rules. The system of block exemptions for beer and petrol would continue. (2) Wider block exemptions. (3) More focused block exemptions. This option proposes to limit the exemption given by current block exemptions to companies with market shares below a 40% threshold. (4) Reduced scope of Article 85 (1) of Treaty of Rome. This is a response to the criticism that block exemptions have had a straitjacket effect and that Article 85 (1) has been applied too widely without reference to the economic and market context. The option 'proposes for parties with a market share less than [20%] to introduce a rebuttable presumption of compatibility with Article 85 (1)' (p. xi).
5. The growth of anti-dumping as an issue can also be shown by the number of countries with AD laws in place: these increased from 10 in 1979 to 24 in 1990 and 40 in 1993 (Lipstein, 1997).
6. The Commission will have wider powers to vet mergers if a new proposal is approved. Mergers will be vetted when they require three or more national filings, when the companies involved have a combined global turnover of Ecu 2.5bn. and an EU turnover of Ecu 100m. each, and

where in each member state involved at least two of the merging companies have a turnover of Ecu 25m. or more.

7. In December 1991, France filed a complaint with the European Court of Justice alleging that the Commission had exceeded its authority in entering into this agreement. A joint Council-Commission decision of April 1995 approved the agreement and declared it applicable from the date it was first signed by the Commission.
8. The weakness of the WTO in respect of competition policy emerged recently in relation to a dispute settlement case in the photofilm market. This involved claims by Eastman Kodak of the USA that its sales in Japan were blocked by a series of government measures introduced to limit competition with its Japanese rival Fujifilm. The US non-violation complaint concerned competition issues, which the Japanese argued is not covered by WTO rules and, therefore, cannot be the subject of a panel ruling (*Financial Times*, 1997g).
9. To illustrate the difficulties, Korea announced in 1997 an easing of US rules on mergers and acquisitions following its entry into the OECD. Despite this, several Korean *chaebol* (conglomerates) announced that they would act jointly to prevent any hostile takeover bids in an effort to prevent domestic companies falling into foreign hands. The EU and the USA also called on the South Korean government to disown 'anti-import behaviour' fostered by the country's 'frugality' campaign (see *Financial Times*, 1997h, 1997i).

Appendix 9.1

Reviews of the 1976 OECD Guidelines for Multinational Enterprises Pertaining to Competition

1984 Recommendations

'Para. 27. In contemplating new legislation, action under existing legislation or other exercise of jurisdiction which may conflict with the legal requirements or established policies of another Member country and lead to conflicting requirements being imposed on multinational enterprises, the Member countries should:

(i) Have regard to relevant principles of international law;

(ii) Endeavour to avoid or minimize such conflicts and the problems to which they give rise by following an approach of moderation and restraint, respecting and accommodating the interests of other Member countries;

(iii) Take fully into account the sovereignty and legitimate economic, law enforcement and other interests of other Member countries;

(iv) Bear in mind the importance of permitting the observance of contractual obligations and the possible adverse impact of measures having a retroactive effect.'

1995 Recommendations

'Section 5 suggests that the member countries take the following coordinating steps [with respect to an investigation or proceeding in a member country]:

- Provide notice of applicable time periods and schedules for decisionmaking;
- Share factual and analytical information and material, subject to national laws governing the confidentiality of information and the principles relating to confidential information set forth in the recommendation;
- Request, in appropriate circumstances, that the subjects of the investigation voluntarily permit the cooperating countries to share some or all of the information in their possession, to the extent permitted by national laws;
- Coordinate discussions or negotiations regarding remedial actions, particularly when such remedies could require conduct or behavior in the territory of more than one member country;

  and
- In those member countries in which advance notification of mergers is required or permitted, request that the notification include a statement identifying notifications also made or to be made to other countries.

[In Section 6, each member country is to:]

- Assist in obtaining information on a voluntary basis from within the assisting member's country;
- Provide factual and analytical material from its files, subject to national laws governing the confidentiality of information and the principles relating to confidential information set forth in the recommendation;
- Use, on behalf of the requesting member country, its authority to compel the production of information in the form of testimony or documents, where the national laws of the requested member country provide for such authority; and
- Provide information in the public domain relating to the relevant conduct of practice. To facilitate the exchange of such information, member countries should consider collecting and maintaining data about the nature and sources of such public information to which other member countries could refer.

[In Section 10, member countries are recommended to:]

- Use moderation and self-restraint and take into account the substantive and procedural rules in the foreign forum when exercising their investigatory powers with a view to obtaining information located abroad;
- Consider, before seeking information located abroad, whether adequate information is available domestically; and
- Frame any requests for information from abroad in terms that are as specific as possible.'

Source: Warner, 1996: 250–2, citing para.27 of Doc. C/MIN (84) 5 (final) and sections 5, 6, and 10 of Revised Recommendation of the Council Concerning Cooperation Between Member Countries on Anticompetition Practices Affecting International Trade (C (95) 130 / Final).

10

Policy Dilemmas

Developing Countries

10.1 Introduction and Background Issues

As earlier chapters have shown, attitudes (and, therefore, policies) towards multinational firms during the 1970s were openly hostile in some developing countries and negative in most others. Even so, annual flows of FDI to developing economies grew rapidly—by 29 per cent a year in nominal terms on average and 19 per cent in real terms (OECD, 1987). Developing countries' share of worldwide flows rose from an average level of around 20 per cent in the first half of the 1970s to over 32 per cent in the late 1970s, approaching the record shares achieved in the 1960s. The developing nations' share of FDI flows, however, slumped in the first half of the 1980s. This was a consequence of a slowdown in capital flows in general, and more especially the major reduction in US outward FDI. In addition, the market situation in mining and minerals, sectors of major interest to developing countries, was weak; while the severe debt problems in some Latin American countries in particular had a strongly negative impact on FDI, as did restrictive policies in some of the developing economies. The outcome was a continuing decline in developing countries' share of FDI inflows to a low point of 16.5 per cent in 1990, as Table 10.1 reveals.

By contrast, the developing countries' FDI position in the 1990s has been very buoyant. This has been linked on the recipient side to progress on macroeconomic stabilization and structural and financial sector reforms, including privatization programmes and the liberalization of trade and investment regimes. And on the investor side, FDI growth into developing economies has been driven by the globalization of production, with technological advances and declining transportation and communication costs encouraging worldwide production and purchasing. Developing nations' share of worldwide FDI flows peaked at a figure of 38.6 per cent in 1994, and was the major factor in sustaining the continued upward trend in net private capital flows.

Some cautionary remarks are in order, nevertheless, since both private capital flows overall and FDI flows were heavily concentrated in a small group of middle-income countries in East Asia together with China; the latter alone accounted for two-fifths of all flows into developing countries in 1994 and was the second largest country recipient of FDI after the United States (overtaking the UK in the process).

Table 10.1 FDI Inflows to Developing Countries, 1984–1995

(a)

US$ million (annual average)	1984–9	1990	1991	1992	1993	1994	1995[a]
All developing countries of which:	22,195	33,735	41,324	50,376	73,135	87,024	99,670
Africa	2,728	2,303	2,809	2,987	3,300	5,084	4,657
Latin America and Caribbean	7,739	8,900	15,362	17,698	19,456	25,302	26,560
Asia	11,540	22,122	22,694	29,114	49,979	56,266	68,051
Other	188	410	459	577	400	372	402
(China)	2,282	3,487	4,366	11,156	27,515	33,787	27,500
(Least developed countries)	533	154	1,582	1,283	1,636	869	1,120

(b)

Percentage of world total	1984–9	1990	1991	1992	1993	1994	1995[a]
All developing countries of which:	19.2	16.6	26.2	30.0	35.2	38.6	31.6
Africa	2.4	1.1	1.8	1.8	1.6	2.3	1.5
Latin America and Caribbean	6.7	4.4	9.7	10.5	9.4	11.2	8.4
Asia	10.0	10.9	14.4	17.3	24.0	24.9	21.6
Other	0.2	0.2	0.3	0.3	0.2	0.2	0.1
(China)	2.0	1.7	2.8	6.6	13.2	15.0	11.9
(Least developed countries)	0.5	0.1	1.0	0.8	0.8	0.4	0.4

Note: [a]Provisional.

Source: Calculated from UNCTAD, 1996*a*: annex table 1.

By contrast, as UNCTAD (1995: p. xxv) commented: 'Africa remains marginalized. The FDI boom in developing countries has largely bypassed that continent . . . Most FDI in African countries continues to be concentrated in a small number of countries endowed with natural resources, especially oil.'

The basic argument of this volume is that it is desirable to extend international investment agreements to a world stage. This has become easier with the shift towards market-based policies, including increasingly favourable regulatory frameworks and attractive investment climates overall. Attitudes and policies towards MNEs, while not universally favourable and liberal, are generally much more positive, reflecting acceptance of the supremacy of market forces. Developing countries would benefit from an international accord which would guarantee a secure and stable environment for investors; curb beggar-thy-neighbour investment incentive schemes which favour rich countries with deep pockets; eliminate potential discrimination by regional agreements; and take into account the needs of the poorest countries which receive little inward FDI.

In extending international investment rules to developing economies, however, a number of problems need to be resolved. The first concerns the question of whether and how to incorporate a developmental component into multilateral FDI instruments. Especially perhaps in the poorer countries of Latin America, Asia, and Sub-Saharan Africa, there are still hangovers of suspicion in respect of alleged neo-colonialist behaviour by multinational firms. More objectively, there is opposition in some quarters to the Structural Adjustment Programmes imposed by the World Bank and International Monetary Fund, because of the very slow responsiveness of private capital inflows and indigenous private sector expansion to fiscal and monetary reform.[1] In addition, there are concerns about the potentially adverse distributional effects of MNEs' activities, even if these are globally welfare enhancing.

A second and linked issue concerns the nature of international investment rules. The thrust of the debate has swung sharply towards an emphasis on the rights of firms and obligations of countries, and away from the rights of nations and obligations of companies. Yet the 1976 OECD Guidelines for Multinational Enterprises, for example, while voluntary, emphasize the need 'to ensure that the operations of these enterprises are in harmony with national policies of the countries where they operate and to strengthen the basis of mutual confidence between enterprises and States' (OECD, 1976*a*: introduction para. 6).

The concerns of developing countries are shared to some extent by the trade unions who have expressed serious concerns about the dislocation of employment associated with the globalization of the firm and with the adverse social effects of multinational activities.[2] In regard to the latter, attention has focused upon five core labour standards, namely, elimination of child labour exploitation; prohibition of forced labour; freedom of association; the right to organize and bargain collectively; and non-discrimination in employment. The view of many developing countries is that the emphasis upon some of these issues, as with that of environmental standards, is simply an ill-disguised attempt at protectionism.[3] Nevertheless, there has been some support for a global but voluntary system of 'social labelling' from the International Labour Organization: this would guarantee that internationally traded goods are produced under humane working conditions (essentially defined to include the core labour standards listed above) (*Financial Times*, 1997*j*).

The third issue relates to the forum for negotiating international roles incorporating developing countries. The WTO is the obvious forum, but a core group of developing nations including India, Pakistan, Egypt, Tanzania, and Malaysia has expressed opposition to this. Their concerns relate to the limitations which might be placed on their ability to pursue their own development strategies and industrial policies (although in fact their flexibility in this regard is very limited anyway); and they would like discussion confined within UNCTAD (*Financial Times*, 1996*d*).

10.2 The Economic Impact of MNEs in Developing Countries

Latin American writers led the way in the 1970s in analysing the problems of developing countries in terms of radical and dependency models: the multinational enterprise was the key player in these analyses, acting as an agent of imperialism and creating a global hierarchy of economic dependence. Because of their assumptions, the models left little scope for objective analysis of development and they have had limited influence recently (Lall, 1996). In truth, development theory generally, with its focus upon interventionism, has for the time being lost its way (Leys, 1996).

The application of conventional models is, however, still hampered by the counterfactual problem: would the generation of national capabilities with different degrees of reliance on inward direct investment be better or worse for long-term development in developing nations? Even without this problem, there are methodological difficulties in specifying direct causal linkages between FDI and economic growth; the two are interactive over time and exhibit variability across countries and through time (Jun and Brewer, 1997). Nevertheless, the scatterplot of FDI and GDP for thirty developing countries shown in Figure 10.1 suggests a positive relationship. Furthermore, there is ample evidence (based on academic research and country cases) providing strong support for the positive role of FDI in promoting economic growth in developing host countries: for example, the ratio of inward FDI to total output was found to have a positive influence on growth (Blomström et al., 1996). Furthermore, the positive growth impact of FDI flows was more significant compared with other types of external flows (Husain and Jun, 1992) and compared with domestic investment (Borenstein et al., 1994). At the same time, FDI flows respond positively to recent increases in GDP and presumably to expectations of future increases.

Given the difficulties of disentangling cause and effect, researchers have resorted to an analysis of the constituents of economic impact, namely, the effects of MNE activities on capital flows and domestic savings, technology, innovation and business practices, trade and human capital, etc. Lall's (1996) summary of the evidence concludes that MNEs '*generally offer net benefits*' (p. 62) to host developing countries, largely related to their ownership and internalization advantages as compared with indigenous firms. He adds (p. 63):

> exceptions to that generalisation are nevertheless possible when TNCs engage in undesirable practices like tax evasion (e.g. by transfer pricing) or predatory behaviour to local competition, or where they give inadequate attention to potential local suppliers, do not strike up links with local technological institutions, invest too little in local research and development, or fail . . . to exploit the export competitiveness of their affiliates.

There are also trade-offs among the different advantages offered by MNEs, e.g. local linkages versus exports; and MNE strategies of globalization and regionalization and integrated international production have changed the balance of the benefits offered. In reality these conclusions apply equally to recipient developed countries and have represented the policy challenge in all host economies for the last thirty years.

Fig. 10.1 FDI and Host Country Economic Growth

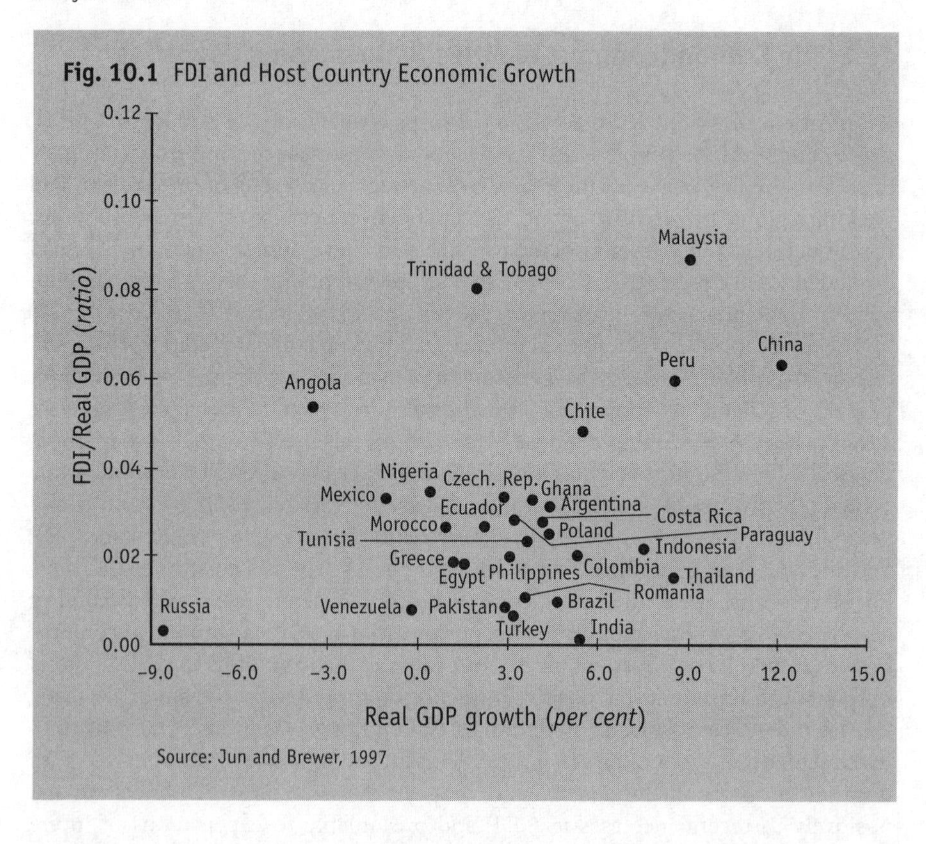

Source: Jun and Brewer, 1997

There are a number of more specific findings which are important for this study. One is that MNEs' role as engines of growth is likely to vary according to the state of development of the host country (UN, 1992). Thus the contribution may be more substantial for middle- and high-income developing nations than for low-income countries at early stages of development. Dunning's (1987) investment development cycle provides a helpful description of country patterns of inward and outward investment and GNP growth as an illustration of this point.) The poorer developing countries do not offer attractive markets because of limited purchasing power or a low-cost, factory-disciplined labour force. Their interests, namely raising agricultural productivity, improving basic infrastructure, and raising the standards of education and nutrition in their societies, are marginal to those of multinational firms in general. At early stages of development, countries have relied more on official aid. But aid policies are now heavily criticized since they have been used in some countries to support anti-market policies; while aid creates a mentality of dependency (Ryrie, 1995). Since the alternative market-based policies require foreign direct capital inflows there is no clear development model for the poorer countries.

A second important area of findings concerns the trade orientation of MNEs and developing countries. The classic work of Lall and Streeten (1977) (and supported by other studies subsequently) revealed that investments in protected, import-substituting regimes generated much lower benefits than those that were undertaken within export-oriented environments or those that were exposed to significant foreign competition. UNCTAD (1995) also concludes that both Asian and Latin American experience indicates that MNEs prefer to control their export-oriented affiliates through high ownership shares, with access to their international marketing network being viewed as a proprietary asset. As will be shown below, nevertheless, export orientation in newly industrializing countries has gone hand in hand with active policies to transfer foreign technology into the indigenous sector, high levels of trade intervention to protect infant industries, infrastructural upgrading, and stable macroeconomic regimes.

A number of concerns have been expressed about other possible effects of MNEs which are specific to developing countries. These relate, for example, to culture, politics, environment, and women and labour generally. The notion of 'sustainable development' has been employed to encompass not only the economic objectives of growth and efficiency but also ecological and social objectives. It is widely accepted that failure to address challenges such as the environment will reduce the capacity for long-term development in host developing countries. As yet, however, there has been only limited analysis of the impact of MNEs in these areas and methodological problems are rife (Jun and Brewer, 1997).

The debate has been given added urgency in an international investment policy context by the calls by some developed nations for rules to address environmental protection and fair labour standards. These may lead to new barriers to trade and investment that will penalize developing countries with divergent (weaker and less stringent) policies and thereby hamper market integration (Hart, 1995). Protectionism is justified by proponents on moral grounds: environmentalists believe that it is the moral duty of the state to protect the environment and prevent MNEs escaping regulation by relocation to developing countries; and similar arguments are presented by trade unions with respect to minimum levels of labour legislation or by human rights activists in regard to child labour etc. In fact, economic growth in developing countries is not a threat but an opportunity to create rising living standards and generate huge markets. An overview of environmental issues and international investment agreements is presented in Box 10.1.

Most debate has occurred on the effects of global liberalization and developing nations' exports on levels of income inequality in developed economies (Krugman, 1996; Lawrence, 1996). Widening levels of earnings inequality in, for example, the United States and the United Kingdom are a reality. And so are rising imports from developing countries: in the mid-1990s these accounted for about one-third of US imports compared with 14 per cent in 1970, while in the EU the proportion of imports from developing economies rose from 5 to 12 per cent in the same period (*Financial Times*, 1995*c*, 1995*d*). With a number of strong assumptions, trade can be regarded as an alternative to the physical movement of labour and capital, and will equalize the worldwide returns on the two factors. Hence the abundancy of skilled labour in developing economies would drive down the wages of unskilled workers in developed nations while benefiting skilled workers and owners of capital. Careful research by Lawrence (1996) concludes that the quantitative effects of changes in trade explain

Box 10.1

Environmental Issues and International Investment Agreements

In general, it is probably the case that MNEs operate with improved environmental standards as compared with equivalent national companies and provide leadership on environmental protection issues. Nevertheless, multinational firms are very visible in environmentally polluting industries. And differences in host nation environmental protection rules and practices can influence investment decisions and lead to the relocation of pollution-creating industries in countries with lax regulations.

Environmental issues were initially included on the international policy agenda in 1971 when a Working Group on Environmental Measures and International Trade was established by GATT contracting parties. Interest waned and the group did not meet until the 1990s; then in a WTO context it was reincarnated as a Committee on Trade and the Environment. Its role is to investigate aspects of the relationship between environmental and trade (and presumably FDI) policies. As Hoekman and Kostecki (1995: 262) note: 'One issue that will have to be addressed . . . is the need to expand the coverage of GATT Article XX to include environmental objectives, and if so, how to ensure that such an expansion does not become another loophole in the GATT allowing for discriminatory trade restrictions to be imposed.'

Provisions on protection of the environment have been included in various international investment instruments as shown below:

WTO Subsidies and Countervailing Measures (SCMs) agreement. In principle, the SCMs agreement applies to FDI subsidies, but the scope and significance of the conditions that limit its application to FDI projects are not yet clear. There is also a Trade and Environment Work Programme in progress.

OECD Multilateral Agreement on Investment. The draft text provides (in Section III, Article 91) for subsequent negotiations of limits on incentives, with a recognition that incentives include environmental policy aspects. The draft also provides for national treatment and most favoured nation treatment in FDI incentives policies.

NAFTA Chapter 11 (Investment) and the Supplemental Agreement on Environmental Cooperation. Although there are no provisions concerning investment subsidies, there are provisions concerning the relaxation of environmental standards as an investment incentive.

APEC Non-binding Investment Principles. The provision on investment incentives includes a pledge not to relax health, safety, and environmental regulations.

ECT Article 19 and Energy Efficiency and Related Environmental Aspects Protocol. There are declarations of intentions, which are excluded from investment arbitration (Articles 26 and 27).

While progress has been limited to date, UNCTAD (1996*a*: 188) rightly observe that: 'The question of environmental protection is thus increasingly seen as part of a framework of rules that seek to promote the orderly operation of economic activity.'

only about 10 per cent of the rising income differential between high school and college educated workers in America. Furthermore the impact of trade on the relative demand for college versus high school educated labour was only around one-third of the effects of deindustrialization (see also *Financial Times*, 1996e).

Some of the current debate has parallels in earlier concerns in the United States about the effects of outward direct investment on home country employment, and more recently about the impact of NAFTA on US jobs. In respect of the former, the impacts are critically dependent on the assumptions concerning the counterfactual situation. But most studies (summarized in Hood and Young, 1979: 311–21) have indicated large positive employment effects resulting from the creation of non-production jobs in the USA, only partially offset by reductions in low-skilled jobs in America; adjustment costs were estimated to be substantial (see also Krugman, 1996: 60–4).

Although the debate will continue, there is reasonable agreement amongst professionals rejecting protectionism against developing country imports. The best solution is vastly improved education and training for the unskilled in developed countries. This could be allied to compensation to unskilled workers for their declining relative wages through the tax and benefit system (*Financial Times*, 1995*d*).

In concluding this section on impact, it is important to observe one outcome of economic development processes which is the emergence of multinational enterprises from developing countries (so-called Third World MNEs (TWMNEs)). Outward direct investment is an inevitable consequence of the growing resources and competitiveness of indigenous firms. Early work (Wells, 1983) focused upon FDI in neighbouring countries with similar tastes but lower wages. More recently, Tolentino (1993) has presented a developmental model of the outward FDI of developing nations in which investment commences in resource-based production or in simple forms of manufacturing; at later stages the sectoral path of FDI evolves towards more technologically sophisticated manufacturing investments and support activities, allowing for independent technological development trajectories. Although research is still in its early stages, the technological learning from outward FDI (especially that in developed countries: see Young et al., 1996) may be very significant for corporate development and hence developing country economic impact.

Outward FDI from developing nations is still small in global terms: for the period 1990–4 their share of worldwide outflows was 10 per cent, but this proportion had doubled from 5 per cent in the years 1980–4. TWMNEs are also highly concentrated by source country, with China, Hong Kong, Korea, Singapore, and Taiwan accounting for over 70 per cent of outward stock and 90 per cent of outward flows from developing nations in 1993 (UNCTAD, 1995).

The phenomenon of TWMNEs represents an important further driver for liberalization, as developing countries recognize the importance of market access for FDI as well as trade, and of international competitiveness for long-term development in a global era.

10.3 Investment and Trade Policies in Developing Countries

Country policies

The 1980s trend to liberalize national laws and policies regarding FDI continued and deepened during the 1990s. Associated with this trend was a growing number of bilateral investment treaties concluded by developing countries. Latin America and the Caribbean and especially Sub-Saharan Africa, however, lag significantly behind other parts of the developing world. Since BITs set basic standards of protection of investments from political risks, provide for the repatriation of profits and capital, etc., it is apparent that there is still some considerable way to go in improving the investment climate in many parts of the developing world.

In observing this widespread policy liberalization, it is instructive to note the factors in Asian economic growth.[4] The World Bank (1993) analysis of eight high-performing East Asian economies highlights six key policy fundamentals, namely ensuring low inflation and competitive exchange rates; building human capital; creating effective and secure financial systems; limiting policy distortions; limiting the bias against agriculture; and absorbing foreign technology. In respect of the latter, all the countries were open to foreign technology: Japan, Korea, and to a lesser extent Taiwan relied heavily on licensing, machinery imports, and reverse engineering; Hong Kong, Singapore together with Indonesia, Malaysia, and Thailand, in addition, welcomed foreign direct investment. Foreign multinational enterprises were, therefore, primarily regarded as one but not the only way of acquiring technical and managerial know-how, which could be assimilated by indigenous industry and in turn promote the competitiveness and internationalization of domestic firms. A second role of inward investing MNEs was to support the export-push strategies of these economies. As with the countries' technology acquisition policies, the export-push strategies were associated with different forms of interventionism: in Japan, Korea, and Taiwan, for example, substantial protection of the domestic market was combined with compulsion or strong incentives to export, targeted to specific industries. The more recent export growth efforts of Indonesia, Malaysia, and Thailand have relied less on targeted export incentives, and more on phased reductions in import protection; this has been allied to a regime of duty-free inputs for exports and the attraction of export-oriented FDI.

Therefore, the notion that deregulation and free market economics alone created high growth rates is singularly inadequate. The crises of 1997–8 in several countries in the region suggested, furthermore, that close relationships between government and business have been an important part of the growth story, but also one source of the currency and debt crises of that period.

In respect of the theme of this volume the general country policy trends towards liberalization of FDI are undoubtedly desirable from the perspective of both national and global efficiency and growth. Investment policies are only one constituent of a package, nevertheless, which should include sound macroeconomic measures plus investment in human capital, research and technological development, and so on. It is evident, moreover, that measures to support export orientation (including export-oriented FDI) may be necessary. In addition, policies to assist technology transfer, assimilation, and diffusion are critically important. Hence selective interventions are essential to support liberalization. Given the experience of East Asia, where such interventions were undoubtedly in part culture-specific, it seems necessary to devise developmental strategies which are complementary to social and cultural dynamics in the poorer developing nations also.

International trade policy and developing countries

Study of multilateral trade policy with respect to developing countries is clearly instructive for international investment rule-making. Table 10.2 summarizes the main developments over the fifty years since the formation of the GATT. At inception, a clause permitting protection for infant industries was the major development-specific provision in the GATT and it was not directed solely at developing countries. It was not until the establishment of UNCTAD that demands for special status for developing nations was reflected in GATT rules: thus in 1965 a new Part IV of the GATT was adopted, defining the concept of non-reciprocity for developing economies. Under the terms of this non-legally binding clause, countries in the developing world were not expected to provide tariff concessions and establish a tariff schedule (bind tariffs); instead they were granted free-rider status through the operation of the MFN principle. This mainly applied to ex-colonies which did not have separate tariff schedules, whereas countries that were not ex-colonies generally had to bind tariffs.

The principle of non-reciprocity—applied such that reciprocal reductions in tariff barriers were not provided by developing nations—operated during the Tokyo Round negotiations (1973–9), despite the dissatisfaction of many developed countries. An 'Enabling Clause' was also approved, creating a permanent legal basis for the implementation of the Generalized System of Preferences (GSP). Articles XII and XVIII relating to the use of trade measures for balance of payments purposes were clarified and codified. This gave developing nations 'flexibility' in operating trade measures to meet their 'essential development needs'.

From the late 1970s numerous criticisms of the concept of 'special and differential treatment' (S & D) for developing nations were voiced. These related in part to wider criticism of import-substitution policies in developing countries, which supported isolationism and uncompetitive industries: the S & D system effectively reinforced import substitution and did not provide encouragement or any incentive to export industries. Hoekman and Kostecki (1995) suggest that the GATT did little to persuade governments to adopt more outward-looking trade policies, and even carefully avoided discussion on a definition of 'developing countries' (with the exception of the group of least developed countries, where the UN definition is applied).

Free-riding was, moreover, not particularly beneficial to developing nations, since trade negotiations were basically conducted among developed countries which focused upon their own trade agendas. And sectors of major importance to developing economies like agriculture or textiles and clothing were excluded from the GATT or dealt with on an *ad hoc* basis. Indeed observers considered that the long-standing protectionist Multifibre Agreement and its predecessors (operational since 1962) are

Table 10.2 GATT/WTO and Developing Countries

Date	Event
1947	Ten low-income countries accede to the GATT on essentially the same terms as developed countries. An infant-industry protection clause (Article XVIII) is the main development-specific provision in GATT. Only one Balance of Payments (BOP) Article existed: Article XII.
1954–5	Article XVIII is modified to include XVIII:b allowing for Quantity Restrictions (QRs) to be used for BOP purposes whenever foreign exchange reserves are below what is considered necessary for economic development. This vague test constitutes much weaker discipline than Article XII, and it has been invoked extensively.
1964	Establishment of UNCTAD. A committee for Trade and Development is created in the GATT to address development-related concerns; the International Trade Centre (ITC) is charged with assisting developing countries to promote exports.
1965	A new Part IV on Trade and Development is added to the GATT, which defines the notion of non-reciprocity for developing countries. However, Part IV contains no legally binding obligations.
1968	The USA accepts the Generalized System of Preferences (GSP)—as called for by UNCTAD—under which industrialized countries were to grant tariff preferences to developing countries on a non-reciprocal basis. Such preferences were voluntary, not mandatory, and granted unilaterally. The ITC became a joint venture with UNCTAD
1971	A GATT waiver is granted authorizing tariff preferences under the GSP. Another waiver is adopted for the Protocol on Trade Negotiations among Developing Countries (Geneva Protocol).
1973–9	More than 70 developing countries participate in the Tokyo Round. The Enabling Clause is adopted which introduces the concept of 'special and differential treatment' (S & D) *inter alia* making the 1971 waivers permanent and including language on graduation. Most developing countries abstain from signing the various Tokyo Round codes.
1986	Developing countries approve launching of the Uruguay Round with a ministerial declaration that contains many references to S & D.
1994	All developing-country GATT contracting parties join the WTO, adopting the results of the Uruguay Round as a Single Undertaking.
1997	China applied to join the GATT in the 1980s but failed to reach agreement on joining the WTO at its start date. Prospects of joining the WTO looked brighter in 1997.

Source: Adapted from Hoekman and Kostecki, 1995: table 10.1.

a reflection of the sidelining of developing countries and developing country interests in the GATT. Finally, the value of special and differential treatment diminished with each Round of GATT negotiations as tariffs were cut, and any preferences to developing countries were granted and could be removed unilaterally.

Overall, as Hart (1995: 227) observes: 'The GATT/IMF trade and payments regime . . . failed miserably in preparing developing countries for the reality of an international, let alone a global economy. By acquiescing in their quest for special treatment, the old regime relegated them to second class citizenship.'

The changing philosophies of the 1980s, which emphasized market-led reforms, economic orientation, and the attraction of inward FDI, were reflected in a very different stance by developing countries in the Uruguay Round negotiations. It was agreed that the outcomes of the Uruguay Round would apply to all members, with all having schedules of concessions and commitments. Developing nations had an important influence on issues such as GATS, TRIMs, and dispute settlement and on sectors like textiles and clothing, tropical products, and agriculture.

Nevertheless, special and differential treatment remains in the World Trade Organization, with explicit provisions for developing countries in terms of (Hoekman and Kostecki, 1995): a lower level of obligations; more flexible implementation timetables; best endeavour commitments by developed countries; more favourable treatment for least developed countries; and technical assistance and training (see Table 10.3). The Committee on Trade and Development, a subsidiary of the General Council of the WTO, deals with the trade-related concerns of the least developed nations.

The special and differential treatment provisions which remain under the WTO include Article XVIII (where application is essentially negotiated on an *ad hoc* basis) and Article XVIII:b allowing for the imposition of quantitative restrictions for balance of payments purposes. No additional provisions were sought by developing countries but longer transition periods and technical assistance to implement negotiated agreements were approved. In general, no criteria for graduation from developing country status was agreed. The Subsidies Agreement, however, specifies that a developing country which has achieved a global market share of 3.5 per cent for a product is required to phase out export subsidies; there is also a per capita GDP level of US$1,000 below which developing nations' export subsidies will not be countervailed.

Among the Uruguay Round agreements which encompassed both trade and FDI, concern for development is apparent in the GATS. As is illustrated in Box 10.2, however, this is based on relative reciprocity and development compatibility and not on special treatment as in the GATT. Transitional arrangements to take account of the needs of developing nations are also included in the TRIPs and TRIMs agreements. In both of these issues, the interests of developing and developed nations are very different, which explains the limited progress made in the Uruguay Round and the narrowly circumscribed provisions. As discussed elsewhere, the developed countries have agreed that TRIMs (especially local content, trade balancing, and export requirements) cause distortions in patterns of trade and development, whereas developing nations regard them as important tools to promote development objectives and strengthen trade balances.

By contrast, developing nations have sought control over investment incentives. But despite distortions caused by competitive bidding for investments and the fact that they discriminate in favour of the richer countries (this is true even within the industrialized world), developed nations have been unwilling or unable to agree on controlling incentives (Brewer and Young, 1997). There are self-interests on both sides of course. Performance requirements in developing countries serve the inter-

Table 10.3 References to Developing and Least Developed Countries in the WTO

Subject	Concession							
	Lower level of obligation		Best-endeavour commitment		Longer time frame[a]		Technical assistance	
	LDCs	LLDCs	LDCs	LLDCs	LDCs	LLDCs	LDCs	LLDCs
WTO				✓		✓	✓	
Balance of payments	✓	✓					✓	
Safeguards	✓		✓					
Anti-dumping			✓					
Subsidies	✓	✓	✓		✓	✓		
TRIMs	✓		✓	✓	✓	✓		
Import licensing	✓		✓	✓	✓			
Customs valuation	✓		✓		✓		✓	
Pre-shipment inspection							✓	
Rules of origin								
Technical barriers	✓		✓				✓	✓
Sanitary / Phytosanitary			✓	✓	✓	✓	✓	
Agriculture	✓	✓	✓	✓	✓			✓
Textiles and clothing								
Services	✓		✓	✓	✓	✓	✓	✓
TRIPs	✓		✓	✓	✓	✓	✓	✓
Dispute settlement			✓	✓			✓	
Trade policy review	✓	✓					✓	✓

Note: LDCs=developing countries; LLDCs=least developed countries.
[a]Longer time frame refers to longer transitional periods for implementing negotiated disciplines.

Source: Adapted from Hoekman and Kostecki, 1995: annex 6.

ests of local producers which have grown up as protected monopolies, while MNEs are obviously the beneficiaries of incentive contests. Still, it is hard to argue with UNCTC / UNCTAD (1991: 9–10) in their observation that:

> In seeking to proscribe the kind of investment packages most compatible with developing country circumstances while leaving equivalent investment packages of the developed world intact, the Uruguay Round TRIMs effort could also be regarded in itself, as distortionary . . . More beneficial would be an attempt to achieve a multilateral agreement to limit all locational incentives, perhaps as part of an expanded subsidies code.

A similar type of debate emerges in respect of TRIPs, where the developed country interest is in strong laws in respect of intellectual property rights, and is justifiable in terms of appropriating the rents from investment in R & D. The developing nation

Box 10.2

The Development Dimension in the GATS

An important objective of the GATS is to promote development of developing countries. The second preambular paragraph reads as follows: 'wishing to establish a multilateral framework of principles and rules for trade in services with a view to the expansion of such trade under conditions of transparency and progressive liberalization and as a means of promoting the economic growth of all trading partners and the development of developing countries', and the fifth preambular paragraph states: 'desiring to facilitate the increasing participation of developing countries in trade in services and the expansion of their service exports including, *inter alia*, through the strengthening of their domestic services capacity and its efficiency and competitiveness.'

Countries agreed during the Uruguay Round that participation of developing countries should be based on the principle of relative reciprocity/development compatibility, and should not be seen as 'special treatment' along the lines of GATT Part IV. Article IV of GATS commits members to facilitate the participation of developing countries in trade in services through negotiated specific commitments relating to the strengthening of their domestic services capacity, including through access to technology on a commercial basis, improved distribution channels and information networks, and the liberalization of market access in sectors and modes of supply of export interest to them. Article IV also provides for the establishment of contact points to facilitate access to information on commercial and technical aspects of the supply of services, registration, recognition and obtaining of professional qualifications, and the availability of service technology.

Article XIX of GATS calls for successive rounds of negotiations, aimed at achieving a progressively higher level of liberalization. Article XIX:2 provides that the process of liberalization will take place with due respect for national policy objectives and the level of development of individual parties, both overall and in individual industries. Appropriate flexibility is foreseen for individual developing countries for opening fewer industries, liberalizing fewer types of transactions, progressively extending market access in line with their development situation, and, when making access to their markets available to foreign service suppliers, attaching to it conditions aimed at achieving the objectives referred to in Article IV.

Article XIX:3 provides for an assessment of trade in services in overall terms and on a sectoral basis with reference to the objectives of GATS, including those set out in paragraph 1 of Article IV for the purposes of establishing negotiating guidelines.

Finally, by covering all factors of production, including the temporary movement of natural persons, the GATS opens opportunities for increased services exports from developing countries, an innovation of considerable importance to these countries. Furthermore, by using a positive-list approach (i.e. market access and national treatment are subject to specific negotiations), each country can strategically negotiate the individual service industries of transactions that it is ready to open up (subject to specific conditions and limitations), in pursuance of long-term progressive liberalization.

Source: UNCTAD, 1996*a*: box V.1.

interest is in ease of access to technology where intellectual support can be provided from the characteristics of knowledge as a public good and the spillovers generated by freely available information.

International investment policy

The international investment instruments which pay special attention to development related matters are the OECD Guidelines for Multinational Enterprises of 1976 and the UNCTC draft code of conduct (1983). Both are voluntary, but only the former has been ratified.

In its statement of General Policies, the OECD Guidelines (1976*a*: 13) specify that:

Enterprises should
1. take fully into account established policy objectives of the Member countries in which they operate;
2. in particular give due consideration to those countries' aims and priorities with regard to economic and social progress, including industrial and regional development, the protection of the environment, the creation of employment opportunities, the promotion of innovation and the transfer of technology;
4. favour close cooperation with the local community and business interests.

And again under the guidelines of Science and Technology, it is stated that (OECD, 1976*a*: 17):

Enterprises should
1. endeavour to ensure that their activities sit satisfactorily into the scientific and technological policies and plans of the countries in which they operate, and contribute to the development of national scientific and technological capacities, including as far as appropriate the establishment and improvement in host countries of their capacity to innovate;
2. to the fullest extent practicable, adopt in the course of their business activities policies which permit the rapid diffusion of technologies with due regard to the protection of industrial and intellectual property rights;
3. when granting licenses for the use of industrial property rights or when otherwise transferring technology do so on reasonable terms and conditions.

In the reviews of the Guidelines post-1976, some amendments have been made to these rules. For example, paragraph 2 of the General Policies chapter now reads: 'the protection of the environment *and consumer interests*, the creation of employment opportunities.' So there is evidence of flexibility and adaptability in the Guidelines, which provide a helpful umbrella framework in support of development. In the years since 1976, with the regulatory tide flowing strongly in favour of the rights of firms as opposed to their obligations, the developmental aspects of the OECD Guidelines have had only limited influence. However, their long-standing existence is recognition of the rights of countries which cannot be ignored, and they could prove a very significant bargaining tool for developing countries in negotiations concerning comprehensive multilateral investment rules.

The UNCTC draft code of conduct, while much weakened in its various drafts, is still more strongly development—and developing country—oriented than the OECD Guidelines. The aim is to 'maximize the contributions of transnational cor-

Box 10.3

UN Draft Code of Conduct on Transnational Corporations: Selected Provisions Relating to Economic Development

'10. Transnational corporations should carry out their activities in conformity with the development policies, objectives and priorities set out by the Governments of the countries in which they operate and work seriously towards making a positive contribution to the achievement of such goals at the national and, as appropriate, the regional level, within the framework of regional integration programmes. Transnational corporations should co-operate with the Governments of the countries in which they operate with a view to contributing to the development process and should be responsive to requests for consultation in this respect, thereby establishing mutually beneficial relations with these countries. . . .

21. Transnational corporations should make every effort so to allocate their decision-making powers among their entities as to enable them to contribute to the economic and social development of the countries in which they operate. . . .

24. Transnational corporations should contribute to the managerial and technical training of nationals of the countries in which they operate and facilitate their employment at all levels of management of the entities' enterprises as a whole. . . .

28. Transnational corporations should, where appropriate, contribute to the promotion and diversification of exports in the countries in which they operate and to an increased utilization of goods, services and other resources which are available in these countries.

29. Transnational corporations should be responsive to requests by Governments of the countries in which they operate, particularly developing countries, concerning the phasing over a limited period of time of the repatriation of capital in case of disinvestment or remittances of accumulated profits, when the size and timing of such transfers would cause serious balance-of-payments difficulties for such countries. . . .

36. (a) Transnational corporations shall conform to the transfer of technology laws and regulations of the countries in which they operate. They shall co-operate with the competent authorities of those countries in assessing the impact of international transfers of technology in their economies and consult with them regarding the various technological options which might help those countries, particularly developing countries, to attain their economic and social development.

(b) Transnational corporations in their transfer of technology transactions should, in accordance with the criteria set forth in the Set of Multilaterally Agreed Equitable Principles and Rules for the Control of Restrictive Business Practices, avoid restrictive practices which adversely affect the international flow of technology, or otherwise hinder the economic and technological development of countries, particularly developing countries.

(c) Transnational corporations should contribute to the strengthening of the scientific and technological capacities of developing countries, in accordance with the science and technology established policies and priorities of those countries. Transnational corporations should undertake substantial research and development activities in developing countries and should make full use of local resources and personnel in this process.'

Source: UNCTAD, 1996*d*.

porations to economic development and growth and to minimize the negative effects of the activities of these corporations' (UNCTAD, 1996*d*). The provisions specifically relate to disclosure of information by MNEs, environmental and consumer protection, restrictive business practices, the avoidance of corrupt practices and transfer pricing, parent–affiliate relations, as well as labour relations and working conditions. Some of the provisions which relate specifically to the development issues are included in Box 10.3. Despite the substantial amendments to the code in its successive drafts, developed nations view the document as lacking in balance and as excessively strident in both tone and substance; the lack of agreement on the code in the UN, moreover, means that it is not acceptable to many developing nations either.

10.4 **Conclusion**

The evidence of this chapter is that the main development problem which confronts the world economy concerns the poorest of the developing countries and the need to generate a momentum of growth. Market reforms and economic liberalization (including liberalization of investment rules) are essential but not be sufficient. Of course in a number of the poorer countries the implementation of reforms to date has been inadequate; in others, there are major political and social problems and poor leadership, and the slow response of the private sector to economic reforms brings a chorus of calls for a return to interventionism.

The economic benefits associated with inward direct investment have been fairly widely recognized and these are reflected across the world in more attractive investment regimes and investment climates generally. Further liberalization is still necessary in respect, for example, of speeding up of approval procedures and reducing bureaucracy, and the extension of bilateral investment treaties is clearly desirable in some countries. A major lesson from the East Asian economies, however, concerns the significance of parallel measures of selected intervention to improve the benefits from technology transfer (with FDI as one technology transfer mechanism) and to support an export orientation strategy (including export-oriented FDI). Alongside other measures for technology assimilation and diffusion, performance requirements are one illustration of the former; and export subsidies and duty-free imported inputs for export sectors an example of the latter. Another policy, to encourage export-oriented FDI, which has grown rapidly in importance in recent years has been the establishment of export processing zones (EPZs). They have, however, been heavily criticized (UNCTAD, 1995). FDI activity in EPZs has generally taken the form of low-skilled, export platform assembly. Linkages with the rest of the economy are very limited since a characteristic of EPZs is the reliance on imported inputs, and the potential for upgrading local value added is low. These features also mean that EPZ investments are footloose, subject to cost competition and relocation.

To bring developing countries (especially the poorer economies) within the body of international rules, therefore, requires mechanisms to tolerate measures which seem to signal a reversal of liberalization. The principles underlying such measures which are designed to improve the benefits of the FDI are contained within the

OECD Guidelines (and the draft UN code), but these are voluntary in general. A way ahead would seem to require exceptions to agreed international investment rules for the poorer developing economies (defined according to an income per head criterion). Any such approvals for, say, local content rules would have to be conditional upon the formulation of World Bank/IMF-agreed integrated development strategies. This is essential if the general market reform and liberalization programmes are to continue. And in order to prevent any reversion to protectionism, approved measures would need to have carefully defined objectives and time scales. Further work is necessary to identify the types of approved measures, which would extend beyond export subsidies and performance requirements to possibly improved terms for technology transfer through licensing etc. Because of the trade/FDI linkages, pref-

Box 10.4

Extending Trade Preferences to FDI

Under the Generalized System of Preferences (GSP), industrial countries offer more favourable treatment to the import of manufactures and semi-manufactures from developing countries, particularly the least developed, thereby providing them a competitive edge in the industrial market (i.e. in terms of a price advantage relative to imports from non-beneficiary countries). The GSP is an agreed departure from the most favoured nation principle of the GATT. The GSP arrangements are drawn up by individual preference-giving countries, who specify beneficiaries, product coverage, and other requirements, principally relating to rules of origin.

In an effort to extend GSP schemes to FDI, industrial countries have begun to apply the 'donor country content' rule under which the preference-giving country allows inputs (materials, parts, and components) of its manufacture, when supplied to a preference-receiving country and used there in a production process, to be regarded as originating in the preference-receiving country for the purpose of determining whether the finished products qualify for GSP treatment. This facility is granted by Australia, Canada, Japan, New Zealand, several Central and Eastern European countries, and, as of 1 January 1995, the European Union. Norway and Switzerland are in the process of introducing the facility. Although the United States does not provide it, TNCs have voiced strong support for it to be included in the new United States GSP scheme.

A number of home countries offer incentives to their firms to invest in the least developed countries. Although these schemes have had only limited impact, they could be coupled with trade preferences through the FDI facility of the GSP to reinforce each other, and constitute a more comprehensive system of investment–trade preferences offered by developed countries to the least developed countries. With business as a new home country constituency, the erosion of support for trade preferences could also be counteracted. Supportive measures of this type are a necessary complement to the liberalization measures enacted by most least developed countries to attract FDI, which still amounts to less than 1 per cent of the total flow to developing countries.

Source: UNCTAD, 1995: box VI.2.

erential trade policy rules are also necessary. The link is beginning to be recognized through efforts to extend the Generalized System of Preferences scheme to FDI, as is shown in Box 10.4.

Aside from the difficulties of obtaining agreement from developed nations, a potential major obstacle to the FDI-led development efforts of industrializing nations is a threat of protectionism, especially in the United States but also in Europe. As discussed earlier, this is dressed up in terms of a requirement for harmonized labour and environmental standards. The liberalization trends which have been evident in the recent past are far from irreversible.

Notes

1. Structural adjustment is designed to create the conditions for private sector-led growth, but in countries where there is only a very small private sector at the start of the process, the supply response is bound to be slow. However, some commentators have also alleged that part of the problem in Africa is that adjustment programmes have not been implemented effectively (Ryrie, 1995).
2. In its submission regarding negotiations on the OECD Multilateral Agreement on Investment (MAI), TUAC (the Trade Union Advisory Committee to the OECD) argued that the OECD Guidelines should be incorporated within the MAI.
3. In truth, core labour standards are not an important determinant of competitive advantage in international business. This was the conclusion of an OECD study, *Trade, Employment and Labour Standards: A Study of Core Workers' Rights and International Trade*, discussed at an OECD Workshop in October 1996. Two of the key findings of the study were that low (or absent) core standards were not an important determinant of competitive advantage in international trade; and that there was a mutually reinforcing relationship between trade liberalization and the enforcement of core standards (OECD, 1996*b*).
4. This book went to press in early 1998 in the midst of the Asian currency and debt crises, and the analysis therefore does not generally reflect those events. However, two early lessons seemed to be the need for effective government regulation of financial markets and the associated need to deal with problems of corruption in business–government relations.

Part IV

Implications

11

Current and Future Challenges

11.1 Introduction

This volume has considered the multilateral system for investment from a variety of analytic perspectives—the theory of FDI and MNEs (Chapter 1), patterns and trends in the economic-political context of the system (Chapter 2), key developments in its history over half a century (Chapters 3–6), and a series of current policy problem areas (Chapters 7–10). Major challenges for international policy-making in the multinational enterprise and foreign direct investment area have been identified. The purpose of this final chapter is to present an overview of the book as a whole, and to point the way forward into the future. The underlying philosophy of the book is based on the economic principles of free markets and economic efficiency tempered by considerations of equity and political feasibility. To assist an understanding of the past and project this into the future, however, it is important to accept the reality of the policy-making process; and a politically focused perspective is therefore explicitly included in this chapter.

Investment rule-making has evolved over time; however, the pattern in this evolution has not been consistent, except in the period since the early 1980s when a strong liberalization trend has been evident at all policy levels. As a starting point for review and analysis, Table 11.1 summarizes the characteristics of the major multilateral and regional investment agreements which were operative in the late 1990s; in addition, it should be noted that a Multilateral Agreement on Investment was being negotiated in the OECD as at the time of writing.

11.2 The Shifting Policy Pendulum

It will be recalled from Chapter 1 that the liberalization conditions for market efficiency require two types of government policies. First are liberal government policies that create internationally open economies and facilitate MNEs' activities that transfer funds, technology, goods, services, and people internationally and that entail cross-national control relationships among firms in different countries; these can be defended on the grounds of efficiency. The argument is similar to that of traditional trade theory based on comparative advantage which establishes a rationale for the relatively free movement of goods and services by unrelated firms. Second, governance policies that encourage competition and discourage restrictive business

Table 11.1 Summary Characteristics of Major Multilateral and Regional

Characteristics	Multilateral				
	WTO[b]			OECD[c]	
	GATS	TRIMs	TRIPs	Cap	Cur
Binding	yes	yes	yes	yes	yes
Year	1994	1994	1994	1963	1963
Country coverage (number)	124[g]	124[g]	124[g]	26	26
Objectives	Establish services trade and investment framework	Limit performance requirements in manufacturing	Protect intellectual property rights	Liberalize restrictions on capital transactions	Liberalize restrictions on capital transactions
Features	Complex architecture	Narrowly focused	Includes technology protection and technology transfer	Covers many types of capital transfers	Focused on balance of payments current account transactions

Notes: [a] Strictly agreements which include investment provisions, since they may also relate to trade, technology, etc. The European Union has been excluded from this table, because it does not formally include an investment agreement; but the EU is far ahead of other organizations in terms of its degree of integration, and the inclusion of elements such as competition policy which would be included in a comprehensive investment agreement.

[b] WTO agreements are: GATS—General Agreement on Trade in Services; TRIMs—Trade Related Investment Measures; TRIPs—Trade Related Intellectual Property Rights. TRIPs is not an investment agreement *per se* but has major, direct implications for MNEs and FDI.

[c] OECD agreements are: Cap—Code of Liberalization of Capital Movements; Cur—Code of Liberalization of Current Invisible Operations; NTI—National Treatment Instrument; MNE—Guidelines for

practices can also be readily defended on the grounds that MNEs and FDI tend to exist in oligopolistic industries. Given the nature of the multinational enterprise, multilateral investment rules are desirable since the range of existing instruments and agreements at national, bilateral, regional, and, indeed, multilateral levels creates an inefficient patchwork; MNEs may be able to circumvent and exploit this policy patchwork and extract rents in the process. Avoidance of inefficiency also requires multilateral policies which are coherent across issues, are neutral as between modes of market servicing and ensure market contestability.

Yet the evidence of Chapters 2–6 showed that there have been significant shifts over time in the mix of liberalization-regulation tendencies and in the prevailing atti-

Investment Agreements[a]

		Regional / Sectoral	Regional	
		ECT[d]	NAFTA[e]	APEC[f]
NTI	MNE			
no	no	yes	yes	no
1976	1976	1994	1993	1994
26	26	51	3	18
Establish national treatment principles	Establish guidelines for firms' behaviour	Liberalize energy trade and investment in Central and Eastern Europe	Liberalize regional trade and investment	Liberalize regional trade and investment
Many sectoral exceptions	Brief statements on selected issues	Detailed sector-specific and region-specific coverage	Detailed coverage of numerous issues	General principles to follow in establishing national rules

Multinational Enterprises. As at the time of writing a Multilateral Agreement on Investment (MAI) was being negotiated.

[d] Energy Charter Treaty.

[e] North American Free Trade Agreement.

[f] Asia Pacific Economic Cooperation (APEC) Non-binding Investment Principles.

[g] Number of countries increased in early years of WTO.

Source: Extended from Brewer and Young, 1996.

tudes and policies towards MNEs and FDI. Initially, during the 1940s, when the creation of the ITO was being negotiated, there was a balanced mix of both tendencies. When the ITO failed to materialize and the GATT emerged as the key international organization for trade policy-making during the 1950s and 1960s, the liberalization of government policies dominated as MNEs enjoyed their honeymoon period. During the 1970s, the policy pendulum shifted sharply—to a focus on control and regulation of MNEs, not only in UN fora, but also at both regional and national levels, in developing countries especially. In the 1980s and into the 1990s, the pendulum shifted yet again—to a nearly exclusive focus on liberalization of government policies (albeit without much progress on the critical issue of governance rules relating to competition policy).

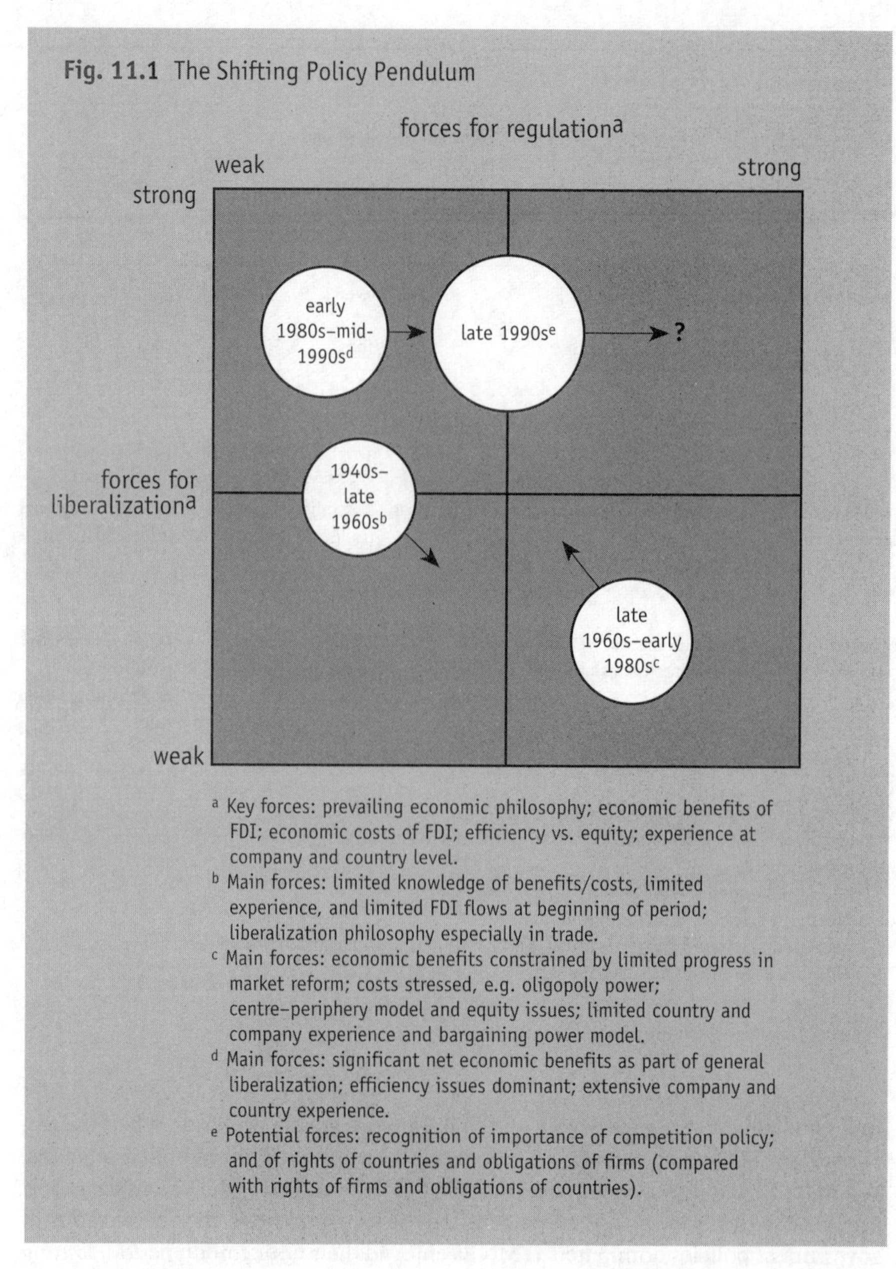

Fig. 11.1 The Shifting Policy Pendulum

[a] Key forces: prevailing economic philosophy; economic benefits of FDI; economic costs of FDI; efficiency vs. equity; experience at company and country level.

[b] Main forces: limited knowledge of benefits/costs, limited experience, and limited FDI flows at beginning of period; liberalization philosophy especially in trade.

[c] Main forces: economic benefits constrained by limited progress in market reform; costs stressed, e.g. oligopoly power; centre–periphery model and equity issues; limited country and company experience and bargaining power model.

[d] Main forces: significant net economic benefits as part of general liberalization; efficiency issues dominant; extensive company and country experience.

[e] Potential forces: recognition of importance of competition policy; and of rights of countries and obligations of firms (compared with rights of firms and obligations of countries).

Figure 11.1 highlights some of the key forces determining the policy balance over fifty years. It is important to recognize that FDI policy cannot be dissociated from the more general economic policy philosophy prevailing at particular periods of time. Hence the honeymoon period in the immediate post-war years was associated with an international organizational framework designed to facilitate liberalization, even though the investment arm of this framework did not materialize. In the 1980s and 1990s, investment liberalization was linked to a widespread process of market reform, deregulation and privatization. This latter period was also characterized by a high degree of understanding of the economic benefits (and costs) associated with multinational activity, and by extensive experience among both companies and countries in handling relationships. At host nation level, the attraction of inward FDI has become a sophisticated marketing exercise (backed by subsidies), targeted on countries, sectors, and subsectors, and value-adding activities (assembly, R & D, regional headquarters, etc.).

The policy balance is expressed in terms of a pendulum because in both economic and political terms it is reasonable to suppose that there could be a shift towards a different mix of liberalization and regulation at the end of the twentieth and into the twenty-first century, especially if national governments attempt to reassert their sovereignty. The liberalization trend is sufficiently well established at all levels that it can be expected to continue for several more years, though there will be significant variability across industries and countries in the liberalization trend. It is noteworthy that, even within the traditionally highly protectionist agriculture, textile, and steel sectors, for instance, the liberalization process has gained much momentum.

A continued FDI liberalization momentum requires that there are identifiable gains from market reforms generally at country level and these may be questionable at least within a reasonable time scale. For example, among some developed host countries in Europe, continuing high levels of unemployment may create pressures for protection and regulation; in other developed countries, rising income inequality could stall or reverse liberalization. Among the poorer developing nations and some of the economies in transition, continuing progress in market reforms and FDI liberalization is dependent upon recognizable benefits from existing deregulation and privatization programmes.

Aside from the changing liberalization-regulation mix, a key policy dimension in the post-war years has been the level at which policy developments have occurred. Some of the major influences are shown in Figure 11.2. Following the non-ratification of the ITO, attitudes and, therefore, policies towards MNEs were generally benign. From the late 1960s, there were attempts to regulate the MNE at all levels; whereas into the 1980s the liberalization thrust occurred at all levels.

In the late 1990s and into the 2000s, the continued expansion of FDI and globalization factors will undoubtedly encourage rule-making at the multilateral level. By contrast there are two major constraints working against multilateral rules at the dawn of the millennium. The first concerns enforcement possibilities, which also relate to the status of investment instruments as between voluntary and required. The preference is clearly for binding rules which would lock in the liberalization which has been achieved, and this was part of the thinking behind the MAI negotiations in the OECD; however, a number of the OECD investment rules from the past have been non-binding and, therefore, weak. The binding rules emanating from the Uruguay Round negotiations were bolstered up by improved dispute settlement mechanisms in the WTO. Nevertheless, the WTO patchwork of rules creates problems for enforcement; these difficulties are exacerbated by a diminished US commitment to multilateralism (as discussed later in the chapter).

The second major problem for multilateral rules concerns the complexity of agreements, and, therefore, of negotiations (this was, indeed, an argument used by proponents in favour of the OECD as opposed to the WTO forum in efforts to conclude a multilateral investment pact). While the GATT had an enormous influence on multilateral tariff-cutting in the post-war period, many saw the beginnings of its demise in the rise of non-tariff barriers in the 1970s. The difficulties of eliminating NTBs are paralleled by problems in removing investment barriers; indeed, the two represent different sides of the same coin in many industries (e.g. anti-dumping duties restrict trade and induce investment).

The suggestion of Figure 11.2 is that problems in multilateral negotiations will promote regionalism into the twenty-first century. Economic ties encourage RIAs; enforcement possibilities are easier, especially where there is a regional hegemon (the USA in NAFTA) or hegemonic axis (Germany and France in the EU); and agreements are less complex. Chapter 7 analysed the marked revival of interest in RIAs in the 1990s, and the importance of NAFTA both as an investment cum trade agreement, and as a vehicle for developing state-of-the-art rules and deep integration (in some areas). The EU has major lessons for other areas, too, especially in its competition policy, Single Market programme, and, potentially, the Social Chapter of the Maastricht Treaty (and its focus upon the rights of nations and obligations of firms). There is an extensive literature criticizing the discriminatory trade provisions of regional agreements; and similar fears exist in respect of their investment provisions, hence the debate over 'building blocks versus stumbling blocks'. Assuming there is no reversion to unilateralism and bilateralism (which seems likely), the main impetus to investment rules whose objective is economic efficiency is likely to come at the regional level and plurilateral level (see the EU proposals on Competition Policy in Chapter 9).

11.3 **Policy Issues**

Principles of non-discrimination

National treatment means that a government treats a foreign-owned corporation no less favourably than a domestically owned corporation—that is, it does not discriminate against foreign investors in favour of locally owned firms. The nominal commitment to national treatment, however, is substantially diluted by each country's industry-specific exceptions—which are evident in the NAFTA, the OECD National Treatment Instrument, and the GATS. These industry exceptions are central to the negotiation of any international investment agreement providing for liberalization of government restrictions on the right of establishment for foreign investors; these negotiations are often conducted on a bilateral basis within the larger regional or multilateral negotiations. The intensity of the desire to seek exceptions varies

Fig. 11.2 Factors Influencing FDI Policy (by level of agreement)

Influencing factors	*Policy level* National	Bilateral	Regional	Multilateral
Growth of FDI and the MNE	+	+	+	++
Net economic benefits	+	+	+	+
Economic ties	+	++	++	+
Enforcement possibilities	+	+	+–	––
Complexity of agreements	+	+	+–	––
Balance of domestic vs. global interests at national level	++ or ––	++	– or +	–– or ++

Legend: ++ factors strongly favourable to policy at particular level
+ factors favourable to policy at particular level
– factors unfavourable to policy at particular level
–– factors strongly unfavourable to policy at particular level

across industries or countries, but there are some recurrent patterns—such as exceptions for national security-sensitive industries (e.g. nuclear energy) or highly regulated industries (e.g. banking and insurance) or other industries where there are monopolies and/or significant government ownership (e.g. transportation and communications). In addition there are industries that are so central to the economy (e.g. petroleum in some countries) or are politically sensitive for other reasons (e.g. culturally sensitive industries such as film) or have yet other features that give them special status in the political system that they can gain exemption from national treatment. In some instances, the negotiations on specific industries become sufficiently problematic and idiosyncratic that there are semi-autonomous negotiations for separate agreements (e.g. textiles in the Uruguay Round), or deferred negotiations on the contents of an annex (e.g. financial services in the GATS), or overlapping negotiations on separate chapters with extensive industry-specific provisions that cut across more general investment-related provisions (e.g. the automotive industry in NAFTA).

Aside from national treatment, the other core principle of non-discrimination is *most favoured nation (MFN) treatment*—i.e. the commitment to extend the same level of liberalized policy measures to investors from all signatory countries regardless of their nationality. There are accordingly provisions for MFN in the APEC principles, the ECT, the NAFTA, and the GATS; the language of the NAFTA is particularly expansive in this regard.

While the MFN principle is firmly embedded in existing international agreements, as with national treatment, there are many exceptions to it in practice. In recent years, two tendencies have been undermining MFN as a keystone of the international trade regime, and by implication threaten to undermine efforts to reform the investment regime. The first tendency is to approach issues bilaterally through a focus on bilateral disputes (e.g. Japanese–US trade in the motor vehicle industry) and on conditional MFN in negotiations (e.g. financial services and other industries in the GATS). It should be noted, however, that there is a fundamental difference between MFN on trade issues such as tariff levels, and on investment issues such as the right of establishment. Whereas tariff levels can be negotiated down incrementally, the right of establishment is categorical, except for any industry exceptions that are negotiated.

Another tendency has been to seek 'carve-outs' for regional organizations in agreements. This has become an issue, for instance, for the EU in the OECD negotiations on the MAI. The two major recent documents of the European Commission (1995*a*, 1995*b*) that deal with investment issues are nearly silent on a commitment to MFN. The only reference to MFN is in the context of a brief discussion of bilateral investment treaties:

> Without [global MFN], attempts to provide equal treatment for foreign investors will be thwarted by those who continue to discriminate through the use of non-standardised BIT(s). MFN should be supported by a standstill agreement which will prevent countries from reducing access to all of its trading partners. Equally, it will be important to assure equal treatment for host countries.

In contrast, the APEC espousal of 'open regionalism' can be interpreted as a commitment not to undermine the traditional multilateral systemic principle of MFN, though many of the statements of the principle of open regionalism with regard to APEC have in fact omitted any reference to MFN. Along with the half-century commitment to MFN in the GATT/WTO agreements on trade (and now selectively for investment as well in the GATS), at the same time there has been the acceptance of regional agreements even though they inherently violate the MFN principle (see the discussion in Chapter 7).

There is little disagreement in international agreements on the core principles of freedom of entry, national treatment, most favoured nation treatment, and investment protection. Similarly, the ECT and NAFTA agreements provide state-of-the-art provisions which could be widened in a forum such as the OECD's MAI. Progress will not be easy in a wider forum, and even the ECT and NAFTA contain exceptions and conditions which require to be whittled away. Also national treatment and MFN have been increasingly undermined in recent years by the bilateral and regional emphases of some countries' policies and by the concomitant adoption of conditional (reciprocal) non-discriminatory policies.

The OECD National Treatment Instrument forms a natural starting point for future negotiations on this subject. The major limitations of the OECD instrument concern the range of exceptions and reciprocity conditions. An objective of future negotiations, therefore, should be to secure standstill in both of these areas, together with progressive rollback. Prime target sectors for the latter should be industries in which FDI flows are of the greatest significance, either currently or potentially—for instance, banking, insurance, and other financial services and air transport. High priority should be given to reductions in the signatories' industry exceptions to national treatment.

Sector-specific issues

The international agreements considered in this volume have addressed sector-specific issues through several different architectural arrangements.[1] Although the architecture varies, there is a fundamental similarity in the net results—namely, a further complication of the already complex patchwork of agreements. There is also a further *de facto* dilution of national treatment and MFN. Two prominent examples are the automotive industry and financial services. The separate NAFTA chapter annex on the automotive industry, for instance, includes elaborate and discriminatory, industry-specific provisions concerning rules of origin, which have far-reaching implications for firms' FDI decisions as well as the more obvious trade implications. As for financial services, the separation of financial services from the other sectors covered by the GATS and the associated deferral of the completion of negotiations have made possible a more effective domestic political campaign in the United States by that industry to resist the completion of those negotiations. On the other hand, the development of semi-autonomous industry-specific agreements may facilitate the horizontal integration across policy areas; thus investment policy–trade policy and investment policy–technology policy linkages can perhaps be more directly addressed on a sectoral basis. For example, the linkages between trade performance requirements and trade subsidies, on the one hand, and investment incentives, on the other, are central issues in the automotive industry, but not in financial services. In contrast, the linkages between domestic regulatory issues such as capital requirements for banks, on the one hand, and obstacles to establishment for foreign investors, on the other, are obviously of special interest in financial service industries. There is then an issue about how best to address industry-specific questions without unduly complicating or diluting more generic agreements. The diversity in the architecture of existing agreements reflects the complexity of the varying requirements of diverse industries and the political realities of international and domestic negotiations.

Binding versus non-binding agreements—and dispute settlement

Theory does not assist in terms of a preference for legally binding agreements, as opposed to soft law policy measures. The World Bank (1992*a*) has pointed out that efforts of international agencies to develop codified, universally agreed laws on FDI in the past have been protracted and ended either in no agreement or with some limited agreement representing the lowest common denominator. This has meant limited progress in terms of encouraging desirable practice and a more attractive investment climate. It was for this reason that World Bank efforts have been directed towards setting out *guidelines* on what may constitute acceptable and desirable standards (World Bank, 1992*a*). In a similar vein, Fatouros (1996: 60) has argued that: 'The prospect of a binding agreement may "freeze" states (and other actors) in positions intended to maximize bargaining advantage and thereby hinder and perhaps distort moves to liberalization.' It is true that voluntary guidelines which are in some sense an 'ideal' are helpful in setting aspiration levels, provided they are complementary to existing sets of rules. However, there is a danger of non-binding agreements being ignored or sidelined, and the OECD Guidelines for Multinational Enterprises have suffered from this problem (Hamilton, 1983). Self-evidently, legally binding agreements have greater status, especially when there is still a proliferation of FDI agreements which may confuse participating actors. And even if the standards set are lower than with voluntary codes, the liberalization gains cannot readily be reversed. In truth, it may not be a choice between binding or non-binding agreements: in order to make progress on a series of fronts, a combination of approaches may be utilized.

Disputes

Dispute settlement procedures nearly always arise as an issue with binding agreements, in which the distinction between state–state and state–investor disputes is essential to an understanding of provisions for dispute settlement procedures. The Uruguay Round / WTO Dispute Settlement Understanding and related agreements address only state–state disputes, while the NAFTA addresses both types. The newly strengthened GATT / WTO dispute settlement procedures can include investment disputes directly as a result of disputes concerning either the GATS or TRIMs agreement; or indirectly through cross-retaliation procedures whereby retaliation in trade disputes, in limited circumstances, can involve investment policies (Brewer, 1995*a*, 1995*b*). The generally tighter schedules for the operation of the dispute settlement process, the requirement of a unanimous vote to reverse a panel finding and the creation of an appeals process have all significantly strengthened the state–state dispute process in the WTO. In NAFTA, there are extensive provisions for investor–state dispute settlement processes as well.

Governments' competition policies and firms' restrictive business practices

Anti-competitive behaviour by firms becomes a major concern in an era of globalization of markets. The nature of anti-competitive behaviour has also changed with the growing importance of strategic alliances and joint ventures. Within the context of competition policy, too, should be added the behaviour of state monopolies. These, and other issues, such as the increasing industry concentration as a result of international mergers and acquisitions in many industries, and the inherent difficulties of unilateral national government attempts to regulate restrictive business practices, suggest that interest in international agreements on competition policy is likely to (and should) continue to increase.

The WTO negotiations scheduled for 1998–2000 (Table 6.1) allow for the possibility of including competition policy on the TRIMs agenda. Into the next century, therefore, it is possible that there will be growing activity that will create the tangible beginnings of a significant competition policy regime, including specific country coordination; and the EU, for example, is pushing for progress on a plurilateral agreement (Chapter 9).

Environmental regulation

Another regulatory topic that is already receiving institutionalized interest at the WTO is environmental policy, although primarily as it relates to trade. Any artificial separation of trade from investment in the consideration of environmental issues, however, could easily produce weak, ineffective agreements. To date, linkages between international environmental issues and international investment issues have been mostly addressed at the regional level, within NAFTA in particular, and to a lesser extent in APEC. However, the increasing interest in those linkages within the UN system and the World Bank, as well as the WTO and OECD, suggests that environmental regulatory issues will become an important element of the liberalization-regulation mix of international investment regime issues.

Investment incentives

This is an issue area of particular complexity and controversy because it entails questions of both liberalization and regulation. There are liberalization issues because many investment incentives represent inefficient and inequitable government intervention and lead to wasteful, beggar-thy-neighbour bidding between nations. There are also regulation aspects because some incentives are economically justifiable due to positive or negative externalities; thus, incentives can be useful elements of environmental protection policies, for instance. Further, like environmental issues, incentive issues often have an underpinning of conflicts between developing and developed countries, and this adds to the inherent technical difficulties of developing an international regime that can distinguish among incentives that are and are not economically justifiable. Investment incentives are particularly problematic because of the very limited progress that has been made to date in any fora on those issues.

Reflecting this situation, a report by UNCTAD (1996*b*) suggests a step-by-step approach to international cooperation on incentives. Standstill with progressive rollback would be compatible with this approach. Within the WTO, this could be accomplished by extensions of the agreement on TRIMs and the agreement on Subsidies and Countervailing Measures (Brewer and Young, 1997). In the OECD, provisions for standstill and rollback on both incentives and performance requirements are desirable, building on the (quite limited) existing agreement on incentives. Since such multilateral disciplines will primarily act as constraints on developed nations, there may be greater tolerance by developing countries of international rules generally. Questions of definition and scope and types of disciplines need to be addressed (OECD, 1996*a*). Discussions on incentives will also need to include investment-distorting mandatory performance requirements which are frequently linked.

Developing countries

As reflected in the above comments on incentives, recognition needs to be given to the differing interests of developed and developing nations. The latter states are particularly concerned about the developmental implications of MNEs and technology transfer. Attention has been drawn in recent work (see Chapter 10) to the continued relevance of theories of underdevelopment where firms lack competitive, indigenously generated technological capacities, and to the problems of technology transfer into lower-income developing countries. Recognition by developed nations of these issues and concerns is important for the future of multilateral rules. The agreements on intellectual property rights and services in the WTO were widely regarded as reflecting developed country priorities and agendas. The relative weakness of the TRIMs agreement reflected the inability of developed and developing countries to make progress on performance requirements.

Market contestability, modal neutrality, and policy coherence

While the key issues for the future have been discussed above as discrete policy areas, it is critically important that efforts are made to develop a holistic framework for rule-making around the concepts of market contestability, modal neutrality and policy coherence. This is highly complex because of the number of dimensions of policy, including:

- type of international business transactions or relationships that transcend international boundaries (movement of funds, goods, services, technology, people); control / ownership of firms;
- sectors and industries (agriculture, manufacturing, etc.);
- issue areas (investment, trade, technology, etc.);
- level of policy (national, bilateral, regional, multilateral);
- binding or non-binding agreements.

Yet it is also crucial, not only to ensure that genuine progress is being made towards facilitating improved economic efficiency, but also to ensure that companies and countries recognize this. In the case of the first point, it is entirely possible that a supposed policy improvement could be detrimental to economic efficiency by exacerbating the patchwork. And unless the actors are convinced of improvement, they will be reluctant to participate enthusiastically in further negotiations.

11.4 Politics

Because all of the policy questions discussed in this book are subject to a variety of political forces as well as economic forces, any conclusions must explicitly take into account key political considerations.[2] Whether answers are being sought concerning explanatory or predictive or evaluative questions about policy, it is useful to include six elements of political processes in the analysis:

- issues—the central questions about policy, i.e. what should and should not be done;
- interests—the kinds of interests that are at stake in the issues;
- ideology—the basic beliefs and values that shape opinions on specific issues;
- conflicts—the principal lines of conflict (and cooperation) and thus the composition of coalitions in the conflicts;
- power relationships—the actors that are in relatively strong (and weak) positions to try to make their preferences prevail;
- institutional outcomes—the policies that are accepted (and rejected) at the multilateral, regional and bilateral levels.

Each of these elements is incorporated into Box 11.1, where a summary is presented of the politics of the evolution of the international investment system covered in Chapters 3–6.

In the aftermath of the collapse of the effort to create the ITO during the 1940s, shared interests in post-war economic reconstruction, avoidance of another depression, and cooperation in the early years of the cold war all led to a period of relative quiescence on investment issues. Aside from capital control liberalization initiatives within the OECD, which was strongly European in its orientation, and the creation of the European Common Market, with its competition policy provisions, the early period was marked by the emergence of bilateral investment treaties as the predominant form of international arrangements on investment issues. These regional and bilateral outcomes were in substantial part the result of US preferences (which included much pressure for European integration) and US hegemony. Similarly, the absence of a multilateral institution with significant authority on investment issues was also the result of US policy, which in the end reflected congressional opposition to such an organization. Because many developing countries were only gaining their political independence during this period, neither they—nor the communist countries—had significant involvement in any of the efforts after the collapse of the ITO in the early post-war years.

Box 11.1

Key Features of Politics

A. Mid-1940s–Late 1960s

- *Issues*: Whether to create international institutions with authority for investment and competition policies; how to protect investors.
- *Interests*: Economic recovery from war and economic development in former colonies as well as industrial countries.
- *Ideologies*: Liberal international economic regime and private investment are essential to economic growth.
- *Conflicts*: USA and other developed countries wanted emphasis on liberalization while India and other developing countries wanted emphasis on development; within countries, especially the USA, split over whether to include regulatory authority.
- *Power relationships*: US hegemony in multilateral institutions; emergence of France, Germany, and UK as European leaders; independence of former colonies.
- *Institutional Outcomes*
    - — Multilateral: Defeat of ITO; creation of GATT, IBRD, and IMF; neglect of investment, except in OECD.
    - — Regional: Establishment of EEC with competition focus.
    - — Bilateral: Development of bilateral investment treaties for investor protection.

B. Late 1960s–Early 1980s

- *Issues*: Whether and how to control MNEs.
- *Interests*: Governments' control over national economies.
- *Ideologies*: MNEs are threat to national sovereignty and centre–periphery differences are inequitable.
- *Conflicts*: North–south differences on roles of MNEs and international institutions in world economy.
- *Power relationships*: Increasing international economic interdependence enhances bargaining position of developing countries.
- *Institutional outcomes:*
    - — Multilateral: Prolonged, inconclusive negotiations on UN codes; formulation of OECD and other guidelines.

C. Early 1980s–Mid-1990s

- *Issues*: Whether to include investment liberalization in trade agreements.
- *Interests*: Recovery from 'stagflation' in developed countries and external debt crises in developing countries; integration of Central and East European countries into world economy.
- *Ideologies*: Liberalization of international economic policies of all types is desirable to take advantage of markets.
- *Conflicts:* Differences over methods and pace of liberalization, as well as market access, with USA often having most ambitious agenda; increasing USA–Japan and USA–EU conflict.
- *Power relationships:* US hegemony in decline.

- *Institutional outcomes:*
  - — Multilateral: Investment policy included in GATT negotiations for first time; establishment of WTO, with investment policies in many industry sectors.
  - — Regional: Investment policy provisions included as central elements in NAFTA.
  - — Bilateral: Large increase in number of BITs.

D. Late 1990s

- *Issues*: How to implement Uruguay Round agreements on investment in WTO; whether to expand investment agenda in OECD and/or WTO; how to include China in system; how to reconcile regional and multilateral agreements.
- *Interests*: Sustainable development.
- *Ideologies*: Efficiency requires regulation as well as liberalization.
- *Conflicts*: Inconsistent US negotiating strategy and style; increasing differences among developed countries and developing nations on specific issues.
- *Power relationships*: Assertion of EU leadership role, tempered by member governments' differences; continued US initiatives.
- *Institutional outcomes:*
  - — Multilateral: Modest expansion of WTO's and OECD's investment activities.
  - — Regional: Proliferation of agreements.
  - — Bilateral: More BITs.

During the 1970s, the USA actively opposed the development of a multilateral agreement on investment in the UN, despite widespread advocacy by an increasingly vociferous group of developing countries, whose concerns were focused more on equity than efficiency. After a long history of conflict, the issue was finally dropped in the UN. Instead, the principal tangible outcome of the period occurred in the OECD, where the USA successfully sought a non-binding code among more like-minded developed countries. Thus, although US hegemony may have been in decline during the period, it was, nevertheless, powerful enough again to see its preferences prevail.

During the 1980s, after having been rebuffed in earlier efforts to include investment issues on the GATT agenda, the USA was successful in getting investment into the Uruguay Round. The issues of this period were fundamentally different from the 1970s: the liberalization of government policies replaced the regulation of MNEs' practices as the central issues. Issues were more often seen in terms of the rights of firms and obligations of governments. Although ideology and interests had shifted, however, there was still significant reticence about full-scale liberalization of investment policies. The principal outcome at the multilateral level, therefore, was an uneven treatment of investment issues because of the negotiating trade-offs that were made. Thus, whereas liberalization of TRIMs in the manufacturing sector was negligible, the beginning of liberalization in services through the GATS framework and the inclusion of intellectual property rights through the TRIPs agreement both marked significant departures for the new WTO, in comparison with the GATT. In addition, during the early 1990s NAFTA was created with significant investment provisions—entailing both liberalization within the region and discrimination against firms outside the region.

As of the mid-1990s, therefore, there had been a long history of outcomes that reflected American preferences and power, as well as shifting economic and political conditions in all parts of the world. The circumstances at the end of the millennium, however, were quite different. The frequent use of the new WTO dispute settlement procedures, particularly by developing countries, led to a more legalistic and public approach to conflicts over investment issues as well as trade issues. Furthermore, conflicts between the EU and the USA over investment issues became sharper as countries began to shape the new agenda in the WTO. Similarly, the USA and the other OECD member countries encountered difficulties in reaching agreement on an MAI. Yet there were also historically important sectoral liberalization agreements on telecommunications in the WTO and on energy in the European Energy Charter Treaty. Thus, several key features of the political processes affecting development of the international investment system had changed. The issues were more about tangible implementation procedures, review procedures, and sector-specific agreements. Interests, lines of conflict/cooperation, and power relationships were all more complex and fluid. At the same time, the tenets of liberalization were still widely accepted and provided a common ideological underpinning to the process. Thus, the complexities and uncertainties about interests, power, and shifting political alignments were more about strategy, tactics, and next steps than about the basic nature and directions of the system. It was widely agreed that the system needed to be strengthened further at the multilateral level. Issues about how and where and at what pace to do it, however, provided ample grounds for disagreement.

International agreements can be especially effective in these circumstances as a way to bolster national governments against domestic political pressures. In this respect, international investment agreements are like international trade agreements: they are much more than instruments of international economics; they are also instruments of domestic politics. Indeed, precisely because international investment agreements (in comparison with trade agreements) tend to have more extensive domestic economic implications and thus domestic political repercussions, it is essential that they be politically viable within the domestic political systems of key countries; in the same way they must obviously also be politically viable internationally.

Both political viability tests, furthermore, depend on the (perceived and actual) distribution of the benefits and costs of the agreements. Economic equity thus becomes a central evaluative criterion along with economic efficiency. In recent years, the efficiency gains of liberalization have been the dominant economic criterion in the efforts to develop the international investment regime at all levels—bilateral and regional as well as multilateral. However, as the agenda of investment issues at the WTO in particular continues to expand, equity issues will become more salient; it has been noted, for instance, that there are equity reasons as well as efficiency reasons for developing international restraints on investment incentives.

It is, therefore, expected that the scope of discussions about international investment agreements will be expanded significantly in coming years in both their political and economic dimensions. Politically, the discussions will include much more attention to domestic political questions. Economically, the discussions will include more attention to equity questions. The issues will become more salient as well as more complex and contentious. The stakes, furthermore, will continue to increase—for individual consumers and workers as well as for firms and governments.

US policy

One of the most important features of the political context of international policy-making on investment issues, in general, and the development of the multilateral regime, in particular, is the position of the US government. During the period covered by this book, there have been two fundamental changes in the role of the US government on international economic issues. First, there has been a decline in US power, often stated in terms of the end of US 'hegemony' (Keohane, 1985), a purported trend that has stimulated much controversy as to its accuracy and implications. Despite the controversy, it seems clear that US influence (in the sense of impact on the outcomes of specific issues) has in fact declined over the past half-century; yet, it is also clear that US influence continues to be substantial in general, greater than that of any other single country on most issues, and even dominating on some issues. Though it may have a veto power on some issues, however, so do other countries or groups of countries. Yet, the US position on nearly any issue is still of great significance.

The underlying approach (the philosophy or ideology) of US policies has changed as well. In particular, there has been a decline in US support for multilateralism and an increased use of plurilateral agreements in international trade (Green, 1995). This shift in policy preferences was in part the result of the presumed decline of US influence in international policy-making fora, especially multilateral fora. The turning point in US attitudes occurred in the early 1980s, when US policy-makers became enamoured with the possibility of using regional fora (where they presumably had more influence) to develop regional free trade agreements, which could then be used as building blocks for an eventual worldwide free trade regime.

As this heightened interest in regional agreements continued through three US administrations from the early 1980s into the late 1990s, the active US support for free trade agreements of diverse types led to the NAFTA, the APEC forum, the Free Trade for the Americas initiative and even a Trans-Atlantic Dialogue. Although these arrangements were principally seen as ways to liberalize and otherwise address trade issues, they also included investment issues on their agendas. As for investment issues, in particular, however, there has also been a strong bias toward bilateral agreements. Thus, the already long-standing tradition of US bilateral treaties of friendship, commerce, and navigation (FCN) was instrumental in the US defeat of the ITO, and the more recent use of bilateral investment treaties (BITs) has established standards of investment protection and policy liberalization that the USA fears could be undermined by multilateral agreements. Further, there have been occasional surges of unilateralism as well—as in the Section 301 legislation providing for unilateral US sanctions outside the GATT/WTO dispute settlement process, and the attempts to assert US anti-trust laws outside US territory to foreign affiliates of US parents or in some instances even to unrelated foreign firms. In addition to these regional, bilateral, and unilateral tendencies in US policy, there has also been an increasing sectoral focus that has cut across international agreements at all levels. This sectoral approach has been manifest in numerous industry-specific US–Japanese agreements, in the sector-specific chapters of NAFTA, and in the sector-specific annexes of the GATS in the WTO.

Altogether, this 'plurilateral' approach and its departure from the traditional US focus on multilateralism has tended to create uncertainties about US willingness to assume a leadership role in the development of multilateral arrangements. Though there are legitimate issues (such as free-rider problems) involved in these policy choices, and though the USA has surely not been alone in adopting these plurilateral approaches, these changes in US policy have fundamentally altered the political dynamics of multilateral regime issues from the earlier era of multilateralism and hegemony.

11.5 Conclusion

1. The MNE is a ubiquitous and holistic business organization, the activities of which encompass production, service, trade, R & D, investment, and other management operations, both within and across national borders. When developing international investment rules, the focus should be on the MNE as an international business organization rather than only FDI *per se*.
2. Similarly, it should be recognized that FDI entails much more than international capital movements. It involves cross-border control of a firm in one country by a firm in another country as well as other types of international business relationships.
3. A multilateral investment regime is required to facilitate improved economic efficiency and world welfare in the era of the multinational enterprise. The growing globalization of business, with MNEs as the leading players, reinforces the arguments for multilateral investment rules.
4. Market efficiency conditions require a policy framework which has a twin-track liberalization focus to remove impediments to international business operations and to constrain the anti-competitive activities of international oligopolists.
5. A series of other conditions are also necessary to ensure efficiency, namely, market contestability, modal neutrality, and policy coherence. The attainment of these conditions is necessary if firms are to be free to choose their own methods of market servicing, are to have free access to and compete for all factors of production, and are to operate in an environment in which policies are integrated to avoid distortions.
6. These conditions for efficiency are not being fulfilled. Some progress has been made in the liberalization conditions for market efficiency. However, widespread distortions exist, with a patchwork of policies operating at different levels, involving different organizations, applying to different sectors, and discriminating among different methods of market servicing. And, except for the EU, virtu-

ally no progress has been made in introducing the necessary governance (e.g. competition policy) rules for market efficiency.

7. The framework under items (4) and (6) above needs to be applied consistently in the development of new agreements and in upgrades of existing rules, if the prevailing patchwork is not to be exacerbated.
8. Progress is hampered in part by the fact that the benefits of international investment rule-making are not well understood at country level; this is true, for example, of efforts to reduce incentives among industrialized countries or to limit performance requirements by developing nations. The lack of understanding is compounded by the continued reference to 'international trade agreements' when these may include investment components. The terms 'international trade and investment agreement' or 'international business agreement' are surely preferable.
9. Additional multilateral agreements are desirable to lock in efficiency-enhancing rules. However, progress seems likely to be slow and patchwork-oriented in the WTO, partly because of its focus on trade thus far.
10. Whatever the final outcome of the discussions on the Multilateral Agreement on Investment at the OECD, they will prove to have been of substantial value as a learning process. The intensive analytic efforts which went into the MAI negotiations will prove invaluable for the future. Many of the points discussed in this book were developed as part of the research programmes initiated by the announcement of MAI negotiations. Yet, there has been rather limited progress on tangible measures within the OECD in the lengthy period since the Codes of Liberalization were agreed more than thirty years ago.
11. There is likely to be much progress in the development of regional integration agreements which proliferated in the 1990s. Efforts, therefore, also need to be made in multilateral fora to agree on acceptable characteristics for RIAs which would avoid increased discrimination against outsiders in respect of both investment and trade. Existing WTO rules have been shown to be weak and have been heavily criticized in this regard.
12. Multilateral investment rule-making needs to take into account equity as well as efficiency. Efforts to develop the multilateral system are likely to be stalled if consideration is not given to the needs of poor countries. This book covers one period—from the late 1960s to the early 1980s—when equity considerations were more conspicuous than in the 1990s, but FDI flows continued to expand rapidly.
13. The philosophy of international agreements has swung markedly away from the obligations of firms and rights of governments to firms' rights and governments' obligations. This is a reflection of the changing attitudes and priorities at the host country level and the recognition of the beneficial contribution of international investment. For future negotiations, it will be unrealistic to ignore issues concerning the obligations of firms, given the bargaining power of MNEs and the distributional implications of their actions, especially in developing countries. The next decade may thus see a substantial change in the nature of MNE/government relations.

14. The objectives and responsibilities of governments are more complex than those of firms. Governments are, therefore, understandably concerned about the implications of MNEs' activities for national macroeconomic conditions and for national security. Provisions in international agreements for 'safeguards' concerning balance of payments, public order, and national security are thus likely to continue to be problematic issues.
15. The future evolution of international agreements for investment and MNEs will depend as much on domestic politics as on economic diplomacy.

Notes

1. In some instances (e.g. telecommunications), there are industry-specific technical issues that purportedly require special treatment; in others (e.g. banking), there are distinctive regulatory issues; and in yet others (e.g. textiles, maritime transport, air transport), there are long-standing traditions of protectionism that create particularly strong political resistance to liberalization measures.
2. There is an extensive body of political science literature on the politics of multilateral regimes—especially regime change. However, it has focused on trade and neglected investment (see Haggard and Simmons, 1987; Brewer, 1997; Yarbrough and Yarbrough, 1992). An important exception is Preston and Windsor, 1992.

References

AGMON, T., and VON GLINOW, M. A. (1991), *Technology Transfer in International Business* (Oxford: Oxford University Press).

ALIBER, R. Z. (1970), 'A Theory of Direct Foreign Investment', in C. P. Kindleberger (ed.), *The International Corporation* (Cambridge, Mass.: MIT Press): 17–34.

ALLENDE, S. (1975), 'Speech to the United Nations', in H. Radice (ed.), *International Firms and Modern Imperialism* (Harmondsworth: Penguin Books): 233–47.

ASTOLFI, E. G. (1994), 'UNCTAD Report: Investment–Technology Transfer Interrelationship', *Les Nouvelles*, 29 (3): 162–4.

Asia-Pacific Economic Cooperation (1994), *Guide to the Investment Regimes of the APEC Member Economies*, 2nd edn. (Singapore: APEC).

BAIN, J. S. (1956), *Barriers to New Competition* (Cambridge, Mass.: Harvard University Press).

BAKKER, A. F. P. (1996), *The Liberalization of Capital Movements in Europe* (Dordrecht: Kluwer Academic Publishers).

BARAN, P. A., and SWEEZY, P. M. (1966), *Monopoly Capital* (New York: Monthly Review Press).

BARNET, R. J., and MÜLLER, R. E. (1974), *Global Reach:The Power of the Multinational Corporations* (New York: Simon & Schuster).

BARTLETT, C. A., and GHOSHAL, S. (1997), 'The Evolution of the Transnational', in I. Islam and W. Shepherd, *Current Issues in International Business* (Cheltenham: Edward Elgar): 108–31.

BAUTISTA, L. R. (1990), 'Expectations, Needs of Developing Countries', *Les Nouvelles*, 25 (1): 39–43.

BECERRIL, O. M. (1996), 'NAFTA Countries in Harmony, Now', *Les Nouvelles*, 31 (3): 100–4.

BELL, J., and YOUNG, S. (1998), 'Towards an Integrative Framework of the Internationalisation of the Firm', in G. Hooley, R. Loveridge, and D. Wilson (eds.), *Internationalisation:Process, Context and Markets* (London: Macmillan; New York: St Martin's Press).

BERGSTEN, C. F. (1974), 'Coming Investment Wars', *Foreign Affairs*, Oct.: 136–7.

—— and KRASNER, S. D. (1976), 'One, Two, Many OPECs. . . ?' in K. P. Sauvant and F. G. Lavipour (eds.), *Controlling Multinational Enterprises* (London: Wilton House): 195–213.

BHAGWATI, J. (1993), 'Regionalism and Multilateralism: An Overview', in J. de Melo and A. Panagariya (eds.), *New Dimensions in Regional Integration* (Cambridge: Cambridge University Press): 22–51.

—— and PANAGARIYA, A. (1996), *The Economics of Preferential Trade Agreements* (Washington: American Enterprise Institute).

BHATTACHARYYA, B. (1994), *Liberalisation in the External Sector: India's Experience* (New Delhi: Indian Institute for Foreign Trade).

—— (1995*a*), *Synthesis Report on Policy Impediments to Foreign Direct Investment in India* (New Delhi: Indian Institute for Foreign Trade).

—— (1995*b*), *Synthesis Report on Policy Impediments to Foreign Trade in India* (New Delhi: Indian Institute for Foreign Trade).

BIAC Committee on International Investment and ⅞ultinational Enterprises (1982), *National Treatment: A Major Investment Issue of the 1980s* (Paris: OECD), Dec.

BLACK, R., BLANK, S., and HANSON, E. C. (1978), *Multinationals in Contention: Responses at Governmental and International Levels* (New York: The Conference Board).

BLOMSTRÖM, M., LIPSEY, R. E., and ZEJAN, M. (1996), 'Is Fixed Investment the Key to Economic Growth?', *Quarterly Journal of Economics*, 111 (1): 269–76.

Boddewyn, J. (1974), *Western European Policies toward US Investors* (New York: New York University).

Bora, B. K. (1995), 'Apec's Non-binding Investment Principles: A Step Forward?', in C. J. Green and T. L. Brewer (eds.), *Investment Issues in Asia and the Pacific Rim* (New York: Oceana): 137–56.

—— and Graham, E. M. (1995), 'Nonbinding Investment Principles in APEC', *CAPA Report*, 49, Jan: 1–2.

Borenstein, E., De Gregorio, J., and Lee, J.-W. (1994), 'How Does Foreign Direct Investment Affect Economic Growth?', Working Paper (Washington: International Monetary Fund).

Brander, J. A., and Spencer, B. J. (1985), 'Export Subsidies and International Market Share Rivalry', *Journal of International Economics*, 18 (Feb.): 83–100.

Breland, E. A. C., and Cordell, V. V. (1996), 'Conflicting Competition Policies in a Globalized Business Environment: Prospects for International Cooperation and Convergence', paper presented at a conference on Globalization and Regionalization of Trade and International Investment, Université Paris I Pantheon Sorbonne, 29–30 May.

Brewer, T. L. (1995*a*), 'International Investment Dispute Settlement Procedures: The Evolving Regime for Foreign Direct Investment', *Law and Policy in International Business*, 26 (3): 633–73.

—— (1995*b*), 'Investment Issues in the WTO and Implications for APEC', in Carl J. Green and Thomas L. Brewer (eds.), *Investment Issues in the Asia Pacific Region and the Role of APEC* (New York: Oceana): 113–33.

—— (1996), 'International Investment Dispute Settlement Mechanisms: Agreements, Institutions and Issues', in OECD, *Toward Multilateral Investment Rules* (Paris: OECD): 85–105.

—— (1997), 'International Political Economy and MNEs' Strategies: New Directions for Interdisciplinary Research', in I. Islam and W. Shepherd, *Current Issues in International Business* (Cheltenham: Edward Elgar): 69–83.

—— and Young, S. (1995*a*), 'The Multilateral Agenda for Foreign Direct Investment: Problems, Principles and Priorities for Negotiations at the OECD and WTO', *World Competition*, 18 (4), June: 67–83.

—— —— (1995*b*), 'Towards a Multilateral Framework for Foreign Direct Investment: Issues and Scenarios', *Transnational Corporations*, 4 (1): 69–83.

—— —— (1995*c*), 'European Union Policies and the Problems of Multinational Enterprises', *Journal of World Trade Law*, 29 (1): 33–52.

—— —— (1996), 'Investment Policies in Multilateral and Regional Agreements: A Comparative Analysis', *Transnational Corporations*, 5 (1): 9–35.

—— —— (1997), 'Investment Incentives and the International Agenda', *World Economy*, 20 (2): 175–98.

Bronz, G. (1969), 'The International Trade Organization Charter', *Harvard Law Review*, 62: 1089–125.

Brown, W. A. (1950), *The United States and the Restoration of World Trade: An Analysis and Appraisal of the ITO Charter and the General Agreement on Tariffs and Trade* (Washington: Brookings Institution).

Buckley, P. J., and Casson, M. (1976), *The Future of the Multinational Enterprise* (London: Macmillan).

Cantwell, J. A. (1989), *Technological Innovation and Multinational Corporations* (Oxford: Basil Blackwell).

—— (1991), 'A Survey of Theories of International Production', in C. N. Pitelis and R. ugden (eds.), *The Nature of the Transnational Firm* (London: Routledge): 16–63.

Caves, R. E. (1971), 'International Corporations: The Industrial Economics of Foreign Investment', *Economica*, 38: 1–27.

—— (1996), *Multinational Enterprise and Economic Analysis*, 2nd edn. (Cambridge: Cambridge University Press).

Christy, P. B. (1991), 'Negotiating Investment in the GATT: A Call for Functionalism', *Michigan Journal of International Law*, 12 (4), Summer: 743–98.

CLEGG, J. (1996), 'US Foreign Direct Investment in the EU—The Effects of Market Integration in Perspective', in F. Burton, M. Yamin, and S. Young (eds.), *International Business and Europe in Transition* (London: Macmillan; New York: St Martin's Press): 189–206.

COASE, R. H. (1937), 'The Nature of the Firm', *Economica*, 4: 386–405.

COMANOR, W. S., GEORGE, K., JACQUEMIN, A., JENNY, F., KANTZENBACH, N., ORDOVER, J. A., and WAVERMAN, L. (1990), *Competition Policy in Europe and North America: Economic Issues and Institutions* (Chur: Harwood Academic Publishers).

Commission of the European Communities (1993), *XXIInd Report on Competition Policy 1992* (Luxembourg: Office for Official Publications of the European Communities).

—— (1997), *Green Paper on Vertical Restraints in EC Competition Policy*, COM (96) 721 final, Brussels, 22 Jan. 1997.

COWLING, K., and SUGDEN, R. (1987), *Transnational Monopoly Capitalism* (Brighton: Wheatsheaf).

CROOM, J. (1995), *Reshaping the World Trading System* (Geneva: World Trade Organization).

CURHAN, J. P., DAVIDSON, W. H., and SURI, R. (1977), *Tracing the Multinationals: A Sourcebook on US-based Enterprises* (Cambridge, Mass.: Ballinger Publishing Co.).

D'CRUZ, J. R., and RUGMAN, A. M. (1993), 'Developing International Competitiveness: The Five Partners Model', *Business Quarterly*, 58 (2): 60–72.

DE MELO, J., MONTENEGRO, C., and PANAGARIYA, A. (1992), *Regional Integration: Old and New*, WPS 985 (Washington: The World Bank).

DE VRIES, M. G., and HORSEFIELD, J. K. (1969), *The International Monetary Fund 1945–1965: Twenty Years of International Monetary Cooperation* (Washington: International Monetary Fund).

DIEBOLD, W. (1952), 'The End of the ITO', *Princeton Essays in International Finance* (16), Princeton University.

DIXIT, A. K., and GROSSMAN, G. M. (1986), 'Targeted Export Promotion with Several Oligopolistic Industries', *Journal of International Economics*, 21 (Nov.): 233–49.

DUNNING, J. H. (1987), 'The Investment Development Cycle and Third World Multinationals', in S. Lall (ed.), *Transnational Corporations and Economic Development*, United Nations Library on Transnational Corporations 3 (London: Routledge): 135–66.

—— (1988), 'The Eclectic Paradigm of International Production', *Journal of International Business Studies*, 19, 1–31.

—— (1991), 'Governments—Markets—Firms: Towards a New Balance?', *CTC Reporter*, 31 (Spring): 2–7.

—— (1992), 'The Global Economy, Domestic Governance, Strategies and Transnational Corporations: Interactions and Policy Implications', *Transnational Corporations*, 1 (3): 7–45.

—— (1993), *Multinational Enterprises and the Global Economy* (Wokingham: Addison-Wesley).

—— (1994*a*), 'Globalization, Economic Restructuring and Development', The Raúl Prebisch Lectures, No. 6 (Geneva:UNCTAD): 29 Apr.

—— (1994*b*), 'Re-evaluating the Benefits of Foreign Direct Investment', *Transnational Corporations*, 3 (1): 23–51.

—— (1995), 'Reappraising the Eclectic Paradigm in an Age of Alliance Capitalism', *Journal of International Business Studies*, 26 (3), 461–91.

—— and ROBSON, P. (1988), 'Multinational Corporate Integration and Regional Economic Integration', in J. H. Dunning and P. Robson (eds.), *Multinationals and the European Community* (Oxford: Basil Blackwell): 1–23.

DYKER, D., and BARROW, M. (1994), *Monopoly and Competition Policy in Russia* (London: The Royal Institute of International Affairs).

EATON, J., and GROSSMAN, G. M. (1986), 'Optimal Trade Policy and Industrial Policy under Oligopoly', *Quarterly Journal of Economics*, May: 383–406.

Economist Intelligence Unit (1994), *The EIU Guide to the New GATT* (London: EIU).

—— (1996), 'China', in *Investment, Licensing and Trading Conditions Abroad* (London: EIU, looseleaf).

EDEN, L., and APPEL. M. M. (1993), 'The NAFTA's Automotive Provisions', C. D. Howe Institute, *The NAFTA Papers*, No. 53, Nov.

European Commission (1995*a*), *Competition Policy in the New Trade Order: Strengthening International Cooperation and Rules* (Luxembourg: Office for Official Publication of the European Communities), July.

—— (1995*b*), *Conference on Competition Policy*, organized by the European Commission in cooperation with the Office of Economic Competition of Hungary (Brussels), 19–21 June.

—— (1996*a*), *Report on United States Barriers to Trade and Investment* (Brussels: EC).

—— (1996*b*), 'Draft Horizontal Framework on Regional Aid for Larger Investment Projects', Directorate-General XVI Regional Policy and Cohesion (Brussels, mimeo).

FATOUROS, A. A. (1996), 'Towards an International Agreement on Foreign Direct Investment', in OECD, *Toward Multilateral Investment Rules* (Paris: OECD): 47–67.

Financial Times (1995*a*), 'A Maturing Marks Copyright Deal' (28 July).

—— (1995*b*), 'Case for More Discipline' (16 Feb.).

—— (1995*c*), 'Wage Pressures from the South' (1 June).

—— (1995*d*), 'Haunted by the Trade Spectre' (24 July).

—— (1996*a*), 'Less Lean But Considerably More Agile' (10 May).

—— (1996*b*), 'Extra Aid Wins $650m. BMW Factory' (16–17 Nov.).

—— (1996*c*), 'An Unhealthy Trade-Off' (29 Oct.).

—— (1996*d*), 'WTO Push for Investment Rules Pact' (17 Oct.).

—— (1996*e*), 'Trade is Not to Blame' (10 Dec.).

—— (1996*f*), 'Multinationals Raise Profiles in Nigeria' (17 Oct.).

—— (1997*a*), 'Forex Move by Tokyo Lights Fuse' (24 Feb.).

—— (1997*b*), 'Andean Pact Begins to Crumble' (23 Apr.).

—— (1997*c*), 'MERCOSUR: Trade Pact Sets the Pace for Integration' (4 Feb.).

—— (1997*d*), 'Vietnam and US in Piracy Pact' (17 Apr.).

—— (1997*e*), 'Push to Head off Clash on Burma Trade' (24 Apr.).

—— (1997*f*), 'Van Miert Denies Air Row is Settled' (26 Feb.).

—— (1997*g*), 'Shadow Cast over WTO' (15 Apr.).

—— (1997*h*), 'Chaebols Act to Ban Korean Takeovers' (12 Mar.).

—— (1997*i*), 'Seoul Challenged to Disown Imports Attack' (12 Mar.).

—— (1997*j*), 'ILO Chief in Appeal for Social Labelling' (24 Apr.).

—— (1997*k*), 'Governments behind Tiger Success' (10 Mar.).

Foreign and Commonwealth Office / Department of Trade and Industry (UK) (1996), *Free Trade and Foreign Policy: A Global Vision*, Cm. 3437, London, Nov.

FOX, E. (1995), 'Competition Law and the Next Agenda for the WTO', in OECD, *New Dimensions of Market Access in a Globalising World Economy* (Paris): 169–94.

FRANKO, L. (1976), *The European Multinationals* (New York: Harper).

General Agreement on Tariffs and Trade (1955), *Basic Instruments and Selected Documents*, 3rd Supplement (Geneva: GATT).

—— (1959), *Basic Instruments and Selected Documents*, 8th Supplement (Geneva: GATT).

—— (1994*a*), *Guide to GATT Law and Practice*, 6th edn. (Geneva: GATT).

—— (1994*b*), *The Results of the Uruguay Round of Multilateral Trade Negotiations: The Legal Texts* (Geneva: GATT).

Georgetown University (1995), *Forum on U.S.–India Business Development* (Washington: Georgetown University School of Business).

GESTRIN, M., and RUGMAN, A. M. (1994), 'The North American Free Trade Agreement and Foreign Direct Investment', *Transnational Corporations*, 3(1): 77–95.

—— (1996), 'The NAFTA Investment Provisions: Prototype for Multilateral Investment Rules', in OECD, *Market Access after the Uruguay Round* (Paris:OECD): 63–78.

Gold, J. (1965), *The International Monetary Fund and International Law: An Introduction* (Washington: International Monetary Fund).

Goldberg, P. M., and Kindleberger, C. P. (1970), 'Toward a GATT for Investment: A Proposal for Supervision of the International Corporation', *Law and Policy in International Business*, 2 (2): 295–323.

Goldfarb, L. H. (1995), 'Trade and Competition Policies in the Global Market Place', in OECD, *New Dimensions of Market Access in a Globalising World Economy* (Paris): 125–7.

Graham, E. M. (1978), 'Transatlantic Investment by Multinational Firms: A Rivalistic Phenomenon?', *Journal of Post-Keynesian Economics*, 1 (Fall): 82–99.

—— (1995*a*), 'Competition Policy and the New Trade Agenda' in OECD, *New Dimensions of Market Access in a Globalising World Economy* (Paris): 105–18.

—— (1995*b*), 'Toward an Asia Pacific Investment Code', in C. J. Green and T. L. Brewer (eds.), *Investment Issues in Asia and the Pacific Rim* (New York: Oceana): 15–40.

—— (1996), *Global Corporations and National Governments* (Washington: Institute for International Economics).

—— and Krugman, P. R. (1995), *Foreign Direct Investment in the United States*, 3rd edn. (Washington: Institute for International Economics).

—— and Richardson, J. D. (1997), *Global Competition Policy* (Washington: Institute for International Economics).

—— and Wilkie, C. (1994), 'Multinationals and the Investment Provisions of the NAFTA', *International Trade Journal*, 8: 9–38.

Gray, H. P. (1996), 'The Eclectic Paradigm: The Next Generation', *Transnational Corporations*, 5 (2): 51–65.

Green, C. J. (1995), 'Plurilateralism and its Discontents', in C. J. Green and T. L. Brewer (eds.), *Investment Issues in Asia and the Pacific Rim* (New York: Oceana): 211–29.

—— and Brewer, T. L. (eds.) (1995), *Investment Issues in Asia and the Pacific Rim* (New York: Oceana).

—— and Rosenthal, D. E. (eds.) (1996), *Competition Regulations in the Pacific Rim* (New York: Oceana).

Guisinger, S. E. (1995), 'Putting an Investment Code to Work: Harmonizing Incentive Policies in the Asia Pacific', in C. J. Green and T. L. Brewer (eds.), *Investment Issues in Asia and the Pacific Rim* (New York: Oceana): 157–68.

—— and associates (1985), *Investment Incentives and Performance Requirements* (New York: Praeger).

Haggard, S., and Simmons, B. (1987), 'Theories of International Regimes', *International Organization*, 41: 491–517.

Hamilton, G. (1983), 'International Codes of Conduct for Multinationals', *Multinational Business*, 1: 1–10.

Hart, M. (1995), 'What's Next: Negotiating Rules for a Global Economy', in OECD *New Dimensions of Market Access in a Globalising World Economy* (Paris: OECD): 221–42.

Helleiner, G. K. (1983), *Towards a New Bretton Woods: Challenges for the World Financial and Trading System* (London: Commonwealth Secretariat).

Hellmann, R. (1977), *Transnational Control of Multinational Corporations* (New York: Praeger).

Hertner, P., and Jones, G. (1986), *Multinationals: Theory and History* (Aldershot: Gower).

Hindley, B. (1994), 'Two Cheers for the Uruguay Round', in B. Hindley and D. Lall (eds.), *Trade Policy Review 1994* (London: Centre for Policy Studies), Sept.

Hoekman, B. M., and Kostecki, M. M. (1995), *The Political Economy of the World Trading System* (Oxford: Oxford University Press).

—— and Mavroidis, P. C. (1994), 'Anti-trust-Based Remedies and Dumping in International Trade', Discussion Paper No. 1010 (London: Centre for Economic Policy Research).

Hood, N., and Young, S. (1979), *The Economics of Multinational Enterprise* (London: Longman).

Hooke, A. W. (1983), *The International Monetary Fund: Its Evolution, Organization, and Activities* (Washington: International Monetary Fund).

Horsefield, J. K. (1969), *The International Monetary Fund 1945–1965: Twenty Years of International Monetary Cooperation* (Washington: International Monetary Fund).

Houde, M.-F. (1994), 'Mexico and Foreign Investment', *OECD Observer*, 190: 10–13.

—— (1996), 'Foreign Direct Investment', *OECD Observer*, 176: 9–13.

Hufbauer, C. C., and Schott, J. J. (1993), *NAFTA: An Assessment* (Washington: Institute for International Economics).

Hufbauer, G., and Erb, J. (1984), *Subsidies in International Trade* (Washington: Institute for International Economics).

Husain, I., and Jun, K. W. (1992), *Capital Flows to South Asian and ASEAN Countries: Trends, Determinants and Policy Implications*, Policy Research Working Paper No. 842 (Washington: The World Bank).

Hymer, S. H. (1976), *The International Operations of National Firms: A Study of Direct Investment* (Cambridge, Mass.: MIT Press).

Inside US Trade (1996*a*), 'US Proposal on FTAA Competition Policy Working Group' (12 Jan.).

—— (1997*a*), 'Results of US–China Business Council Survey on WTO Accession' (7 Feb.).

—— (1997*b*), 'Draft Text of the Multilateral Agreement on Investment' (24 Feb.).

International Chamber of Commerce (1972), *Guidelines for International Investment* (Paris: ICC).

International Confederation of Free Trade Unions (1975), *Multinational Charter* (Brussels: ICFTU).

International Labour Office (1977), *Tripartite Declaration of Principles Concerning Multinational Enterprises and Social Policy* (Geneva: ILO).

International Monetary Fund (1997), 'IMF Wins Mandate to Cover Capital Accounts: Debt Initiative Put in Motion', *IMF Survey*, 26 (9): 129–32.

Itoh, M., and Nagaoka, S. (1997), 'VERs, VIEs and Global Competition', in E. M. Graham and J. D. Richardson (eds.), *Global Competition Policy* (Washington: Institute for International Economics).

Jackson, John H. (1997), *The World Trade System* (Cambridge, Mass.: MIT).

Johanson, J., and Vahlne, J.-E. (1977), 'The Internationalization Process of the Firm: A Model of Knowledge Development and Increasing Foreign Market Commitment', *Journal of International Business Studies*, 8 (1): 23–32.

Julius, DeAnne (1990), *Global Companies and Public Policy* (London: The Royal Institute of International Affairs / Pinter Publishers).

Jun, K. W., and Brewer, T. L. (1997), 'The Role of Foreign Private Capital Flows in Sustainable Development', paper prepared for the UN Fourth Expert Group Meeting on Financial Issues of Agenda 21, *Finance for Sustainable Development: The Road Ahead* (Santiago): 8–10 Jan.

Karl, J. (1996), 'Multilateral Investment Agreements and Regional Economic Integration', *Transnational Corporations*, 5 (2): 19–50.

Kent, C. (1993), 'NAFTA, TRIPs Affect IP', *Les Nouvelles*, 28 (4): 176–81.

Keohane, R. (1985), *After Hegemony: Cooperation and Discord in the World Political Economy* (Princeton: Princeton University Press).

Keon, J. (1988), 'TRIPs in Current GATT Negotiations', *Les Nouvelles*, 23 (4): 203–6.

Khalil, M. I. (1992), 'Treatment of Foreign Investment in Bilateral Investment Treaties', *ICSID Review: Foreign Investment Law Journal*, 7: 339–83.

Kindleberger, C. P. (1969), *American Business Abroad: Six Lectures on Direct Investment* (New Haven: Yale University Press).

Knickerbocker, F. T. (1973), *Oligopolistic Reaction and Multinational Enterprise* (Boston: Division of Research, Graduate School of Business Administration, Harvard University).

Kobrin, S. J. (1995), 'Regional Integration in a Globally Networked Economy', *Transnational Corporations*, 4 (2), 15–33.

Kojima, K. (1978), *Direct Foreign Investment: A Japanese Model of Multinational Business Operations* (London: Croom Helm).

—— (1990), *Japanese Direct Investment Abroad*, Monograph Series No. 1 (Tokyo: International Christian University Social Science Research Institute).

Krugman, P. R. (ed.) (1986), *Strategic Trade Policy and the New International Economics* (Cambridge, Mass.: MIT Press).

—— (1992), 'A Global Economy is not the Wave of the Future', *Financial Executive*, Mar./Apr.: 10–13.

—— (1996), *Pop Internationalism* (Cambridge, Mass.: MIT Press).

Laird, S. (1996), 'Fostering Regional Integration', in OECD, *Regionalism and its Place in the Multilateral Trading System* (Paris:OECD): 169–91.

Lall, S. (1974), 'Less-Developed Countries and Private Foreign Direct Investment', *World Development*, Apr.–May: 43–8.

—— (1996), 'Transnational Corporations and Economic Development', in UNCTAD Division on Transnational Corporations, *Transnational Corporations and World Development* (London: International Thomson Business Press): 44–72.

—— and Streeten, P. (1977), *Foreign Investment, Transnationals and Developing Countries* (London: Macmillan).

Lan, P., and Young, S. (1996), 'Foreign Direct Investment and Technology Transfer: A Case Study of Foreign Direct Investment in North-East China', *Transnational Corporations*, 5 (1): 57–83.

Lawrence, R. Z. (1995), 'Emerging Regional Agreements: Building Blocks or Stumbling Blocks?' in J. A. Frieden and D. A. Lake (eds.), *International Political Economy* (New York: St Martin's Press): 407–15.

—— (1996), *Single World, Divided Nations?* (Washington: Brookings Institution, Paris: OECD Development Centre).

Leidy, M. (1995), 'Unfair Trade or Unfair Remedy?', *Finance and Development*, 32 (1): 27–29.

Ley, R. (1989), 'Liberating Capital Movements: A New OECD Commitment', *OECD Observer*, 159 (Aug.–Sept.): 22–6.

—— (1996), 'Multilateral Rules to Promote the Liberalisation of Investment Regimes', in OECD, *Towards Multilateral Investment Rules* (Paris:OECD): 69–73.

Leys, C. (1996), *The Rise and Fall of Development Theory* (Oxford: James Currey).

Lipstein, R. A. (1997), 'Using Antitrust Principles to Reform Antidumping Law', in E. M. Graham and J. D. Richardson (eds.), *Global Competition Policy* (Washington: Institute for International Economics).

Low, P., and Subramanian, A. (1995), 'TRIMs in the Uruguay Round: An Unfinished Business?' mimeo (Washington: The World Bank).

McCulloch, R., and Owen, R. (1983), 'Linking Negotiations on Trade and Foreign Direct Investment', in C. P. Kindleberger and D. B. Audretsch (eds.), *The Multinational Corporation in the 1980s* (Cambridge, Mass.: MIT): 334–58.

Malott, R. H. (1989), '1990s Issue: Intellectual Property Rights', *Les Nouvelles*, 24 (4): 149–53.

Mansfield, E. (1974), 'Technology and Technological Change', in J. H. Dunning (ed.), *Economic Analysis and the Multinational Enterprise* (London: George Allen & Unwin): 147–83.

Minor, M. S. (1994), 'The Demise of Expropriation as an Instrument of LDC Policy, 1980–1992', *Journal of International Business Studies*, 25(1): 177–88.

Moncarz, R. (1995), 'International Trade and the New Economic Order: An Introduction', in R. Moncarz (ed.), *International Trade and the New Economic Order* (Oxford: Elsevier/Pergamon): 1–10.

Montagnon, P. (1990), 'The Trade Policy Connection', in P. Montagnon (ed.), *European Competition Policy* (London: The Royal Institute of International Affairs/Pinter Publishers).

Morgan, E. J. (1997), 'Industrial Restructuring and the Control of "Concentrations" in the European Market', in G. Chryssochoidis, C. Millar, and J. Clegg (eds.), *Internationalisation Strategies* (Basingstoke: Macmillan; New York, St Martin's Press): 91–112.

Mossinghoff, G. J. (1996), 'IP Protection Increases R & D Worldwide', *Les Nouvelles*, 31 (4): 159–63.

NEWFARMER, R. S. (ed.) (1985), *Profits, Progress and Poverty: Case Studies of International Industries in Latin America* (Notre Dame, Ind.: University of Notre Dame Press).
O'CONNOR, D. H. (1995), 'TRIPs: Licensing Challenge', *Les Nouvelles*, 30 (1): 16–18.
OHMAE, K. (1985), *Triad Power: The Coming Shape of Global Competition* (New York: The Free Press).
—— (1990), *The Borderless World* (London: Collins).
OLIVER, R. W. (1971), *Early Plans for a World Bank* (Princeton: Princeton University, Department of Economics, International Finance Section).
OMAN, C. (1984), *New Forms of International Investment in Developing Countries* (Paris: OECD).
Organization for Economic Cooperation and Development (1976*a*), *Guidelines for Multinational Enterprises* (Paris: OECD).
—— (1976*b*), *International Investment and Multinational Enterprises* (Paris: OECD).
—— (1987), *Recent Trends in International Direct Investment* (Paris: OECD).
—— (1993*a*), *Code of Liberalisation of Capital Movements* (Paris: OECD).
—— (1993*b*), *Code of Liberalisation of Current Invisible Operations* (Paris: OECD).
—— (1994*a*), *National Treatment for Foreign-Controlled Enterprises*, OECD Working Papers No. 34, vol. ii (Paris: OECD).
—— (1994*b*), *The OECD Guidelines for Multinational Enterprises* (Paris: OECD).
—— (1994*c*), *Merger Cases in the Real World: A Study of Merger Control Procedures* (Paris: OECD).
—— (1995), *New Dimensions of Market Access in a Globalising World Economy* (Paris: OECD).
—— (1996*a*), *Towards Multilateral Investment Rules* (Paris: OECD).
—— (1996*b*), 'Labour Standards: First Talks with Non-members', *OECD Letter*, 5 (9): 3.
OSTRY, S. (1992), 'The Domestic Domain: The New International Policy Arena', *Transnational Corporations*, 1 (1): 7–26.
PETERS, E. (1995), 'Restructuring of Scotland's Information Technology Industries: Strategic Issues and Responses', in A. Amin and J. Tomaney (eds.), *Behind the Myth of European Union* (London: Routledge): 263–81.
PITELIS, C. N., and SUGDEN, R. (eds.) (1991), *The Nature of the Transnational Firm* (London: Routledge).
PORET, P. (1992), 'Liberalising Capital Movements', *OECD Observer*, 176: 4–8.
—— (1994), 'Mexico and the OECD Codes of Liberalisation', *OECD Observer*, 189 (Aug. / Sept): 9–12.
PORTER, M. E. (1990), *The Competitive Advantage of Nations* (London: Macmillan).
PRESTON, L., and WINDSOR, D. (1992), *The Rules of the Game in the Global Economy: Policy Regimes for International Business* (Boston: Kluwer).
Proceedings and Documents of the United Nations Monetary and Financial Conference, Bretton Woods, New Hampshire (1944) (Washington: United States Government Printing Office), vols i and ii.
QUINN, D. (1997), 'The Correlates of Change in International Financial Regulation', *American Political Science Review*, 91(3): 531–53.
ᶠIVOLI, P., and ALORIO, E. (1996), 'Foreign Direct Investment and Investment Under Uncertainty', *Journal of International Business Studies*, 27(2): 335–57.
RODRIK, D. (1994), 'Comments on Maskus and Eby-Konan', in A. Deardorff and R. Stern (eds.), *Analytical and Negotiating Issues in the Global Trading System* (Ann Arbor: University of Michigan Press): 447–50.
ROSENTHAL, D. E., and KNIGHTON, W. M. (1982), *National Laws and International Commerce* (London: The Royal Institute of International Affairs / Routledge & Kegan Paul).
ROSENTHAL, D. E., and NICOLAÏDES, P. (1997), 'Harmonizing Anti-trust: The Less Effective Way to Provide International Competition', in E. M. Graham and J. D. Richardson (eds.), *Global Competition Policy* (Washington: Institute for International Economics).
RUGMAN, A. M. (1977), 'The Regulation of Foreign Investment in Canada', *Journal of World Trade Law*, 11 (4), July–Aug.: 322–33.
—— (ed.) (1994), *Foreign Investment and NAFTA* (Columbia: University of South Carolina Press).
—— and GESTRIN, M. V. (1991), 'US Trade Laws as Barriers to Globalisation', *World Economy*, 14 (3): 335–52.

—— and VERBEKE, A. (1990), *Global Corporate Strategy and Trade Policy* (London: Routledge).

—— —— (1997), 'Global Strategies for Multinational Enterprises', in I. Islam and W. Shepherd (eds.), *Current Issues in International Business* (Cheltenham: Edward Elgar): 132–50.

RYRIE, W. (1995), *First World, Third World* (Basingstoke: Macmillan Press).

SAFARIAN, A. E. (1993), *Multinational Enterprises and Public Policy* (Aldershot: Edward Elgar).

SAKURAI, M. (1995), 'Japan's Foreign Investment in Southeast Asia: Facts and Legal Problems', in C. J. Green and T. L. Brewer (eds.), *Investment Issues in Asia and the Pacific Rim* (New York: Oceana): 65–88.

SAUVANT, K. P. (1977), 'Controlling Transnational Enterprises: A Review and Some Further Thoughts', in K. P. Sauvant and H. Hasenpflug (eds.), *The New International Economic Order* (London: Wilton House Publications): 356–433.

—— and LAVIPOUR, F. G. (eds.) (1976), *Controlling Multinational Enterprises* (London: Wilton House).

SAUVÉ, P. (1994), 'A First Look at Investment in the Final Act of the Uruguay Round', *Journal of World Trade*, 28 (5): 5–16.

—— (1995), 'Assessing the General Agreement on Trade in Services: Half Full or Half Empty?', *Journal of World Trade*, 29 (4): 125–45.

—— and SCHWANEN, D. (eds.) (1996), *Investment Rules for the Global Economy* (Toronto: C. D. Howe Institute).

SCHERER, F. M. (1994), *Competition Policies for an Integrated World Economy* (Washington: The Brookings Institution).

SCHOTT, J. J. (1994), *The Uruguay Round: An Assessment* (Washington: Institute for International Economics).

SCHRÖTER, H. G. (1993), 'Continuity and Change', in G. Jones and H. G. Schröter (eds.), *The Rise of Multinationals in Continental Europe* (Aldershot: Edward Elgar): 24–48.

SCHWAMM, H., and GERMIDIS, D. (1977), *Codes of Conduct for Multinational Companies: Issues and Positions* (Brussels: European Centre for Study and Information on Multinational Corporations (ECSIM)).

SELL, S. K. (1989), 'Environment for Technology Transfer Grows Tighter', *Les Nouvelles*, 24 (4): 180–5.

SERVAN-SCHREIBER, J. J. (1968), *The American Challenge* (New York: Atheneum).

SHIELLS, C. (1995), 'Regional Trade Blocs: Trade Creating or Diverting?', *Finance and Development*, 32 (1): 30–2.

SMITH, A. (1996), 'The Development of a Multilateral Agreement on Investment at the OECD: A Preview', in OECD, *Towards Multilateral Investment Rules* (Paris:OECD): 31–8.

SORNARAJAH, M. (1994), *The International Law on Foreign Investment* (Cambridge: Cambridge University Press).

SOUTHARD, Jr., F. A. (1979), *The Evolution of the International Monetary Fund*, Department of Economics, International Finance Section (Princeton University).

The Stakes of Bretton Woods: A Statement on International Policy of the National Planning Association (1945) (Washington: National Planning Association).

STRANGE, R. (1997), 'Trading Blocs, Trade Liberalisation and Foreign Direct Investment', in G. Chryssochoidis, C. Millar, and J. Clegg (eds.), *Internationalisation Strategies* (London: Macmillan; New York: St Martin's Press): 19–42.

SUNKEL, O. (1972), 'Big Business and Dependencia', *Foreign Affairs*, Apr.: 517–31.

TAMURA, J. (1995), 'The Administrative Procedure Law: Encouraging Foreign Direct Investment in Japan by Making Administrative Guidance More Transparent', in C. J. Green and T. L. Brewer (eds.), *Investment Issues in Asia and the Pacific Rim* (New York: Oceana): 201–10.

TEECE, D. J. (1986), 'Transaction Cost Economics and the Multinational Enterprise', *Journal of Economic Behavior and Organization*, 7: 21–45.

THARAKAN, P. K. M. (ed.) (1991), *Policy Implications of Antidumping Measures* (Amsterdam: Elsevier Science / North Holland).

THORSTENSEN, V. (1996), 'Connections and Interlinkages between Regional Integration Arrangements and the Multilateral Trading System: The Perspective of MERCOSUL' in OECD, *Regionalism and its Place in the Multilateral Trading System* (Paris: OECD): 103–11.

TOLENTINO, P. E. E. (1993), *Technological Innovation and Third World Multinationals* (London: Routledge).

TYSON, L. D'A. (1992), *Who's Bashing Whom? Trade Conflict in High Technology Industries* (Washington: Institute for International Economics).

UL HAQUE, N., MATHIESON, D., and SHARMA, S. (1997), 'Causes of Capital Inflows and Policy Responses to Them', *Finance and Development*, Mar., 3–6.

United Nations (annual), *World Economic Survey* (New York: UN).

—— (1973), *Multinational Corporations in World Development*, Doc. No. ST/ECA/190 (New York: UN).

nited Nations Centre on Transnational Corporations/International Chamber of Commerce (1992), *Bilateral Investment Treaties 1959–1991* (New York: UN).

——/ nited Nations Conference on Trade and Development (1991), *The Impact of Trade-Related Investment Measures on Trade and Development* (New York: UN).

United Nations Conference on Trade and Development (1976), *Trade and Development Issues in the Context of a New International Economic Order*, UNCTAD/OSG/104/Rev.1 (New York: UN).

—— (1993), *World Investment Report 1993: Transnational Corporations and Integrated International Production* (New York: UN).

– (1994), *World Investment Report 1994: Transnational Corporations, Employment and the Workplace* (New York: UN).

– (1995), *World Investment Report 1995: Transnational Corporations and Competitiveness* (New York: UN).

—— (1996*a*), *World Investment Report 1996: Investment, Trade and International Policy Arrangements* (New York: UN).

– (1996*b*), *Incentives and Foreign Direct Investment*, UNCTAD/DTCI/28, Current Studies, Series A, No. 30 (New York: UNCTAD).

—— (1996*c*), *International Investment Instruments: A Compendium*, i: *Multilateral Instruments* (Geneva: UN).

—— (1996*d*), 'Draft United Nations Code of Conduct: Transnational Corporations (1983 Version)', in *International Investment Instruments: A Compendium*, i (Geneva: UN): 161–80.

——/World Bank (1994), *Liberalizing International Transactions in Services: A Handbook* (New York: UN).

nited Nations Economic and Social Council (1974), *Report of the Group of Eminent Persons on the Impact of MNC on the Development Process and on International Relations* (New York: UN).

—— (1976), *Transnational Corporations: Issues Involved in the Formulation of a Code of Conduct*, Centre on Transnational Corporations, E/C.10/17 (New York: UN).

—— (1978), *Transnational Corporations in World Development*, Commission on Transnational Corporations, 4th Session, E/C.10/38 (New York: UN).

United Nations—Transnational Corporations and Management Division (1992), *World Investment Report 1992: Transnational Corporations as Engines of Growth* (New York: UN).

US Department of State (1946), *Suggested Charter for an International Trade Organization of the United Nations* (Washington).

—— (1947*a*), *Draft Charter for the International Trade Organization of the United Nations* (Washington).

—— (1947*b*), *Havana Charter for an International Trade Organization and Final Act and Related Documents* (Washington).

—— (1948), *Havana Charter for an International Trade Organization, Including a Guide to the Study of the Charter* (Washington).

US Government (1993), *North America Free Trade Agreement between the Government of the United States of America, the Government of Canada and the Government of the United Mexican States* (Washington: US Government Printing Office).

US Office of the Trade Representative (1997), 'National Trade Estimate, China', web site, 10 Mar.

US Senate (1976), *Senate Resolution 516*, 94th Cong. 2nd Session, Report No. 94–1307, 1 Oct.

Van den Bulcke, D. (1992), 'Multinational Companies and the European Community', in B. Nelson and D. Roberts (eds.), *The European Community in the 1990s* (New York: Berg): 106–23.

—— Boddewyn, J. J., Martens, B., and Klemmer, P. (1979), *Investment and Divestment Policies of Multinational Corporations in Europe* (Farnborough: Saxon House; in association with Brussels: ECSIM).

Van Miert, K. (1996*a*), 'Transatlantic Relations and Competition Policy', *Competition Policy Newsletter*, 2 (3): 1–5.

—— (1996*b*), 'The Proposal for a European Competition Agency', *Competition Policy Newsletter*, 2 (2): 1–4.

Vaupel, J. W., and Curhan, J. (1973), *The World's Multinational Enterprises: A Sourcebook of Tables* (Boston: Division of Research, Harvard Business School).

Vernon, R. (1966), 'International Investment and International Trade in the Product Cycle', *Quarterly Journal of Economics*, 80, 190–207.

—— (1971), *Sovereignty at Bay* (New York: Basic Books).

Viner, J. (1950), *The Customs Union Issue* (New York: Carnegie Endowment for International Peace).

Vogelaar, T. (1977), 'Multinational Enterprises: The Guidelines in Practice', *OECD Observer*, May: 7–8.

Wallace, C. D. (1982), *Legal Control of the Multinational Enterprise* (The Hague: Martinus Nijhoff).

Warner, M. A. A. (1996), 'Private and Public Impediments to Market Presence: Exploring the Investment/Competition Nexus', in P. Sauvé and D. Schwanen (eds.), *Investment Rules for the Global Economy*, Policy Study 28 (Toronto: C. D. Howe Institute), Sept.: 219–59.

—— and Rugman, A. M. (1994), 'Competitiveness: An Emerging Strategy of Discrimination in U.S. Antitrust and R & D Policy', *Law and Policy in International Business*, 25 (3): 945–82.

Weinberg, P. J. (1978), *European Labor and Multinationals* (New York: Praeger).

Wells, L. T., Jr. (1983), *Third World Multinationals* (Cambridge, Mass.: MIT Press).

Wilcox, C. (1949), *A Charter for World Trade* (New York: Macmillan; reprinted by Arno).

Wilkins, M. (1970), *The Emergence of Multinational Enterprise: American Business Abroad from the Colonial Era to 1914* (Cambridge, Mass.: Harvard University Press).

—— (1989), *The History of Foreign Investment in the United States* (Cambridge, Mass.: Harvard University Press).

Wilks, S. (1994), *The Revival of Japanese Competition Policy and its Importance for EU–Japan Relations* (London: The Royal Institute of International Affairs).

Williamson, O. E. (1985), *The Economic Institutions of Capitalism* (New York: The Free Press).

Witherell, W. (1996), 'Towards an International Set of Rules for Investment', in OECD, *Toward Multilateral Investment Rules* (Paris: OECD): 17–29.

Womack, James P., et al. (1990), *The Machine that Changed the World* (New York: Rawson).

Woolcock, S. (1996), 'Rules of Origin', in OECD, *Regionalism and its Place in the Multilateral Trading System* (Paris: OECD): 195–212.

World Bank (1992*a*), *Guidelines on the Treatment of Foreign Investment* (Washington: The World Bank).

—— (1992*b*), *Legal Framework for the Treatment of Foreign Investment*, ii: *Guidelines* (Washington: The World Bank).

—— (1993), *The East Asian Miracle* (New York: Oxford University Press).

World Trade Organization (1995*a*), *Regionalism and the World Trading System* (Geneva: WTO).

—— (1995*b*), *International Trade, Trends and Statistics, 1995* (Geneva: WTO).

—— (1996*a*), 'Ministerial Declaration on Trade in Information Technology Products' (Singapore), 13 Dec.

—— (1996*b*), 'Trade and Foreign Direct Investment: New Report by the WTO Secretariat', Geneva, 9 Oct.

World Trade Organization (1997*a*), 'The WTO Negotiations on Basic Telecommunications', web site, 17 Feb.
—— (1997*b*), 'WTO Basic Telecommunications Services Agreement', web site, 3 Mar.
—— (1997*c*), 'Press Brief: Information Technology Agreement', web site, 3 Mar.
—— (1997*d*), 'Summary of the State of Play of WTO Disputes', web site, 23 Dec.
YARBROUGH, B., and YARBROUGH, R. (1992), *Cooperation and Governance in International Trade: The Strategic Organizational Approach* (Princeton: Princeton University Press).
YOUNG, S. (1975), 'Trade Creation and Trade Diversion in the EEC: A Case Study for Milk', *Journal of Agricultural Economics*, 26 (2): 197–208.
—— HAMILL, J., WHEELER, C., and DAVIES, J. R. (1989), *International Market Entry and Development* (Hemel Hempstead: Harvester Wheatsheaf/Prentice Hall).
—— MCDERMOTT, M., and DUNLOP, S. (1991), 'The Challenge of the Single Market', in B. Bürgenmeier and J. L. Mucchielli (eds.), *Multinationals and Europe 1992* (London: Routledge): 3–21.
—— Huang, C.-H., and MCDERMOTT, M. (1996), 'Internationalization and Competitive Catch-up Processes: Case Study Evidence on Chinese Multinational Enterprises', *Management International Review*, 36 (4): 295–314.
ZAMPETTI, A. B. (1995), 'The Uruguay Round Agreement on Subsidies: A Forward-Looking Assessment', *Journal of World Trade*, 29 (6): 5–29.
—— and SAUVÉ, P. (1995), 'New Dimensions of Market Access: An Overview', in OECD, *New Dimensions of Market Access in a Globalising World Economy* (Paris: OECD): 13–22.

Index

Notes:

1. Page references in **bold** indicate major topics
2. Page references in *italics* refer to boxes and Appendices